ACHIEVE BUSINESS ANALYSIS CERTIFICATION

A Concise Guide to PMI-PBA®, CBAP®, and CPRE EXAM SUCCESS

KLAUS NIELSEN, PMP, PMI-PBA, PMI-ACP, CPRE-FL

J.ROSS PUBLISHING

Copyright © 2016 by Klaus Nielsen

ISBN-13: 978-1-60427-111-9

Printed and bound in the U.S.A. Printed on acid-free paper.

10 9 8 7 6 5 4 3 2 1

Library of Congress Cataloging-in-Publication Data

Nielsen, Klaus, 1972- author.
   Title: Achieve business analysis certification : a concise guide to PMI-PBA, CBAP
      and CPRE exam success / by Klaus Nielsen, PMP, ACP, Certified Scrum Master.
   Description: Plantation, FL : J. Ross Publishing, [2015] | Includes index.
   Identifiers: LCCN 2015041295 | ISBN 9781604271119 (pbk. : alk. paper)
   Subjects: LCSH: Business analysts--Certification. | Business analysts—Examinations,
      questions, etc.
   Classification: LCC HD69.B87 N54 2015 | DDC 658.40076—dc23 LC record available at
      http://lccn.loc.gov/2015041295

Phone: (954) 727-9333
Fax: (561) 892-0700
Web: www.jrosspub.com

Contents

Preface. ix
Acknowledgments. xi
About the Author xiii
WAV™ Page. xiv

Part 1   **Overview, How to Use This Guide, Study Tips, and Pre-Test Knowledge
Assessments** 1

Chapter 1   **Business Analysis Certification Overview** 3
     1.1   Brief Introduction: Certification. 3
     1.2   Business Analysis Certification Organizations 3
     1.3   Business Analyst Certification and Body of Knowledge 4
     1.4   The Value of Business Analyst Certifications 5
     1.5   Target Groups for Business Analyst Certifications. 7
     1.6   PMI-PBA® Exam Content 7
     1.7   Using This Book to Pass Business Analyst Certification Exams. 11

Chapter 2   **Study Tips and How to Pass the PMI-PBA® Exam** 13
     2.1   Brief Introduction: Study Tips. 13
     2.2   Exam Basics 13
     2.3   Before the Exam 14
     2.4   During the Exam. 17

Chapter 3   **Organizational Need for Business Analysts.** 19
     3.1   Brief Introduction: Organizational Need. 19
     3.2   Business Analyst Role. 20
     3.3   The Relationship Between the Business Analyst and the Project Manager. 21

Chapter 4   **Pretest Knowledge Assessments for Business Analyst Certification Exams.** 23
     4.1   Brief Introduction: Knowledge Assessment 23
     4.2   Pretest Questions for the PMI-PBA® Designation 23
     4.3   Pretest Answers for the PMI-PBA® Designation 26
     4.4   Pretest Questions for the IIBA CBAP® Designation 28
     4.5   Pretest Answers for the IIBA CBAP® Designation. 31
     4.6   Pretest Questions for the IREB CPRE-FL Designation 33
     4.7   Pretest Answers for the IREB CPRE-FL Designation 36

Part 2   The Domains...**39**

Chapter 5   Needs Assessment Domain...**41**
Terms to Know 41
5.1   Brief Introduction: Needs Assessment..................................42
5.2   Define Business Requirements 43
5.3   Define Value Proposition 47
5.4   Develop Project Goals 55
5.5   Identify Stakeholders 57
5.6   Analyze Stakeholders 62
5.7   Relating PMI-PBA® Practices to *PMBOK® Guide—Fifth Edition* Practices ..68
5.8   Relating PMI-PBA® Practices to Agile Practices 68
5.9   Chapter Summary..69
5.10   Posttest: Take Five 71
5.11   Posttest: Correct Answers 72

Chapter 6   Planning Domain...**73**
Terms to Know 73
6.1   Brief Introduction: Planning 73
6.2   Determine Project Context 74
6.3   Plan Requirement Traceability 78
6.4   Develop Requirement Management Plan 83
6.5   Plan Requirement Change Control......................................87
6.6   Plan Document Control..91
6.7   Define Project Expected Outcome 93
6.8   Relating PMI-PBA® Practices to *PMBOK® Guide—Fifth Edition* Practices 97
6.9   Relating PMI-PBA® Practices to Agile Practices 97
6.10   Chapter Summary..98
6.11   Posttest: Take Five 100
6.12   Posttest: Correct Answers 102

Chapter 7   Analysis Domain **103**
Terms to Know 103
7.1   Brief Introduction: Analysis..104
7.2   Elicit Requirements...105
7.3   Elaborate Requirements 115
7.4   Validate Requirements 119
7.5   Allocate Requirements 122
7.6   Get Requirement Signoff 129
7.7   Document Requirements...129
7.8   Verify Requirements..138
7.9   Specify Requirements: Expected Results 141
7.10   Relating PMI-PBA® Practices to *PMBOK® Guide—Fifth Edition* Practices 143
7.11   Relating PMI-PBA® Practices to Agile Practices 143

	7.12	Chapter Summary	144
	7.13	Posttest: Take Five	146
	7.14	Posttest: Correct Answers	148
Chapter 8	**Traceability and Monitoring Domain**		**149**
	Terms to Know		149
	8.1	Brief Introduction: Traceability and Monitoring	149
	8.2	Track Requirements	150
	8.3	Monitor Requirements	155
	8.4	Update a Requirements Status	157
	8.5	Communicate Requirements Status	159
	8.6	Manage Changes to Requirements	161
	8.7	Relating PMI-PBA® Practices to *PMBOK® Guide—Fifth Edition* Practices	162
	8.8	Relating PMI-PBA® Practices to Agile Practices	163
	8.9	Chapter Summary	163
	8.10	Posttest: Take Five	164
	8.11	Posttest: Correct Answers	166
Chapter 9	**Evaluation Domain**		**167**
	Terms to Know		167
	9.1	Brief Introduction: Evaluation	167
	9.2	Validate Test Results	168
	9.3	Analyze Solution Gaps	170
	9.4	Obtain Stakeholder Acceptance of the Solution	173
	9.5	Evaluate Solution Results	175
	9.6	Relating PMI-PBA® Practices to *PMBOK® Guide—Fifth Edition* Practices	176
	9.7	Relating PMI-PBA® Practices to Agile Practices	177
	9.8	Chapter Summary	177
	9.9	Posttest: Take Five	179
	9.10	Posttest: Correct Answers	180
Part 3	**Knowledge, Skills, Methodologies, and Standards**		**181**
Chapter 10	**PMI-PBA® Knowledge, Skills, Tools, and Techniques**		**183**
	Terms to Know		183
	10.1	Brief Introduction: Knowledge Concepts and Skills	184
	10.2	Tools and Techniques Overview	184
	10.3	Analytic Tools and Techniques	184
	10.4	Backlog Management	196
	10.5	Business Rule Analysis Tools and Techniques	199
	10.6	Change Control Tools and Techniques	201
	10.7	Collaboration Tools and Techniques	202
	10.8	Communication Skills	204
	10.9	Conflict Management and Resolution Tools and Techniques	207

10.10 Contingency Planning 211
10.11 Data Analysis Tools and Techniques 212
10.12 Decision-Making Tools and Techniques 213
10.13 Development Methodologies. 215
10.14 Document Management Tools and Techniques 219
10.15 Elements of a Requirements Management Plan 220
10.16 Elicitation Tools and Techniques 220
10.17 Estimating Tools and Techniques 220
10.18 Facilitation Tools and Techniques. 224
10.19 Interface Analysis 226
10.20 Leadership Principles and Skills 227
10.21 Lessons Learned and Retrospectives 232
10.22 Measurement Tools and Techniques 234
10.23 Negotiations Tools and Techniques 235
10.24 Organization Assessment. 237
10.25 Planning Tools and Techniques. 241
10.26 Political and Cultural Awareness. 246
10.27 Prioritization Tools and Techniques. 249
10.28 Problem Solving and Opportunity Identification Tools and Techniques 249
10.29 Process Analysis Tools and Techniques 251
10.30 Project Methodologies 251
10.31 Quality Management 262
10.32 Reporting Tools and Techniques. 262
10.33 Requirements Traceability Tools and Techniques 264
10.34 Requirement Types 264
10.35 Root Cause Analysis 265
10.36 Scheduling Tools and Techniques. 266
10.37 Stakeholder Analysis. 267
10.38 System Thinking 269
10.39 Validation Tools and Techniques 270
10.40 Valuation Tools and Techniques 270
10.41 Verification Tools and Techniques 270
10.42 Version Control Tools and Techniques 270

Chapter 11 Professional Ethics and Conduct Standards 273
11.1 Brief Introduction: Ethics and Conduct. 273
11.2 PMI and IIBA Standards 273

Chapter 12 The PMI-PBA® and the *PMBOK® Guide* 281
12.1 Brief Introduction: *PMBOK® Guide* 281
12.2 Process Groups and Knowledge Areas. 281
12.3 PMI-PBA® Overview. 283

Chapter 13   Agile Methodologies and Manifesto **287**
    13.1   Brief Introduction: Agile 287
    13.2   Agile Principles and Practices 287
    13.3   Scrum 292

Part 4   IIBA CBAP® and IREB CPRE Knowledge Areas and Alignment **297**

Chapter 14   The IIBA CBAP® and the *BABOK® Guide* **299**
    14.1   Brief Introduction: *BABOK® Guide* 299
    14.2   IIBA CBAP®: Overview 301
    14.3   IIBA—Business Analysis Planning and Monitoring 302
    14.4   IIBA—Elicitation and Collaboration 302
    14.5   IIBA—Requirements Life Cycle Management 303
    14.6   IIBA—Strategy Analysis 303
    14.7   IIBA—Requirements Analysis and Design Definition 304
    14.8   IIBA—Solution Evaluation 304
    14.9   IIBA—Underlying Competencies 304
    14.10 IIBA—Techniques 305

Chapter 15   The IREB CPRE and Foundation Level Syllabus **309**
    15.1   Brief Introduction: Foundation Level Syllabus .309
    15.2   IREB CPRE: Overview 309

Part 5   Practice Exam **313**

Chapter 16   PMI-PBA® Full Practice Exam **315**
    16.1   Brief Introduction: Simulated PMI-PBA® Exam 315

Part 6   Appendices **345**

Appendix 1   Glossary and Acronyms 347
Appendix 2   Bibliography 359
Index 363

Preface

I clearly remember the day when the Project Management Institute (PMI) announced the Professional in Business Analysis (PMI-PBA)® designation. Call me odd, but I was delighted. Shortly after, I entered into a contract with J. Ross Publishing, a leader in the project management field and publisher of several noteworthy books on business analysis, including the best-seller *Seven Steps to Mastering Business Analysis*. Drew Gierman, the publisher at J. Ross, had already foreseen the need and quickly embraced the concept of a self-study guide for individuals who are interested in becoming certified as a business analysis professional—but not just any self-study guide.

We discussed the concept of *knowledge that sets you apart*. From our discussions we formed the goal of creating a guide that would enable *you*—business analysis practitioners with varied titles and backgrounds, as well as students of the discipline—to gain both the recognized credentials and professional development and knowledge needed to help set you apart in the marketplace.

This meant developing a guide that would provide practitioners and students far more than the bare minimum needed to pass the PBA certification offered by PMI. When I started, my sole focus was on the PMI-PBA certification. However, during its development, more and more techniques, tools, and concepts from two other recognized sources of knowledge that preceded PMI's involvement in business analysis arose, and they turned out to be well-aligned with one another. So in keeping with the concept of *knowledge that sets you apart* and our goal, this book evolved into a complete guide to passing the PMI-PBA, IIBA CBAP® version 3, and IREB CPRE-FL certification exams in a very synergistic way, becoming a resource of greater value than the sum of its parts.

With the growing demand to do more with less, most every employed professional is very busy these days. In fact, I'm guessing that many of you work nearly seven days a week, just as I do. This meant conveying all relevant content efficiently and effectively, in a manner that builds the confidence that comes from gaining knowledge. I remember passing my first certification exam, which was a wonderful feeling. I also remember taking certification exams without knowing whether I was properly prepared to pass the exams or not—I hated that!

Achieve Business Analysis Certification: The Complete Guide to PMI-PBA®, CBAP®, and CPRE Exam Success provides ample high-quality exercises, practice quizzes, and simulated exams, as well as supplemental aids and tips gained through significant experience. It conveys not only the knowledge needed to be confident about passing almost any exam on business analysis, but the level of knowledge that will help *set you apart* from your peers on the job in the real world.

Many of the tips I've shared—with the roughly 300 practitioners whom I provide exam prep training to each year and now here with you—come from firsthand experience. I currently hold more than ten different certifications of my own. Many of the other tips supplied in this guide are based on years of feedback gained from my students who were successful in passing certification exams with high scores on their first attempt. The proven systematic approach used in this guide has been applied quite successfully to several different certification exams, such as the PMI-ACP®, PMI-RMP®, and the PMI-PMP® certification exams, among others. The substantial knowledge delineated in this guide comes from a wide variety of resources including, but not limited to, books and articles written by most of the world's leading experts in this field and a couple previous books of my own.

I took some time off at work and traveled to green Ireland, land of poets and legends, to develop this study guide. I wrote it with the goal of it being one of the first, most effective, most extensive, and yet efficient guides to mastering the content of the PMI-PBA, the Certified Business Analysis Professional (CBAP®), and the Certified Professional for Requirements Engineering (CPRE) certification exams. The goal for the reader is to enable you to achieve one or all of these certifications on your first attempt, and in the process gain an anthology of *knowledge that sets you apart*.

If you should have any ideas on how to improve this guide or would like to share your success in using it, I'd love to hear from you at kni@itu.dk.

Klaus Nielsen

By the way—*Harvard Business Review* (Hillman, 2013) calls the position of business analyst or data scientist the "sexiest job of the 21st century," so you better start reading . . .

Acknowledgments

Acknowledgments are the recognition or favorable notice of an act or achievement, and were numerous in the creation of this work. My only plea is forgiveness for any who are not mentioned, but not by any means forgotten. First of all, I would like to extend my thanks and gratitude to the people who have helped to make this work a reality. By doing so, I need to acknowledge all the leaders, practitioners, students, and experts with whom I have interacted within the fields of project management, agile methodologies, and business analysis. Writing this book has been a research process performed while standing on the shoulders of giants. The Project Management Institute has set the standard high with the *Examination Content and Practice Guide*, which I have interpreted based upon the reference material, and aligned it with top contributors and certifications from the International Institute of Business Analysis and the International Requirements Engineering Board. In addition, this book is supported by a wide range of research, knowledge, articles, and academic sources from ACM digital library, IEEE, and a range of industry resources and professional business and academic books.

Also, I learned a lot (although I did not always realize it at the time) from the world-class educators at the University of Cambridge and the fellows of Trinity College. Hard time spent comes back tenfold.

A large number of people have contributed over the years to the evolution of this book, as many of the ideas in this book have been formed, sharpened, and aired at meetings, training sessions, debates, and lectures.

Thanks to Paul Words for beginning the editing process of this book and making it readable. Thanks to Drew Gierman, the publisher at J. Ross Publishing, Inc., for making this dream possible and providing a wonderful experience. This work would not have been possible without the support of all the people who have taken part, one way or another, in ensuring the quality of this book. Thank you. I owe you my greatest gratitude.

My deepest appreciation goes to Nina, the most patient and most supportive coworker any author or man could ever dream of.

Finally, the greatest of thanks to my family, that has put up with my absence for more birthdays and evenings than I like to think about while writing this book.

Any errors, of course, are mine.

Klaus Nielsen

"With grandiose resolve a man endeavors to soar above all obstacles, but thus encounters a hostile fate. He retreats and evades the issue. The time is difficult. Without rest, he must hurry along, with no permanent abiding place. If he does not want to make compromises within himself, but insists on remaining true to his principles, he suffers deprivation. Nevertheless he has a fixed goal to strive for, even though the people with whom he lives do not understand him and speak ill of him."

The Book of Changes: Darkening of the Light

About the Author

Klaus Nielsen is Cambridge (UK) educated and holds two MBAs (HRM and Technology). He has worked in both project and program management, and as a professional business analyst for more than 15 years; and has been embracing Project Management Institute (PMI), IIBA, and IREB tools, techniques, knowledge, skills, and methodologies for the last 10.

Klaus holds PMP®, PMI-PBA®, PMI-ACP®, and PMI-RMP® credentials from PMI. His other relevant professional certifications include: Certified Scrum Master (CSM), ISTQB, PRINCE2 practitioner, Managing Successful Programmes (MSP), Six Sigma, CPRE-FL, and ITIL.

He is the author of *I am Agile*, *Better Business Case*, and *Mastering the Business Case* and has written numerous industry-related articles that have been published worldwide. For the last few years, Klaus has taught part-time at the IT University of Copenhagen as a faculty lecturer.

Mr. Nielsen is the founder of Global Business Development (gbd.dk), a PMI Registered Education Provider (R.E.P.) and SHRM training company, where he trains and consults for businesses ranging from small start-ups to Fortune 500 companies worldwide. He is also a frequent speaker at events, conferences, and tradeshows. Klaus Nielsen's current programs, at the time of this writing, include:

- PBA® Certification Exam Preparation Course
- ACP® Certification Exam Preparation Course
- RMP® Certification Exam Preparation Course
- PMP® Certification Exam Preparation Course
- Mastering the Business Case based upon the book by Klaus Nielsen and Martin Ernst
- Mastering Projects, Programs, and Portfolios
- SHRM Certified Professional (SHRM-CP)
- SHRM Senior Certified Professional (SHRM-SCP)

As the demand for new professional certifications courses grows, we do our best to meet this need. For a complete listing on Nielsen's programs, products, high-profile clients, and speaking schedule, visit the Global Business Development website at www.gbd.dk. To book him for your next conference, event, or in-house training, please e-mail at kni@itu.dk or connect at LinkedIn.

Web
Added
Value™

This book has free material available for download from the
Web Added Value™ resource center at *www.jrosspub.com*

At J. Ross Publishing we are committed to providing today's professional with practical, hands-on tools that enhance the learning experience and give readers an opportunity to apply what they have learned. That is why we offer ancillary materials available for download on this book and all participating Web Added Value™ publications. These online resources may include interactive versions of material that appears in the book or supplemental templates, worksheets, models, plans, case studies, proposals, spreadsheets and assessment tools, among other things. Whenever you see the WAV™ symbol in any of our publications, it means bonus materials accompany the book and are available from the Web Added Value Download Resource Center at www.jrosspub.com.

Downloads for *Achieve Business Analysis Certification* include:

- Directions for how to use the online test bank with your unique serial number found on the inside front cover of this book
- Hundreds of downloadable practice questions for the IIBA CBAP® and IREB CPRE certification exams
- PowerPoint slides for trainers and instructors

Part 1

Overview,
How to Use This Guide,
Study Tips, and
Pre-Test Knowledge Assessments

Business Analysis Certification Overview

1

1.1 BRIEF INTRODUCTION: CERTIFICATION

For every project, investment, or pitch for new products, a compelling requirement specification is vital in order to succeed. This powerful, easy-to-use, and concise book is that tool for enhancing your professional development and greatly improving your chances of passing these world-recognized business analysis certifications.

Based upon the knowledge and experience of numerous experts on business analysis and packed with additional material from leading researchers, this comprehensive study guide, used in conjunction with the *Project Management Body of Knowledge (PMBOK® Guide)*, provides all you need to know about the Project Management Institute Professional in Business Analysis (PMI-PBA)® examination content, PMI recommended reference material, and the *Business Analysis for Practitioners: A Practice Guide*, to successfully pass the PMI-PBA certification exam. This authoritative reference gives you a unique look into the PMI-PBA exam content, from needs assessment to planning, analysis, traceability, monitoring, and evaluation; and enables you to learn from the best in an easy and timely manner.

Used in conjunction with *A Guide to the Business Analysis Body of Knowledge (BABOK® Guide) v3* and the Agile Extension, you will also have all you need to know to successfully pass the International Institute of Business Analysis (IIBA®) Certified Business Analysis Professional (CBAP®) exam. Furthermore, this study guide provides the knowledge covered in the Certified Professional for Requirements Engineering (CPRE)-Foundation Level (FL) syllabus and all you need to achieve the CPRE-FL designation offered by the International Requirements Engineering Board (IREB).

Some of the materials that you will need to pass these three business analysis certifications will be made available to you in electronic format; the rest is presented in this one book. The first chapter will set the stage and introduce you to how you can maximize the value of the book in order to pass the certifications within a relatively short period of time and with a high level of knowledge and confidence. After reading the first chapter, you will be ready to begin your journey toward achieving exam success and learning the value of the business analyst certifications.

1.2 BUSINESS ANALYSIS CERTIFICATION ORGANIZATIONS

"The Project Management Institute is the world's leading not-for-profit professional membership association for the project, program, and portfolio management profession. Founded in 1969, PMI delivers value for more than 2.9 million professionals working in nearly every country in the world through global advocacy, collaboration, education, and research" (PMI, 2015).

PMI delivers the wide range of certifications listed below, with corresponding frameworks including processes, tools, and techniques for project success, as well as program and portfolio management:

- Professional in Business Analysis (PMI-PBA)®
- Project Management Professional (PMP)®
- Agile Certified Professional (PMI-ACP)®
- Risk Management Professional (PMI-RMP)®
- Program Management Professional (PgMP)®
- Portfolio Management Professional (PfMP)®
- Scheduling Professional (PMI-SP)®
- Certified Associate in Project Management (CAPM)®

As highlighted throughout this book, the PMI-PBA certification is very much entangled with the PMP-ACP, as well as the PMI-RMP certification, because it is the business analyst who delivers the organizational needs throughout projects.

The IIBA was founded in Toronto in 2003, and is globally recognized today for the IIBA standard for practice of business analysis, which is a generally accepted practice for business analysts. The standard for practices are found and verified in the CBAP® designation, which is a professional certification for individuals with extensive business analysis experience.

Since 2007, the IREB has certified business analysts with their CPRE exam, which includes Foundation, Advanced, and Expert levels. As of 2014, the exam has been taken by practitioners in 51 countries, with 17,000 successfully passing, of which a large number are based in European, German-speaking countries.

1.3 BUSINESS ANALYST CERTIFICATION AND BODY OF KNOWLEDGE

The business analyst certification (PMI-PBA) is based upon a role delineation study (RDS) where leaders, skilled practitioners, and key organizational stakeholders—who span a wide variety of industries and geographies in order to maintain a broad and all-encompassing perspective—were taken into account, in order to create the best practice body of knowledge for business analysts. By doing so, PMI employs the very best of project management, and it is reflected in the *PMBOK® Guide—Fifth Edition* and in the Body of Knowledge from the PMI-ACP certification, in order to create a competitive and relevant business analyst designation.

The CBAP® from the IIBA is based upon the *BABOK® Guide v3*, while the CPRE-FL has a syllabus and recommended reading materials, which are to the degree needed, included in this study guide.

A business analyst's work is partly project management related, and partly requirements management related—with both, project management as well as requirements management, being fields with a growing demand. However, there are areas where many projects have the possibility of doing much better. The following research highlights some of the challenges that requirements management is facing today:

- PMI's 2014 Pulse of the Profession® study said that poor requirements management is a major cause of project failure—second only to changing organization priorities. That same Pulse study found that 37 percent of organizations report inaccurate requirements gathering as a primary reason for project failure.

- Business Analysis Benchmark 2009: The Path to Success, a study by IAG consulting, found that poor requirements definition and management maturity undermines organizational competitiveness.
- Poor requirements management made the list of *Top 5 Project Failure Reasons, or Why My Project Fails*, by Eric McConnell.
- Companies with poor business analysis efforts will have three times as many project failures as successes (Ellis, BA Benchmark Report, 2009).
- Companies pay a premium of as much as 60% in time and budget when they use poor requirement practices on their projects (Ellis, BA Benchmark Report, 2009).
- 50% of defects are related to requirement errors (Schwaber, 2006).
- Getting requirements right early in the project can save you one-third or more of your overall project budget (Hooks and Farry, 2001).
- 90% of projects that delivered on time and on budget did not deliver expected business outcomes (Burdette, 2013).
- On average, large information technology (IT) projects run 45% over budget and 7% over in time, while delivering 56% less value than predicted (Forrester, 2012).

Additionally, the benefits of increasing the quality and value of requirements management are tremendous, as costs associated with fixing a defect in the requirements later in the project are very high, and symptoms for inadequate requirements engineering are as numerous as their causes.

1.4 THE VALUE OF BUSINESS ANALYST CERTIFICATIONS

When it comes to career and professional development, education is important, and in order to determine the value of certifications, professionals should ask, "How can a specific certification help me achieve my career goals?"

Part of the answer to this question is related to the organization behind the certification. Professionals and organizations alike need to put trust in the organizations that have developed the certifications. The PMI-PBA certification is developed and managed by PMI, an entity that is well-known and trusted by organizations and their hiring managers for their credential standards. If we examine PMI a bit closer, the statistics of interest, as of May 31, 2014, show 450,011 active members and 650,000 certified individuals globally; these numbers depict an organization that delivers value to 2.9 million professionals working in nearly every country in the world, through global advocacy on a yearly basis. A vast majority of the 650,000 certified individuals are PMPs. However, the PMI-PBA designation is brand new and will quickly gain popularity. When examining the organization, one may also examine the alternative—which for a business analysis professional is the IIBA. The IIBA has over 28,000 members as of 2014 within six continents and is well-known for the Certification of Competency in Business Analysis (CCBA®) and CBAP® certifications. In Europe, the alternative is the IREB. The conclusion is that the amount of people being certified along with the demand from the industry will increase the value of these certifications for most professionals.

The second part to answering the question is related to the content of the certifications, and to some degree, to the requirements in the industry. What is also of significant value is the fact that leading researches and publications are part of the certification, as reference materials, and are not just supported by a single piece of reference. PMI does not endorse specific review courses, resources, references, or other materials for certification preparation. However, PMI does publish a reference list as a courtesy for professionals. The reference list contains best practice sources on business analysis, which are an integrated part of the PMI-PBA certification. The same goes for the IIBA and IREB designations.

The third part to answering the question with regard to the value of a certification relates to the individual and the organization (see Tables 1.1 and 1.2).

The last part of answering the question is associated with deciding whether certification training fits with your current or desired lifestyle. This really has to do with personal and career goals and your current situation in life.

Table 1.1   Value of the certification for individuals

Demonstrates knowledge of the skills necessary to be an effective business analyst	Recognition of professional competence by peers and management
Develops a professional level of competence in the principles and practices of business analysis	Advances career potential by creating a separate and distinct career path within the IT industry and business community
Participates in a recognized professional group	Demonstrates dedication to the business analysis profession
May obtain an increase in salary with certification	May follow market demands and job requirements more effectively
May apply the knowledge and skills to a higher degree than non-certified professionals	Increases professional versatility in business analyst knowledge and skills

Table 1.2   Value of the certification to organizations

Certificate holders are acknowledged as competent individuals who perform a role that is increasingly recognized as a vital component of any successful project	Certificate holders can demonstrate the ability to transfer knowledge across the organization
Global knowledge of the working methods and standards of the organizations	Certificate holders can be identified as individuals with an advanced level of knowledge and qualifications
Certifications follow established standards outlined by PMI, IIBA, and IREB	Certificate holders demonstrate a commitment to quality and may increase the attractiveness of working for the organization
Certificate holders obtain a high relative value, as the effort to pass the certification and the costs associated with it are exceeded by the gains	Certificate holders produce reliable, quality results with increased efficiency and consistency

1.5 TARGET GROUPS FOR BUSINESS ANALYST CERTIFICATIONS

The target groups for business analyst certifications are fairly comprehensive since business analysis is about evaluating the organization's needs. Business analysis is a broader perspective on requirements management, and works closely with project and program management to deliver the organization's needs. The projects may be delivered in a plan-based (Waterfall approach) manner, or by the use of agile (Spiral model) methodologies, which also highlights the importance of varied competence and target groups for business analyst certifications (see Figure 1.1).

Figure 1.1   Target groups for business analyst certifications

1.6 PMI-PBA® EXAM CONTENT

As mentioned previously, early in 2012, PMI initiated an RDS in order to examine the best practice for a PBA designation. The findings were documented as tasks, knowledge, and tools and techniques. The findings were aligned with *A Guide to the Project Management Body of Knowledge*, known as the *PMBOK® Guide—Fifth Edition*, and were published in the PMI-PBA examination content outline, which is available for free at the PMI website at http://www.pmi.org. Early in 2015, PMI published *Business Analysis for Practitioners*, which serves as a practice guide.

The PMI-PBA examination outline describes the content of the certification, which is divided into five domains and 40 sets of knowledge and skills. Table 1.3 illustrates the five domains, the amount of tasks contained in each domain, and the percentage of items tested on the actual exam.

The five domains contain a total of 28 tasks, ranging from four to eight tasks in each domain. The tasks are detailed descriptions of the content of the domain. A task can be explained as a process by which we *define or review a business problem or opportunity using problem and opportunity analysis techniques in order to develop a solution scope statement and/or to provide input to create a business case.* In addition to the domains, the PMI-PBA examination content outline also includes 40 sets of knowledge and skills. An example of content in the knowledge and skills section would be *negotiations tools and techniques.*

The PMI-PBA exam contains 175 scored questions and 25 pretest questions, which are not counted towards the final score. The allocated examination time includes a tutorial in the beginning before time begins, then four hours of exam time, followed by a survey of 15 minutes at the end. Table 1.4 contains the PMI-PBA exam blueprint with the exam and pretest questions. The exam questions on the knowledge and skills are found throughout the domains. Chapter 10 includes an overview of the knowledge and skills mapped to the domains.

The passing score is not published by PMI. However, in order to pass the examination, the level is similar to other PMI certifications. This estimate is around 110–120 correct answers or a score of 63-69%.

As demonstrated earlier, the PMI-PBA examination content outline is an excellent resource on your journey toward your business analyst certification. The second key resource is the PMI-PBA handbook, as it describes the PMI-PBA credential process, including the PMI-PBA eligibility requirements and continuing certification requirements program.

Table 1.3   PMI-PBA domains

Domain	Tasks	Percentage of items on test
Domain 1 – Needs Assessment	5	18%
Domain 2 – Planning	6	22%
Domain 3 – Analysis	8	35%
Domain 4 – Traceability and Monitoring	5	15%
Domain 5 – Evaluation	4	10%

Table 1.4   PMI-PBA exam blueprint

Domain	Exam questions	Pretest questions
Domain 1 – Needs Assessment	32	4
Domain 2 – Planning	38	5
Domain 3 – Analysis	61	9
Domain 4 – Traceability and Monitoring	26	4
Domain 5 – Evaluation	18	3

The PMI-PBA designation emphasizes education and experience, testing competence, and ongoing development for the business analyst. The PMI-PBA credential process is conducted online at the PMI website at http://www.pmi.org, and is highlighted by the timeline of the PMI-PBA credential process:

- Application submission
- Application completeness review
- Application payment process
- Audit process
- Multiple choice examination eligibility
- Certification cycle
- Certification maintenance
- Certification renewal
- Certification suspension
- Credential expiration

On your journey toward business analyst certification, you need to fulfill the PMI-PBA eligibility requirements. These are found in Table 1.5, and contain requirements related to your educational background, business analyst experience, general project experience, and training in business analysis. Two sets of requirements are present, depending on your educational background, as the PMI-PBA eligibility requirements are reduced if you have a bachelor or higher degree.

However, passing the PMI-PBA eligibility requirements and the actual exam is one thing; another aspect is the Continuing Certification Requirements (CCR) program. The CCR program is an online application created in order to enhance ongoing professional development, foster learning opportunities, and sustain the global recognition and value of certification. This is managed by collecting 60 professional development units (PDUs) within a 3-year cycle. The CCR program includes educational activities, as well as *giving back to the profession* activities. Tables 1.6 and 1.7 describe the activities and the maximum PDUs obtained within each category. In general, one PDU is awarded for one hour.

As of December 2015, PMI has changed the CCR program due to the evolution of the profession. One change is that PDUs can be given in smaller size segments of 0.25 in order to reflect how learning has changed. Another part of this update is the new PMI Talent Triangle, which represents the skill set that global organizations have deemed as critical for project practitioners. The Talent Triangle illustrates the three skill areas employers need: Technical Project Management (i.e., requirements gathering, risk management), Strategic and Business Management (i.e., business acumen, legal, finance) and Leadership (i.e., conflicts resolution, motivation).

Table 1.5 PMI-PBA Eligibility requirements

Educational background	Business analyst experience	General project experience	Training in business analysis
Secondary degree	7,500 hours earned within the last eight years	2,000 hours earned within the last eight years	35 contact hours
Bachelor or higher degree	4,500 hours earned within the last eight years	2,000 hours earned within the last eight years	35 contact hours

Table 1.6 Education

Education (35 PDU minimum)	Maximum PDUs within the category in a 3-year cycle
Courses offered by PMI R.E.P. chapters and communities	None
Continuing education	None
Self-directed learning	30 PDUs
No maximum PDUs within a 3-year cycle	

Table 1.7 Giving back to the profession

Giving back to the profession	Maximum PDUs within the category in a 3-year cycle
Creating new project management knowledge	45 PDUs
Volunteer service	45 PDUs
Work as a professional in project management	45 PDUs
No maximum PDUs within a 3-year cycle	

The education requirement is a minimum of 35 PDUs for the PMI-PBA certification. A minimum of 8 PDUs must be obtained within each of the three areas of the Talent Triangle. The remaining 11 PDUs can be obtained in any area of the triangle.

Review this list of activities. Can you tell which ones are accepted by PMI as PDUs?

- Attending a conference on IT practices?
- Attending a work meeting on business analysis?
- Reading a book on business analyst practices?
- Taking part in a free online webinar?
- E-learning from the Institute of Electrical and Electronics Engineers (IEEE) or the Association for Computing Machinery (ACM)?
- Completing a business analysis two-day course?
- Doing extra work on a project?

Interestingly, all of these activities can be considered for PDUs. However, the amount of PDUs may vary depending on the actual activity. This also stresses the fact that PDUs are not necessarily costly or bound to PMI. It's all about ongoing professional development and fostering learning opportunities in order to sustain the global recognition and value of the certification.

Chapters 14 and 15 describe the IIBA CBAP® and the IREB CPRE-FL certifications, content, and requirements.

1.7 USING THIS BOOK TO PASS BUSINESS ANALYST CERTIFICATION EXAMS

The PMI-PBA examination content outline sets the boundaries for the examination. And as mentioned previously, in order to cover the material, PMI has published a list of reference materials for the PMI-PBA certification. Table 1.8 highlights this reference material.

This book summarizes most of the relevant content for the certification exam from the material on the PMI list of reference materials, which represents approximately 5,000 pages in total. Thus, your savings in terms of time and costs are tremendous with this book. In addition, an extensive range of sources have been added to significantly increase your chance of exam success on the very first try—in a quick and easy manner—for the professional business analyst who wants or needs more than to *just pass* the exam. The content of the book is structured around five main bodies as illustrated here:

- Part 1 (Chapters 1–4) gives an introduction to the area of business analysis and cover all the relevant certification issues. Pretest exams are provided for all three business analysis certifications—study tips are provided as well.
- Part 2 (Chapters 5–9) contains the five domains: Needs Assessment; Planning; Analysis; Traceability and Monitoring; and Evaluation, which are demonstrated by the tasks highlighted by PMI. This part is the main bulk of knowledge you need to learn.

Table 1.8 Reference materials for the PMI Professional in Business Analysis (PMI-PBA) Certification

Title	Author	Publisher
A Guide to the Project Management Body of Knowledge (PMBOK® Guide)	Project Management Institute	Project Management Institute
Business Analysis: Best Practices for Success	Steven Blais	Wiley
Business Analysis Techniques: 72 Essential Tools for Success	James Cadle, Paul Turner, and Debra Paul	British Informatics Society Ltd.
Seven Steps to Mastering Business Analysis	Barbara Carkenord	J. Ross Publishing
The Software Requirements Memory Jogger: A Pocket Guide to Help Software and Business Teams Develop and Manage Requirements	Ellen Gottesdiener	Goal QPC Inc.
Unearthing Business Requirements: Elicitation Tools and Techniques	Kathleen Haas and Rosemary Hosenlopp	Management Concepts, Inc.
Customer-Centered Products: Creating Successful Products Through Smart Requirements Management	Ivy F. Hooks and Kristin A. Farry	AMACOM
The Business Analyst's Handbook	Howard Podeswa	Cengage Learning PTR
Mastering the Requirements Process: Getting Requirements Right	Suzanne Robertson and James Robertson	Addison-Wesley Professional
Data Modeling Essentials	Graeme Simsion and Graham Witt	Morgan Kaufmann
Software Requirements 2	Karl Wiegers	Microsoft Press
Business Analysis for Practitioners: A Practice Guide	Project Management Institute	Project Management Institute

- Part 3 (Chapters 10–13) includes the 40 knowledge and skills areas highlighted by PMI along with what you need to know about traditional project management and agile project management. This is the second main part of knowledge to be learned. In addition, the PMI Code of Ethics & Professional Conduct is included.
- Part 4 (Chapters 14–15) gives an overview of the IIBA and IREB certifications and alignment to the PMI-PBA certification.
- Part 5 (Chapter 16) contains one full PMI-PBA practice exam with 175 questions and should be completed within 4 hours. You should not begin the practice exam until you have finished the book. Additionally, with the purchase of a new, physical copy of this book, readers will have 45 days of free access to an online PMI-PBA test bank with over 800 practice exam questions (see this book's WAV material on page xiv for more details).
- Part 6 contains a glossary and a number of acronyms which may be useful as references and for test-prep memorization.

The beginning of most chapters includes a list of the key terms you are required to know by PMI. You may start with these terms, but if you already have solid knowledge of them, then you may consider skipping that chapter. However, once you have finished reading the chapter, you can refer back to the list and test your knowledge.

Each chapter also explains the examination content outline tasks, knowledge, and skills, so you can easily follow your progress and ensure that nothing is missed. Most tasks include relevant exercises that you can complete to get an increased understanding of the content and/or hands-on experience. Furthermore, some chapters have an exercise where you need to match the key terms to their definitions, which will help you memorize the content.

At the end of each chapter, the content is aligned with *PMBOK® Guide* and agile practices in order to set the domains, tasks, knowledge, and skills respectively, and increase the mode of application. This is also quite useful as many examination questions relate to these practices.

Each chapter with exam content has a posttest at the end of the chapter, which is a small practice exam with just five questions to be completed in six to seven minutes. These questions are relevant to the chapter that has just been completed, and taking a posttest is an easy way to measure your own progress.

Study Tips and How to Pass the PMI-PBA® Exam

2

2.1 BRIEF INTRODUCTION: STUDY TIPS

This section will explain exam basics, study tips to know before taking the exam, which can be useful to read at an early stage, and details about the topics included in the exam, which may be useful to read shortly before the actual exam.

2.2 EXAM BASICS

The Project Management Institute's Professional in Business Analysis (PMI-PBA)® examination contains 175 multiple-choice questions with four hours allocated for answers—that is just a little more than 75 seconds to answer each question. During the actual exam, the testing aids required are calculators that are built into the software, along with paper and pencils, or markers and note boards.

The exam will test your knowledge of business analysis domains and tasks, as well as knowledge and skills documented in the PMI-PBA examination content outline and covered in detail throughout this book. You will need to understand the many terms that are used to describe the work of a business analyst. In addition, you will be tested on your ability to apply established business analysis practices in a variety of hypothetical situations. It will be necessary to demonstrate a comprehensive understanding of certain project management and agile methodologies. However, you also need to understand the PMI testing basics.

During the exam, you will encounter 175 well-written, multiple-choice questions with these attributes:

- Most of the wording should be in the question stem.
- Answer choices should be brief and parallel.
- Each question should address a single topic.
- There should be four answer choices. Of those:
  - One choice should be the unambiguous correct answer.
  - One choice should be almost correct. The intent is to distinguish between those who truly know the content from those whose knowledge is more superficial.
  - A third choice may be similar to the previous one, or it could be less correct, while still sounding plausible to the uninformed.
  - One choice should be clearly wrong (but in the same context).

The full practice exam in Chapter 16, the Chapter 4 pretests, the end-of-chapter practice exam questions, and the online exam questions will illustrate and test you on this.

2.3 BEFORE THE EXAM

The certification exams are, in most cases, passed or failed before actually attending the exam, which is highlighted by the alteration of a passage from Sun Tzu, a famous sixth-century BC Chinese military strategist. The reason for this is that only one aspect is the actual exam content; another aspect is mastering the exam by preparing for the actual exam. You need to do both well:

> It is said that if you know your 'examination content outline' and know how to 'learn, memorize, and perform' at the exams, you will not be imperiled in a hundred exams; if you do not know your 'examination content outline' but do know how to 'learn, memorize, and perform' at the exams, you will win one and lose one; if you do not know your 'examination content outline' or how to 'learn, memorize, and perform' at the exams, you will be imperiled in every single exam.

The following section will provide you with some tips on how to learn, memorize, and perform at the exam. Commonsense guidance is not included (such as underlining text with different colored pens, utilizing post-it notes, and other similar tips). Every individual is unique, so what works for you may not work for others, but the following techniques have been tried and tested by many professionals in the past.

If you follow these techniques while preparing with this book, you will most likely pass the PMI-PBA exam. The content of the exam is structured around the application of business analysis theory, practice, and reflection. A multiple-choice exam requires that you know your glossary and have completed as many practice questions and exams as possible because this will help you to learn the content and the exam format. This is the reason that most chapters in this book include terms to know, a posttest, and preparatory exercises. In addition, this book has three 25-question pretests (one for each certification) and a full PMI-PBA practice exam with 175 questions (see Chapter 16) in order to prepare for the actual exam as best as possible. So, follow the chapter outline, do the exams and exercises, and after you have read and completed all of the material, consider the practice of *rinse and repeat*. And in addition to that, please make use of the online material as well.

You may find it advantageous to use some techniques for remembering/memorizing important terms while working with the material in this book. Three techniques which have been proven useful for passing certification exams and for competing in world memory championships are: *mnemonics, the journey method*, and *mind maps*. The techniques are explained below and exercises have been suggested for you to test yourself.

Mnemonics are most commonly used for lists, numerical sequences, knowledge, skills, and techniques. Table 2.1 is an example of estimating techniques with the mnemonics of BIRDS, which makes it easier to remember.

Table 2.1   Mnemonics with BIRDS

- **Brainstorming**
- **Interviewing**
- **Root Cause Analysis**
- **Delphi**
- **SWOT Analysis**

Exercise 2.1—As you continue through this study guide, develop mnemonics of your own for material you will find on the exam.

The journey method is a powerful, flexible, and effective mnemonic device based around the idea of remembering landmarks on a well-known journey. Oddbjørn By, a Norwegian who has been taking part in memory championships, wrote a book called *Memo,* which the example in Table 2.2 is based upon. The idea in this case is to memorize the 10 biggest countries in the world. The journey method of doing this is by connecting the countries to landmarks—in this case, a house I know very well.

Table 2.2   Journey map

Room	Country
At the front door	Russia
Hallway	Canada
Powder room	USA
Game room	China
Bedroom	Brazil
Bathroom	Australia
Kitchen	India
Living room	Argentina
Utility room	Kazakhstan
Cellar	Sudan

The journey method virtualizes the countries in the rooms. After a few minutes to memorize this, you should be able to recall the countries by walking through the house in your memory. At the front door, I see a Russian, meaning Russia. Something else meaning Russia may also be useful, if it is easier to remember. If you need bigger or smaller journeys, you can simply add more to it. Please keep in mind that you cannot add content to the rooms in your memory if you do not understand it properly.

Exercise 2.2—Try the journey method on an exam study topic and include your own landmarks.

A mind map is a diagram used to visually organize information. A mind map for the PMI-PBA exam would include the five domains and the 40 knowledge types and skills. For the exam-content-driven chapters in this book, a similar version called *wordly* is applied, which highlights the content that is present in the chapter. A mind map is usually created around a single concept, drawn as an image in the center of a blank page. Other related images and words are added to the center image, typically connected directly to the central concept like tree branches coming out from its trunk (the core concept).

Exercise 2.3—Develop a mind map or wordly on another study area from this book.

Table 2.3 explains some general study tips for passing the exams.

Table 2.3 Study tips

Study tips	Explanations
Pair up	Describe it to someone, have someone describe it to you, discuss the content and application.
Read, reread, reread	Practice makes perfect.
Explain it to someone	Challenge your understanding—even better, use it at work.
Don't book yourself solid	Apply knowledge and skills.
Build skills in the right order	Don't jump around in the content before you have completed it all, unless you already know it all.
Success spirals	Complete one chapter and have success with the posttest before moving on.
Set realistic expectations	Think Pareto—with a 20% effort, you can master 80% of the content and you will pass the exam. However, if you want the last 20% correct as well, it would require that you learn all the content of the book by heart, which would require 80% more effort.
Time management	Before and during the exam.
Memorize all formulas and definitions	Check the glossary and chapter exercises.
Practice takes time	Take at least three months for the whole preparation—do not try to attempt the exam without being prepared.
Freeze your exam date well in advance	Do it at least three months before since the preferable exam dates may not be available as there is always a high demand for business analyst exams.
Read the *PMBOK® Guide* or *BABOK® Guide*	Even though the exam content is covered in this book, these titles are a must for a thorough understanding.
Read *Business Analysis for Practitioners: A Practice Guide*	Even though the exam content is covered in this book, the practice guide will give you an even better understanding of the BA practice.
Don't read additional literature, as you only need to be an expert on the actual exam syllabus	Focus on the PMI reference list if in need of additional literature, but it should not be necessary since what you need to know is covered here.

2.4 DURING THE EXAM

During the exam, you should consider the general strategies that are highlighted in Table 2.4.

Table 2.4   General strategies

General strategies	Comments
Pace yourself	You have a little more than one minute for each question.
First questions are always tough	Keep your spirit up as you get into rhythm.
Use all of the allotted time	When you get to the end, go back to consider the ones that you were in doubt of or skipped. If all are completed, just double-check and enjoy.
Answer each question the first time you read it	It takes time to read and answer a question—if you read it but don't answer it, time is wasted. Mark the question after answering it if you are not sure.
Use the tutorial	This will teach you how to use the program, which can save you time during the actual exam.
Use the *mark question* feature	If you're not sure of your answer, mark it so that if you have time you can go back and examine it again. Always make sure you answer the question just in case you run out of time and can't make it back.
Take a break or two	Take a break if you feel that you are answering the questions a bit too fast, can't concentrate, or when you have completed all the questions the first time through. A lot of wrong answers are due to lack of a clear mind rather than a lack of knowledge. You will find time for a break or two during the four-hour exam.

Answering the questions should follow the process as illustrated in Figure 2.1.

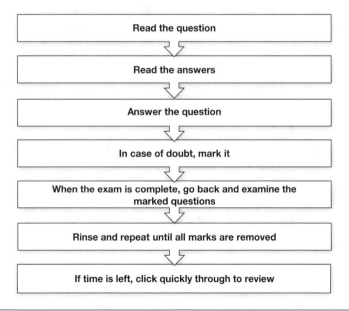

Figure 2.1   Answering the questions

In order to answer the exam questions as successfully as possible, consider the advice that is given in Table 2.5 for handling questions.

Exercise 2.4—How Much Time Left? The PMI-PBA exam consists of 175 multiple choice questions with 4 hours allocated to finish the exam. If you have completed the following number of questions, how much time do you have left for the rest of the questions if each question takes an equal amount of time to solve? (Answers are found under Table 2.5.)

1. 25 questions answered
2. 40 questions answered
3. 75 questions answered
4. 100 questions answered
5. 120 questions answered

Table 2.5   Strategies for answering the exam questions

Strategies for questions	Comments
Read the question.	A critical step to passing the exam is to read and understand each question.
Read ALL the choices.	Reading each of the four answers is just as important as carefully reading the questions.
Use a process of elimination.	Remove the clearly wrong answers first so you can use the time on the two likely answers.
Guessing.	You are well prepared, have read the material, and completed the book, so trust your instinct—it is not there by chance.
Remember that you're looking for the best answer.	One or two answers might seem correct—however, you need to pick the best one.
There are certain questions that contain extra information.	This information is irrelevant and does not relate to the correct answer. Beware of such questions and remember, it isn't necessary to use all the information provided to answer the question.
Each question has only one correct answer.	You need to select the most appropriate answer.
You need to answer the questions from a PMI perspective—not from your own perspective, which you acquired through experience.	Remember that PMI is trying to present an ideal environment for business analysts, which might be different from your own experience.
Beware of answer choices that represent generalizations that may be characterized by words such as always, never, must, or completely.	These are often the incorrect choices.
Look out for choices that represent special cases. These choices tend to be correct and are characterized by words such as often, sometimes, may, generally, and perhaps.	The correct answer may not be grammatically correct.

Answers to *Exercise 2.4*: 3 hours and 25 minutes, 3 hours and 5 minutes, 2 hours and 17 minutes, 1 hour and 43 minutes, and 1 hour and 15 minutes.

Organizational Need for Business Analysts

3

3.1 BRIEF INTRODUCTION: ORGANIZATIONAL NEED

Every project starts with a need; projects without a need don't fail at the end, they fail at the beginning. This is why we need the business analyst to connect the dots and ensure project success—because unclear or incomplete requirements are the main cause of project failure. In the list of reasons for canceled projects by The Standish Group (2006), incomplete requirements and changing requirements are in the top 10 every year. The Project Management Institute's (PMI's) 2014 annual global Pulse of the Profession® study revealed that 47% of unsuccessful projects fail to meet goals due to poor requirements management. Furthermore, the same study revealed that *inaccurate requirements gathering* remained a primary cause of project failure—37% in 2014 (up from 32% in 2013). PMI research highlights that when executive sponsors give value to requirements management as a critical competency, it leads to better project performance—and, of course, poor requirements lead to inadequate performance. However, only 49% of organizations report that they have the necessary resources in place to properly perform requirements management. The research indicates that high-performing organizations, as a whole, are significantly more likely to value requirements management as a critical competency versus low-performing organizations. This highlights the importance of effective requirements management as one of the key factors in determining project success (Burke, 2010). On the other hand, unclear or incomplete requirements could possibly be fixed at a later time—however, costs may then be relatively high (Pflegeer, 2000) as illustrated in Table 3.1, based upon data from the Department of the Air Force Software Technology Support Center.

Table 3.1 Cost of fixing requirements

Phase in which fixed	Relative cost multiplier
Requirements	1
Design	3–6
Development	10
Testing	15–40
Acceptance testing	30–70
Operations	40–1000

3.2 BUSINESS ANALYST ROLE

The business analyst is the person who manages requirements. However, requirements change rapidly (Reifer, 2000). A survey of 4,000 European companies by Sommerville in 2000 indicated the lack of proper management of changing requirements as one of the main drivers and links to the lack of project success. With an increase in complexity due to a wide range of factors—such as globalization, technology, systems, processes, and resources—the role of the business analyst is more vital and complex than ever before. Furthermore, we need business analysts more than ever. A survey by McKinsey and Company, "Big Data Report" (Hillman, 2013), found that by 2018 the United States alone needs between 140,000–190,000 professionals with deep analytical skills, such as business analysts.

The business analyst can be an independent assessor or a catalyst for change that can create a positive attitude of collaboration, in order to overcome internal inertia against change. He/she is a self-confident analyst of change, which requires analytical thinking and conflict resolution skills. Often, creative problem solving is also needed, combined with empathy and communication skills.

The British Computer Society (BCS) proposes the following definition of a business analyst: *An internal consultancy role that has the responsibility for investigating business systems, identifying options for improving business systems, and bridging the needs of the business with the use of IT.*

One of the basic objectives of a PMI-Professional in Business Analysis (PBA)® is to correlate business analysis and project management activities together. These roles share many responsibilities, and this is why some people get confused about what differentiates the two roles. A project manager is accountable for the successful completion of a project, which is measured by the fact that objectives of the project have been achieved. A business analyst, on the other hand, is accountable for the product scope of the project, which needs to be defined correctly and delivered. Therefore, requirement processes will be seen in elaborated form in a PMI-PBA, and the business analyst will ensure that product vision is in line with the benefits mentioned in the business case.

Business analysis is the evaluation of an organization's needs, followed by the identification and management of requirements, to arrive at a solution. In other words, it is the discipline of working with stakeholders to define an organization's requirements in order to shape the output of projects and ensure that the output delivers the expected business benefits.

The business analyst works closely with both the business and the development community (see Table 3.2). The business analyst defines the product or solution which solves a business problem. The defined solution is then produced by the development community and project.

According to the PMI global standard, *Business Analysis for Practitioners* (2015), "a business analyst is the application of knowledge, skills, tools, and techniques to:

- Determine problems and opportunities;
- Identify and recommend viable solutions for meeting those needs;
- Elicit, document, and manage stakeholders requirements in order to meet business and project objectives; and
- Facilitate the successful implementation of the product, service, or end result of the program or project."

Table 3.2 The business analyst blueprint

Business community		Upper-level management		Development community
	Business manager		IT manager	
Problem owner		BA		Project manager
Process workers		Defines		Solution team
Problem	**Solve**	**Solutions**	**Produce**	**Projects**

In order to make this happen, we need the business analysis to relate to project management, as: *project management is the application of knowledge, skills, tools and techniques to project activities to meet project requirements. Requirements are an inherent aspect of project management (and program management) and business analysis is an important function that identifies, analyzes, and manages those requirements in order to ensure the goal of the project is achieved* (PMI, 2014).

In addition, we need the business analysis to relate to requirements management, as: *business analysis is a discipline of the broader practice of requirements management. Risk, complexity, change, and stakeholder and communications management are components of requirements management but are only useful if you successfully identify and plan for them within the project and/or program plan* (PMI, 2014).

This emphasizes the wide range of competencies needed by the business analyst in order to perform in alignment with project management and requirements management. Some of these competencies are: business intelligence, business process management, requirements management, decision analysis, enterprise architecture, compliance issues management, quality control, organizational change management, project management, program management, software improvements, and strategic planning. All of these are highlighted throughout this book, where the domains melt together with knowledge and skills from project and requirements management.

Exercise 3.1—What is a Business Analyst Really? Explain with your own words the variation in definitions of a business analyst as defined by BCS and PMI. (An answer is found on the bottom of page 22.)

3.3 THE RELATIONSHIP BETWEEN THE BUSINESS ANALYST AND THE PROJECT MANAGER

The relationship between the business analyst and the project manager is often not clear—at best, slightly confusing. On the surface, the project manager manages the project, while the business analyst conducts business analysis—however, it's not that simple, nor should it be. The business analyst is responsible for a subset of activities in the project that need to be aligned and managed collaboratively. If business analysis activities fail, the project will most likely fail, with scope challenges resulting in the wrath of stakeholders.

If business analysis activities are successful, the likelihood of success for the project increases, with product scope well-defined and managed. As this book will demonstrate, the business analyst needs to identify and manage stakeholders, risks, communication, and a range of business analysis planning activities which also are activities involving the project manager. In *Business Analysis for Practitioners* (2015), these duties are defined as collaboration points where the business analyst and the project manager should work together since joining forces may increase the value of the work more than doing it individually. The project manager and business analyst are both leaders within their area of expertise, which requires some degree of alignment and cooperation to work. In order to make the partnership work, to avoid rework and stakeholder confusion, the roles and responsibilities of the business analyst and the project manager need to be coordinated and communicated. Some may see the relationship between the business analyst and the project manager as a competition; however, that should not be the case, as each one is needed for the other to be successful. As a result, more and more successful business analysts and project managers have experience with both roles.

Answer to *Exercise 3.1*: The BCS defines the business analyst as an internal consultant with a more narrow focus than PMI where the application of knowledge, skills, and tools and techniques are more explicit. PMI also sees the business analyst as having a wider range of roles and a greater impact on the successful implementation of the project.

Pretest Knowledge Assessments for Business Analyst Certification Exams

4

4.1 BRIEF INTRODUCTION: KNOWLEDGE ASSESSMENT

This chapter is intended to test your current knowledge of business analysis. These pretests should be completed before moving on to further chapters. It will help you focus on those areas of your knowledge and experience that are weakest, and save you time by allowing you to skim over areas in which you are already knowledgeable and strong. These assessments may also help you decide whether you need to take a special course before attempting a certification exam.

4.2 PRETEST QUESTIONS FOR THE PMI-PBA® DESIGNATION

This pretest includes 25 Project Management Institute Professional in Business Analysis (PMI-PBA)® practice exam questions. Use no more than 30 minutes to complete this pretest. Please answer the questions in the answer section next to the questions in Table 4.1. You will find the correct answers to the questions, explanations, and areas of knowledge (such as domains or knowledge and skills) in the following section (see Table 4.2). These pretest questions are also good training if you are aiming for the Certified Business Analysis Professional (CBAP®) or Certified Professional for Requirements Engineering-Foundation Level (CPRE-FL) exams.

Table 4.1   PMI-PBA pretest questions and answers section

No.	Question	Answer
1	Who signs off in a Scrum project? a) The stakeholders b) The product owner c) The Scrum Master d) The development team	
2	The business case is developed for: a) The current solution b) The proposed solution c) All scenarios d) All stakeholders' identified needs	
3	Traceability tools are *not*: a) Specification trees b) Text-based references and hyperlinks c) Trace matrices d) Trace requirement documents	
4	Which of the following aspects may influence the context of a system? a) People b) Systems not in operation c) Former events d) Obsolete documentation	
5	Which of the following diagrams are *not* used in a root cause analysis? a) Cause and effect b) Ishikawa c) Fishbone d) Use case	
6	What is business value? a) A concept that is unique to each organization and includes tangible and intangible elements b) A concept that is unique to each organization and includes costs and benefits c) A concept that is unique to each organization and includes the cost-benefit analysis d) The result of the business case	
7	In Scrum, requirements are called: a) User stories b) Features c) Requirements d) Epics	
8	In conflict management, which step may be involved? a) Conflict assessment b) Conflict navigation c) Conflict resolution d) Conflict management	
9	Organization assessment for change would follow which category? a) People change b) System change c) Cultural change d) Valuation change	

10	You are gathering information about the business. What kind of material are you likely to use? a) Job descriptions b) Trouble-shooting documents c) Financial reports d) All of the above	
11	Which technique would you use to elicit requirements that are categorized in the Kano model as dissatisfiers? a) Observations b) Document-centric techniques c) Both of the above d) Survey techniques	
12	If you are using three-point estimates, one being optimistic, which technique are you using? a) Parametric estimating b) Delphi c) Program evaluation and review technique (PERT) d) Expert judgment	
13	One approach to requirements elicitation on a high level is the Brown Cow Model which includes: a) Future b) Past c) Why d) Near future	
14	Using Schein's iceberg on culture, what would you describe the company logo as? a) An artifact b) A basic assumption c) A belief d) A company item	
15	Traceability and monitoring manage the life cycle of the requirements and entails: a) Ongoing progress and control b) Ongoing communication and collaboration c) Configuration management d) Change management	
16	You have identified opportunities and challenges to a process. In which document is the result most likely documented? a) Project scope description b) Vision document c) Statement of the problem d) Project charter	
17	Risks can be identified as opportunities or challenges. In a project, where/when would the business analyst most likely find the answers to how to classify these risks? a) During the risk analysis b) Documented in the risk register c) Identified by the stakeholders d) In the business case, risk management section	
18	You are using the PLUME model. What does the *M* stand for? a) Management b) Memorability c) Memory d) Mastery	

19	The voice of the customer may *not* be derived from: a) Business requirements b) The impact analysis c) Constraints d) Solution ideas	
20	Which statement is most true? a) Requirement changes happen all the time due to stakeholders' changing goals. b) Requirement changes are inevitable. c) Requirement changes happen all the time due to a lack of requirement management competence. d) Requirement changes are always very costly.	
21	How does a business analyst analyze solution-identified gaps? a) Using quality assurance tools b) Using time schedules c) Using the control scope process d) Interview the stakeholders	
22	How would you document the system context? a) Use case diagrams b) User stories c) Value stream mapping d) Software requirement specifications	
23	Categorizing the requirements according to the Kano model; Delighters are: a) Explicitly demanded system properties b) Unexpected system properties c) Properties of the system that are self-evident d) Properties of the system that are taken for granted	
24	Business analyst tasks with regard to traceability do *not* involve: a) Updating the traceability matrix b) Updating requirement documentation c) Communicating requirement status d) Communicating configuration status	
25	Who owns the requirement management plan? a) The project manager b) The business analyst c) The product owner d) The Scrum Master	

4.3 PRETEST ANSWERS FOR THE PMI-PBA DESIGNATION

The answers correspond to the questions with the same numbers—in other words, Answer 1 goes with Question 1, and so forth. In addition to the explanations, the *chapter column* directs you to where relevant information will be found.

Table 4.2 Answer sheet to the PMI-PBA pretest

No.	Answer	Explanation	Chapter
1	B	In Scrum the signoff is done by the product owner. The development team has influence on the work performed, the Scrum Master guides the process, while the stakeholders provide input to the product owner.	Chapter 9
2	A	The business case is developed for the current solution; it contains risk and is aligned with stakeholder needs.	Chapter 5
3	D	Traceability tools include text-based references, hyperlinks, trace matrices, trace graphs, specification trees, specialized templates, traceability chains, and requirement/tracing tools.	Chapter 8
4	A	Aspects that may influence the context of a system are people (stakeholders or groups of stakeholders), systems in operation, processes (technical or physical processes, business processes), events (technical or physical), and documents (e.g., laws, standards, system documentation).	Chapter 6
5	D	Cause and effect diagrams, Ishikawa diagrams, and fishbone diagrams are the same kind of diagrams and are all used for root cause analysis.	Chapter 10
6	A	Business value is defined as *a concept that is unique to each organization and includes tangible and intangible elements*. Tangible and intangible elements include costs and benefits, which are found in the cost-benefit analysis of the business case.	Chapter 5
7	A	In Scrum, the requirements are called user stories. Large user stories are called epics and may be divided into user stories and features.	Chapter 8
8	C	Conflict management includes conflict identification, conflict analysis (who, what, why, when) and conflict resolution.	Chapter 10
9	A	Organizational change, people change, or benefit management.	Chapter 10
10	D	For gathering information, the following sources are often used: business plans, strategic plans, marketing plans, business rules procedures, process flow charts, enterprise architecture, job descriptions, trouble-shooting documents, financial reports, business cases, business needs, and solution scope.	Chapter 5
11	C	Observations and document-centric techniques are both widely applied for this purpose in the Kano model.	Chapter 7
12	C	The program evaluation and review technique (PERT) is a three-point estimation method based upon an optimistic, most likely, and pessimistic estimate. Delphi implies asking several experts not in the same location, parametric would imply use of data, while expert judgment is advice from one or more experts.	Chapter 10
13	A	The Brown Cow Model includes four quadrants: Future, Now, How, and What.	Chapter 7
14	A	The company logo is a company item, however, it is described by Schein as an artifact.	Chapter 10
15	B	Traceability and monitoring manage the life cycle of the requirements, which include ongoing communication and collaboration.	Chapter 8
16	B	The result is in the vision document which is translated into the project scope description and also contains the statement of the problem. The documents are input to the project charter.	Chapter 5
17	A	Opportunities and challenges surrounding risk are found during risk analysis. The risk register is completed during risk analysis. Stakeholders take part in risk analysis. The business case includes risks, which also are included in the risk analysis.	Chapter 5

18	B	Memorability.	Chapter 9
19	C	The voice of the customer may be derived from business requirements, the impact analysis, and solution ideas.	Chapter 7
20	B	Requirement changes happen all the time and are inevitable. Changes are not always costly or due to lack of competence.	Chapter 6
21	A	The business analyst needs to analyze and communicate the solution-identified gaps and deltas using quality assurance tools and methods in order to enable stakeholders to resolve discrepancies between solution scope, requirements, and the developed solution.	Chapter 9
22	A	The typical documentation of the system context contains use case diagrams, data flow diagrams, context diagrams, and work scope diagrams.	Chapter 6
23	B	Delighters are unexpected system properties that would impress stakeholders.	Chapter 7
24	D	The business analyst tasks with regard to traceability involve keeping track of changes, collecting requirement traceability information, tracking and reporting requirement status, updating requirement documentation, communicating requirement status and changes, and maintaining and updating the traceability matrix.	Chapter 8
25	B	The requirement management plan is owned by the business analyst while the project manager owns the project plan. The product owner is the one responsible in Scrum while the Scrum Master guides the process.	Chapter 6

4.4 PRETEST QUESTIONS FOR THE IIBA CBAP® DESIGNATION

This pretest includes 25 exam-related practice questions for the International Institute of Business Analysis (IIBA®) CBAP® designation. Use no more than 30 minutes to complete this pretest. Please answer the questions in the answer section, next to the question. You will find the correct answers to the questions, explanations, and areas of knowledge (such as domains or knowledge and skills) in the following section. These pretest questions are also good training if you are aiming for the PMI-PBA or International Requirements Engineering Board (IREB) CPRE-FL exams. Table 4.3 contains the questions and answers section, and the answer sheet is found in Table 4.4, which includes the correct answers and explanations.

Table 4.3 CBAP® pretest questions and answers section

No.	Question	Answer
1	You are part of a process in which a stakeholder map is developed and some stakeholders are mapped as *keep informed* due to: a) The stakeholders have high impact and high influence b) The stakeholders have low impact and high influence c) The stakeholders have low impact and low influence d) The stakeholders have high impact and low influence	
2	You are in the process of *Planning Stakeholder Engagement.* Which knowledge area are you working in? a) Business Analysis Planning and Monitoring b) Requirements Analysis and Design Definition c) Communication d) Business Procedures	
3	Which of the following is *not* a reason for changing requirements? a) Change in rules and regulations by regulatory bodies b) Lack of consensus c) Business need changes d) Lack of resources	
4	You are in need of price quotes from a range of vendors. Which form would be the best option? a) Price form b) RFI c) RFQ d) RFP	
5	Which of the following options represent a competency of a business analyst? a) Emotional intelligence b) Technical knowledge c) Software development know how d) Behavioral characteristics	
6	Which of the following can be used in a root cause analysis? a) A cause and effect diagram b) An Ishikawa diagram c) A Fishbone diagram d) All of the above	
7	In the RACI model, *A* is short for: a) Accepted b) Approval c) Advisor d) Accountable	
8	What does MoSCoW stand for? a) Must, should, could, won't b) Must, shall, could, won't c) Must, should, can, won't d) Must, shouldn't, could, will not	
9	Is the business analyst stakeholder in all business analysis activities? a) Yes b) No, just in some of the business analysis activities c) A business analyst is not a stakeholder d) Maybe, depends on the project	

10	Which of the following techniques are best for confirming the stated requirements and stakeholder concerns? a) Observation b) Focus groups c) Workshops d) Prototypes	
11	Which of the following forms of financial analysis would *not* be found in the business case? a) Payback period b) NPV c) IRR d) Asset management ratios	
12	Which of the following is *not* a knowledge area? a) Strategy Analysis b) Requirement Management c) Elicitation and Collaboration d) Solution Evaluation	
13	Which of the following is a procurement document? a) Work breakdown structure b) Product backlog c) Project charter d) Request for proposal	
14	Which of the following tasks are *not* included in the knowledge area of Elicitation and Collaboration? a) Prepare Elicitation Package b) Conduct Elicitation c) Communicate Business Analysis Information d) Confirm Elicitation Results	
15	What is the use of a requirements repository? a) A method for versioning b) A method of identifying and storing requirements c) A method of storing requirements d) A method used in conjunction with change management	
16	Which knowledge area is used to identify the current state? a) Business Analysis Planning and Monitoring b) Solution Evaluation c) Requirements Analysis and Design Definition d) Elicitation and Collaboration	
17	Which one of the following techniques is most likely applied in the Plan Business Analysis Approach? a) Fagan inspection b) Business rules c) GAP analysis d) Decision analysis	
18	You are shadowing a coworker for a day in order to elicit requirements. This technique is a variant of: a) Workshops b) Observation c) Interviewing d) Prototyping	

19	Which of the following is a table of all stakeholders, showing the mapping of which stake-holders will contribute information to other stakeholders? a) Solution scope management plan b) Organizational breakdown structure c) RAM chart d) Communications management plan	
20	Which one of the following is most likely a domain subject matter expert? a) Any individual with in-depth knowledge of a topic relevant to the business need or solution scope b) End users of the solution c) People who will be indirect users of the solution, such as managers d) All of the above	
21	Which of the following types of charts shows which resources are needed in the project and allows you to group the resources by project phase or other attributes? a) Organizational breakdown structure b) Gantt chart c) Root cause analysis d) Resource breakdown structure	
22	In the Business Analysis Planning & Monitoring knowledge area, which one of the following is *not* an organizational process asset? a) COBIT™ b) Sarbanes-Oxley c) Planning poker d) V-model	
23	Decision analysis uses the following theory: a) Total quality management b) Decision matrix c) Game theory d) Decision flow analysis	
24	You are conducting Plan Business Analysis Governance; which task have you just completed? a) Trace Requirement b) Prepare Requirements Package c) Plan Stakeholder Engagement d) Assess Risks	
25	Which document is considered to be the most important for the go-ahead approval of a project? a) The business case b) The solution scope c) The enterprise analysis d) The requirement specification	

4.5 PRETEST ANSWERS FOR THE IIBA CBAP® DESIGNATION

The answers correspond to the questions with the same numbers—in other words, Answer 1 goes with Question 1, and so forth. In addition to the explanations, the *chapter column* directs you to where relevant information can be found.

Table 4.4 Answer sheet to the CBAP® pretest

No.	Answer	Explanation	Chapter
1	B	The stakeholders with low impact and high influence are kept informed.	Chapter 5
2	A	The task, *Plan Stakeholder Engagement*, is conducted in the Business Analysis Planning and Monitoring knowledge area.	Chapter 14
3	D	The common reasons for change are: change in perceived value, change in technology, change in rules and regulations by regulatory bodies, lack of consensus, business need changes, and lack of traceability.	Chapter 7
4	C	RFQ is a request for quote.	Chapter 10
5	D	The business analyst's underlying competencies are: analytical thinking and problem solving, behavioral characteristics, business knowledge, communication skills, interaction skills, and tools and technology.	*BABOK® Guide v3*
6	D	Herringbone, Ishikawa, and Fishbone diagrams are all cause and effect diagrams used in root cause analysis.	Chapter 10
7	D	*A* is short for accountable which is the only decision maker.	Chapter 5
8	A	MoSCoW means must, should, could, won't.	Chapter 7
9	A	By definition, the business analyst is a stakeholder in all business analysis activities.	*BABOK® Guide v3*
10	C	Workshops or interviews.	Chapter 7
11	D	The most common financial analyses applied in the business case are return on investment (ROI), discounted cash flow, net present value (NPV), internal rate of return (IRR), cost-benefit analysis, and payback period (PP).	Chapter 5
12	B	The knowledge areas are Elicitation and Collaboration, Business Analysis Planning and Monitoring, Requirement Life Cycle Management, Strategy Analysis, Requirement Analysis and Design Definition, and Solution Evaluation.	Chapter 14
13	D	An invitation to bid or RFP (request for proposal).	Chapter 10
14	A	Prepare for Elicitation, Conduct Elicitation, Confirm Elicitation Results, Communicate Business Analysis Information, and Manage Stakeholder Collaboration are tasks included in the Elicitation and Collaboration knowledge area.	Chapter 14
15	C	A requirements repository is a method of storing requirements, including those under development, those under review, and approved requirements.	Chapter 7
16	A	Business Analysis Planning and Monitoring describes how business analysts identify the current state.	Chapter 14
17	D	Decision analysis, process modeling, and structured walkthrough are applied in this task.	*BABOK® Guide v3*
18	B	Shadowing and apprenticing are variants of observation.	Chapter 7
19	B	Organizational breakdown structure.	Chapter 10
20	D	A domain subject matter expert is any individual with in-depth knowledge of a topic relevant to the business need or solution scope. This role is often filled by people who will also be end users or people who will be indirect users of the solution, such as managers, process owners, legal staff (who may act as proxies for regulators), consultants, and others.	*BABOK® Guide v3*
21	D	Resource breakdown structure.	Chapter 10

22	C	Include the elements of existing business analysis approaches in use by the organization. Organizational process assets that may be useful in defining the business analysis approach include methodologies for process change or software development, tools or techniques that are in use or understood by stakeholders, corporate governance standards (such as COBIT™, Sarbanes-Oxley, and Basel II), and templates for deliverables.	*BABOK® Guide v3*
23	C	Game theory.	*BABOK® Guide v3*
24	C	The order of tasks in Business Analysis Planning and Monitoring are: Plan Business Analysis Approach, Plan Stakeholder Engagement, and Plan Business Analysis Governance.	*BABOK® Guide v3*
25	A	The business case is designed to provide a narrative that describes the cost-benefit of the project.	Chapter 10

4.6 PRETEST QUESTIONS FOR THE IREB CPRE-FL DESIGNATION

The pretest includes 25 exam-related practice questions for the IREB CPRE-FL designation. Use no more than 30 minutes to complete this pretest. Please answer the questions in the answer section, next to the question. You will find the answers to the questions, explanations, and areas of knowledge (such as domains or knowledge and skills) in the following section. These pretest questions are also good training if you are aiming for the PMI-PBA or IIBA CBAP® exams. Table 4.5 contains the questions and answers section, and the answer sheet is located in Table 4.6, which includes the correct answers and explanations.

Table 4.5 CPRE-FL pretest questions and answers section

No.	Question	Answer
1	An evaluation consists of activities to determine how well the developed solution fulfills: a) The contract b) The project charter and defined solution c) The defined solution and business needs d) The stakeholders requirements	
2	What is the *system context*? a) Part of the system environment that is relevant for the definition as well as the understanding of the requirements b) A specific context that can only be interpreted correctly by the business analyst c) It is the context that separates the system to be developed from its environment d) All aspects within the system	
3	What is a disadvantage of survey techniques? a) Can't uncover subconscious requirements b) Time consuming c) Costly in any scale d) Gathers requirements that the requirement engineer already knows	
4	Why is requirement elicitation like a good murder novel? a) It is a bit of a mystery b) It requires a lot of skills to master c) It requires some time and energy to complete d) It is error prone	

5	Which sentence best characterizes the term *requirement*? a) A thing that is needed or wanted. b) A thing that is compulsory; a necessary condition. c) A condition or capability needed by a user to solve a problem or achieve an objective. d) A condition or capability needed by a user to solve a range of problems.	
6	Sources and sinks help to identify the interfaces the system has with its environment. Which answer best describes a *sink*? a) A sink is an output from the system to be developed b) A sink is an input to the system to be developed c) A sink is the medium by which to interact with the system to be developed d) All of the above	
7	Which of the following describes an Entity-Relationship diagram? a) Graphical representation of entities b) Display structure and content c) Sometimes suited for requirements modeling d) Logical structure of files	
8	Which of the following *two* conceptual models may be used for requirements documentation? a) Cause and effect diagram b) Use case diagram c) Activity diagram d) User story	
9	What are among the most commonly used traceability tools? a) Enterprise environment factors b) Organizational process assets c) Specialized templates d) Traceability path	
10	Which of the following statements best characterizes a stakeholder during elicitation? a) A person or an organization that has little or no direct influence on the requirements of the system b) Essential in engineering c) A source of requirements d) A key decision maker	
11	Which *two* items best characterize the documentation of the system context? a) E/R diagrams b) Use case diagrams c) Data flow diagrams d) Prototypes	
12	Which activity conducted during requirements validation supports traceability? a) Specification checking b) Authoring c) Traceability modeling d) Visual modeling	
13	Which statements characterizes the term *requirements specification*? a) A requirements specification is a systematically represented collection of requirements b) Description of a system to be developed c) A formal depiction of requirements d) All of the above	

14	What is an alternative to the requirement traceability matrix? a) Requirement documents b) Traceability chain c) Use case diagrams d) Websites	
15	Which of the following statements characterize the goals of requirements engineering? a) Understand the relevant requirements b) Achieve a consensus about the requirements among the stakeholders c) Document requirements according to given standards d) All of the above	
16	Which of the following is a type of requirement source? a) Stakeholders b) Legal documents c) Systems in operation d) All of the above	
17	What is a common use of a requirement repository? a) A requirement specification b) A WIP board c) A requirement matrix d) A website with folders for requirement documents	
18	Which of the following is *not* true regarding using natural language to document requirements? a) It does not require preparation time to be read b) It is understood by stakeholders c) It can be used to describe any type of circumstance d) It has no disadvantages	
19	At a control board meeting, which role on the change control board analyzes and assesses a change request? a) Originator b) Modifier c) Verifier d) Evaluator	
20	Which of the following is *not* a characteristic of a requirements engineer? a) Management skill b) Analytical thinking c) Empathy d) Communication skill	
21	Under the Kano model, dissatisfiers are concerned with: a) Subconscious properties b) Conscious properties c) Unconscious properties d) System properties that the stakeholder does not know or expect and discovers only while using the system	
22	System archaeology belongs to what kind of group of techniques? a) Support techniques b) Document-centric techniques c) Observation techniques d) Creativity techniques	

23	Which of the following statements best characterizes the relationship between a requirements engineer and a stakeholder in the role of a tester? a) The requirements engineer delivers input for the work of the stakeholder b) The output from the requirements engineer is managed by the stakeholder who also acts as Scrum Master c) The requirements engineer delivers input for the stakeholders who adapt it for the product owner d) The stakeholder monitors the work of all involving the requirements engineer	
24	Which diagram is *least* suited for the representation of the delimitation of an IT system? a) Cause and effect diagram b) Activity diagram c) Use case diagram d) Context diagram with data flows	
25	Which of the following is a type of requirement? a) Functional requirement b) Quality requirement c) Constraint d) All of the above	

4.7 PRETEST ANSWERS FOR THE IREB CPRE-FL DESIGNATION

The answers correspond to the questions with the same numbers—in other words, Answer 1 goes with Question 1, and so forth. In addition to the explanations, the *chapter column* directs you to where relevant information will be found.

Table 4.6 Answer sheet to the CPRE-FL pretest

No.	Answer	Explanation	Chapter
1	C	The evaluation consists of activities to determine how well the developed solution fulfills the defined solution and business needs. This involves validating the solutions and business needs with the use of acceptance criteria.	Chapter 9
2	A	System context is the part of the system environment that is relevant for the definition and understanding of the requirements of a system to be developed.	Chapter 6
3	B	Time consuming.	Chapter 7
4	D	Requirement elicitation is error prone, therefore a structured approach and documentation is emphasized, almost like a good murder novel.	Chapter 7
5	C	A requirement is defined as a condition or capability needed by a user to solve a problem or achieve an objective.	Chapter 7
6	A	A sink is an output from the system to be developed.	Chapter 6
7	A	The Entity-Relationship diagram is a graphical representation of entities.	Chapter 7
8	B,C	Use case diagram, activity diagram, and class diagram.	Chapter 7
9	C	Text-based references and hyperlinks, trace matrices, trace graphs (over different development artifacts), specification trees, specialized templates, traceability chain (foundation for impact analysis), and requirement/tracing tools.	Chapter 8
10	C	A stakeholder is essential in requirements engineering and is the most important source of requirements.	Chapter 5
11	B,C	System context documentations are, in most situations, use case diagrams and data flow diagrams.	Chapter 6
12	A	Requirement validation activities include specification checking, simulation design, and test case automation.	Chapter 8
13	D	All are correct.	Chapter 7
14	B	The requirement traceability matrix is an effective tool. However, some alternatives could be textual reference, hyperlinks, and trace graphs (over different development artifacts) or traceability chains (linking relations). Most of these tools are integrated in most automated requirement management tools.	Chapter 6
15	D	All are correct.	Not included
16	C	Stakeholders, legal documents, and systems in operation can all be requirement sources.	Chapter 7
17	C	Requirement repository (i.e., the requirement matrix).	Chapter 6
18	D	Natural language can have several disadvantages, such as misunderstandings.	Chapter 7
19	D	The role of evaluator analyzes and assesses a change request.	Chapter 6
20	A	Analytical thinking, empathy, communication skill, conflict resolution skill, moderation skill, self-confidence, and persuasiveness are characteristics of a requirements engineer.	Not included
21	A	Dissatisfiers—properties of the system that are self-evident and taken for granted (subconscious).	Chapter 7
22	B	Document-centric techniques	Chapter 7

23	A	The requirements engineer delivers input for the work of the stakeholder.	Not included
24	A	A cause and effect diagram is used for root cause analysis.	Chapter 7
25	D	All are correct.	Chapter 7

Part 2

The Domains

Needs Assessment Domain

5

TERMS TO KNOW

The list at the beginning of each chapter highlights the key terms you are required to know by the Project Management Institute (PMI). Hence, you should start with these terms. If you already have solid knowledge of them, you may consider skipping this chapter. However, once you have finished reading the chapter, you can refer back to this list and test your knowledge. The concepts are:

- Identifying stakeholders
- Techniques for identifying stakeholders
- Stakeholder register
- Analyzing stakeholders
- Techniques for analyzing stakeholders
- Responsible, accountable, consulted, and informed (RACI) and responsibility assignment matrix (RAM)
- Investigating problems and opportunities

- Conducting current state assessment
- Stakeholder salience
- Scope
- Business case
- Project charter
- Analytical techniques
- Business value
- Value proposition
- Project goals

5.1 BRIEF INTRODUCTION: NEEDS ASSESSMENT

PMI defines the Needs Assessment domain as the *activities related to understanding a business problem or opportunity and evaluating various inputs to help develop an effective solution.* The main points from this domain are illustrated in Figure 5.1, as emphasis is on understanding the business needs of the various stakeholders in the form of goals. Goals then turn into objectives, business needs, a business case, and project and product scope—with an agreement being made on what people want before attempting to create effective solutions. In the process, the current capabilities of the organization are assessed in order to identify gaps in organizational capabilities.

The business needs arise from a business problem or opportunity as described in Section 5.1. Then, in Section 5.2, we examine the value proposition to determine whether it is worth the effort. The business needs, being valued as goals and objectives, are then defined in Section 5.3, while Sections 5.4 and 5.5 identify and analyze the stakeholders in order to ensure their proper involvement. *Business Analysis for Practitioners* (2015) illustrates the needs assessment as the following steps:

- Identify problem or opportunity
- Assess current state of the organization
- Recommend action to address business needs
- Assemble the business case

The process initiates with high focus being given to the stakeholders' needs and develops through the five domains into useful business cases for final evaluation. This is illustrated in Figure 5.2.

If we decompose the requirements' pyramid slightly by adding some examples of requirement types and documents as illustrated in Table 5.1, we see a clear journey ahead of us—with each of the five domains playing a separate and vital role.

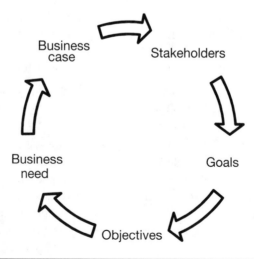

Figure 5.1 Needs assessment

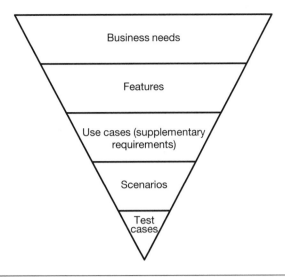

Figure 5.2   The requirements' pyramid adapted from Zielczynski

Table 5.1   Requirements and documents created in each domain

Steps	Requirement types	Documents
Needs Assessment	Stakeholders' needs	Stakeholders' requests
Planning	Features	Vision/Situation statement
Analysis	Use cases, scenarios	Use case specifications
Traceability and Monitoring	Test cases	Test cases
Evaluation	Test cases	Delivered solution

5.2 DEFINE BUSINESS REQUIREMENTS

As business analysts, we are often faced with two general business analysis scenarios; one being plan-driven, another being change-driven. In a plan-driven scenario, the general requirements are identified and the need for change is well understood. In a change-driven scenario, general requirements are either not known or not well understood. Thus, the business analyst needs to investigate to a higher degree than with a plan-driven approach by using problem and opportunity analysis techniques.

In order to do so, we must first define the problems and opportunities, and assess organizational capacities and gaps—before forming the first phase of the solution scope and developing a business case for the proposed solutions. When the business case is created, we use it as an input for the *develop project charter* process, and initiate the project with the aim to deliver the change.

In this regard, the business analyst should seek out the relevant documentation beforehand with an emphasis on gathering information about the business. This needs to be done as soon as a potential client expresses interest in a project. Some of the documentation that is most likely to be available include:

- Business plan
- Strategic plan
- Marketing plan
- Business rules procedures
- Process flow charts
- Market analysis
- Enterprise architecture
- Job descriptions
- Troubleshooting documents
- Financial report
- Business case
- Business needs
- Solution scope
- Benchmarking (cycle time, website visitors, market size, increase in sales, etc.)

As the business analyst gathers relevant data to evaluate the situation, a situation statement may be developed which documents the current problems that need to be solved or opportunities to be explored. The following analysis describes how business analysts identify plans to extract business needs, and help in defining a solution scope that can easily be implemented by the business. The following pages highlight the general ideas to be formed by the business analyst during the preliminary analysis.

Defining the Problems and Opportunities

Whether the scenario is plan-driven or change-driven, it often originates from problems with existing solutions or opportunities in order to attain new solutions. During the defining problem and opportunities process, the techniques are derived from the PMI knowledge area of quality management as we are faced with a major problem, its root causes, and effects that we need to change. Changing the current situation may have a significant cost, which is described in the value proposition as part of the business case, highlighting the benefits and costs associated with the proposed solution and change. Table 5.2 illustrates the identify opportunities and challenges process. Some of the applied techniques for root cause analysis and opportunity analysis in the situation are:

- Five whys
- Cause and effect diagrams
- Interrelationship diagrams
- Process flows

Table 5.2 Identify problems and opportunities

Questions	Where to document the answer
Major problems	Pareto chart
Why the problem occurs	Cause/effect diagram
Cost to the business	Value proposition
Features customers want	Cause/effect diagram
Risk involved	Risk analysis

The result of the identify problems and opportunities process would be the situation statement or vision document, which is *a document that defines the high-level scope and purpose of a program, product, or project*. A clear statement of the problem, proposed solution, and the high-level features of a product help establish expectations and reduce risks. The vision document is, in PMI terms, translated into the project scope and product scope. The product scope is defined as *the features and functions that characterize a product, service, or result*, to which we add the project scope description, which is defined as *the documented narrative description of the project scope*. The business analyst will obtain stakeholder approval for the situation statement (problem, effect, and impact) or vision document.

Assessing Organizational Capacities and Gaps

Next, we need to assess the organizational capacities and gaps in order to determine how to change the current situation into a future situation or solution, which often closes the gaps in between by involving a changed scenario.

The techniques applied for this purpose are illustrated in Chapter 10. However, in most cases, the following techniques are widely used:

- GAP analysis
- Process flows
- Enterprise and business architectures
- Capability framework
- Business process reengineering
- Value stream mapping techniques

As a result, capability tables, affinity diagrams, and benchmarking may prove useful to determine the required capabilities needed to address the situation.

Forming the First Phase of the Solution Scope

At this stage, we have to examine the documents and identify a problem or opportunity. However, we do not yet have a formal project structure to work within. For this, we would have to identify and analyze the stakeholders (discussed later in this chapter) to elicit the information required in order to understand interfaces, data, processes, goals, and business rules.

Developing the business needs is a continuation of the identification, verification, and narrative of the needs that bring about the project requirements, which then leads to the solutions and deliverables. In order to assess the sponsor needs, stakeholder needs, organizational assets, capabilities, and other relevant needs, a range of techniques is applied, as shown in Table 5.3.

Table 5.3 Techniques

Qualitative	Quantitative	Documenting the results
Interviewing	Questionnaires	Risk pictures
Workshops	Sampling	Mind maps
Observations	Special-purpose records document analysis	Context diagrams
		Use case diagrams
		Feature levels
		System events

Exercise 5.1—Qualitative or Quantitative? The following techniques are used for defining the solution scope. Classify them as qualitative, quantitative, or part of the documentation. (The answer is found on page 72.)

1. System events _____
2. Workshops _____
3. Observations _____
4. Mind maps _____
5. Sampling _____

Developing a Business Case for Proposed Solutions

Now it is time to develop a business case for the proposed solution. The business case is defined as *a documented economic feasibility study used to establish validity of the benefits of a selected component lacking sufficient definition and that is used as a basis for the authorization of further project management activities.* Later in this chapter, we will examine the value proposition in greater detail, as it is vital for the business analyst and organization to understand the benefits and costs associated with the proposed business case. When the business case is complete, we have the input for the *develop project charter* process where the project can be initiated.

The business case is important because it recommends actions to address the business needs, including a high-level approach for adding capabilities and providing alternative options for satisfying them. This implies identifying constraints, assumptions, and risks for each option and assessing the feasibility and organizational impact of each option. The business case is the most viable option to address business needs.

Business Analysis for Practitioners (2015) has identified risk planning as a collaboration point where the business analyst may draw upon the project manager's expertise and knowledge. The project manager may focus on project risks while the business analyst may focus on product risks.

The *Project Management Body of Knowledge (PMBOK® Guide)* approach to *develop project charter* is by Process 4.1 *Develop project charter*, which is illustrated in Table 5.4. (The overview of the processes included in this domain can be found at the end of this chapter.)

Table 5.4 Develop project charter

Input	Tools and Techniques	Output
• Project statement of work • Business cases • Agreements • Enterprise environment factors • Organizational process assets	• Expert judgment • Facilitation techniques	• Project charter

Once we have investigated plans, strategies, outside influences, and so forth, the work covered up to this stage is used as enterprise environment factors and organization process assets. The problem and opportunity statement is then transformed into the vision statement, which is used as input for the business case and the statement of work (SOW). The SOW is *a narrative description of products, services, or results to be delivered by the project.* The result of this process is the project charter, which is *a document issued by the project initiator or sponsor who formally authorizes the existence of a project and provides the project manager with the authority to apply organizational resources to project activities.*

5.3 DEFINE VALUE PROPOSITION

During the *define value proposition* stage, we seek to collect and analyze information from a variety of sources using valuation tools and techniques to contribute to the determination of the value proposition of the initiative. First, we examine business value before determining the value proposition of the initiative within the business case and its financial measurements.

Business value is defined as *a concept that is unique to each organization and includes tangible and intangible elements.* Through the effective use of project, program, and portfolio management disciplines, organizations will possess the ability to employ reliable, established processes to meet enterprise objectives and obtain greater business value from their investment. The elements are costs and benefits, which are found in the business case.

Business Analysis for Practitioners (2015) has identified the development of the business case is a collaboration point where the business analyst and the project manager should work together since each role represents different expertise. In addition to this, we examine value proposition as a promise of value to be delivered and acknowledged; and a belief from the customer that value will be experienced. A value proposition can apply to an entire organization, parts thereof, customer accounts, or products and services. The value proposition is basically benefits minus costs, which are highlighted in the business case.

Before going into the details of the business case, the following are additional methods for value proposition analysis:

- Strengths, weaknesses, opportunities, and threats (SWOT) analysis
- Value chain analysis
- Financial forecasts
- Options thinking
- Roadmapping
- Linkage grids
- Political, economic, social, technological, legal, and environmental (PESTLE) analysis

Additionally, it is also important to view the value proposition from the customer's perspective with regard to an organization. Table 5.5 illustrates this.

Table 5.5 Value propositions are the customer's perspective with regard to an organization

		Customers		
		Owner	Partner	End customer
Value categories	Timing			Arrival of products
	Financial		Discount rate	
	Quality	Reputation of organization		

For some stakeholders, values are closely related to the benefits and features received by an initiative, which can also be highlighted as part of the value proposition analysis as Table 5.6 illustrates.

Table 5.6 Benefits and features

Customer benefits	Supporting features
New support staff can quickly learn how to use the product	A knowledge base supports personnel
Management can identify problems	Trends and distribution reports

The business case describes from a business perspective whether or not the project is worth the required investment, which is input for the *develop project charter* process and leads to the summary budget.

The *PMBOK® Guide*'s approach to *plan cost management* is by Process 7.1 *Plan cost management*, which is illustrated in Table 5.7. The overview of the processes in this domain can be found at the end of this chapter.

Table 5.7 Plan cost management

Input	Tools and Techniques	Output
• Project management plan • Project charter • Enterprise environmental factors • Organizational process assets	• Expert judgment • Analytical techniques • Meetings	• Cost management plan

The analytical techniques covered in the *plan cost management* section are similar to the techniques we use to develop the business case and its value propositions so let's examine these techniques further.

"Show me the money, Yeah! Louder! Show me the money!" This is a well-known phrase uttered by characters in the 1996 film, *Jerry Maguire. Show me the money* is also an essential element of a solid business case. Management compares business cases based on how good they are at showing them the money. In this section, we will discuss financial management within the business case, to show the money to the stakeholders.

The solid business case is designed and created upon a solid financial model for it seems that "Justifying IT investments is moving from art to science as executives look for business cases they can understand and embrace" (Apfel, 2003). The financial management of the business case is important because it aims "to quantify, qualify, and prioritize the ways IT contributes to the bottom line" (Mayor, 2002).

Thus, it is mainly about measuring the costs and benefits of the business case, and doing the necessary calculations to create a solid base for good management decisions. "Anything is measurable in a way that is superior to not measuring it at all" (DeMarco, 2002).

Costs and Benefits

Costs and benefits are fundamental, central, and primary factors of business case accounting. Thus, in order to measure the business case accurately, the business case analyst needs to identify the various costs and benefits, which are often more complicated than first glance.

Costs and benefits can be categorized as either tangible or intangible. Tangible assets—whether costs or benefits—are something we can measure. Intangible assets—whether costs or benefits—are much more difficult to measure. A tangible asset might be goods produced while intangible assets may be knowledge or vision, which are more immaterial and abstract to some degree, making them more difficult to measure.

Business Analysis for Practitioners (2015) has identified cost/benefit analysis as a collaboration point where the business analyst and the project manager should work together to prepare financial estimates.

These basic approaches cover the key financial concepts and initial business case calculations found in the cost/benefit section of the business case. The nine methods covered in this section are:

- Present value (PV)
- Net present value (NPV)
- Future Value (FV)
- Return on investment (ROI)
- Internal rate of return (IRR)
- Payback period (PP)
- Discounted cash flow (DCF)
- Benefit-cost ratio (BCR)
- Profitability index (PI)

This list is not comprehensive, but it encompasses the most commonly applied calculations found in a solid business case.

Present Value

PV is one of the first set of calculations that the business case analyst can use to demonstrate the value of the business case. PV is a way of factoring the time value of money to calculate a project's worth. PV calculations are very useful in comparing one potential project or opportunity to another.

The formula is: $PV = FV/(1 + r)^n$

Exercise 5.2—Let us calculate the present value if the future value is $8,000 in 4 years with a discount rate of 5%. Would that leave us with $7,634, $6,775, $6,582 or $6,575 in PV?

The unit of currency makes no difference in calculating PV; whether dollars or euro, the formula is still the same. Therefore, if the discount rate (r) is 5%, $8,000 in 4 years is now worth: $8,000/(1 + 0.05)^4$, which equals $6,582. *Note*: Most basic approaches are fairly easily calculated in Microsoft Excel or similar spreadsheet programs.

Net Present Value

NPV is another way of factoring the time value of money to calculate a project's worth. However, NPV also considers the project's costs in the equation. NPV calculations enable an *apples-to-apples* comparison of investment alternatives in terms of the value of cash today versus the interest-adjusted value of cash for various times in the future.

The formula is: NPV = PV (all cash inflows) − PV (all cash outflows)

If the PV of all cash inflows is $500,000 and outflows are $350,000, then the NPV is $150,000. NPV decision rules are:

- A business case with positive NPV should be accepted
- A business case with negative NPV should be rejected
- In case of mutually exclusive projects, the one with a higher NPV should be selected

A basic example of NPV with an initial investment of $900,000 and using a discount rate of 10% is illustrated in Table 5.8.

Table 5.8 Financial results per year—NPV

Year	Annual cash flow (inflows-outflows)	Discount factor (10%)	NPV	Cumulative NPV
0	–$900,000	1.00	–$900,000	–$900,000
1	$550,000	.909	$499,950	–$400,050
2	$650,000	.826	$536,900	$136,850
3	$750,000	.751	$563,250	$700,100

Table 5.9 shows a slightly more advanced NPV calculation of a server consolidation project versus a virtualization project.

Table 5.9 Using NPV to choose between options

Year	Discount factor (10%)	Server consolidation		Virtualization	
		Cash flow	PV of cash flow	Cash flow	PV of cash flow
0	1	–$1,000,000	–$1,000,000	–$1,000,000	–$1,000,000
1	0.909	–$500,000	–$454,500	–$1,000,000	–$909,000
2	0.826	$500,000	$413,000	$750,000	$619,500
3	0.751	$500,000	$375,500	$750,000	$563,250
4	0.683	$600,000	$409,800	$750.000	$512,250
5	0.621	$600,000	$372,600	$750,000	$465,750
Totals		**$700,000**	**$116,400**	**$1,000,000**	**$251,750**

The expected NPV of a project can be calculated by assigning probabilities (p) to various scenario NPVs:

$$\text{Expected NPV} = (\text{Scenario NPV} \times p)$$

The best case scenario has an NPV of $80,000 and a probability of 0.2 (20% chance)

The middle case scenario has an NPV of $50,000 and a probability of 0.6 (60% chance)

The worst case scenario has an NPV of $30,000 and a probability of 0.2 (20% chance)

Expected NPV = ($80.000 × 0.2) + ($50.000 × 0.6) + ($30.000 × 0.2) = $52,000

A discount rate of 5% has been used in this example. It can be seen from the sum of all the discounted values that: Project 1 in Table 5.10 has an NPV of –$2.01 million, while Project 2 in Table 5.11 has an NPV of +$0.82 million. Project 2 is the preferred option based on a higher NPV.

Table 5.10   Cash flow for Project 1 over five years (in millions)

Project 1	Year 0	Year 1	Year 2	Year 3	Year 4	Year 5
Initial non-recurring costs	–15.00					
Benefits		3.00	3.00	3.00	3.00	3.00
Discounted values	12.99	2.86	2.72	2.59	2.47	2.35
Net present value	–2.01					

Table 5.11   Cash flow for Project 2 over five years (in millions)

Project 2	Year 0	Year 1	Year 2	Year 3	Year 4	Year 5
Initial non-recurring costs	–10.00					
Benefits		2.50	2.50	2.50	2.50	2.50
Discounted values	10.82	2.38	2.27	2.16	2.06	1.96
Net present value	0.82					

The project illustrated previously had the same discount rate. However, in the example in Table 5.12, three different discount rates are applied.

Table 5.12   Illustrates the NPV with three different discount rates

Year	Cash flow	Discount rate 10%		Discount rate 15%		Discount rate 20%	
		Factor	Amount	Factor	Amount	Factor	Amount
0	–$1,000,000	1.000	–$1,000,000	1.000	–$1,000,000	1.000	–$1,000,000
1	$300,000	0.909	$273,000	0.870	$261,000	0.833	$250,000
2	$300,000	0.826	$248,000	0.756	$227,000	0.694	$208,000
3	$300,000	0.751	$225,000	0.658	$197,000	0.579	$174,000
4	$300,000	0.683	$205,000	0.572	$172,000	0.482	$145,000
5	$300,000	0.621	$186,000	0.497	$149,000	0.402	$121,000
Total	$500,000		NPV = $137,000		NPV = $6,000		NPV = –$102,000

Future Value

FV is the value of an asset at a specific date in the future.

The formula is: $FV = PV/(1 + r)^n$

If PV = $177,700, the effective annual interest rate (r) is 3%, and the time period (n) is 4 years, the future value would be roughly $200,000.

Return on Investment

ROI is often used to demonstrate the percentage return that an organization makes by investing. The higher the ROI, the better it is for the company.

The ROI formula is: ((Benefits − Costs)/Costs) × 100

If benefits are $230,000 and costs are $200,000, then $230,000 − $200,000 = $30,000/$200,000 = 15% ROI. A percentage above 0 means that the benefits are higher than the costs. Still, management may have other business cases with a higher ROI, which may be more profitable to initiate. Table 5.13 expands Table 5.8 to include ROI after each year of the project.

Table 5.13 Financial results per year—ROI

	Annual cash flow (inflows-outflows)	Discount factor (10%)	NPV	Cumulative NPV	ROI
0	−$900,000	1.00	−$900,000	−$900,000	−100%
1	$550,000	.909	$499,950	−$400,050	−44.5%
2	$650,000	.826	$536,900	$136,850	15.2%
3	$750,000	.751	$563,250	$700,100	77.8%

Internal Rate of Return

IRR also takes into account the time value of money. It analyzes an investment project by comparing IRR to the minimum rate of return that the company requires to fund an investment. IRR shows us the discount factor that makes the NPV exactly $0. We are interested in the IRR because any discount factor (rate) that is higher than the IRR would cause the NPV to be negative and the project would not be approved.

IRR = Discount rate for which NPV = $0

Under this method, if IRR promised by the investment project is greater than or equal to the minimum required rate of return, the project is considered acceptable. Otherwise, the project is rejected. IRR is the upper bound of the discount factor for a positive NPV.

IRR decision rule: The project is acceptable if the rate (r) < IRR.

In Table 5.14, we can see that the IRR for a hypothetical project is 12%. If the company needs to borrow money at a higher rate than 12% or requires a rate of return higher than 12% to fund this project, the investment should not be approved.

Table 5.14 Use IRR to find the rate at which NPV is $0.

Discount factor (%)	NPV
10	$1,500
11	$725
12	**$0**
13	−$685
14	−$1445

Payback Period

PP determines the point in time at which cumulative net cash flows exceed zero. This method involves dividing the annual returns from a proposal by the initial investment amount, and then it identifies the number of years it will take for an investment to *pay for itself*. Under the PP method, projects with a shorter PP are preferred. This method is easy to use since it does not take into account the time value of money. However, by itself, the PP is an unsatisfactory decision rule because it takes no direct account of the timing of benefits, it assumes future cash flows are fixed, and it takes no account of any costs or benefits occurring after the payback date.

The formula is: cost of project/annual cash inflows = PP

PP is usually expressed in years. Start by calculating net cash flow for each year: net cash flow Year 1 = cash inflow Year 1 − cash outflow Year 1. Then, calculate the cumulative cash flow = (net cash flow Year 1 + net cash flow Year 2 + net cash flow Year 3, ..., etc.). Accumulate by year until cumulative cash flow is a positive number—that year is the payback year. The method is illustrated in Table 5.15.

Table 5.15 Payback period—what it looks like

	Server consolidation	Virtualization
	Investment: $1 million	Investment: $1 million
Year	Savings per year	
1	$333,333	$250,000
2	$333,333	$250,000
3	$333,333	$250,000
4	—	$250,000
5	—	—
Total	$1 million	$1 million
Payback period	3 years	4 years

In some circumstances it might be relevant to know how certain the payback period is, in which case, the business analyst could add a sensitivity analysis to it. Sensitivity analysis is a process which helps us to understand what will happen to the value of our project if any of our key inputs or assumptions were to change. The basic process for conducting a sensitivity analysis involves changing each input variable one at a time, and assessing the effect that has on the total project value. The main reasons to conduct a sensitivity analysis are to determine which variables have the biggest impact on project value, how much each variable would have to be adjusted to make the project unprofitable, and which variables we need to be estimated more accurately. A Monte Carlo Simulation is a much more complex, but much more powerful form of scenario analysis.

Discounted Cash Flow

DCF converts future cash flow into present value cash flow. DCF analysis is simple, widely used, and accepted—which works well to determine the NPV for income or costs to be incurred over future years. It answers the question, "Will we be better off investing in this proposal, or investing in an alternative opportunity?"

The formula is: cash flow/$(1+$ discount rate$)^n$ + cash flow/$(1+$ discount rate$)^n$...

The PV of $1,000 in 10 years, with a discount rate of 6.3 percent, is $1000/(1 + 0.063)^{10} = \$532.73$.

The challenge with the DCF is that non-financial measurements are ignored and it is, to some extent, too simple and inflexible.

Benefit-Cost Ratio

The BCR is the ratio of the PV of benefits to the PV of costs. A proposal is usually worthwhile when the PV of benefits is greater than the PV of costs. Thus, this method acts like an alternative decision criterion. The BCR is given by the PV of benefits (cash inflows) over the analysis period divided by the net present cost (NPC).

The formula is: discounted value of incremental benefits/discounted value of incremental costs

As an example, let's assume that a project that costs $6 million and accrues $24 million in benefits has a BCR of 4 ($24 million divided by $6 million). A BCR of 4 means that management can expect $4 in benefits for every $1 in costs. A BCR greater than 1 means the benefits outweigh the costs and the investment should be considered. If the ratio is less than 1, the costs outweigh the benefits. If the BCR is equal to 1, the benefits equal the costs.

Profitability Index

PI, also known as a profit investment ratio (PIR) or value investment ratio (VIR), is the ratio of payoff to investment of a proposed project. It is a useful tool for ranking projects because it allows you to quantify the amount of value created per unit of investment.

The formula is: (PV of future cash flows/initial investment)

For example, the initial investment is $40,000 and over a period of 5 years will generate future cash flows of $18,000, $12,000, $10,000, $9,000, and $6,000. Using a discount rate of 10%, the cumulative present value of these future cash flows equals $43,679. Thus the PI = $43,679/$40,000 = 1.092.

PI decision rules are:

- Business case with a PI that is greater than one should be accepted
- Business case with a PI that is less than one should be rejected

Exercise 5.3—Business Case Ready or Not? Which of the following must be true if you are to approve the business case? (The answer is found on page 72.)

1. The PI is less than one
2. The discounted value of incremental benefits is $500M while the discounted value of incremental costs is $575M
3. The payback period is more than 20 years
4. The IRR is positive
5. The ROI is not positive

Advanced approaches for assessing the value of an investment and the value propositions of the business case are:

- Breakeven analysis
- Value chain analysis
- Investment opportunity analysis
- Sensitivity analysis
- Trend analysis
- Value stream mapping and gap analysis
- Snapshot approach
- Cost effectiveness analysis
- Least cost analysis
- DuPont analysis

5.4 DEVELOP PROJECT GOALS

This section puts an emphasis on collaboration during the development of project goals and objectives by providing clarification of business needs and solution scope in order to align the product with the organization's goals and objectives.

Business needs may arise from market demands, strategic opportunities/business needs, social needs, environmental considerations, customer requests, technological advancements, legal requirements, or in the context of a strategic plan. The business needs are defined in the relationship between project management, operations management, and organizational strategy. Organizational strategy could propose strategic opportunities, which are delivered by project. Day-to-day operations management could also encounter new legal requirements, which would result in the creation of a project to deliver the changes in order to bring the firm into compliance. A new lean strategy may also affect operations management, which is carried out as a project. In the heart of all these activities is the business analyst.

Business needs consist of project goals and objectives. Project goals are those that the organization wants to accomplish, and the objectives are the means by which the organization will meet its goals. The project goal is the highest level of requirement. One goal may result in one or more objectives. Thus, when working with project goals and objectives, ensure that they are SMART (specific, measurable, achievable, relevant, and time-sensitive) within the context of your projects and responsibilities. Each objective may result in one or more business needs and plans to support them, such as a marketing or technology plan. Objectives are business needs documented in the business case.

At this stage, it can be useful as part of the identification and assessment of stakeholders to map them with goals and requirements. Mapping stakeholders with requirements is illustrated in Table 5.16 while Table 5.17 illustrates stakeholders with goals.

Table 5.16 A goal is something stakeholders want to achieve

Goals (stakeholders)	Requirements (product)
May be an ideal, unattainable, indicating what is hoped for	Must be realizable within limits of budget, time, technology, and skills available
May conflict	Must not conflict

Table 5.17 Stakeholders' goals

Stakeholders	Goals
Finance	Reduce costs
Legal	Document handling
Human Resources	Competence mapping

The business needs are eventually translated into the SOW and used as an input to the process called *develop project charter*. This enables the project—that is, *a temporary endeavor undertaken to create a unique product, service, or result*—to achieve business needs. It is supported by project management, which is *the application of knowledge, skills, and techniques to execute projects effectively and efficiently*.

The product scope identifies what portion of the product vision the project will address; while the product vision (document) and situation statement aligns all stakeholders in a common direction. The product vision is broken into smaller deliveries or releases, as illustrated in Figure 5.3.

In order to define and document the project scope, you must understand why the project has been initiated (the project statement of purpose) and what the goals of the project (the project objectives) are. As the business analyst, you need to stay true to the organization's project boundaries and analyze the business problem without jumping to an immediate solution.

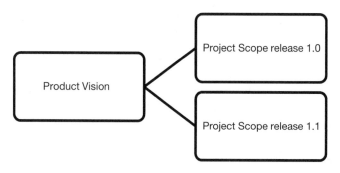

Figure 5.3 Product vision

The project scope is very important because it defines the boundaries and constraints for the project and the product. In addition, scope also includes needs, goals, objectives, business case, assumptions, constraints, and responsibilities. When working on scope, whether project or product, the lead roles and deliverances need to be firmly agreed upon. Table 5.18 illustrates one approach to defining the lead roles.

Table 5.18   Project scope and product scope

	Project scope	Product scope
Lead roles	Project manager	Business analyst
Deliverables	Project plans	Requirement management plan

5.5 IDENTIFY STAKEHOLDERS

Stakeholder analysis has always been important. Pulitzer prize-winning historian Barbara Tuchman illustrates this in her sobering history *The March of Folly: From Troy to Vietnam*, which recounts a series of disastrous misadventures that followed in the footsteps of ignoring the interests of, and information held by, key stakeholders.

We need to identify stakeholders to ensure that the appropriate parties are represented, informed, and involved. Stakeholders are one of the key sources for requirements and for this, you need to know the number of stakeholders that you are eliciting information from. By knowing the number, you can determine which elicitation techniques work best.

During needs assessment, it is important to identify stakeholders in order to answer these questions:

- Which sponsor is responsible?
- Which stakeholders can benefit from the project?
- Which stakeholders can provide financial support or other benefits?
- Which stakeholders need the solution?
- Which stakeholders may require changes?
- Which stakeholders may help implement the solution?
- Which stakeholders may support the solution?

Stakeholders are vital for project success. Some may recall the butterfly effect, where a butterfly may spread it wings in China and cause a flood in Europe. Stakeholders—identified and analyzed or not—have a similar capability to influence the project. Typical stakeholders would have the following roles:

- Business analyst
- Customer
- End user
- Subject matter expert
- Project manager
- Sponsor
- Supplier
- Tester

Although stakeholders are in no way related to donkeys, let's start with the tale of two donkeys to further explain stakeholder influence on a project. The two donkeys, as illustrated in Figure 5.4, were bound by a rope and unable to reach their food. When both donkeys moved in opposite directions, neither of the donkeys was able to reach its food. At some point, one of the donkeys moved toward the other donkey and they were able to eat some of the food before moving together to the other side.

This story highlights the importance of stakeholders; and the need to know how they move and what kind of "food" triggers them. If stakeholders move in opposite directions with conflicting requirements, the products cannot be scoped. If stakeholders can agree on the goals and scope, and move in the same direction, the road ahead can clearly be described by the business analyst. The story of the two donkeys may be viewed from one of the donkey's perspective or an individual perspective. Alternatively, a more systematic view that we apply during stakeholder analysis is the one in which stakeholders are viewed on a high level and not just from one perspective.

Surveys of more than 8,000 projects show that most project failures involve stakeholder problems (Johnson, 1999). Stakeholder management is the process of identifying the right stakeholders and ensuring the stakeholders' engagement in the project or activities.

PMI (2014) defines a stakeholder as: *an individual, group, or organization who may affect, be affected by, or perceive itself to be affected by a decision, activity, or outcome of a project.* The various stakeholders are illustrated in the stakeholders' wheel in Figure 5.5. *Business Analysis for Practitioners* (2015) has

Figure 5.4 Tale of the two donkeys adapted from Charles West

Figure 5.5 Stakeholders' wheel

recognized that the processes where stakeholders are identified and analyzed are areas where the business analyst and the project manager should collaborate and avoid duplicating activities.

The fundamental problem of stakeholder management is a failure to see that the needs of each stakeholder group, including shareholders, are different; and that for the best results, all of these different needs must be met accordingly. In simple terms, this means that a stakeholder is a person or an organization that has a direct or indirect influence on the requirements of the system and is essential in requirements management, as well as being the most important source of requirements. The stakeholders are those who are affected by the success or failure of the solution. They are the users or customers that may approve the solution and have an interest in it.

Exercise 5.4—Stakeholders? You work as a business analyst in the IT department on a public sector project and are in the process of identifying stakeholders. The project is a new IT system for administration and payrolls. Which of the following will you most likely identify as stakeholders? (The answer is found on page 72.)

1. Your boss
2. A data entry clerk who will use the new system
3. Other business analysts working on other projects
4. The project department PMO
5. A member of your firm's legal department

The *PMBOK® Guide*'s approach to *identifying stakeholders* is by Process 13.1 *Identify stakeholders,* which is illustrated in Table 5.19. The overview of the processes in this domain can be found at the end of this chapter.

Table 5.19 Identifying stakeholders

Input	Tools and Techniques	Output
• Project charter • Procurement documents • Enterprise environmental factors • Organizational process assets	• Stakeholder analysis • Expert judgment • Meetings	• Stakeholder register

The output of the *identifying stakeholders* process is the stakeholder register, as shown in Figure 5.6, which is a project document including the identification, assessment, and classification of the project stakeholders. The assessment and classification of the stakeholders will be covered in the next section.

The input for the process of *identifying stakeholders* is the project charter since it is the formal authorization document. However, in this case, we also need the inputs which have gone into the creation of the project charter because it explains what the project is all about and which stakeholders are possibly involved. In addition to this, the sponsor or project initiator who has signed the document is also needed since we would most likely interview them as part of identifying stakeholders.

Several tools and techniques for identifying stakeholders involve documentation analysis or organizational charts, which PMI defines as organizational process assets (plans, processes, policies, procedures, and knowledge bases that are specific to and used by the performing organization).

STAKEHOLDER REGISTER

Project Title:_____ Date Prepared:_____

Name	Position	Role	Contact Information	Requirements	Expectations	Influence	Classification

Figure 5.6 Stakeholder register

Some stakeholders would most likely be identified as external stakeholders who may have influence or control over enterprise environment factors, which are: *conditions, not under the immediate control of the team, that influence, constrain, or direct the project, program, or portfolio.*

During needs assessment, we must identify the right stakeholders. Regardless of which methodology a business analyst or team uses, it is critical that the right people should be involved in the activities, and that communication flows smoothly with the stakeholders. Table 5.20 has listed some of the commonly used techniques for identifying the correct stakeholders.

Table 5.20 Techniques for identifying stakeholders

Technique	Description
Brainstorming	Brainstorming is a creative technique by which group or individual efforts are made to find stakeholders by gathering a list of possible stakeholders spontaneously contributed by its member(s).
Brain writing	A written form of brainstorming where each participant writes one stakeholder on a piece of paper before passing it on.
Interviews	One-on-one interviews (i.e., ask your sponsor).
SWOT analysis	Strengths, weaknesses, opportunities, and threats.
PEST/PESTLE	Political, economic, social, and technological analysis (legal and environmental).
Pre-mortem	The team imagines that a project has failed or succeeded, and then works backward to determine what stakeholders could lead to the success or failure of the project.
Change of perspective—Edward de Bono: Six Thinking Hats (see Table 5.21)	Sequence of methods for the identification of stakeholders. Clarification of the situation. Putting on the white hat to collect facts and figures relevant to the topic (Flipchart, Post-its on pin wall). Putting on the black hat (e.g., to identify stakeholders).
Analogy	Comparison with similar projects. Documentation analysis and prior business analyst experience.
Organization chart	Examine the organization chart for relevant stakeholders.
Onion model	See Figure 5.7.
Analyzing the context of the project	Covered in the next chapter.

The *Onion* model (Figure 5.7) is based upon the two-tier Freemanns (2007) model, which is a common way to show your findings in terms of primary and secondary stakeholders of the project.

Exercise 5.5—Using the method of Six Thinking Hats by Edward de Bono, as shown in Table 5.21, identify the correct stakeholders for a new downtown public library.

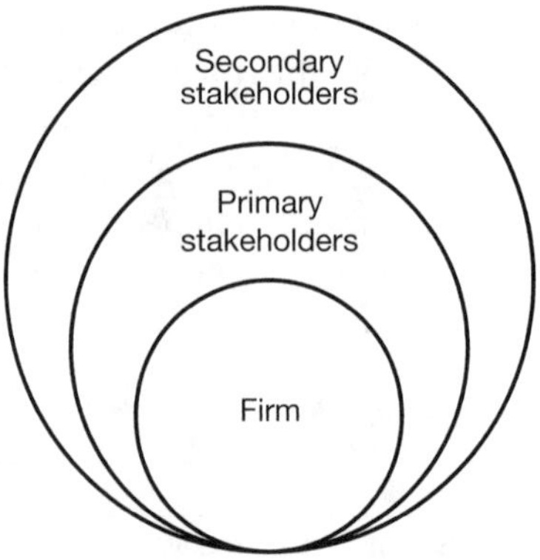

Figure 5.7 *Onion* model

Table 5.21 Six Thinking Hats

Hats	Description
White hat	Factual view of the subject of discussion
Red hat	Emotional, let one's emotions run wild
Black hat	Find negative aspects and risks (pessimist)
Yellow hat	Discover positive aspects (optimist)
Green hat	Creative, search for alternatives (usual brainstorming)
Blue hat	Controlling and organization of the thinking process

Sequence of methods for the identification of stakeholders:

1. Clarification of the situation
2. Putting on the white hat to collect facts and figures relevant to the topic (Flipchart, Post-its on pin wall)
3. Putting on the black hat (e.g., to identify stakeholders who may want the project to fail)

Exercise 5.6—Use the method of Pre-mortem to identify the right stakeholders for the new downtown library being built in your city.

Exercise 5.7—Explain the variation in results from Exercises 5.5 and 5.6.

5.6 ANALYZE STAKEHOLDERS

Previously, stakeholders were identified as a source for requirements. Next is the stakeholder analysis, which is defined as *a technique of systematically gathering and analyzing quantitative and qualitative information to determine whose interests should be taken into account throughout the project.*

Stakeholder analysis takes place during the process, *Identify stakeholders* (Table 5.22). However, this section will emphasize obtaining information about the stakeholders in order to determine their values regarding the product by using elicitation techniques to provide a baseline for prioritizing requirements.

Table 5.22   13.1 Identify stakeholders

Input	Tools and Techniques	Output
• Project charter • Procurement documents • Enterprise environmental factors • Organizational process assets	• Stakeholder analysis • Expert judgment • Meetings	• Stakeholder register

First, we need to determine the stakeholder's values, which is done during value identification, and includes the value proposition and value delivery. Value identification aims at finding the stakeholder's value, which provides a baseline for establishing stakeholder expectations and contributions. The next step is then aimed at aligning each stakeholder around the program value stream structure. Each stakeholder will contribute their efforts or resources to the value stream regarding the ways in which they can derive value. In addition, stakeholder analysis aims at establishing a clear communication of balanced expectations with all stakeholders. With this in mind, we can prioritize stakeholders and achieve a consensus about the requirements among the stakeholders.

The *analyze stakeholders* process aims at getting insights on the stakeholders with regard to various factors, which we will examine in greater detail. The obvious part of the stakeholder's value proposition is understanding their values. Table 5.23 highlights how a stakeholder's values can be analyzed.

Table 5.23   Stakeholder's value

Stakeholder group		
Stakeholder name		
Ask the stakeholder what they value. What do they expect to get from their involvement with your project?	On a scale of 1 to 5, how important is this value to the stakeholder?	On a scale of 1 to 5, is this project the best use of resources to increase sales?
Increased sales	4	4

The stakeholder analysis highly emphasizes stakeholders' needs, which also includes priorities and concerns. In addition, it also needs to be related to the current and proposed solution because the business analyst has to focus on a better solution than the current one—Table 5.24 illustrates this.

Table 5.24   Stakeholders' needs

Need	Priority	Concerns	Current solution	Proposed solution
Increased sales	High	Stagnant sales	Low sales	Sales increase of 25%

In most stakeholder analyses, the stakeholders' interests and contributions play a vital role in how they will interact during the project work. First, we will demonstrate how to keep the analysis separate, as shown in Tables 5.25, 5.26, and 5.27, before examining models for several variances.

Table 5.25 Stakeholders' interests

Stakeholders' interest in the project		
Customers	Faster buying cycle	Better service
Employees	Online access	Less work

Table 5.26 Stakeholders' contributions

Stakeholders' contributions to the project			
Customers	Money	Ideas	Feedback
Employees	Manpower	Expertise	

Table 5.27 Stakeholders' supporters or opponents matrix

Support	Weak supporters	Strong supporters
Opposition	Weak opponents	Strong opponents
	Weak stakeholder power	**Strong stakeholder power**

The next step is stakeholder management, which would include a quality assessment of causes of the different stakeholders. In this case, the methods for mapping is Mitchell's framework (1997), which divides the stakeholders with respect to power, legitimacy, and urgency. The numbers illustrate whether or not the stakeholders hold power and/or legitimacy and/or urgency. The only types of stakeholders holding them all are represented as number 7. Aside from this, additional knowledge of the stakeholders' relationships, risk potentials, or moral claims may also be of value. This approach is defined as *stakeholder salience,* as shown in Table 5.28.

Table 5.28 Stakeholder salience

Type of stakeholder	Power	Legitimacy	Urgency	Level of Salience or Priority	Ranking (0-7)
Dormant stakeholder	YES	NO	NO	High Priority	7
Discretionary stakeholder	NO	YES	NO	Medium Priority	6
Demanding stakeholder	NO	NO	YES	Medium Priority	5
Dominant stakeholder	YES	YES	NO	Medium Priority	4
Dangerous stakeholder	YES	NO	YES	Low Priority	3
Dependent stakeholder	NO	YES	YES	Low Priority	4
Definitive stakeholder	YES	YES	YES	Low Priority	1
Non-stakeholder	NO	NO	NO	Low Priority	0

Power: Ability to influence the organization, deliverables, or project outcomes
Legitimacy: Relationship and actions in terms of desirability, properness, or appropriateness
Urgency: Perceived time sensitivity and criticality of responses to expectations

The stakeholder analysis also needs to take into consideration how stakeholders interact. Table 5.29 illustrates this with five types of relationships and five variables, such as trust and power, which should be tailored to your situation (a similar tool for this is a radar diagram).

Table 5.29 How stakeholders interact

		Relationship type				
		Allied	**Cooperative**	**Neutral**	**Competitive**	**Threatening**
Asset Criteria	**Orientation & evaluation mode**	Cooperative strategic		Individual Operative		
	Trust		Knowledge-based			Distrust
	Communication			Direct content Low frequency		
	Learning				Single loop	
	Power	Very low				Very high

A range of techniques for analyzing stakeholders should be known and employed by the business analyst. Table 5.30 highlights the techniques that are used to analyze stakeholders. These techniques are to some degree illustrated in the following text as well.

Table 5.30 Major techniques that are used to analyze stakeholders

Technique	Description
Power/interest grid	See below
Extended power/interest grid	See below
Stakeholder influence diagram	A variation of the *Onion* model
Waterdrop model	A variation of the *Onion* model
Network model	Use the *Onion* model with arrows
Onion models/diagrams	Use the *Onion* model with arrows
CATWOE	Customer, actor, transformation, world view, owner, environment
VOCATE	Viewpoint, owner, customer, actor, transformation, environment
PARADE	Perspective, activity, recipient, actor, decision-maker environment
Business activity modeling (BAM)	Defines business activities involving the stakeholders
Responsibility assignment matrix (RAM)	A grid that shows the project resources assigned to each work package
Outline your stakeholders' personalities	MBTI, Belbin, DISC, Strength-based leadership
Learning style	Are they visual people? Auditory people? Kinesthetic people? Everyone has a primary learning and interaction style. Knowing your stakeholders' preferred style puts you in a better position to tailor your message to your audience.
RACI	A common type of responsibility assignment matrix that uses responsible, accountable, consulted, and informed statuses to define the involvement of stakeholders in project activities.

Exercise 5.8—Objective Assessment of Stakeholders: Use Table 5.30 to help perform this exercise. Which of the techniques explained in this chapter for analyzing stakeholders are objective assessments as opposed to subjective assessments? (The answer is found on page 72.)

The power and interest grid is a common technique used to actively manage the stakeholders in order to keep them satisfied and informed; keeping some of them on your side while maintaining a low profile with others who exhibit low power and interest. Table 5.31 illustrates this model.

Table 5.31 Power/interest grid

Level of power	High power/Low interest	High power/High interest
	Low power/Low interest	Low power/High interest
	Level of interest	

If the stakeholder analysis process is more extensive or complex, it may be useful to use the extended power and interest grid analysis as illustrated in Table 5.32, which has a higher degree of details.

Table 5.32 Extended power/interest grid

Power/Influence	**High**	High power/Low interest		High power/High interest
	Medium	Medium power/Low-high interest		
	Low	Low power/Low interest		Low power/Medium-high interest
		Low	**Medium**	**High**
		Level of interest		

Waterdrop models, network models, and the *Onion* model (or *Onion* diagram), are also common methodologies for analyzing stakeholders. The concept is to identify the stakeholders and the impact for those stakeholders. The closer you get to the center, the higher the impact is for the stakeholders. The stakeholders' influence diagram is a variant of the *Onion* model—Figure 5.8 illustrates this.

Figure 5.8 Impact on stakeholders

So far, stakeholder analysis has focused on attaining more insights on the stakeholders. However, an important part of this process is also on the focus of roles and responsibilities. With the stakeholders, we need to know who is doing what. The techniques to be used are the RACI and RAM, both of which link project resources to each work package. A less common variant of the RAM and RACI is the RASCI model, which includes Responsible, Accountable, Supportive, Consulted and Informed or PARIS (Participants, Accountable, Review needed, Input needed, and Sign-off required). Table 5.33 illustrates the RASCI technique.

Table 5.33 RASCI

	Sponsor	Project manager	Business analyst
Plan stage	A	I	R/C
Approve change request	S	R	C/I

Overall, the business analyst's work of identifying and assessing stakeholders with the team would likely include most of the tasks in the following list. The results would be categorized in a matrix for stakeholder management:

- Brainstorm regarding who the key stakeholders are—and why
- List potential stakeholders or form pairs of clusters of stakeholders
- Differentiate and group stakeholders
- Determine stakeholder influence and importance
- Address stakeholder perception
- Identify conflicting ideas and shared views on the problematic situation
- Clarify key stakeholder objectives
- Identify shared and conflicting objectives
- Identify roles
- Experience
- Location and availability
- Assess performance in each role
- Identify gaps and overlaps
- Develop criteria for assessing linkage
- For each stakeholder, list their information needs
- For each stakeholder, check whether stakeholders receive the information they are in need of
- Indicate the likely gains or losses

As a more advanced business analyst, you can also assess and incorporate community and stakeholder values to add quality to the stakeholders. The idea is to map stakeholders with values, which also would highlight common ground and possible conflicts. The values should be high level such as: vision, servant leadership, trust, collaboration, honesty, learning, courage, openness, adaptability, and leading change. Also, it can be useful to group the analyzed stakeholders where supporting techniques are job analysis or by the use of personas.

Exercise 5.9—Find two sample RACIs or RAMs online from different industries. What are the similarities or differences?

5.7 RELATING PMI-PBA® PRACTICES TO *PMBOK® GUIDE—FIFTH EDITION* PRACTICES

This domain emphasizes processes that are a part of the Initiating process groups, as well as being a part of the introduction to the *PMBOK® Guide*.

Table 5.34 *PMBOK® Guide* framework for Chapter 5

Knowledge areas	Project management process groups				
	Initiating	Planning	Executing	Monitoring and Controlling	Closing
	Domain—Needs Assessment				
Project integration management	4.1 Develop project charter				
Project scope management					
Project time management					
Project cost management		7.1 Plan cost management			
Project quality management					
Project human resource management					
Project communication management					
Project risk management					
Project procurement management					
Project stakeholder management	13.1 Identify stakeholders				

5.8 RELATING PMI-PBA PRACTICES TO AGILE PRACTICES

Value-based prioritization is about delivery of the software to the customer in a manner that gives the greatest value. It is all about project justification and business needs assessment. Business needs assessment determines if the project is worth the effort. It involves forecasting value to the customer or the market and evaluating the project against other projects, no matter how the project is being managed.

We sought to plan and assess value of the project and product in this chapter. Others would call this value-driven delivery since our deliveries are driven by what gives value to our customers. We need to start, as all projects must, by describing the project. "Agile projects are born the same way as traditional projects" (Crowe, 2012).

5.9 CHAPTER SUMMARY

Key concepts

- Stakeholders are sources for requirements
- Determine stakeholder values
- Stakeholder salience
- Extract business needs

- The business case describes from a business perspective whether or not the project is worth the required investment
- The project goal is the highest level of requirement

Exercise 5.10—Match the Key Words to Their Definitions: Match the business analyst key words to their definitions. You will have to match the key words from Table 5.35 to the definitions from Table 5.36. Table 5.37 is suitable as a score sheet and Table 5.38 contains the correct answers.

Table 5.35 Key words

No.	Key words
1	Responsibility assignment matrix (RAM)
2	Product
3	Stakeholder register
4	Project charter
5	Project
6	Organizational process assets
7	Product scope
8	RACI
9	Statement of work (SOW)
10	Scope
11	Stakeholder
12	Business case
13	Objective
14	Project scope description
15	Enterprise environmental factors

Table 5.37 Answer and score sheet

Number of key word	Letter of definition
1	
2	
3	
4	
5	
6	
7	
8	
9	
10	
11	
12	
13	
14	
15	

Table 5.36 Definitions

Letter	Definitions
A	Plans, processes, policies, procedures, and knowledge bases that are specific to and used by the performing organization.
B	A narrative description of products, services, or results to be delivered by the project.
C	An individual, group, or organization who may affect, be affected by, or perceive itself to be affected by a decision, activity, or outcome of a project.
D	The sum of the products, services, and results to be provided as a project.
E	An artifact that is produced, is quantifiable, and can be either an end item in itself or a component item.
F	A common type of responsibility assignment matrix that uses responsible, accountable, consulted, and informed statuses to define the involvement of stakeholders in project activities.
G	Something toward which work is to be directed, a strategic position to be attained, a purpose to be achieved, a result to be obtained, a product to be produced, or a service to be performed.
H	Conditions, not under the immediate control of the team, that influence, constrain, or direct the project, program, or portfolio.
I	The documented narrative description of the project scope.
J	A project document including the identification, assessment, and classification of the project stakeholders.
K	A documented economic feasibility study used to establish validity of the benefits of a selected component lacking sufficient definition and that is used as a basis for the authorization of further project management activities.
L	The features and functions that characterize a product, service, or result.
M	A document issued by the project initiator or sponsor that formally authorizes the existence of a project and provides the project manager with the authority to apply organizational resources to project activities.
N	A temporary endeavor undertaken to create a unique product, service, or result.
O	A grid that shows the project resources assigned to each work package.

5.10 POSTTEST: TAKE FIVE

The posttest contains five exam-related questions in the PMI-PBA format so that you can check your knowledge of the content presented in this chapter and check your readiness for the PMI-PBA exam. The answers will be provided on the following page. You should time the posttest and not use more than six or seven minutes.

1. Some scenarios are plan-driven while others are:

   a) Cost-driven

   b) Stakeholder-driven

   c) Change-driven

   d) Technical-driven

2. As a business analyst, you are in the process of *identify opportunities and challenges* where you are investigating major quality problems. Which tool or technique is most suitable?

   a) Pareto chart

   b) Cause and effect diagram

   c) Risk analysis

   d) SWOT analysis

3. You are examining the value proposition. However, you're in need of some financial measurements. Where would you most likely find them?

   a) In the project charter

   b) In the cost-benefit analysis

   c) In the business case

   d) In the scope statement

4. Which categories would be useful in examining the value proposition from the customer's perspective?

   a) Quality

   b) Timing

   c) Financial

   d) All of the above

5. An investment is projected to be worth $25,000 at the end of Year 3. What is the value of it at Year 0 using a discount rate of 12%

   a) $15,551

   b) $17,279

   c) $17,936

   d) $19,126

Table 5.38 Correct answers

Key words	Definitions
1	O
2	E
3	J
4	M
5	N
6	A
7	L
8	F
9	B
10	D
11	C
12	K
13	G
14	I
15	H

5.11 POSTTEST: CORRECT ANSWERS

1. Answer: C
2. Answer: A
3. Answer: C
4. Answer: D
5. Answer: C

Answers to *Exercise 5.1*: Documentation, Qualitative, Qualitative, Documentation, and Quantitative.

Answer to *Exercise 5.3*: Number four is the correct answer. The IRR must be positive.

Answer to *Exercise 5.4*: One and two are likely stakeholders and should be identified. Four and five are also somewhat likely stakeholders, but these are typically not included when identifying stakeholders. Three is not relevant.

Answer to *Exercise 5.8*: None. All methods for analyzing stakeholders are to some degree subjective, which implies different people may reach different results depending on who applies the technique and what inputs are used.

Planning Domain

6

TERMS TO KNOW

The list at the beginning of each chapter highlights the key terms you are required to know by the Project Management Institute (PMI). Hence, you should start with these terms. If you already have solid knowledge of them, you may consider skipping this chapter. However, once you have finished reading the chapter, you can refer back to this list and test your knowledge. The concepts are:

- System context
- Validating requirements
- Change control
- Change management
- Configuration management

- Traceability
- Requirement management plan
- Project expected outcome
- Business metrics
- Stakeholder engagement

6.1 BRIEF INTRODUCTION: PLANNING

The Planning domain focuses on creating solid fundamentals for the project, and for the activities that are to be conducted within the project. Business analysis planning involves ensuring what is and what is not within the project context, and defining—in collaboration with the stakeholders—the project's expected outcome. In order to deliver the project's expected outcome, the business analyst needs confirmation from the stakeholders that a validated requirements management plan is in place, and that there are plans and procedures for handling changes, traceability, and documents. The business analyst should also ensure that all of it is of the right quality and confirmed by the stakeholders. *Business Analysis for Practitioners* (2015) illustrates business analyst planning as the following steps:

- Conduct or refine the stakeholder analysis
- Create the business analysis plan
- Plan the business analysis work

6.2 DETERMINE PROJECT CONTEXT

In this section, we will review the business case and the project goals and objectives in order to provide context for business analysis activities. The business analyst has to understand the extent of the work and the broader context. Requirements for a system do not appear out of nowhere and they must be identified systematically. A business analyst needs to work within the organizational influence on project management, within the project, and within the business requirement activities, with the aim of separating the system from its environment and highlighting those parts that are relevant and affect the requirements.

On a high level, the organizational influence on project management can be observed in a magnitude of areas, such as:

- Communication
- Structures
- Culture
- Organizational process assets
- Enterprise environmental factors
- Stakeholders and governance
- Project life cycle
- Phases

This sets the standards for how we work, communicate, and behave within a project. Project information is collected, analyzed, and transformed into the dynamic context of the execution. Part of this is the process called *develop project charter*, in which the business case is used as input.

The *Project Management Body of Knowledge (PMBOK® Guide)* approach to the *develop project charter* procedure is by Process 4.1 *Develop project charter*, which is illustrated in Table 6.1. The overview of the processes in this domain can be found at the end of this chapter.

Table 6.1 Develop project charter

Input	Tools and Techniques	Output
• Project statement of work • Business cases • Agreements • Enterprise environmental factors • Organizational process assets	• Expert judgment • Facilitation techniques	• Project charter

At this stage, we need to review the business case and the project charter to ensure that the objectives and goals are clear because we need them to set the boundaries in order to conduct our requirements management work. The business analyst has to understand the extent of the work—and in order to do so, we need to isolate activities that are to be studied from those that are not to be studied. This is sometimes classified as *context analysis*. The purpose of the context analysis is to separate the system from its environment and highlight those parts that are relevant and affect the requirements.

First, we need to establish a *system context*, which is defined as *the part of the system environment that is relevant for the definition, as well as the understanding of the requirements of a system to be developed.*

Possible factors that influence the context of a system are:

- People (stakeholders or groups of stakeholders)
- Systems in operation (other technical systems or hardware)
- Processes (technical or physical processes, business processes)
- Events (technical or physical)
- Documents (e.g., laws, standards, system documentation)

If the system context is considered incorrect or incomplete during the context analysis, the consequences for the requirements and system will be extensive. The consequences of an ill-defined system context would be that an incorrect system or requirement is considered, or requirements would be missing, as systems are not within context. In other cases, requirements would be included, but would not be relevant for the system. This would increase costs, workload, reduce the use of the systems, and so forth. In a worst-case scenario, an incorrect and/or incomplete system context would cause system failures. Figure 6.1 illustrates the consequences of system context considerations.

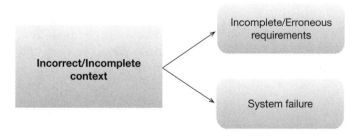

Figure 6.1 Consequences of system context consideration

The system context and the requirement context are closely related as the source of a system's requirement. Both of these are present within the context of the system to be developed. A requirement is defined for a specific system context and can only be interpreted correctly in regard to that specific system context. With a better understanding of the system context of a requirement, there is a greater likelihood that the business analyst will make the correct interpretation of the requirement.

Next, we need to examine the system boundary, which separates the system to be developed from its environment. It is the system boundary that separates the system to be developed from its environment—that is, it separates the part of the reality that can be modified or altered by the development process from aspects of the environment that cannot be changed or modified by the development process. Figure 6.2 illustrates these boundaries.

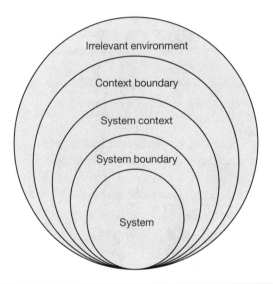

Figure 6.2 System boundary

If we examine the system boundary closely, we will see several types of aspects within the system context. Figure 6.3 highlights the types of aspects within the system context.

These aspects will be covered in greater detail when we document the system context since these aspects are what we seek to illustrate to foster accurate communication with the stakeholders.

The system boundary, which separates the system to be developed from its environment, can—and most likely would—be altered during system development. Within contexts and boundaries, there are interfaces, which are mediums by which the sources and sinks interact with the system to be developed. (Sources are inputs to the systems, while sinks are outputs.) Ignoring interface problems just makes them bigger. Thus, it is vital to resolve them. One approach is to identify and treat interfaces as demonstrated in Table 6.2.

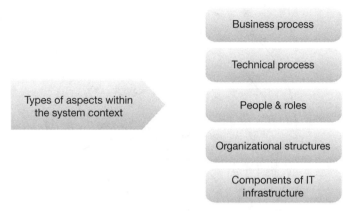

Figure 6.3   Types of aspects within the system context

Table 6.2   Interfaces

Type of interface	Example	How to discover this	Treatment

Sources and sinks help to identify the interfaces that the system has within its environment. For example, there may be an interface between stakeholders and existing systems. We use the inputs and outputs to help the system provide functionality, monitor processes, influence parameters, and control operations of the environment. Types differ for a system depending on the type of source or sink. Types can impose specific constraints or additional sources of requirements on the system to be developed.

Next, we need to consider the context boundary, as shown in Figure 6.4, which is the boundary that separates the relevant part of the environment of a system to be developed from the irrelevant part. In other words, the part that does not influence the system to be developed and thus, does not have to be considered during requirements engineering.

The context boundary is important, as it separates the relevant from the irrelevant. As a business analyst, we want to do our work correctly, so drawing the lines early on is important for setting the stage—otherwise, we would have an incorrectly defined scope with severe consequences. In order to contest the matter, one may argue that gray zones exist in the system boundaries and need to be handled as they constantly change so that the result will be a dynamic boundary that can easily be managed.

When you have a good idea of the work to be done, you can document the system context. The system context supplies the scope description with an established boundary, along with a connection between the system we develop and everything else. The documentation of the system context is also important because it fosters clear and accurate communication with and among the stakeholders. The documentation of the system context is typically conducted by the following methods:

- Use case diagrams
- Data flow diagrams
- Context diagrams
- Work scope diagrams

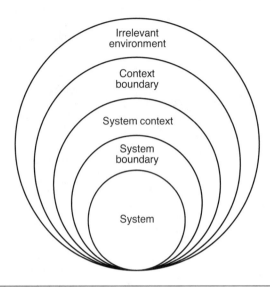

Figure 6.4 Context boundary

When the documentation is completed, it is important to confirm or check the diagrams against the stakeholders, business case, organization requirements goals, and project charter, which concludes this project and system context loop. As a result, the business analyst would review the business case and the project goals and objectives, which may have been changed due to the system context.

Exercise 6.1—What's in a Name? What is the name of the diagram that uses inputs, outputs, drawn databases, and customers? (The answer is found on page 102.)

1. Use case
2. Data flow
3. Context
4. Work scope

6.3 PLAN REQUIREMENT TRACEABILITY

At this point in time, the business analyst needs to define strategy for business requirement traceability using traceability tools and techniques in order to establish the level of traceability necessary to validate and monitor the requirements. In doing so, we first examine why requirement traceability is so important; next, we examine the process, techniques, and tools to deliver a strategy for business requirement traceability. Requirement traceability is about requirements decomposition and documentation. Once requirements are identified, they are broken down into their components. The components are then traced to their objectives. The logic behind how a need and requirement are identified should be documented for analysis in case it is needed later in the analysis—this is called *tracing*.

Business Analysis for Practitioners (2015) has identified collaboration points where traceability is an area in which the business analyst and the project manager should work closely together because the right level of traceability may reduce risks of the project—while too much may hinder the project. Finding the right level is not an independent task. It is related to several project factors that the project manager is responsible for, nevertheless, the business analyst is the specialist on traceability and should actively be involved.

Requirement traceability is a manually intensive task, which would most likely increase the development cost. However, it is an excellent tool with long-term benefits and the ability to reduce product life cycle costs. As a developer, have you ever missed a requirement? This is a valid question. Whether the answer is yes or no, with requirement traceability you can document whether it is the case. Presently, this demand is more and more evident with customers and also useful for satisfying stakeholders. Requirement traceability helps with managing software development through requirement, and demonstrates compliance with contract, specification, or regulation—as you can trace the requirements forward and backward. Forward and backward traceability is illustrated in Table 6.3.

Table 6.3   Forward and backward traceability

Forward Traceability	Backward Traceability
1. Sources of the requirement	3. Sources of the requirement
2. Requirements	2. Requirements
3. Work products that implement the requirements	1. Work products that implement the requirements

Project managers have several options for tracing: nonsystematic ad hoc tracing as default practice, basic tracing as mandated by standards, and extended tracing with a schema that captures rationale for (unusual) requirements in order to support requirements clarification and tracing requirements back to stakeholder value models. These tracing options help to better understand the alignment of requirements with stakeholder value propositions, as illustrated in Figure 6.5.

Requirement traceability is a good practice that works well with design and test work, and prevents inconsistencies. By tracing, the requirement can be followed all the way back to goals, objectives, the business, assumptions, and the project charter. Table 6.4 demonstrates a simple approach to mapping requirements to goals of the stakeholders.

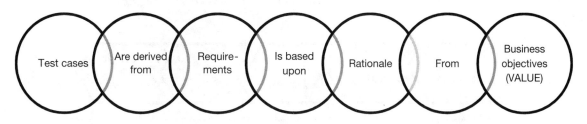

Figure 6.5   Alignment with stakeholder value

Table 6.4 Requirements and goals

ID	Requirement	Goal

Have no doubts about traceability support system development, which is done in many ways—and in case of doubt, ask yourself, "why is it here?" The feature can be traced back to the requirement and the origin. Table 6.5 shows a collection of the advantages of traceable requirements.

Table 6.5 Advantages of traceable requirements

Advantages of traceable requirements	Description
Verifiability	Requirements can be verified whether or not they have been implemented
Identification of gold-plated solution in the system	Identification of unneeded properties
Identification of gold-plated solution in the requirements	Identification of unneeded properties
Change impact analysis	Effect during change management
Reuse/Reengineering	Reuse of requirements for other projects and for reengineering
Project tracking	Project progress by requirements tracking
Risk reduction	Document interconnections, which reduce risk if key team members leave
Accountability	Ability to account for and ensure all activities involved in the development of the requirement are included
Maintenance	Cause and effect of failures and similar
Certification	Certifying safety-critical product that all requirements are implemented

Requirement traceability is a lot of work and should be purpose-driven since it is not possible to capture all of the information that supports the traceability of requirements. Information to be recorded should also be selected with respect to the purpose it serves. In order to complicate matters slightly, the literature suggests different kinds of traceability requirements.

Prerequirement specification (prior inclusion), postrequirement specification (results from inclusion), and traceability between requirements have some similarities with forward and backward traceability as illustrated in Figure 6.6.

Let's examine the process. First, we need a *requirement management plan*, which PMI defines as *a component of the project or program management plan that describes how requirements will be analyzed,*

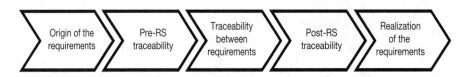

Figure 6.6 Traceability

documented, and managed. The requirement management plan is output in the *plan scope management* process. The requirement management plan contains, in this regard, a traceability structure to reflect which requirement attributes will be captured on the traceability matrix.

The *PMBOK® Guide* approach to the *plan scope management* procedure is by Process 5.1 *Plan scope management*, which is illustrated in Table 6.6. The overview of the processes in this domain can be found at the end of this chapter.

Table 6.6 Plan scope management

Input	Tools and Techniques	Output
• Project management plan • Project charter • Enterprise environmental factors • Organizational process assets	• Expert judgment • Meetings	• Scope management plan • Requirement management plan

With the developed requirement management plan or strategy for business requirements, we can initiate the process called *collect requirements*, where the requirement management plan is input.

The requirement management plan covers all planning decisions for both product and project while the business analysis plan refers to all the business planning activities and is considered a sub-plan of the requirement management plan.

Business Analysis for Practitioners (2015) has identified collaboration points where the business analyst and the project manager should work together toward developing the plan because business planning activities from the business analysis plan should be included in the overall requirement management plan. In addition, collaboration may be required in order to attain key stakeholder buy-in.

The business analysis plan may include some of the following points:

- Type of elicitation activities to be conducted
- Requirement analysis models that are required or expected
- Requirement documentation
- Requirement communication
- Roles and responsibilities
- Acceptance criteria
- How requirements are validated
- Requirement tracking

The *PMBOK® Guide* approach to the *collect requirements* procedure is by Process 5.2 *Collect requirements*, which is illustrated in Table 6.7. The overview of the processes in this domain can be found at the end of this chapter.

Table 6.7 Collect requirements

Input	Tools and Techniques	Output
• Scope management plan • Requirement management plan • Stakeholder management plan • Project charter • Stakeholder register	• Interviews • Focus groups • Facilitated workshops • Group creativity techniques • Group decision-making techniques • Questionnaires and surveys • Observations • Prototypes • Benchmarking • Context diagrams • Document analysis	• Requirement documentation • Requirement traceability matrix

The output in the *collect requirements* process is the requirements documentation and the requirement traceability matrix, which we need in order to establish the level of traceability necessary to validate and monitor the requirements.

The *requirements documentation* is *a description of how individual requirements meet the business need for the project*—which includes the business and project objectives for traceability. The second output of the *collect requirements* process is the *requirement traceability matrix*, which is defined as *an S grid that links product requirements from their origin to the deliverables that satisfy them*. This means that the attributes associated with each requirement can be recorded in the requirement traceability matrix. The requirement traceability matrix comes in many forms. However, Table 6.8 illustrates some of the questions that the requirement traceability matrix should answer in most cases.

Table 6.8 Requirement traceability matrix

What?	
When?	
Where?	
Why?	
What to show stakeholders?	
What to show team members?	
Standards	
Complementary tools	

The requirement traceability matrix is an effective tool. However, some alternatives could be:

- Cross-referencing schemes
- Textual reference
- Key phrase dependencies
- Hyperlinks/text
- Trace graphs (over different development artifacts)

- Templates and matrices
- Integration documents
- Traceability chain (linking relations)

The majority of these tools are integrated into most automated requirement management tools.

Requirement traceability needs to be conducted on the fly—with too big of a backlog, the effort would increase even more, and the quality of the traceability would decrease in most cases. Therefore, an ongoing audit of the requirement traceability effort is useful in many teams.

Exercise 6.2—A Bad Alternative? Which of the following tools are not an alternative to the requirement traceability matrix? (The answer is found on page 102.)

1. Templates
2. Text
3. Textual reference
4. Matrices
5. Project charter
6. Observations

6.4 DEVELOP REQUIREMENT MANAGEMENT PLAN

Now it's time to develop the requirement management plan by identifying stakeholder roles and responsibilities; communication protocols; and methods for eliciting, analyzing, documenting, managing, and approving requirements in order to establish a roadmap for delivering the expected solutions.

The requirement management plan is important because it is the agreement between the sponsor, all key stakeholders, the project manager, and the business analyst on not only the requirement elicitation approach, but also methods for requirement analysis, specification, documentation, and validation. The requirement management plan may also be called the business analyst work plan, the requirement work plan, or the business analyst work division strategy.

The requirement management plan should be approved by the customer in order to support the benefits. The plan may improve communication and teamwork on requirements, develop a common understanding, set clear expectations, scope the task, and serve as an agreement on tasks that require funding and resources. On the whole, this can increase the odds of project success with multiple benefits for large projects that involve several globally distributed functional units.

Currently, the requirement management plan has been defined as *a component of the project or program management plan that describes how requirements will be analyzed, documented, and managed.* However, this is slightly more complicated than it may sound. So far, we have only been focusing on the traceability aspect of the requirement management plan which is a small element. The requirement management plan was developed during the *plan scope management plan* process.

The *PMBOK® Guide* approach to the *plan scope management* procedure is by Process 5.1 *Plan scope management*, which is illustrated in Table 6.9. The overview of the processes in this domain can be found at the end of this chapter.

Table 6.9 Plan scope management

Input	Tools and Techniques	Output
• Project management plan • Project charter • Enterprise environmental factors • Organizational process assets	• Expert judgment • Meetings	• Scope management plan • Requirement management plan

In spite of being important, the requirement management plan is sometimes not very successful since many practitioners do not have the resources, maturity, knowledge, or skills to develop the plan. When developing the requirement management plan, it is essential to keep it separated from the project management plan because it is a subsidiary element of the project management plan. Table 6.10 highlights some of these differences.

Table 6.10 The project management plan and the requirement management plan

Project management plan (PMP)	Requirement management plan
Owned by the project manager	Owned by the business analyst
Primary project control document	Subsidiary element of the PMP
Document project management objectives to meet constraints	Document product objective throughout the project life cycle

The business analysis plan is a component of the requirement management plan, which is a component of the project or program management plan that describes how requirements will be analyzed, documented, and managed. The implications are that the typical requirement management plan would include the following (though several of the items may be found in the business analysis plan):

- Requirement definition activities (needs assessment, planning, analysis, traceability and monitoring, and evaluation) = domains
- Requirement processes
- Requirement repository, i.e., the requirement matrix
- Assigning types to requirements
- Assigning attributes to requirements
- Views on requirements
- Versioning of requirements
- Configuration management activities (requirement processes)
- Requirement management (formal requirement signoff)
- Management of requirement change (change management/change control)
- Requirement acceptance plan
- Problem and issue reporting

- Baselining
- Requirement-related risks
- Resource estimates for all constraints (time, cost, quality, etc.)
- Naming conventions
- Requirement prioritization process
- Product metrics
- Traceability structure
- Roles and responsibilities
- Applicable tools and methods—i.e., IBM Rationale
- Applicable standards—i.e., IEEE Standard 1233 (1998), 830 (1998), 1220 (1994) and *PMBOK®
Guide*

Most firms have their own standards for requirement management plans that are part of the firm's organizational process assets. Table 6.11 highlights some of the relationships between the requirement management plan and other subsidiary plans of the project management plan.

Table 6.11   Requirement management plan and other subsidiary plans

Requirement management plan	Baseline requirements	Change management plan
	Approved changes	Configuration management plan
	Project scope defined	Scope management plan
	New and changed requirements may issue risks	Risk management plan
	Define how requirements are to be reviewed	Quality management plan
	Define which requirements in which releases	Release management plan
	Planning of the activities	Business analysis plan

Exercise 6.3—Content of the Requirement Management Plan: Which of the following content would you not expect to find in the requirement management plan? (The answer is found on page 102.)

1. Versioning of requirements
2. Naming conventions
3. Traceability structure
4. IEEE Standard 1244

Exercise 6.4—Match the Key Words to Their Definitions: Match the business analysis key words to their definitions. You will find the key words in Table 6.12 and the definitions in Table 6.13. You can use Table 6.14 to record your answers and determine your score. You will find the correct answers in Table 6.15 on page 88.

When you have finished reading this chapter, you can refer back to this exercise and test your knowledge again.

Table 6.12 Key words

No.	Key words
1	Context analysis
2	Requirement management plan
3	System context
4	Requirement traceability matrix
5	Requirements documentation
6	Context boundary
7	Traceability
8	System boundary

Table 6.14 Answer and score sheet

Number of key word	Letter of definition
1	
2	
3	
4	
5	
6	
7	
8	

Table 6.13 Definitions

Letter	Definitions
A	Separates the system from its environment and highlights those parts which are relevant and affect the requirements.
B	Separate the system to be developed from its environment.
C	A description of how individual requirements meet the business need for the project.
D	Separates the relevant part of the environment of a system to be developed from the irrelevant part.
E	The process of documenting the development of requirements and solutions.
F	A grid that links product requirements from their origin to the deliverables that satisfy them.
G	The part of the system environment that is relevant for the definition as well as the understanding of the requirements of a system to be developed.
H	A component of the project or program management plan that describes how requirements will be analyzed, documented, and managed.

6.5 PLAN REQUIREMENT CHANGE CONTROL

In this section we need to select methods for requirement change control by identifying channels for communication requests and processes for managing changes in order to establish standard protocols for incorporation into the change management plan.

Requirement changes happen all the time and are as inevitable as death and taxes. Requirements often change for very good reasons—with some changes being stable, while others are more volatile. Requirements change may arise from requirement errors, conflicts, inconsistencies, evolving stakeholder knowledge, changing priorities, organization changes, technological changes, or enterprise environmental factors, such as new laws. Although these changes are perfectly acceptable, we need to ensure that we have a process that protects the entire plan so that the changes can do no further harm—harmful results may include software with flaws, scope creep, and extensive use of resources.

In general, changes can be required by any stakeholder, and the number of changes does not automatically imply whether the requirements were well-defined from the start or not. However, a high frequency of changes may indicate process quality issues.

First, we need to consider how to manage changes. As discussed earlier, the *plan scope management* process develops the requirement management plan which highlights how changes to the product will be initiated; how impact will be analyzed; how they will be traced, tracked, and reported; and who has the authorization to decide upon the changes.

Business Analysis for Practitioners (2015) has identified determining ownership of the change control documentation as a collaboration point between the business analyst and project manager. This process should be worked out together since the business analysis plan and change management plan are both relevant inputs.

The *PMBOK® Guide* approach to the *plan scope management* procedure is by Process 5.1 *Plan scope management*, which was illustrated in Table 6.9. The overview of the processes in this domain can be found at the end of this chapter.

The *plan scope management* process, along with the development of the requirement management plan, helps us make justified decisions on changes, ensures channels for communication requests, and conducts processes for managing changes in order to establish standard protocols for incorporation into the change management plan. In addition, this helps us control resources. However, we also need a process which is not a barrier to halt changes.

It is difficult to discuss the requirement management plan without considering the requirement documentation and requirement traceability matrix which are the output of the *collect requirements* process.

The *PMBOK® Guide* approach to the *collect requirements* procedure is by Process 5.2 *Collect requirements*, which was illustrated in Table 6.7. The overview of the processes in this domain can be found at the end of this chapter.

In this case, the requirements traceability matrix is the structure to manage changes to the product scope, which we will update during the control scope process. The control scope process manages changes to the scope baseline and ensures all required changes are processed through the *perform integrated change control* process. In addition, any output is updated in the project management plan, which

Table 6.15 Correct answers

Keywords	Definitions
1	A
2	H
3	G
4	F
5	C
6	D
7	E
8	B

includes the change management plan. Furthermore, the project document updates include requirement documentation and the requirement traceability matrix.

The *PMBOK® Guide* approach to the *control scope* procedure is by Process 5.6 *Control scope*, which is illustrated in Table 6.16. The overview of the processes in this domain can be found at the end of this chapter.

Table 6.16 Control scope

Input	Tools and Techniques	Output
• Project management plan • Requirement documents • Requirement traceability matrix • Work performance data • Organizational process assets	• Variance analysis	• Work performance information • Change requests • Project management plan updates • Project documents updates • Organizational process assets update

In our case, the output of the *control scope* process is a requirement change request or just a change request, which is defined as *a formal proposal to modify any document, deliverable, or baseline*. The change request is received as an input to the *perform integrated change control* process. In addition, input is the change management plan, as part of the project management plan; organizational process assets, which include the change control procedures; and work performance reports.

The *PMBOK® Guide* approach to the *perform integrated change control* procedure is by Process 4.5 *Perform integrated change control*, which is illustrated in Table 6.17. The overview of the processes in this domain can be found at the end of this chapter.

Table 6.17 Perform integrated change control

Input	Tools and Techniques	Output
• Project management plan • Work performance reports • Change requests • Enterprise environmental factors • Organizational process assets	• Expert judgment • Meetings • Change control tools	• Approved change requests • Change log • Project management plan updates • Project document updates

In order to reach an approved change requests procedure, we need to complete the change control process *whereby modifications to documents, deliverables, or baselines associated with the project are identified, documented, approved, or rejected.* At this stage, we are at the tools and techniques procedure where a meeting is held by the change control board (CCB), which is *a formally chartered group responsible for reviewing, evaluating, approving, delaying, or rejecting changes to the project; and for recording and communicating such decisions.* In addition, the CCB may estimate effort, and classify and prioritize changes. The participants on the CCB would most likely include the following representatives:

- Change manager (chair)
- Contractor
- Architect
- Configuration manager
- Customer representative
- Product manager
- Project manager
- Quality assurance representative
- Technical support or help desk
- Requirement engineer

The participants (whether one or a team) on the CCB may have different roles, as illustrated in Table 6.18.

Table 6.18 Participants in the change control board

Possible roles on the change control board	Description
CCB chair	Final decision making
Evaluator	Analyzes and assesses the change
Modifier	Implements the change
Originator	Submits the change request
Request receiver	Receives the change request
Verifier	Checks that change is made correctly

The participants in the CCB would have received a change request with some of the following information:

- Identifier
- Date
- Title
- Description
- Justification
- Priority
- Applicant

The purpose of the information given to the CCB would, in addition, add value to the following information:

- Change validator
- Impact analysis status
- CCB decision status
- CCB priority
- Responsibility

The incoming change requests received by the CCB can be classified as:

- Corrective requirement change
- Adaptive requirement change
- Exceptional change

The methods for processing requirement changes depends on their classification. However, most requirement changes would require an impact analysis for assessment.

The work and information illustrated are part of the change control system, which is *a set of procedures that describes how modifications to the project deliverables and documentation are managed and controlled*—and is used with change control tools, which are *manual or automated tools to assist with change and/or configuration management*. At a minimum, the tools should support the activities of the CCB.

At this stage, we need the CCB to make a decision where the following must be taken into consideration:

- The number of CCB members or the key roles necessary to constitute a quorum for making decisions
- Whether voting, consensus, consultative decision making, or some other decision rule is used
- Whether the CCB chair can overrule the CCB collective decision
- Whether a higher level of the CCB or someone else must ratify the decision

With the decision being made, the change log is created, which is *a comprehensive list of changes made during the project*. This typically includes the dates of the changes and impact to the project in terms of time, costs, and risks. In addition, we need to update the traceability information and communicate the changes to the relevant parties. It is also a best practice in many firms to measure the amount of change, along with details about which requirements are changed and so forth, which can highlight general issues and help keep track of the project.

Overall, the requirement change control process enables the possibility to turn problems into requirements with identification of the problem often conducted with the help of forms, feedback, and customer requests. With this information, we analyze and assess the problem/change before the proposed change is required. The assessment is then put up for decision as to whether or not to apply the change control—which, after approval, is implemented.

Exercise 6.5—The CCB Process: What is the right order of the CCB process when a decision has just been made? (The answer is found on page 102.)

1. Create the change log
2. Update the traceability information

3. Communicate the changes to the relevant parties
4. Measure the amount of change

6.6 PLAN DOCUMENT CONTROL

Now we need to select methods for document control by using documentation management tools and techniques in order to establish a standard for requirements traceability and versioning. So far, standards for requirements traceability have been discussed, which leaves us with versioning. Versioning goes hand-in-hand with configuration management. To put it simply, change management also includes configuration management, which implies that we need to manage and control what requirements and documentations we have and what we need to change. This is done in order to avoid confusion, misunderstandings, and conflicts.

If we examine requirement management at a high level and in a fairly generic manner, usually it consists of change control, version control, requirement status tracking, and requirement tracing, as illustrated in Figure 6.7.

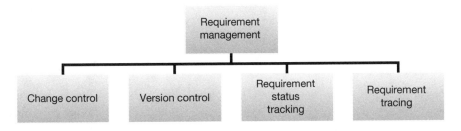

Figure 6.7   Requirement management

If we translate Figure 6.5 into PMI terms, then we need to consider the *plan scope management* process as the output of the requirement management plan, which among other things, describes how requirements are documented and managed. The *PMBOK® Guide* approach to the *plan scope management* procedure is by Process 5.1 *Plan scope management*, which was illustrated in Table 6.9.

The *plan scope management* process will lead us to the process of *perform integrated change control*. The *perform integrated change control* procedure consists of change management and configuration management. Configuration management includes version control.

The *PMBOK® Guide* approach to the *perform integrated change control* procedure is by Process 4.5 *Perform integrated change control*, which was illustrated in Table 6.17.

Configuration management (or the configuration management system) is defined as *a subsystem of the overall project management system*. Hence, it is a collection of formally documented procedures used to apply technical and administrative directions and surveillance, and to identify and document the functional and physical characteristics of a product, result, service, or component. We need to control any changes to such characteristics; record and report each change and its implementation status; and support the audit of the product, results, or components to verify conformance to requirements. It includes the documentation, tracking system, and defined approval levels necessary for authorizing and controlling changes.

Configuration management control is focused on the specification of both the deliverable and the processes. Some configuration management activities are:

- Configuration identification
- Configuration status accounting
- Configuration verification and audit

In order to be able to keep track of the configurations, we need versioning, branching, and baselines of requirements and requirements documents, which also enables reuse of requirements assets at any point in the life cycle and benefits investments across projects.

Requirements are constantly changing, which makes versioning a vital tool to manage the configuration. A small change in a requirement may change it from Version 0.1 to Version 0.2, while a larger change may result in a change from Version 0.3 to Version 1.0. The typical version control used is illustrated in Table 6.19.

Table 6.19 Revision history

Version	Date	Authorization	Responsible	Description

When versions of software are developed for different versions of a product—for example, several clients seek different alterations to the software—then these changes will come in different versions within various branches. Branching is a range of versions related to a given product. A software firm will quite often have many branches to manage version control and configuration management.

Version control includes defining a version identification scheme, identifying requirements documents versions, and identifying individual requirement versions. This implies that versions may be related to products or requirements—as illustrated with branching on a higher level. However, Version 0.2 may fit requirements 1 and 5, while the Version 0.3 may fit with requirements 1 to 5, because bugs have been corrected. This increases the complexity since the amount of items managed by configuration management, whether requirements or codes, would skyrocket. To complicate matters more, requirements have attributes. Requirement attributes would be source, data, version, origin, and the rationale behind the requirements. Requirement attributes change and that means all changes to the requirements are subject to version control.

Requirements are part of our configuration and are managed with the process for *perform integrated change control*, which includes configuration management. A configuration of requirements has the following properties:

- Logical connection
- Consistency
- Unique identification
- Immutable
- Basis for rollbacks

In order to sum this up, we need to mention the requirements baseline since it is closely related and interactive. Requirement baselines are requirements that are committed to be implemented. When requirements are baselined, we have a basis for release planning, estimation of effort, and the tools to develop comparisons. When requirements are baselined, they are frozen. Several requirements are baselined in order to implement them in a given release, and the baseline requirements also function as a point of reference. Baseline requirements are managed with change control.

Exercise 6.6—Requirement Baseline: When requirements are baselined they become a point of reference. What other word can we use to describe them at this point? (The answer is found on page 102.)

6.7 DEFINE PROJECT EXPECTED OUTCOME

In the last task in the planning domain, we need to define business metrics and acceptance criteria in collaboration with stakeholders to evaluate when the solution meets the requirements. Requirements are developed in order to document the desired result. The desired results are defined in the project charter. At this stage, we need to ensure that the quality of the requirements is as expected and that the requirements cover what the stakeholders want. The business analyst should aim for stakeholder approval of the acceptance criteria. Examining requirements may uncover errors—some of the most common are ambiguity, incompleteness, and contradictions. However, we also need to minimize the legal risks and cost overruns, and avoid conflicts with our stakeholders. Requirement validation, which includes business metrics and acceptance criteria, is closely related to negotiation and often goes hand in hand.

Business metrics are standards of measurements by which efficiency, performance, progress, or quality can be assessed. These are often included in our acceptance criteria as nonfunctional requirements. An aim of using quality aspects of requirements with business metrics and acceptance criteria is to check the requirements systematically. Table 6.20 highlights some of the quality aspects of requirements that we need to check for.

Table 6.20 Quality aspects of requirements (content)

Completeness (set of all requirements): Have all relevant requirements for the system to be developed (for the next system release) been documented?	Completeness (individual requirements): Does each requirement contain all necessary information?
Traceability: Have all relevant traceability relationships been defined?	Correctness/adequacy: Do the requirements accurately reflect the wishes and needs of the stakeholders?
Consistency: Is it possible to implement all defined requirements for the system to be developed jointly? Are there any contradictions?	No premature design decisions: Are there any forestalled design decisions present in the requirements not induced by constraints (e.g., constraints that specify the client-server architecture to be used)?
Verifiability: Is it possible to define acceptance and test criteria based on the requirements? Have the criteria been defined?	Necessity: Does every requirement contribute to the fulfillment of the goals defined?

Sometimes the business analyst may encounter a violation of the quality aspects of the documentation of the requirement, which may cause problems for the acceptance criteria, or may not reflect business metrics. Figure 6.8 illustrates some of the common quality aspects of documentation.

Figure 6.8 Quality aspects of documentation

Just before we examine the quality aspects of the content of the documentation, however, it is equally important to validate the quality aspect of the actual documentation, as illustrated in Table 6.21.

Table 6.21 Quality aspect documentation

Conformity to documentation format: Are the requirements documented in the predetermined documentation format? For instance, has a specific requirements template or a specific modeling language been used to document the requirements?	Conformity to documentation structures: Has the structure of the requirements document been maintained? For instance, have all requirements been documented at the proper position in the document?
Comprehension: Can all documented requirements be understood in the context given? For instance, have all terms used been defined in a glossary?	Unambiguity: Does the documentation of the requirements allow for only one interpretation or are multiple different interpretations possible? For instance, does a text-based requirement possess any kind of ambiguity?
Conformity to documentation rules: Have the predetermined documentation rules and documentation guidelines been met? For instance, has the syntax of the modeling language been used properly?	

The third quality aspect contains checks on agreements with the stakeholders. This may be the last opportunity for changes. Requirements validation would focus on these possible outcomes:

- **Agreed**: Is every requirement agreed upon with all relevant stakeholders?
- **Agreed after changes**: Is every requirement agreed upon with all relevant stakeholders after it has been changed?
- **Conflicts resolved**: Have all known conflicts with regard to the requirements been resolved?

Validation denotes checking whether inputs, performed activities, and created outputs (requirements artifacts) of the requirements engineering core activities fulfill defined quality criteria. Validation is performed by involving relevant stakeholders, other requirement sources (standards, laws, etc.), as well as external reviewers, if necessary. The six principles of validation should be followed in order to ensure the expected quality of business metrics and acceptable criteria, which also is a good opportunity for stakeholder engagement (see Table 6.22).

Table 6.22   The six principles of validation

First principle: Involving the right stakeholders	Ensure that relevant company—internal as well as external—stakeholders participate in validation. Pay attention to the reviewers' independence and appoint external, independent stakeholders if necessary.
Second principle: Separating the identification and the correction of errors	Separate defect detection from the correction of the detected defects.
Third principle: Validation from different views	Whenever possible, try to obtain independent views that can be integrated during requirements validation in order to detect defects more reliably.
Fourth principle: Adequate change of document type	Consider changing the documentation format of the requirements into a format that matches the validation goal and the preferences of the stakeholders who actually perform the validation.
Fifth principle: Construction of development artifacts	If your validation approach generates poor results, try to support defect detection by creating development artifacts, such as architectural artifacts, test artifacts, user manuals, or goals and scenarios during validation.
Sixth principle: Repeated validation	Establish guidelines that clearly determine when or under what conditions an already released requirements artifact has to be validated again.

Business Analysis for Practitioners (2015) has identified stakeholder engagement as a collaboration point where the business analyst and the project manager should work together. The project manager is responsible for stakeholder engagement in the project while the business analyst is responsible for stakeholder engagement in the business analyst activities.

In order to complete the six principles of requirements validation, the business analyst can use one or more of the following validation/verification of requirements techniques shown in Table 6.23.

Table 6.23   Validation techniques

Validation techniques	Descriptions
Inspections	An organized examination process of the requirements.
Desk-checks	The author of a requirement artifact distributes the artifact to a set of stakeholders. The stakeholders check the artifact individually. The stakeholders report the identified defects to the author. The collected issues are discussed in a group session (optional).
Commenting	Individual validation of requirements.
Structured walkthroughs	A walkthrough does not have a formally defined procedure.
Prototypes	A prototype allows the stakeholders to try out the requirements for the system and thereby experience them.
Checklists	Quality aspects, experience, error statistics.
Interviews	Interviews applied for validation.
Workshops	Validation through workshops with stakeholders.
Problem tracking	Method to keep track of the validation process and identified problems.

Additional elements of validating requirements involve:

- Checking assumptions
- Defining measurable evaluation criteria
- Defining business value
- Determining dependencies of solution benefits
- Evaluating the alignment of the business case with opportunity cost

This brings us back to the *develop project charter* process, as the inputs and outputs need to be verified/validated one last time with the stakeholders before its baselined.

Exercise 6.7—Validation by Trying it Out: Which of the following validation techniques could be applied when emphasis is on the stakeholders trying out the system? (The answer is found on page 102.)

1. Workshops
2. Prototypes
3. Interviews
4. Wait until the solution is developed

The *PMBOK® Guide* approach to the *develop project charter* procedure is by Process 4.1 *Develop project charter*, which was illustrated in Table 6.1. The overview of the process (and the others listed in this chapter) in this domain can be found in Table 6.24.

Defining the business metrics and acceptance criteria by collaboration with stakeholders is a job for the business analyst. Part of the validation and verification process may involve developers and testers besides the stakeholders. With acceptance criteria for all requirements in place, including the ones involving business metrics, the documentation is quality checked so at some later time in the process the customer can perform acceptance testing to determine whether the system satisfies the acceptance criteria.

6.8 RELATING PMI-PBA® PRACTICES TO *PMBOK® GUIDE—FIFTH EDITION* PRACTICES

Table 6.24 Project management process groups

Knowledge areas	Project management process groups				
	Initiating	Planning	Executing	Monitoring and Controlling	Closing
	Domain—Needs Assessment				
Project integration management	4.1 Develop project charter			4.5 Perform integrated change control	
Project scope management		5.1 Plan scope management 5.2 Collect requirements 5.6 Control scope			
Project time management					
Project cost management					
Project quality management					
Project human resource management					
Project communication management					
Project risk management					
Project procurement management					
Project stakeholder management					

6.9 RELATING PMI-PBA® PRACTICES TO AGILE PRACTICES

In this chapter, the planning domain is described from the standpoint of a plan-based project. In a Scrum-based project, the business context and the project's expected outcome is the sole responsibility of the project owner. If the business context changes, it is up to the product owner to ensure close collaboration with stakeholders. However, the agile methodologies are value-driven, which means that they will be focusing on delivering the most valued project outcome first. A product backlog will be used rather than a requirements management plan. Requirements, in general, will be discussed with the development team. The responsibility of handling changes, traceability, and documents is the task of the members of the development team, who will have a shared responsibility. Changes will be handled in an ongoing process, rather than using boards—and in general, the process is much faster and involves more interaction and collaboration rather than comprehensive documentation. The agile techniques used will be visual and easy to use (i.e., prototypes, storyboards, etc.) for validating, while changes will be managed in an ongoing manner based on the information distribution that is visible to all. At this point, the requirements have not been discussed in detail. However, in the agile methodologies, user stories will be used rather than the types of requirements that have been illustrated so far. In general, the planning is up to the product owner and should be kept to a minimum since changes are inevitable.

6.10 CHAPTER SUMMARY

Key concepts

- The business analyst has to understand the extent of the work *and* the broader context
- Ignoring interface problems just makes them bigger
- Traceability is described as the process of documenting the development of requirements and solutions
- The requirement management plan should be approved by the customer
- The requirement management plan is important because it is the agreement between the sponsor, all key stakeholders, the project manager, and the business analyst—on not only the requirement elicitation approach, but also on the methods for requirement analysis, specification, documentation, and validation
- Changes are inevitable
- Changes can be required by any stakeholder
- Versioning, branching, and baselining of requirements and requirements documents enable reuse of requirements assets at any point in the life cycle, and leverage investments across projects

Exercise 6.8—Match the Key Words to Their Definitions: Match the business analysis key words to their definitions. You will find the key words in Table 6.25 and the definitions in Table 6.26. You can use Table 6.27 to record your answers and determine your score. You will find the correct answers in Table 6.28 on page 100.

When you have finished reading this chapter, you can refer back to this exercise, and test your knowledge again.

Table 6.25 Key words

No.	Key words
1	Change log
2	Change control tools
3	Change control board
4	Change request
5	Change control process
6	Configuration management system
7	Change control system

Table 6.27 Answer and score sheet

Number of key word	Letter of definition
1	
2	
3	
4	
5	
6	
7	

Table 6.26 Definitions

Letter	Definitions
A	A process whereby modifications to documents, deliverables, or baselines associated with the project are identified, documented, approved, or rejected.
B	A comprehensive list of changes made during the project. This typically includes dates of the changes and impacts in terms of time, costs, and risk.
C	A subsystem of the overall project management system.
D	Manual or automated tools to assist with change and/or configuration management. At a minimum, the tools should support the activities of the CCB.
E	A formally chartered group responsible for reviewing, evaluating, approving, delaying, or rejecting changes to the project, and for recording and communicating such decisions.
F	A set of procedures that describes how modifications to the project deliverables and documentation are managed and controlled.
G	A formal proposal to modify any document, deliverable, or baseline.

Table 6.28 Correct answers

Key words	Definitions
1	B
2	D
3	E
4	G
5	A
6	C
7	F

6.11 POSTTEST: TAKE FIVE

The posttest contains five exam-related questions in the PMI-PBA format for you to check your knowledge of the content presented in this chapter and to check your readiness for the PMI-PBA exam. The answers will be provided in the next section. You should time the posttest and not use more than six or seven minutes.

1. What are the advantages of traceable requirements?
   a) Identification of additional costs
   b) Identification of a gold-plated solution in the requirements
   c) It's quick and easy to do
   d) It is a requirement from the stakeholders

2. What is the output of the plan scope management process?
   a) The project charter
   b) Scope management plan and project charter
   c) Scope management plan and requirement management plan
   d) Requirement management plan and requirement management matrix

3. Which question would you *not* ask when developing a requirement traceability matrix?
   a) What
   b) When
   c) Where
   d) Who

4. In a traditional plan-based project, who owns the project management plan?
   a) The project manager
   b) The business analyst

c) The product owner

d) The Scrum Master

5. What is the relationship between requirement management, change control, and version control?

a) Version control is part of configuration management, which includes change management

b) Requirement management includes version control, while change control is part of configuration management

c) Requirement management includes both change control and version control

d) All of the above

6.12 POSTTEST: CORRECT ANSWERS

1. Answer: B
2. Answer: C
3. Answer: D
4. Answer: A
5. Answer: C

Answer to *Exercise 6.1*: Two, it is a data flow diagram.

Answers to *Exercise 6.2*: Five and six are not good alternatives to the requirement traceability matrix. The project charter is input to the collect requirement process while observations are a tool and technique in the collect requirement process.

Answer to *Exercise 6.3*: Four is made up. The IEEE Standard is 1233.

Answer to *Exercise 6.5*: The order is correct.

Answer to *Exercise 6.6*: Frozen

Answers to *Exercise 6.7*: One and three are valid validation techniques, however two is the only correct option (review Table 6.23). Option 4 is entirely incorrect.

Analysis Domain

7

TERMS TO KNOW

The list at the beginning of each chapter highlights the key terms you are required to know by the Project Management Institute (PMI). Hence, you can start by looking over these terms and if you already have solid knowledge of them, then you may consider skipping this chapter. However, once you have finished reading the chapter, you can refer back to this list and test your knowledge. The concepts are:

- Types of elicitation techniques
- Kano model
- Requirement sources
- Group decision-making techniques
- Inspections
- Requirement baseline
- Work breakdown structure

- Techniques for prioritization
- Requirements
- Requirements documentation using a natural language
- Requirements documentation using a model-based language
- Quality

7.1 BRIEF INTRODUCTION: ANALYSIS

The Analysis domain emphasizes requirement management activities. In this domain, requirements are elicited, analyzed, developed, modeled, and managed in all possible forms. However, the domain has close ties to the project management activities and the majority of the activities are conducted in close collaboration with the stakeholders within various parts of the project.

Business Analysis for Practitioners (2015) illustrates requirement elicitation and analysis as the following steps:

- Plan for elicitation
- Prepare for elicitation
- Conduct elicitation activities
- Document outputs from elicitation activities
- Complete elicitation
- Elicitation issues and challenges
- Analyze requirements
- Model and refine requirements
- Document the solution requirements
- Validate requirements
- Verify requirements
- Approval sessions
- Resolve requirement-related conflicts

The needs assessment and planning processes are plan-based processes that must be completed one-by-one before moving on to the next process (see Figure 7.1). However, the analysis process is based on progressive elaboration, which continuously repeats itself from current knowledge to the requirements specifications, until we have an agreement that moves us into the last two domains.

Figure 7.1   Planning

During this chapter, a wide range of tools and techniques will be introduced and explained for the analysis stage, although some may argue that this process is only 20% scientific based on its success in real-life applications. The remaining 80% of the process is considered an art, which consists of approximately 40 knowledge concepts and skills that are explained in Chapter 11. This is illustrated in Figure 7.2.

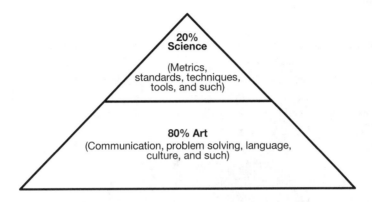

Figure 7.2 Analysis: science or art

7.2 ELICIT REQUIREMENTS

Here, the business analyst needs to elicit or identify requirements using individual and group elicitation techniques in order to discover and capture requirements with supporting details. Requirement elicitation, requirement gathering, requirement discovery, and requirement definition are core activities in requirements engineering. However, while requirement elicitation is critical for the success of our project, it is also very difficult to do. It is error prone, which means the need for a structured approach and proper documentation is crucial. It is also communicatively intensive and should be aligned with stakeholder needs and constraints. Although we need stakeholder input for elicitation, we need to ensure the loudest voice in the room is not the only one that is heard and elicited.

One of the things that makes elicitation difficult is the fact that it is hard to determine when you are done. The theory of requirement elicitation is closely related to selecting and using the appropriate techniques in order to grasp what the businesses are working on and what they want to achieve. This process of eliciting requirements is all about observing, understanding, learning, interpreting, and recording the information gathered—which is why some people say that this method is similar to *fishing* for requirements. It is a challenge for the business analyst to record the voices of the customers—which is usually an unstructured bunch of information containing:

- Business requirements
- Use cases or scenarios

- Business rules
- Functional requirements
- Quality attributes
- External interface requirements
- Constraints
- Data definitions
- Solution ideas

Requirement elicitation may occur from stakeholders (individuals or groups) or other sources (documents). However, the challenge can be obtaining access to stakeholders and other key resources. The elicitation of stakeholders is similar to the scenario illustrated before with regard to the voice of the customer. Some stakeholders may only be able to discuss the current situation, whereas the business analyst (BA) needs to address future needs. In addition to this, BAs also need past information to enhance their knowledge of the organization and avoid mistakes from the past.

One approach to requirement elicitation on a high level is the Brown Cow Model shown in Figure 7.3, which contains the factors of *now, future, how* and *what*. The investigation so far has been focusing on the lower left corner—the *now (current) how* situation, and to some degree, it also targets the *what* of the current situation. However, in order to move from left to right, the business analyst needs to consider the elements of innovation, system thinking, and organizational goals and values.

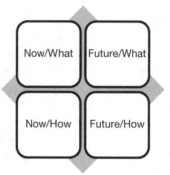

Figure 7.3 Brown Cow Model

Explaining the Types of Requirements Sources

The basis for requirements elicitation is the knowledge that is gained during requirements engineering about the system context of the system to be developed, which comprises the requirements sources that are to be analyzed and queried. These sources include:

- Stakeholders—people or organizations that directly or indirectly influence the requirements of the system
- Documents—often containing important information that can be a source for attaining requirements

- Systems in operation (can be legacy, predecessor, or competing systems)—providing the stakeholders with a chance to try the system out will help them critique the current system so they can then request extensions or changes based on their impressions

Categorizing the Requirements According to the Kano Model

Knowing the importance of requirements for the satisfaction of stakeholders is very helpful for requirements elicitation. Figure 7.4 is a graphical representation of requirement satisfaction using the Kano model. In addition to the properties of the product that determine satisfaction, user satisfaction is classified into three categories:

- Dissatisfiers: requirements or properties of the system that are self-evident, expected, and taken for granted by the stakeholder (subconscious knowledge)
- Satisfiers: requirements or system properties that are explicitly demanded by the stakeholder (conscious knowledge)
- Delighters: requirements or system properties that the stakeholder does not know or expect, and discovers only while using the system—a pleasant and useful surprise (unconscious knowledge)

As time goes by, delighters turn into satisfiers or dissatisfiers, as the stakeholder (user) becomes accustomed to the properties of the system.

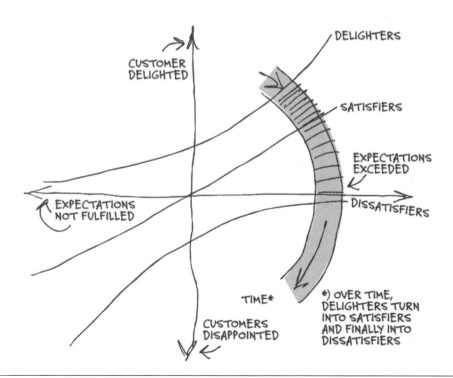

Figure 7.4   Kano model adapted from *I am Agile* by Klaus Nielsen

Table 7.1 demonstrates the properties of the Kano model and connects the model with suitable elicitation techniques.

Table 7.1 The categories of the Kano model

Dissatisfiers	Satisfiers	Delighters
Assumed and must be fulfilled by the system	Consciously known and explicitly demanded	Properties of a system recognized only by using the system
Completely fulfilled dissatisfiers help to avoid massive discontent	Fulfilled satisfiers bring contentment and satisfaction	
Dominantly influenced by existing systems	Any missing property can lead to product unacceptability	
	Satisfaction decreases with each missing satisfier	
Suitable elicitation technique—observation and document-centric techniques	Suitable elicitation technique—survey techniques	Suitable elicitation technique—creativity techniques

Describing the Various Elicitation Techniques

The elicitation of requirements represents an early but continuous and critical stage in the development of software systems. Requirements engineering can be defined as a group of activities that help find and communicate the need, purpose, and context of a system. The requirements for a software system may be spread across many sources. Techniques for requirements elicitation are derived mostly from the social sciences, organizational theory, group dynamics, knowledge engineering, and very often, from practical experience.

The main goal of all elicitation techniques is to support the business analyst in ascertaining the knowledge and requirements of the stakeholders. Every project is mostly unique, with individual constraints and individual characteristics, but there are always common elicitation techniques that are compatible with most projects. There is no universal method for requirements elicitation. A number of factors influence the choice of elicitation technique. They are:

- Distinction between conscious, unconscious, and subconscious requirements
- Time and budget constraints, and stakeholder availability
- The business analyst's experience with a particular elicitation technique
- Chances and risks of the project

Selection of a suitable elicitation technique is dependent on the risk factors involved in a project. These factors can result from the following influences:

- Human influences
- Organizational influences
- Operational influences of the content

A combination of different techniques helps minimize many of the risks that are inherent to the project. *Risk factors* are constraints that are critical to a project (see Table 7.2). They result from human, organizational, and professional influences, along with operational influence of the content and the desired level of requirement details.

Table 7.2 Risk factors

Human influences	Good communication is essential. For high-quality communication, it is important to determine the type of requirement, the desired level of detail, and the experience of the requirements' engineer and the interviewees, using different elicitation techniques.
Organizational influences	These can be the distinctions between fixed price contracts and service contracts, whether the system to be built is a new development or an extension of a legacy system, along with spatial and temporal availability of the stakeholders.
Operational influences of the content	A complex system should employ a structured approach during elicitation in order to deconstruct the operational contents into understandable parts.

It is important to ensure the application of the right techniques during the task analysis. Table 7.3 illustrates how task and requirement techniques can be aligned.

Table 7.3 Alignment of requirements and tasks

	Interviews	Domains	Group work	Ethnography	Prototyping	Goals	Scenarios	Viewpoints
Understanding the domain	X			X	X	X	X	X
Identifying sources of requirements	X	X	X		X	X	X	X
Analyzing the stakeholders		X	X		X	X		
Selecting techniques and approaches		X	X	X				X
Eliciting the requirements			X	X	X	X	X	X

Table 7.4 introduces two approaches to categorizing the requirement elicitation techniques.

Table 7.4 Requirement elicitation methods

Requirement elicitation methods	Techniques
Conversional methods	Interviews Workshops Focus groups
Observational methods	Protocol analysis Ethnography analysis
Analytical methods	Requirement reuse Laddering Card sorting Repertory grid
Synthetic methods	Scenarios Story boards Prototyping JAD/RAD Contextual inquiry

Another influencing factor on the choice of elicitation techniques is the desired level of detail of the requirements. For abstract requirements, the creativity technique is suitable. Inquisitive or observational techniques can be used to get a medium-level detail of requirements, and document-centric techniques can be used for detailed requirements. A combination of different techniques helps minimize many risks that are inherent to the project. Weaknesses and pitfalls of a particular technique can be balanced out through the use of another technique whose strong points lie where the first technique may have deficits. Figure 7.5 illustrates the requirement elicitation techniques that form the toolbox of a business analyst.

Survey Techniques

Survey techniques help to elicit precise and unbiased statements from stakeholders, which are then derived by the business analyst. The survey techniques are interviews, such as personal interviews, structured interviews, unstructured interviews, synchronous interviews (real time), asynchronous interviews (not real time), or group interviews with several stakeholders at once; customer site visits or task analysis; and written surveys in terms of questionnaires. Table 7.5 points out some of the advantages and disadvantages of using interviews for requirement elicitation.

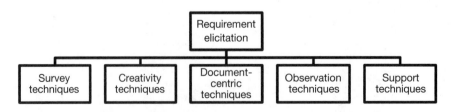

Figure 7.5 Requirement elicitation techniques

Table 7.5   Advantages and disadvantages of using interviews for requirement elicitation

Advantages of interviews	Disadvantages of interviews
• Scripted discussion • Promotes dialogue • Encourages participants • Can observe nonverbal behavior • Allows immediate feedback	• Requires access to committed stakeholders • Requires training and skills to work well • Documentation is subject to interpretation • Conflicts do not get resolved and may be misunderstood • Stakeholders may not be able to describe the future so they are limited to describing the current situation

Exercise 7.1—Discuss in your study or work groups your personal experience with interview and survey techniques for requirement elicitation.

Creativity Techniques

Creativity techniques for requirement elicitation help in developing innovative requirements and elicit excitement factors. Creativity techniques are not suitable for eliciting fine-grained requirements of system behavior. The creativity technique of *brainstorming* can be used in several ways, such as individual brainstorming sessions, open brainstorming during a workshop, structured brainstorming using the work breakdown structure (WBS) for a structured approach, or silent brainstorming using yellow stickers. In addition to this, the brainstorming paradox, as well as the change of perspective and analogy techniques, can be used as creativity techniques for requirements elicitation. Table 7.6 demonstrates advantages and disadvantages of using brainstorming for requirement elicitation.

Table 7.6   Advantages and disadvantages of using brainstorming for requirement elicitation

Advantages of brainstorming	Disadvantages of brainstorming
• Generates multiple ideas quickly • Involves multiple perspectives • Promotes equal participants	• Ideas are not discussed or explored • The true meaning may be misunderstood or ambiguous

Business Analysis for Practitioners (2015) has identified facilitating workshops as a collaboration point where the business analyst and the project manager can team up. The project manager can act as scribe and supporter, while the business analyst can focus on the elicitation.

Exercise 7.2—Go online and find five more specific brainstorming exercises. Try using one to help solve a specific problem.

Document-Centric Techniques

Document-centric techniques begin with existing documents and systems which means that solutions and experiences made with existing systems may be reused. The techniques can also be combined with other elicitation techniques to determine the validity of elicited requirements and to identify new requirements for the new system. The most common document-centric techniques are system archaeology, document review, perspective-based reading, and reuse. The documents used as part of the techniques can vary from old specifications and designs to problem reports and a current list of changes (see Table 7.7).

Table 7.7 Advantages and disadvantages of using document review for requirement elicitation

Advantages of document review	Disadvantages of document review
• Current process documentation for a starting point	• Documentation may be old and out-of-date • Need domain knowledge to judge the documentation • Can be time consuming

Exercise 7.3—What other document-centric techniques for elicitation of requirements for an enterprise resource planning system within a bank can you use?

Observation Techniques

Observation techniques are useful when domain specialists are unable to share their knowledge, and when it is possible to observe stakeholders as they perform their work. Observation techniques help to formulate the potential requirements, identify inefficient processes, and elicit detailed requirements and dissatisfiers. However, they may not be suitable for development of new processes. The most common observation techniques are:

- Field observation
- Passive observation (just observes)
- Active observation (interrupts)
- Participatory observation (takes part)
- Simulation (recreates the work)
- Apprenticing

Table 7.8 illustrates the advantages and disadvantages of using observations and apprenticing for requirement elicitation.

Table 7.8 Advantages and disadvantages of using observations and apprenticing for requirement elicitation

Advantages of observation and apprenticing	Disadvantages of observation and apprenticing
• Get a good feeling about the environment • Discover practical issues and unintended uses • Simulate dialogue • Seeing that a given approach may not work	• May not elicit new requirements • Events may not be typical

Exercise 7.4—What are the biggest pros and cons of using observation techniques at your current workplace, and what can be done to overcome the cons and strengthen the pros?

Support Techniques

Support techniques serve as an addition to the elicitation techniques and help balance out the weaknesses and pitfalls of the selected technique. Support techniques include mind mapping, workshops, class-responsibility-collaboration (CRC) cards, audio/video recordings, personas, use case modeling, Wikis, blogs, discussion forums, requirements prototypes, reverse engineering, and requirement reuse. Table 7.9 illustrates the advantages and disadvantages of using workshops for requirement elicitation.

Table 7.9 Advantages and disadvantages of using workshops for requirement elicitation

Advantages of workshops	Disadvantages of workshops
• Effective at getting real requirements • Can neutralize a predominant voice • Greater chance of getting consensus • Feedback is immediate • Documentation is completed quickly	• Difficult getting the appropriate stakeholders • Can be costly • Success very much depends on the facilitator • Logistic difficulties

With agile methodologies, the use of prototypes has increased over the years. Table 7.10 illustrates some of the advantages and disadvantages of using prototypes for requirement elicitation.

Table 7.10 Advantages and disadvantages of using prototypes for requirement elicitation

Advantages of prototypes	Disadvantages of prototypes
• Reduces time and cost • Improves and increases user involvement	• Poor documentation • Changes user expectation • Unmanageability • Exclusion of some users • Poor system performance • Over-optimistic estimates based upon a prototype

Figure 7.6 illustrates the *prototyping inquiry cycle*, which simply highlights the importance of communication before, during, and after the development of a prototype.

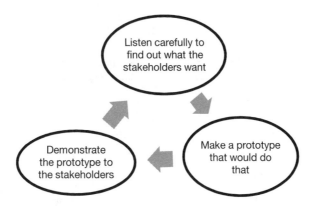

Figure 7.6 The prototyping inquiry cycle

A prototype is not just a prototype. Some are low-fidelity prototypes, which can be created quickly and are simple and low-tech, while high-fidelity prototypes require the use of tools or software to enable the user to interact with the prototype. Table 7.11 illustrates a variety of techniques for building requirements prototypes.

Table 7.11   Techniques for building requirements prototypes

Colored marker pen drawings on a flipchart	Circles and rectangles to form an easily reconfigured mock-up screen	A video of an acted screen
Screen images drawn	Cardboard mock-up	Software implementation
Hypertext of screen views is linked in order to button click to navigate	A scene acted by people	Old version or a competitive product

Exercise 7.5—Which of the Table 7.11 prototypes are low- or high-fidelity?

Requirement elicitation is the heart and soul of the *Project Management Body of Knowledge (PMBOK®
Guide)* approach to the *collect requirements* procedure by Process 5.2 *Collect requirements*, which is illustrated in Table 7.12. The overview of the processes in this domain can be found at the end of this chapter.

Table 7.12   Collect requirements

Input	Tools and Techniques	Output
• Scope management plan • Requirement management plan • Stakeholder management plan • Project charter • Stakeholder register	• Interviews • Focus groups • Facilitated workshops • Group creativity techniques • Group decision-making techniques • Questionnaires and surveys • Observations • Prototypes • Benchmarking • Context diagrams • Document analysis	• Requirement documentation • Requirement traceability matrix

The tools and techniques in the process of *collect requirements* are very similar to the requirement elicitation previously discussed, and Table 7.13 highlights how they fit within that setting.

Table 7.13   Collect requirements alignment with elicitation techniques

Tools and Techniques	Elicitation techniques	Tools and Techniques	Elicitation techniques	Tools and Techniques	Elicitation techniques
Interviews	Survey	Group decision making	None	Benchmarking	Document-centric
Focus groups	Survey	Questionnaires and surveys	Survey	Context diagrams	Document-centric
Facilitated workshops	Several	Observations	Observations	Document analysis	Document-centric
Group creativity techniques	Creativity	Prototypes	Support		

Exercise 7.6—Explain how scenarios with storyboarding and hothousing can be used in requirement elicitation. A bit of research may be required before answering this question.

In some cases it may be useful to highlight the complementary and alternative techniques and approaches as illustrated in Table 7.14. This enables the business analyst to collect the right mix of approaches to cover requirements in a fitting manner.

Table 7.14   Complementary (C) and alternative (A) techniques

	Surveys	Observations	Document-centric
Surveys	--	A	C
Observations	A	--	C
Document-centric	C	C	--

7.3 ELABORATE REQUIREMENTS

After a successful elicitation of the requirements, the business analyst needs to analyze, decompose, and elaborate requirements using techniques such as dependency analysis, interface analysis, and data and process modeling in order to collaboratively uncover and clarify product options and capabilities.

Elaborating requirements is a matter of examining, going into details, and adding knowledge into the elicited requirements. Elaborating requirements can be done with the help of a requirements analysis. Requirements analysis (also called requirements engineering) is the process of determining user expectations for a new or modified product. It is a process of discovery, refinement, modeling, and specification in order to maximize future exploitation possibilities. Requirements analysis also involves frequent communication with stakeholders and system users to determine specific feature expectations. As we expand upon the requirements, the business analyst examines the high-level requirements to determine if they are clear, complete, and free of contradictions before defining the strategy to address these issues. In addition, the business analyst needs to specify the software's operational characteristics that indicate the software's interface with other system elements, and establish constraints that the software must meet.

Requirements analysis allows the business analyst to:

- Elaborate on basic requirements established during earlier requirement engineering tasks
- Build models that depict user scenarios; functional activities; problem classes and their relationships; system and class behavior; and the flow of data as it is transformed
- Identify essential *real-world information*
- Remove redundant, unimportant details
- Clarify unclear natural language statements
- Fill remaining gaps in discussions
- Detect and resolve conflicts between requirements
- Discover the bounds of the software
- Define interaction with the environment

- Elaborate high-level requirements to derive detailed requirements
- Distinguish data and operations

Requirement Classification

Requirements may range from a high-level abstract statement of a service or of a system constraint, to a detailed mathematical functional specification. Currently, we have identified a wide range of requirements and are in the process of elaborating on them. In order to do so, we need to consider what kind of requirements we are working with. Most models for requirements consider two types of requirements: functional requirements, i.e., defining its behaviors; and non-functional requirements, i.e., how it performs them. These are sometimes called strategic requirements. This is explained in more detail in the requirements classification from Table 7.15.

Table 7.15 Types of requirements

Types of requirements	Description	Example
Functional requirement	A requirement concerning a result of behavior that will be provided by a function of the system.	The user shall be able to search either all of the initial set of databases or select a subset from it.
Quality requirement (non-functional)	A requirement that pertains to a quality concern that is not covered by functional requirements. Also called a non-functional requirement.	The user interface for the system shall be implemented as simple HTML without frames or Java applets.
Constraints	A requirement that limits the solution space beyond what is necessary for meeting the given functional and quality requirements. Also called domain requirements.	Because of copyright restrictions, some documents must be deleted immediately on arrival.

PMI defines requirements as *a condition or capability that is required to be present in a product, service, or result to satisfy a contract or other formally imposed specification*. PMI uses the following requirement types:

- Business requirement: high-level needs of the organization
- Stakeholder requirement: needs of the stakeholders
- Solution requirements: functional and non-functional requirements
- Functional requirements: behavior of the product
- Non-functional requirements: environmental condition or quality required
- Transition requirements: temporary capabilities such as training or data conversion

Other classification schemes also describe requirement attributes, such as the level of detail of a requirement, the priority of a requirement, or the degree of legal obligation of requirements. CARA'S SOUPS stands for the following vital requirement attributes—the acronym makes them easier to memorize:

- Complexity
- Absolute reference
- Risks

- Author
- Source
- Stability
- Ownership
- Urgency
- Priority
- Status

Early identification of the quality requirements is important since this has a direct bearing on the design and architecture of the system. Unfortunately, the attributes of the quality requirements are often overlooked and underspecified in early requirement documents, and may cause serious impact in later stages of the software development life cycle. Quality requirements that are not documented, are inadequately documented, or are improperly negotiated can lead to circumstances that can threaten the project's success or the subsequent acceptance of the system that is under development.

A business analyst should place special emphasis on the elicitation, documentation, and negotiation of quality requirements during the development process. Low requirements quality can have expensive consequences during the software development life cycle. Especially if iterations are long and feedback comes late, the sooner a problem is found, the cheaper it is to fix. To document quality requirements, they can be divided into categories under which the classification has to be done (see Figure 7.7).

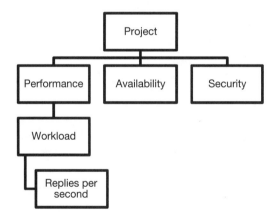

Figure 7.7   Classification of quality requirements

The ISO Standard 9126 (ISO/IEC 9126) classification scheme for quality requirements is used as the standard structure for requirements documentation and as a checklist for requirements elicitation and validation.

Typical categories of quality requirements define the:

- Quality of system functions
- Dependability of functionalities

- Usability of a system
- System efficiency
- Changeability of a system
- Portability of a system

Now, we take a brief look at the *PMBOK® Guide* approach to the *collect requirements* procedure by Process 5.2 *Collect requirements*, which was illustrated in Table 7.13. The overviews of the processes in this domain can be found at the end of this chapter.

Again, the output of the collection process includes the requirement documentation, where PMI defines the following types of requirements:

- Business requirement: high-level needs of the organization
- Stakeholder requirement: needs of the stakeholders
- Solution requirements: functional and non-functional requirements
- Functional requirements: behavior of the product
- Non-functional requirements: environmental condition or quality required
- Transition requirements: temporary capabilities such as training or data conversion

In order to complete the requirements classification, the business analyst also needs to consider the following factors:

- Source
- Product or process requirements
- Priority
- Scope in terms of affected components
- Volatility versus stability

Conceptual Modeling

The last element in elaborating the requirements is conceptual modeling, which is a representation in a semiformal notation and is often a diagrammatic representation, such as:

- Object orientation
- Use cases
- State machines
- Activity diagrams
- Data flow diagrams
- Entity relationship models

The business analyst selects the models and organizes the requirements in order to understand which models are appropriate to include based on the business need; and to understand and clearly communicate the interdependencies and relationships between the various requirements. In addition to this, the business analyst verifies that we are following standards, document dependencies, and interrelationships among requirements; and develops concepts for a consistent set of models and templates to document the requirements.

The common techniques to use for conceptual modeling and requirement analysis are:

- Business rules modeling (decision tree, business rule catalog, and decision table)
- Data modeling (ER diagram, data flow diagram, data dictionary, state table, and state diagram)
- Functional decomposition
- Interface modeling (wireframes, report table, and user interface flow)
- Organization modeling
- Process modeling (use case and user story)
- Scope modeling (context diagram and feature model)

The requirements have now been analyzed and decomposed—which means the requirements have been elaborated and product options and capabilities have been clarified.

Exercise 7.7—Matching Conceptual Models: Match the terms in #1-4 to letters A-D which are all common techniques to use for conceptual modeling and requirement analysis. (The answers are found on page 148.)

1. Business rules modeling
2. Process modeling
3. Interface modeling
4. Data modeling

A. Wireframes
B. User story
C. Data dictionary
D. Business rule catalog

7.4 VALIDATE REQUIREMENTS

Now it's time to validate requirements to product scope by evaluating product options and capabilities using decision-making and valuation techniques in order to determine which requirements are accepted, deferred, or rejected.

First, let us take a brief look at the *PMBOK® Guide* approach to the *validate scope* procedure by Process 5.5 *Validate scope*, which is illustrated in Table 7.16. The overviews of the processes in this domain can be found at the end of this chapter.

Table 7.16 Validate scope

Input	Tools and Techniques	Output
• Project management plan • Requirement document • Requirement traceability matrix • Verify deliveries • Work performance data	• Inspection • Group decision-making techniques	• Accepted deliverables • Change requests • Work performance information • Project document updates

Our input from the *collect requirements* process is the requirement management plan which is a sub-plan to the project management plan; the requirement document which contains all types of requirements and their acceptance criteria; and the requirement traceability matrix which links requirements to their origin and tracks them. The tools and techniques are going to be expanded upon and used in conjunction here because during the inspection we need to decide where the group decision-making techniques can be useful.

One kind of inspection is commenting which is an individual validation of requirements. The author hands over the requirements to another person (coworker) for review, and the coworker identifies issues with regard to the predetermined quality criteria. Identified issues are then marked in the requirements document and briefly explained. Similar types of inspections are peer review/desk checks and pass-arounds.

An inspection is a more systematic review which often is done in several phases with an emphasis on planning overview, defect detection, defect correction, follow-up, and reflection. The inspections may be more formal and include several roles (see Table 7.17).

Table 7.17 Inspection roles

Role	Description
Organizer	Plans and supervises
Moderator	Inspection leader, plans and coordinates with the author and organizer; manages the inspection
Author	Creates and maintains work
Reader	Introduces and guides the inspectors
Recorder	Scribes
Minute-taker	Records time

Some of the typical challenges associated with inspections are in cases with large requirement documents, large inspection teams, or if the geographic locations of the inspectors is an issue. Each challenge would increase the time to complete the inspection, and sets higher demands on the planning and managing of the inspection.

A variation of the inspection is the walk-through which is a lightweight version of a review with roles involved that are slightly differentiated from those mentioned in Table 7.17. Here, the quality flaws within requirements are identified. The process is that the requirements are handed out to all participants for inspection. Requirements are discussed under the guidance of the moderator/reader, and flaws in quality are identified and documented by the recorder.

Perspective-based readings are a kind of validation technique that adopts different perspectives to check the requirements, and are typically applied in conjunction with other review techniques. The validation perspectives would often include:

- User/customer perspective
- Software architect perspective
- Tester perspective

Each perspective would examine the perspective quality aspects in terms of content, documentation, and agreement. Let's examine two more techniques before going into details with the agreement, as it is vital that the business analyst and stakeholders determine which requirements are accepted, deferred, or rejected.

Validation through prototypes is a kind of validation technique that allows experiencing and trying out the requirements. It is an effective method for identifying errors in requirements. The types of prototypes used are evolutionary and throwaway prototypes.

Evolutionary prototype:

- Developed with the goal to be developed further and improved in later steps
- Effort to create is much higher

Throwaway prototype:

- Not maintained once they have been used

Preparations prior to validating requirements by prototype:

- Manual/instructions
- Users of the prototype are supplied with the necessary information to use or apply the prototype
- Done by means of a manual or by means of proper instruction

Validation scenarios:

- Prepare scenarios to be performed with the prototype

Checklist with validation criteria:

- Create checklist of validation criteria

Validation:

- Auditor validates the prototype without being influenced, ensuring that the validation results are created without bias
- Auditor executes alternative and deviant scenarios and uses the prototype to explore and experiment

Documentation:

- Requirements validation through prototypes permits two types of result documentation—protocol of the auditor and observation protocol

Analysis:

- Results of the validation are analyzed after validation is complete
- Change suggestions for the requirements are consolidated

The last validation technique to demonstrate at this point in the process is using checklists for validation. This is a kind of validation technique that is comprised of a set of questions and/or statements, and is applied whenever many aspects must be considered. The checklists can be used in all of the previous requirement validation techniques, can be improved for future use, should not contain ambiguous or outdated questions, and their success depends on their manageability and complexity. To reiterate:

- Before using a checklist, every single question or statement must be defined
- While using a checklist, always look for opportunities to improve the checklist for future use
- Ambiguous questions must be marked and revised
- Outdated or questions that are no longer valid should be removed
- The checklist serves as a guideline for the auditor and as a measure to approach validation in a structured manner
- Application of checklists for requirements validation successfully depends on the manageability and complexity of the checklist

The business analyst and the stakeholders have now validated requirements to product scope by evaluating product options and capabilities. Now, however, we need to use decision-making and valuation techniques in order to determine which requirements are accepted, deferred, or rejected. Sometimes it is easy to decide which requirements are accepted, deferred, or rejected—however, this is not always the case. This is when group decision-making techniques are useful. PMI defines the following group decision-making techniques:

- Unanimity
- Majority
- Plurality
- Dictatorship

Unanimity implies that we all have to agree upon whether a requirement is accepted, deferred, or rejected. In the case of majority, more than half of the participants must agree on the decision while plurality approves the highest vote getter even if it is not a majority. Finally, dictatorship is where one person decides whether the requirements are accepted, deferred, or rejected.

Exercise 7.8—Decision Making: You are in the room with eight other team members. Four options are discussed and a vote is called. One option receives three votes and is called out as the winner. Which decision-making technique was used? (The answer is found on page 148.)

1. Unanimity
2. Majority
3. Plurality
4. Dictatorship

7.5 ALLOCATE REQUIREMENTS

At this stage, the business analyst needs to allocate accepted or deferred requirements by balancing scope, schedule, budget, and resource constraints with the value proposition—using prioritization, dependency analysis, and decision-making tools and techniques in order to create a requirement baseline.

First, we need to balance scope, schedule, budget, and resource constraints with the value proposition. Before we can do this, we need to define scope (the sum of the scope management plan) with the activities for development; the project charter (the high-level project description of scope, schedule, budget, and resources); and the requirements documents (all of the accepted or deferred requirements that will be included in the project).

However, before moving forward, let us take a brief look at the *PMBOK® Guide* approach to the *define scope* procedure by Process 5.3 *Define scope*, which is illustrated in Table 7.18. The overviews of the processes in this domain can be found at the end of this chapter.

Table 7.18   Define scope

Input	Tools and Techniques	Output
• Scope management plan	• Expert judgment	• Project scope statement
• Project charter	• Product analysis	• Project document updates
• Requirement document	• Alternatives generation	
• Organizational process assets	• Facilitated workshops	

Once the input has been discussed, the following tools and techniques can be used:

- Product analysis
- Product breakdown
- System analysis
- Requirement analysis
- System engineering
- Value engineering
- Value analysis
- Alternative generation (brainstorming, lateral thinking, analysis of alternatives)

This gives the business analysis a project scope baseline, which along with the scope management plan, can help us derive the requirement baseline. However, first we need to prioritize the requirements.

Value Proposition Using Prioritization

Requirements (re)prioritization is an essential mechanism of development approaches to maximize value for the clients and to accommodate changing requirements. Once requirements have been identified, the next step is to prioritize them in order to ensure that the team first develops those features that bring the highest value to the business. The prioritization is an exercise where the business analyst meets with the stakeholders or product owners and the team to discuss their priorities. A variation of techniques will be discussed in order to avoid decibel or threat prioritization. However, in some cases, the group decision-making techniques may be more useful. On an overall level, requirements are prioritized using different prioritization criteria, based on their order of implementation. Table 7.19 highlights this.

Table 7.19 Prioritization

Determine the goal and constraints of prioritization	Define the goal of prioritization
	Document the constraints of the prioritization
Determine prioritization criteria	Select a criterion based on the goal
Determine stakeholders	Select appropriate stakeholders based on the goal and criteria
Select artifacts	Select the requirements to be prioritized
Select prioritization technique	Select a prioritization technique(s) based on the properties of the prioritization

The typical prioritization criteria are:

- Cost of implementation
- Risk
- Damage due to an unsuccessful implementation
- Volatility
- Importance
- Law
- Duration of implementation

Alternatively, the business analyst and stakeholders can consider them as input priority, which are provided by the stakeholders; and output priority, which can be realized in a practice design. Another simple approach is to decide whether they are urgent and important. Table 7.20 demonstrates this.

Table 7.20 Prioritization using urgent and important as parameters

	Important	Not important
Urgent	High priority	Very low priority
Not urgent	Medium priority	Low priority

The techniques for requirement prioritization differ with respect to time, cost, risk, volatility, effort, strategic importance, customer importance, and suitability of the different prioritization criteria and project properties. The different techniques (Pohl, et al., 2011) available are illustrated in Tables 7.21 and 7.22.

Table 7.21 Prioritization

Aspect	Technique	Perspective
Strategic importance	AHP	Product manager
Cost	$100	Developers/team
Volatility	Rankings	Business analyst

Table 7.22   Ad hoc and analytical techniques

Ad hoc techniques	Analytical techniques
Majority of the projects implement these techniques Most suitable with regard to resources available	Suitable where the decision process is too incomprehensible or where the results are erroneous
Utilize less time and effort	Utilize more time and effort
For example, ranking, single-criterion classification	For example, AHP, Cost-value analysis, QFD

Overview of the ad hoc and analytical techniques:

- Ranking
- Top-ten/100-dollar
- Single-criterion classification
- Prioritizing user stories
- Multivoting (3 rounds of voting)
- MoSCoW prioritization
- Kano classification
- Karl Wiegers relative weighting/prioritization matrix
- Strategy grids
- Analytical hierarchy process (AHP)
- Cost-value analysis
- Quality function deployment (the house of quality)

Ranking is simply a list where all the requirements are ranked from the highest to the lowest. The list may vary in length, and may be ranked based on a range of objective or subjective criteria. A variation of the *ranking* technique is the Top-ten, which is similar in process. However, it results in only the top-ten requirements. The single-criterion classification may be based on the amount of work, costs, quality, or risks that it takes to complete the item. The result would be a list of items ranked on a single-criterion classification. Ranking, top-ten, and single-criterion classifications are fairly simple techniques to prioritize requirements. In the agile methodologies, prioritization is all about handling the product backlog, and it can be viewed as an iceberg (see Figure 7.8).

Figure 7.8   Agile iceberg from *I Am Agile* by Klaus Nielsen

The requirements or user stories are prioritized, with the most important ones—i.e., those that deliver the highest business value—being placed at the top of the iceberg. They will be part of our next iterations, while the group below that will be part of our future releases. As user stories are developed, completed user stories are removed from the iceberg while others move up in the iceberg. They will be developed when the releases are broken into iterations.

The slightly more advanced techniques to prioritize requirements are the MoSCoW (must have, should have, could have, won't have) prioritization, Kano classification, and Karl Wiegers's relative weighting. Descriptions of these follow.

MoSCoW Prioritization

According to *A Guide to the Business Analysis Body of Knowledge (BABOK® Guide) v3* section on the Agile perspective (pg. 375), the MoSCoW categories are as illustrated in Table 7.23.

Table 7.23 MoSCoW prioritization

Categories	Description
M – MUST	Describes a requirement that must be satisfied in the final solution for the solution to be considered a success.
S – SHOULD	Represents a high-priority item that should be included in the solution if it is possible. This is often a critical requirement, but one that can be satisfied in other ways if absolutely necessary.
C – COULD	Describes a requirement that is considered desirable but not necessary. This will be included if time and resources permit.
W – WON'T	Represents a requirement that stakeholders have agreed will not be implemented in a given release, but may be considered in the future.

Kano Classification

The Kano classification (Pohl, et al., 2011) contains dissatisfiers, satisfiers, and delighters as illustrated in Table 7.24 and back in Figure 7.4.

Table 7.24 Kano classification

	Description
Dissatisfiers	• Must be fulfilled by the system • Completely fulfilled dissatisfiers help to avoid massive discontent • Dominantly influenced by existing systems • Suitable elicitation techniques—observation and document-centric techniques
Satisfiers	• Consciously known and explicitly demanded • Fulfilled satisfiers bring contentment and satisfaction • Any missing property can lead to product unacceptability • Satisfaction decreases with each missing satisfier • Suitable elicitation techniques—survey techniques
Delighters	• Properties of a system recognized only by using the system • Suitable elicitation techniques—creativity techniques

The Kano model also works well in an agile setting for assessing themes. The customer will determine how they feel if the functionality is present (functional) or absent (dysfunctional) in the product. The next step would be to categorize the responses in a matrix (Cohn, 2006), as demonstrated in Table 7.25.

Table 7.25   Kano Model with dysfunctional questions

Categorizing responses		Dysfunctional questions				
		Like	Expect	Neutral	Like with	Dislike
Functional questions	Like	Q	E	E	E	L
	Expect	R	I	I	I	M
	Neutral	R	I	I	I	M
	Like with	R	I	I	I	M
	Dislike	R	R	R	R	Q

M = Must have, L = Linear, E = Exciter, R = Reverse, Q = Questionable, I = Indifferent

Karl Wiegers's relative weighting prioritization matrix is illustrated in Table 7.26. It is similar to Kano. Both include the relative benefits of a feature being present and its negative impacts or relative penalty if it is not present.

Table 7.26   Karl Wiegers's relative weighting prioritization matrix

Feature	Relative benefit	Relative penalty	Total value	Value (%)	Est.	Cost (%)	Priority
Graph event times	8	6	14	42	32	53	0.79
Can upload photos	9	2	11	33	21	34	0.97
Post autobiographical profile	3	5	8	25	8	13	1.92
Total	20	13	33	100	61	100	

Analytical Hierarchy Process

Using the analytical hierarchy process (AHP) (see Figure 7.9), the business analyst can calculate each requirement's relative value and implementation cost and then plot them on a cost-value graph (see below). Cost is typically the x-axis and value is the y-axis. Requirements higher up and close to the y-axis on the graph provide a higher value and are less costly.

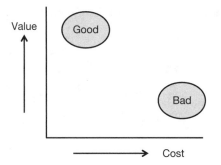

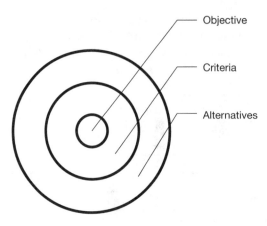

Figure 7.9 Analytical Hierarchy Process

Requirement Baseline

The requirement baseline is developed as part of the Process 5.4 *Create WBS*, which is illustrated in Table 7.27. The overviews of the processes in this domain can be found at the end of this chapter.

Table 7.27 Create WBS

Input	Tools and Techniques	Output
• Scope management plan • Project scope statement • Requirement document • Enterprise environmental factors • Organizational process assets	• Decomposition • Expert judgment	• Scope baseline • Project documents updates

The requirements baseline is the goal that you are working toward achieving during the requirements development stage of the requirements engineering process. The baseline contains the WBS directory, the data models from the elaborated requirements, and the overall scope and vision. The requirement baseline is part of the scope baseline, which is the approved version of a scope statement, and the WBS and its associated WBS dictionary. The scope baseline is subject to the change control process and version control.

The requirement baseline is aligned with the identified need and products, as well as being closely aligned with verification and validation, as illustrated in Table 7.28.

Table 7.28 Requirement baseline

	Verification	Verification
1. Identified Need	**2. Requirement Baseline**	**3. System, Product, or Service**
Validation	Validation	Validation

In order to move from the scope management plan, project scope statement, and requirement document to the scope baseline, the technique of decomposition is used. The concept is to create a WBS, which is defined as *a hierarchical decomposition of the total scope of work to be carried out by the project team to accomplish the project objectives and create the required deliverables.* Alongside the WBS, a WBS directory is created which is *a document that provides detailed deliverables, activity, and scheduling information about each component in the WBS.* This implies that the dependency analysis is conducted during the creation of the WBS directory because all of the scheduling is considered here.

Exercise 7.9—Question for Another Group: In this activity, participants are divided into groups of four to seven people. Together, they develop up to three questions for another group to answer based on the material presented.

7.6 GET REQUIREMENT SIGNOFF

The business analyst needs to obtain signoff on the requirement baseline using decision-making techniques in order to facilitate stakeholder consensus and achieve stakeholder approval. Obtaining signoff on the requirement baseline can be conducted as part of the Process 5.5 *Validate scope*, which was illustrated in Table 7.16.

The signoff is an explicit and collaborative agreement between the team and the stakeholders or product owners. In agile methodologies, this is conducted more informally. However, in plan-based projects a signature is expected. Reaching an agreement is core to the collaboration between the team and the stakeholder because it creates a baseline and fair knowledge about scope—which develops confidence in the project. In spite of this fact, stakeholders and teams need to understand the meaning of signoff in order to avoid turning it into a meaningless ritual. Some people may also use the signoff as a weapon. However, in actuality, it is just another milestone.

The business analyst takes the input and develops group decision-making techniques with the team and stakeholders to reach consensus; after which, the verified project documents may require approvals from the customer or sponsor in the form of signatures or signoffs. This is updated with the project document updates as an output of the process.

7.7 DOCUMENT REQUIREMENTS

Now, it is time to write the requirements specifications using processes (such as use cases, user stories, etc.), data, and interface details in order to communicate requirements that are measurable and actionable or suitable for development.

The requirements specification, software requirements specifications, or recording requirements process is where the business analyst, along with the stakeholders, agree upon the design, types of documents, document structure, and whether the requirements will be documented using a natural language and/or model-based documentation. However, requirements in industry are nearly exclusively written in natural language. Finally, we will examine how it fits within the PMI framework.

Document Design

A requirements specification is a systematically represented collection of requirements, typically for a system or component, that satisfies given criteria. The documentation technique is a formal depiction of requirements that eases communication between stakeholders and increases the quality of the documented requirements. Any kind of documentation technique can be used to document requirements. Figure 7.10 illustrates the three perspectives on requirements:

1. Data perspective: Adopts a static-structural perspective of the system requirements, e.g., services of an external system
2. Functional perspective: Documents the information (data) received from the system context, or manipulated by the system or one of its functions data, that flows back into the system context, as well as documenting the order in which the functions processing the input data are executed
3. Behavioral perspective: Documents system information and explains how it is embedded in the system context

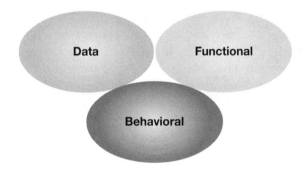

Figure 7.10 The three perspectives on requirements

Three types of perspectives are considered while documenting requirements based on models:

- Data perspective—Entity Relationship (E/R), Unified Modeling Language (UML)
- Functional perspective—Data flow, UML
- Behavioral perspective—Statechart, UML

Each perspective is separately documented using suitable conceptual modeling languages.

Requirements Documentation Using Natural Language

When documenting requirements, you can use a natural language, often your native language. Natural language is inherently ambiguous and special emphasis should be laid on potentially ambiguous statements. The diversity among people may lead to misunderstandings and interpreting the requirements differently. Elicited requirements are frequently documented in natural language as it does not require preparation time to be read and understood by stakeholders and can be used to describe any type of circumstance. However, it has certain disadvantages—subjective perception being one of them.

Transformational effects occur during perception and representation of information and can exhibit different characteristics within every human being. However, transformational effects adhere to certain rules, and hence, are used by the requirements engineer to elicit deep structure from its surface structure. On the whole, transformational effects may cause misunderstandings when reading and understanding the requirements.

Five transformational processes relevant for requirements engineering are:

- Nominalization
- Nouns without reference index
- Universal quantifiers
- Incompletely specified conditions
- Incompletely specified process verbs

Many business analysts use natural language for requirement documentation. Table 7.29 displays the advantages and disadvantages of using natural language.

Table 7.29   Advantages and disadvantages of using natural language

Advantages of using natural language	Disadvantages of using natural language
• Prose is the commonly applied documentation form for requirements • No new notation has to be learned • Any kind of requirement can be expressed	• Ambiguity in requirements • Unintentional mix-up of requirements of different types and perspectives • Leads to difficulty in isolating information of a particular perspective

Some of the disadvantages of using a natural language for requirement documentation can be limited by using templates for requirement construction. The five steps shown in Table 7.30 are an easy-to-use approach.

Table 7.30 Five steps for requirement construction

Step	Description
1	• Determine the degree of legal obligation for a requirement. • Distinguish between legally obligatory requirements, urgently recommended requirements, and future requirements. • Use modal verbs—shall, should, will.
2	• Core of each requirement is the functionality it specifies. • The functionality is referred to as process. • Processes may be described using verbs and should be defined clearly.
3	• System activity for functional requirements can be documented in any one of the three template types: • Autonomous system activity. • User interaction. • Interface requirement.
4	• Potentially missing objects and supplements of objects are identified and added to the requirement.
5	• Quality requirements that describe the conditions under which a requirement is fulfilled are added to the beginning of a requirement as a subordinate clause.

Exercise 7.10—Explain the effects of natural language in requirements documentation.

Requirements Documentation Using Conceptual Models

Requirements documentation using models requires special modeling language. However, they are easy to compact and to understand with conceptual models offering a decreased degree of ambiguity. Some of these important tools are: use case diagram, class diagram, activity diagram, and state diagram. These are illustrated in Figure 7.11 and Table 7.31.

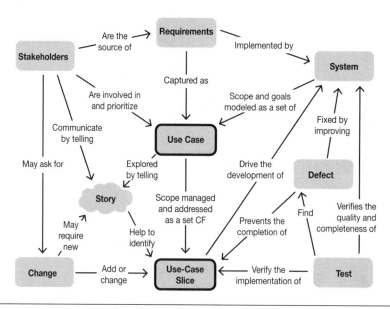

Figure 7.11 Use case concept map from Ivarson's *Use Case 2.0*

Table 7.31   Diagrams

Use case diagram	• Provides a quick overview of the functionalities of a specific system.
	• Describes the system functions offered to the user and their relation with other external entities.
	• Does not describe the responsibilities of the function in detail.
Class diagram	• Documents the static-structural dependencies between system and system context or the complex domain terms in a structured manner.
Activity diagram	• Documents business processes within the system context.
	• Helps to model sequential character of use cases or interaction of functions that process data.
State diagram	• Documents event-driven behavior of a system.

A use case shows all the ways of using a system to achieve a particular goal for a particular user. Taken together, the set of all the use cases gives you all of the useful ways to utilize the system and illustrates the value that it will provide. Use cases clearly state what a system is going to do and by intentional omission, what it is not going to do. They enable the effective envisioning, scope management, and incremental development of systems of any type and any size. Figure 7.11, adapted from Ivar Jacobson, demonstrates the relationship between the use case and the stakeholders and shows the final system being developed.

During model-based documentation of requirements, three types of requirements are documented independently, as shown in Table 7.32, and are used in conjunction with:

- Goals,
- Use cases and scenarios, and
- System requirements.

Table 7.32   Three types of requirements

Goals	• Describes intentions of the stakeholders or groups of stakeholders
	• Can conflict with one another
Use cases and scenarios	• Shows perfect sequences of system usage
	• Scenarios are grouped together in use cases
System requirements	• Describes detailed functions and qualities of the system to be developed
	• Provides complete and precise information to serve as input for subsequent steps

Requirements are mostly documented using models, in addition to natural language, in order to exploit the advantages of models and to minimize the disadvantages.

Goal models are a stakeholder's description of a characteristic property of the system to be developed (see Figure 7.12). The models refine the vision of the system and can be documented using natural language or by using goal models. Use case specifications are based upon goal models.

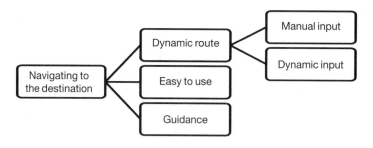

Figure 7.12 Goal model

Document Structure

A requirements document must be well-structured and should be made by using the standardized document structures or by defining custom document structures. Using standard outlines has many advantages and can be tailored with respect to specific project properties to meet the respective constraints. In order to create a well-structured requirements document, use standardized document structures or define custom document structures. Standard outlines offer predefined structures according to which information can be classified. Some of the advantages of standard outlines is that they:

- Simplify incorporation of new members,
- Help in finding the desired content quickly,
- Allow selective reading and validation,
- Allow automatic verification, and
- Allow simplified reuse of the contents.

Three of the most widely used standardized document structures (as shown in Table 7.33) are the:

- Rational Unified Process (RUP)
- Institute of Electrical and Electronics Engineers (IEEE) Standard 830-1998
- V-Model

Table 7.33 Standardized document structures

RUP	• Preferable for software systems developed using object-oriented methods • The structure of the system requirement specification (SRS) is used to document all software requirements • The structures are closely related to the IEEE Standard 830
IEEE Standards 830-1998	• Recommended for documentation of software requirements • According to the standard structure, the requirements document is divided into three main chapters—Introductory Information, General Descriptions of the Software, and Specific Requirements
V-model	• Business modeling and integration defines different structures depending on the creator of the requirements document—customer requirements specification (CRS) and SRS • The CRS is created by the customer and usually describes *what* is made *for what* • The SRS is based on the CRS and contains implementation suggestions. It is a refinement of the requirements and constraints of the CRS

The minimum standard content (see Table 7.34) that should be addressed by any chosen structure is as follows:

- Introduction
- General overview
- Requirements

- Appendices
- Index

Table 7.34 Standard content

Introduction	Contains information about the entire document: • Purpose • System coverage • Stakeholder • Definitions, Acronyms, and Abbreviations • References • Overview
General overview	Contains additional information that increases the ability to understand the requirements. Main sections in this include: • System environment • Architecture description • System functionality • User and target audience • Constraints • Assumptions
Requirements	Contains functional as well as quality requirements.
Appendices	Contains additional information that completes the document. Can include additional documents regarding user characteristics, standards, conventions, or background information of the requirements document.
Index	Typically contains a table of contents and index dictionary.

Writing and documenting requirements is conducted in the *PMBOK® Guide* approach to the *collect requirements* procedure by Process 5.2 *Collect requirements*, which was illustrated in Table 7.12.

The requirement document is the requirement specification. This description is given extreme importance in the beginning of a plan-based approach. However, requirements in agile methodologies are conducted differently and are explained in the following section.

Writing Requirement in Agile Methodologies

In agile development, the user story is a lightweight and more nimble substitute for what has been our traditional means of specifying software requirements. User stories are brief, informal descriptions of requirements written by the system's customers. They illustrate how the system can be used to create value. User stories only provide enough detail to facilitate estimations of how long each story will take to implement with reasonable accuracy. User stories express a capability of the system under development to deliver business value. *A user story describes functionality that will be valuable to either a user or purchaser of a system or software.* User stories are composed of three parts:

- A written description of the story used for planning and as a reminder
- Conversations about the story that serve to flesh out the details of the story
- Tests that convey and document details that can be used to determine when a story is complete (Cohn, 2004)

A user story is a brief statement of intent that describes something the system needs to do for the user. Because user stories are often handwritten, Jeffries (Jeffries et al., 2000) included the following additional three aspects: card, conversation, and confirmation. They capture the components of a user story.

1. Card represents two or three sentences used to describe the intent of the story
2. Conversation represents a discussion between the team, customer, product owner, and other stakeholders
3. Confirmation represents the *acceptance test*, which is how the customer or product owner will confirm that the story has been implemented to their satisfaction

The card could be used in the user story voice and follows this format:

- As a <role> I can <activity> so that <business value>
- As a Consumer, (<role>) I want to be able to see my daily energy usage (<what I do with the system>) so that I can start to understand how to lower my costs over time (<business value I receive>)

User story cards are index cards that hold the user story. Index card information might include:

- Format/information
- ID
- Short description
- Type
- Exploration factor (i.e., uncertainty)

An alternative is the Given-When-Then formula:

- *Given* some context
- *When* some action is carried out
- *Then* a particular set of observable consequences should result

An example of the Given-When-Then formula:

- *Given* my bank account is not negative and I have made no withdrawals recently,
- *When* I attempt to withdraw an amount less than my card's limit,
- *Then* the withdrawal should complete without errors.

Bill Wake (2003) wrote an article entitled *INVEST in Good Stories*, which introduced the INVEST acronym (stated in Table 7.35) for creating effectively written user stories.

Table 7.35 INVEST

Acronym	Terms
I	Independent
N	Negotiable
V	Valuable
E	Estimable
S	Small
T	Testable

This implies that user stories are independent (I) so they do not overlap and can be planned and implemented in any order. Agile requirements are always based on a negotiation (N) with the product owner or business so we need user stories that we are able to discuss. The user stories must have a size and content so the business receives value (V) from them. Sometimes, many user stories may be needed, but only user stories that are valuable to the business need to be developed. If the user story has the right size, the team would be able to estimate (E) it and plan it. Being too big, it would often require additional breakdowns or splitting. The user story must be small (S). Good user stories are small. Being small makes them easier to work with. All user stories must be tested (T), and tested early, by the end users.

An acronym for creating effective goals—SMART (specific, measurable, achievable, relevant, time-boxed)—is often used for the tasks related to the user stories. It is illustrated in Table 7.36.

Table 7.36 SMART

Acronym	Terms
S	Specific
M	Measurable
A	Achievable
R	Relevant
T	Time-boxed

As you discuss stories, write cards, and split stories, the INVEST principles can help in reminding you of the characteristics of good stories. When creating a task plan, applying the SMART attributes can improve your tasks.

Splitting User Stories

A user story generally starts out as a feature or an epic—a large, vague concept of something we want to do for a user. There is no set routine for splitting user stories into iteration-sized bites other than the general guidance to make each story provide a vertical slice (some piece of user value) through the system. Generally, we split user stories when the user story is too large to fit within a single iteration, or in order to make estimates more accurate if the user story is epic.

Epic Stories

As a very large story that may span iterations, epic stories must be disaggregated into their component user stories before being useful at a tactical level. As large blocks of limited functionality, they often should be broken down into smaller stories to be implemented.

Exercise 7.11—An Acronym By Any Other Name: In groups of two to three people, have participants try to come up with some creative acronyms for documenting requirements.

7.8 VERIFY REQUIREMENTS

Next, the business analyst needs to validate requirements using tools and techniques, such as documentation review, prototypes, demos, and other validation methods in order to ensure that the requirements are complete, accurate, and aligned with goals, objectives, and the value proposition.

Let's examine verification and validation here as they are independent procedures that are used together for checking that a product, service, or system meets requirements and specifications, and that it fulfills its intended purpose. *Validation* is defined as *the assurance that a product, service, or system meets the need of the customer and other identified stakeholders.* It often involves acceptance and suitability with external customers. *Verification* is defined as *the evaluation of whether or not a product, service, or system complies with the regulation, requirements specification, or imposed condition.* It is often an internal process. There is overlap between system verification and requirements verification. Verification explains that things are performed in the right way—while validation tells us that the right things have been performed. Verification ensures that requirements are complete and accurate—while validation ensures the requirements are aligned with goals, objectives, and value propositions. Table 7.37 highlights this and illustrates the techniques.

Table 7.37 Verification and validation

	What to check against	Techniques
Verification	Quality requirements for a good requirement	Peer review, walk-throughs, inspections, prototypes, and demos
Validation	Business objectives and stakeholder goals, and measure what the solution is meant to deliver	

Verification is verifying scope against user requirements which highlights the alignment of project scope, user requirements, and the final product (as highlighted in Figure 7.13).

Figure 7.13 Verification adapted from Hans (2013)

In order to verify the quality requirements, review the formal quality criteria according to IEEE Std. 830-1998, as well as the criteria that increase the readers' acceptance of the requirements (as illustrated in Figure 7.14).

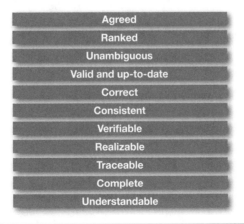

Figure 7.14 Acceptance of the requirements

Some business analysts add the following quality requirements to the list for verification:

- Current
- Testable
- Modifiable

- Independent
- Traceable
- Owned
- Relevant
- Feasible

Verification is conducted in the *PMBOK® Guide* approach to the *quality control* procedure by Process 8.3 *Control quality*, which is illustrated in Table 7.38. The overview of the processes in this domain can be found at the end of this chapter.

Table 7.38 Control quality

Input	Tools and Techniques	Output
• Project management plan • Quality metrics • Quality checklists • Work performance data • Approved change requests • Deliverables • Project documentation • Organizational process assets	• Seven basic quality tools • Statistical sampling • Inspection • Approved change requests	• Quality control measurements • Validated changes • Verified deliverables • Work • Performance information • Change requests • Project management plan updates • Project documents updates • Organizational process assets updates

Quality control also ensures that product quality—including product requirements—are met and validated, and that the requirements correctly describe stakeholder needs, goals, and objectives. In addition, the requirements must be complete and of high quality. Now the requirements meet stakeholder needs in accordance with the early content that was validated versus scope.

At this point you can verify and validate requirements using tools and techniques—such as documentation review, prototypes, demos, tests, inspections, process analysis, product analysis, and other verification and validation methods—in order to ensure requirements are complete; accurate (verified); and aligned (validated) with goals, objectives, and value propositions. This should ensure a smooth signoff.

A verification table illustrated in Table 7.39 may work well to summarize the verifications as the types of requirements are mapped with verification approaches.

Table 7.39 Verification table

Type of requirements	Verification approaches				
	Inspections	Process analysis	Product analysis	Tests	Demos
Functional requirements	OK	OK			
Quality requirements		OK	OK	OK	

Testing as test cases is commonly used in agile approaches. Specifically, test-driven development is an agile method that can help improve verification of requirements since test cases are developed early on in the process..

7.9 SPECIFY REQUIREMENTS: EXPECTED RESULTS

The expected results from the specify requirements process are completed by elaborating and specifying detailed metrics and acceptance criteria using measurement tools and techniques that are used in evaluating whether the solution meets the requirements.

In order to deliver quality, the business analyst needs to plan for it. This is managed in the *PMBOK®* *Guide* approach to the *plan quality management* procedure by Process 8.1 *Plan quality management*, which is illustrated in Table 7.40. The overview of the processes in this domain can be found on page 143.

Table 7.40   Plan quality management

Input	Tools and Techniques	Output
• Project	• Cost-benefit analysis	• Quality management plan
• Management plan	• Cost of quality	• Process improvement plan
• Stakeholder register	• Seven basic quality tools	• Quality metrics
• Risk register	• Benchmarking	• Quality checklists
• Requirement documents	• Design of experiences	• Project documents updates
• Enterprise environmental factors	• Statistical sampling	
• Organizational process assets	• Additional quality planning tools	
	• Meetings	

In order to develop the specific detailed metrics and acceptance criteria for evaluating whether the solution meets the requirements, the business analyst needs to consider the proper tools and techniques. Cost-benefit analysis quantifies and compares the financial and non-financial costs to the benefits gained. Costs of quality relate to costs of conformance and costs of non-conformance (as illustrated in Table 7.41).

Table 7.41   Costs of conformance and costs of non-conformance

Costs of conformance	Costs of non-conformance
Prevention cost	Internal failure cost
Appraisal cost	External failure cost

Our focus is on the cost of conformance, which is also cheaper, although the sooner the non-conformance cost is managed, the better. Prevention cost is about building a quality product where we describe the documentation and level of training needed to use the measurement tools. Appraisal costs are the costs of assessing the quality when the detailed metrics are used in action, and tests are conducted versus the acceptance criteria. The seven basic quality tools—which are all metrics that can be used to describe the quality—are:

- Cause and effect diagrams
- Flowcharts
- Check sheets
- Pareto diagrams
- Histograms

- Control charts
- Scatter diagrams

In addition, benchmarking, design of experiences, statistical sampling, and the additional quality planning tools, such as brainstorming and force field analysis, can be useful in developing the quality management plan and need metrics. The result is a quality management plan that includes all the details on delivering quality. Furthermore, we need quality metrics and quality checklists. In order to deliver quality—which is *the degree to which a set of inherent characteristics fulfills requirements*—a quality metric is useful, as it is *a description of a project or product attribute and how to measure it*. We can combine the quality metrics with a quality checklist, which is *a structured tool used to verify that a set of required steps have been performed*. The business analyst now has the needed tools to elaborate and specify detailed metrics and acceptance criteria that are used to determine whether the solution meets the requirements.

Exercise 7.12—Quality It Is: Which of the following are considered part of the seven basic quality tools? (The answers are found on page 148.)

1. Prevention costs
2. Pareto diagrams
3. Costs of non-conformance
4. Scatter diagrams
5. Cause and effect diagrams

7.10 RELATING PMI-PBA® PRACTICES TO *PMBOK® GUIDE—FIFTH EDITION* PRACTICES

Table 7.42 highlights the project management process groups and knowledge areas applied in this domain.

Table 7.42 Project management process groups and knowledge areas

Knowledge areas	Project management process groups				
	Initiating	Planning	Executing	Monitoring and Controlling	Closing
	Domain—Needs Assessment				
Project integration management					
Project scope management		5.2 Collect requirements 5.3 Define scope 5.4 Create WBS 5.5 Validate requirements			
Project time management					
Project cost management					
Project quality management				8.1 Plan quality management 8.3 Control quality	
Project human resource management					
Project communication management					
Project risk management					
Project procurement management					
Project stakeholder management					

7.11 RELATING PMI-PBA® PRACTICES TO AGILE PRACTICES

The analysis domain puts emphasis on the requirement management activities. In this domain, requirements are elicited, analyzed, developed, modeled, and managed in all possible ways. An agile software development team relies on communication and collaboration to perform requirements engineering activities, rather than on dedicated analysis tools or documentation. Table 7.43 illustrates this iterative process.

Table 7.43 Agile iterative process

Contexts	Definition
Gathering	When the team is introduced to a new requirement, resulting in the need to generate a new story card.
Clarifying	When the team is discussing more detail about an existing story card(s) or when the card(s) is ambiguous or in conflict; also concerns correctness of requirements.
Evolving	When the team's understanding of existing requirements changes (may result in a new card, or a substantial change to an existing card).

When working with agile methodologies, the changes are significant. First of all, the work is conducted by the development team and the product owner who is in close contact with the stakeholders. At a high level, the requirements are elicited by the product owner or his organization before turning them over to the development team that transforms them into user stories. All user stories are prioritized by the product owner based upon a value-driven approach. Here, it is also only the product owner who can provide the signoff for the team. In some cases (e.g., spikes), it will be useful for the team to develop prototypes.

The aspects of quality and metrics also vary within agile methodologies as quality is built into the product and process through the agile way of working with frequent verification and validation. Most teams would use test-first development, test-driven development, and acceptance test-driven development, which combined with continuous integration, continuous deployment, and continuous improvement, can deliver high quality at low costs. In case of too many escaped defects, agile smells refactoring and similar techniques can be employed. Software metrics are used in agile for the purpose of improving and strengthening the development team, not for outside control. For visibility and transparency of already high metrics, velocity, cycle time, and various burn-down and burn-up charts will be developed.

7.12 CHAPTER SUMMARY

Key concepts

- Effective elicitation of requirements is the best defense against requirements risk to the project
- Several types of elicitation techniques exist, and should be tailored before use
- Validate requirements to product scope
- The signoff is an explicit and collaborative agreement between the team and the stakeholders or product owner

- Using requirement documentation with a natural language and model-based language maximizes the advantages and reduces the disadvantages
- There is overlap between system verification and requirements verification
- Quality requires planning

Exercise 7.13—Match the Key Words to Their Definitions: Match the business analysis key words to their definitions. You will find the key words in Table 7.44 and the definitions in Table 7.45. You can use Table 7.46 to record your answers. You will find the correct answers in Table 7.47.

When you have finished reading this chapter, you can refer back to this exercise and test your knowledge again.

Table 7.44 Key words

No.	Key words
1	Perspective-based readings
2	Commenting
3	WBS directory
4	Functional requirement
5	Quality metrics
6	User story
7	Quality checklists
8	Constraint
9	Verification
10	Work breakdown structure (WBS)
11	Quality
12	Quality requirement
13	Validation

Table 7.46 Answer and score sheet

Number of key word	Letter of definition
1	
2	
3	
4	
5	
6	
7	
8	
9	
10	
11	
12	
13	

Table 7.45 Definitions

Letter	Definitions
A	A lightweight and more nimble substitute for what has been our traditional means of specifying software requirements.
B	A requirement that pertains to a quality concern that is not covered by functional requirements. Also called a non-functional requirement.
C	A document that provides detailed deliverables, activity, and scheduling information about each component in the work breakdown structure.
D	The evaluation of whether or not a product, service, or system complies with the regulation, requirements specification, or imposed condition. It is often an internal process.
E	A hierarchical decomposition of the total scope of work to be carried out by the project team to accomplish the project objectives and create the required deliverables.
F	The degree to which a set of inherent characteristics fulfills requirements.
G	A requirement concerning a result of behavior that will be provided by a function of the system.
H	The assurance that a product, service, or system meets the needs of the customer and other identified stakeholders. It often involves acceptance and suitability with external customers.
I	A structured tool used to verify that a set of required steps have been performed.
J	A kind of validation technique that adopts different perspectives to check the requirements, and are typically applied in conjunction with other review techniques.
K	A description of a project or product attribute and how to measure it.
L	A requirement that limits the solution space beyond what is necessary for meeting the given functional and quality requirements.
M	A type of inspection which is an individual validation of requirements.

Table 7.47 Correct answers

Key words	Definitions
1	J
2	M
3	C
4	G
5	K
6	A
7	I
8	L
9	D
10	E
11	F
12	B
13	H

7.13 POSTTEST: TAKE FIVE

The posttest contains five exam-related questions in the PMI-PBA format for you to check your knowledge of the content presented in this chapter, and to check your readiness for the PMI-PBA exam. The answers will be provided in the next section. You should time the posttest and not use more than six or seven minutes.

1. Which technique would you use to elicit requirements categorized in the Kano model as satisfiers?

   a) Observation

   b) Document-centric techniques

   c) Both of the above

   d) Survey techniques

2. One approach to requirement elicitation on a high level is the Brown Cow Model in Figure 7.3. Which of these terms does it not contain?

   a) Past

   b) Future

   c) How

   d) What

3. The voice of the customers may be derived from?

    a) Customer complaints

    b) Business rules

    c) Impact analysis

    d) The business case

4. What makes elicitation difficult?

    a) Choosing the proper techniques

    b) It requires close collaboration with the stakeholders

    c) You hardly ever know when you are done

    d) Uncertain scope

5. Requirement elicitation is communication intensive and should be aligned with:

    a) The stakeholders' needs and constraints

    b) The business case

    c) The requirement management plan

    d) The cost-benefit analysis

7.14 POSTTEST: CORRECT ANSWERS

1. Answer: D
2. Answer: A
3. Answer: B
4. Answer: C
5. Answer: A

Answers to *Exercise 7.7*: 1D, 2B, 3A, and 4C.

Answer to *Exercise 7.8*: The correct answer is plurality. Option 1 would require all votes, option 2 would require five votes, while option 4 only requires the one who is the key decision maker.

Answers to *Exercise 7.12*: The correct answers are two, four, and five.

Traceability and Monitoring Domain

8

TERMS TO KNOW

The list at the beginning of each chapter highlights the key terms you are required to know by the Project Management Institute (PMI). You can start by looking over these terms and if you already have solid knowledge of them, you may consider skipping this chapter. However, once you have finished reading the chapter, you can refer back to this list and test your knowledge. The concepts are:

- Forward traceability
- Backward traceability
- Requirements traceability matrix
- Requirements status
- Traceability artifacts

- Requirements management life cycle
- Project life cycle
- Requirements eleven
- Interactive, push and pull communication
- Impact analysis

8.1 BRIEF INTRODUCTION: TRACEABILITY AND MONITORING

The domain of Traceability and Monitoring manages the life cycle of the requirements—which includes ongoing communication and collaboration with the stakeholders in order to manage, trace, and monitor the requirements throughout the life cycle. Traceability is defined as *the ability to interrelate any uniquely identifiable software engineering artifact to any other, maintain required links over time, and use the resulting network to answer questions of both the software product and its development process.*

Business Analysis for Practitioners (2015) illustrates traceability and monitoring as the following steps:

- Relationship and dependencies
- Approving requirements
- Baselining approved requirements
- Monitoring requirements using a traceability matrix
- The requirements life cycle
- Managing changes to requirements

Software traceability is a sought-after, yet often elusive quality in software-intensive systems. Required in safety-critical systems by many certifying bodies, such as the U.S. Federal Aviation Administration, software traceability is an essential element of the software development process. For instance, at the start of the work during needs assessment, fuzziness or uncertainty is high; but as work progresses, the degree of uncertainty or fuzziness decreases. With traceability and monitoring, the degree of uncertainty or fuzziness is almost as low during evaluation as it is when the work progresses—which is illustrated in Figure 8.1.

8.2 TRACK REQUIREMENTS

As discussed earlier, traceability is important when documenting the life of the requirements. The documentation or traceability may help control the force of change and avoid runaway requirements turning into scope creep. Traceability helps the business analyst get the updated status on the current requirements

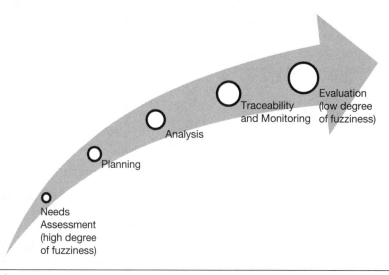

Figure 8.1 Fuzziness

and all its cross references. With traceability, the business analyst can explain why a requirement has been changed, then use the documentation as a basis for testing and as ongoing system documentation. Furthermore, traceability can enhance our ability to understand where requirements are built-in. Traceability can improve quality, reduce risks, and reduce development costs—which may increase our ability to embrace change. The goals of traceability are illustrated in Table 8.1.

Table 8.1 Goals of traceability

ID	Goal	Description
1	Purposed	Traceability is fit-for-purpose and supports stakeholder needs (i.e., traceability is requirements-driven).
2	Cost effective	The return on investment (ROI) from using traceability is adequate in relation to the outlay of establishing it.
3	Configurable	Traceability is established as specified moment-to-moment, and it accommodates changing stakeholder needs.
4	Trusted	All stakeholders have full confidence in the traceability as it is created and maintained in the face of inconsistency, omissions, and change; all stakeholders can (and do) depend upon the traceability provided.
5	Scalable	Varying types of artifacts can be traced at variable levels of granularity and in quantity—as the traceability extends through life and across organizational and business boundaries.
6	Portable	Traceability is exchanged, merged, and reused across projects, organizations, domains, product lines, and supporting tools.
7	Valued	Traceability is a strategic priority valued by all; every stakeholder has a role to play and actively discharges his or her responsibilities.
8	Ubiquitous	Traceability is always there, without ever having to think about getting it there—as it is built into the engineering process; traceability has effectively disappeared without a trace.

Some of the business analyst tasks with traceability are:

- Keep track of changes (evolving requirements)
- Collect requirements traceability information
- Track and report requirements status
- Update requirements documentation
- Communicate requirements status and changes
- Maintain and update the traceability matrix

In order to capture the requirements status, sources, and relationship using artifacts and tools, a wide range of approaches are available to the business analyst. In previous chapters we have discussed prerequirement specification traceability and postrequirement specification traceability. Prerequirement specification traceability, also defined as backward traceability, examines previous artifacts. These may include stakeholders and interview protocols or legacy documentation. Postrequirement specification traceability, also defined as forward traceability, examines current or posterior artifacts. These may include components and test cases. In addition, the business analyst can trace traceability between requirements by mapping dependencies, also defined as horizontal traceability.

The traceability tools are mostly:

- Text-based references and hyperlinks
- Trace matrices
- Trace graphs (over different development artifacts)
- Specification trees
- Specialized templates
- Requirements statement language
- Process entity-relationship models
- The planning and design methodology
- Quality function deployment
- Traceability chain (foundation for impact analysis)
- Requirements tools/tracing tools

In general, traceability is tedious work, and it is easy to make mistakes. This leads to an increase in the use of requirements tools or tracing tools—which to some degree automates the work of managing the requirements.

The requirements traceability matrix is vital in the process, which will be discussed further. However, Table 8.2 illustrates a simple version.

Table 8.2   Requirements traceability matrix

ID	User requirements	System reference
123	Add new user	S1,S2,S3
456	Add long user name	S1
789	Change password	S5

Business Analysis for Practitioners (2015) has identified the requirements traceability matrix as a collaboration point where the business analyst and the project manager should work together, and in coordination with key stakeholders, to determine content and application.

Traceability tables show the relationships between requirements, or between requirements and design components. Requirements are listed along the horizontal and vertical axes, and relationships between requirements are marked in the table cells. Traceability tables for showing requirements dependencies should be defined with requirement numbers used to label the rows and columns of the table. This is illustrated in Table 8.3.

Table 8.3   Requirements traceability tables

	Requirement 1	Requirement 2	Requirement 3
Requirement 1			X
Requirement 2			
Requirement 3			

A simpler approach to the requirements traceability table is the requirements traceability list which is useful for less than 250 requirements. This is illustrated in Table 8.4.

Table 8.4 Requirements traceability lists

Requirements	Depends on
Requirement 1	Requirement 3, Requirement 4
Requirement 2	Requirement 5, Requirement 6

In addition, most of the traceability tools will trace source/content to their relationship—for example, features to use cases, which is illustrated in Table 8.5.

Table 8.5 Traceability

Features to use cases		
Feature key	**Feature name**	**Use case**
FEAT1234	Tracking	UC1234
FEAT5678	Help system	No linkage

During traceability, the business analyst needs to ensure the capturing of the requirements status. The tracking of the requirements status can be conducted in numerous ways. Table 8.6 demonstrates this by suggesting requirements statuses which give a basis to understand the various statuses.

Table 8.6 Suggested requirements statuses

Status	Definition
Proposed	Requested by an authorized source
Approved	Analyzed, estimated, and approved
Implemented	Work complete
Verified	The correct functionality of the requirement has been confirmed
Deleted	An approved requirement has been removed
Rejected	A requirement was proposed, but it was not planned for implementation

The process of tracking requirements is conducted in the *collect requirements* and *perform integrated change control* processes. The *Project Management Body of Knowledge (PMBOK® Guide)* approach to the *collect requirements* procedure by Process 5.2 *Collect requirements* is illustrated in Table 8.7. The overview of the processes in this domain can be found at the end of this chapter.

Table 8.7 Collect requirements

Input	Tools and Techniques	Output
• Scope management plan • Requirements management plan • Stakeholder management plan • Project charter • Stakeholder register	• Interviews • Focus groups • Facilitated workshops • Group creativity techniques • Group decision-making techniques • Questionnaires and surveys • Observations • Prototypes • Benchmarking • Context diagrams • Document analysis	• Requirements documentation • Requirements traceability matrix

The process of *collect requirements* ensures that our requirements documentation and requirements traceability matrix track requirements using traceability artifacts and tools, thereby capturing the requirements status, sources, and relationships. Traceability involves the tracking of evolving requirements, which is conducted in the process of *perform integrated change control*. The *PMBOK® Guide* approach to the *perform integrated change control* procedure is by Process 4.5 *Perform integrated change control*, which is illustrated in Table 8.8. The overview of the processes in this domain can be found at the end of this chapter.

Table 8.8 Perform integrated change control

Input	Tools and Techniques	Output
• Project management plan • Work performance reports • Change requests • Enterprise environmental factors • Organizational process assets	• Expert judgment • Meetings • Change control tools	• Approved change requests • Change log • Project management plan updates • Project documents updates

The result of the process is updated requirements with requirements status, sources, and relationships (including dependencies).

Exercise 8.1—Expert Judgment in Action: You are working on a building project and are in need of an expert when performing change control. Which of the following could be considered experts? (The answer is found on page 166.)

1. An old university professor
2. Colleagues
3. A competitor on a similar project
4. The PMO
5. My boss

8.3 MONITOR REQUIREMENTS

The next stage is monitoring requirements throughout their life cycle using traceability artifacts or tools in order to ensure the appropriate supporting requirements artifacts (such as models, documentation, and test cases) are produced, reviewed, and approved at each point in the life cycle.

Monitoring requirements throughout their life cycle depends upon the project life cycle and the related requirements management life cycle. In general, we have discussed the waterfall or plan-based approach from Royce, which the *PMBOK® Guide* is based upon—and the agile methodologies, which are based upon an iterative/spiral development approach based upon Boehm and similar approaches. In addition, several other development models exist. These are the V-model, B-model, and incremental development model.

The waterfall or plan-based approach by PMI is broken down into project management process groups, which are Initiating, Planning, Executing, Monitoring and Controlling, and Closing. The Project Management Institute Professional in Business Analysis (PMI-PBA)® certification is based upon five domains. These are Needs Assessment, Planning, Analysis, Traceability and Monitoring, and Evaluation. During the domains and project management process groups, a range of requirements management activities take place—such as requirements elicitation, requirements analysis, requirements development, and requirements modeling. Table 8.9 highlights the variation of process groups, domains, and requirements activities.

Table 8.9   Life cycle

Initiating	Planning	Executing	Monitoring and Controlling	Closing
	Requirements elicitation Requirements analysis	Requirements specification Requirements validation	Requirements management	
	Requirements definition	Requirements validation Requirements documentation	Requirements management	
Needs Assessment	**Planning**	**Analysis**	**Traceability and Monitoring**	**Evaluation**

Overall, the requirements life cycle can be a complicated process involving a number of phases and should be aligned with project and program life cycle management as illustrated. With a view of the project and requirements life cycle, the business analyst needs to monitor requirements throughout their life cycle using traceability artifacts or tools in order to ensure the appropriate supporting requirements artifacts. Table 8.10 illustrates how and when the requirements life cycle and traceability artifacts or tools can be deployed.

Table 8.10   Traceability and life cycle

Requirements definition	Requirements validation	Requirements documentation	Requirements management
Authoring Traceability Visual modeling	Specification checker Simulation designer Test case automation	Document management Custom reports Diagram modeling	Share data

What is visible is the concept of different requirements and process traceability tools and artifacts to be used in various stages of the project and requirements life cycle. Table 8.11 demonstrates another view on this approach where traceabilities are mapped with requirements domains and explained within the headlines.

Table 8.11 Traceability activities (from Anne Hartly Consulting)

Domain	Headline	Traceability activities
Planning Traceability and Monitoring	Planning and monitoring	Stakeholder and business requirements, solution Scope, constraints, requirements plan, tracking
Analysis	Development	Elicitation Elaboration Analysis Design/Prototype
Analysis	Validation and verification	Proposed solution Design validation Prototype feedback Constructed Solution Testing Traceability oversight
Analysis Traceability and Monitoring	Change management	Agreed protocol Change control Approvals Signatures

A business analyst must apply a requirement's status, such as being produced, reviewed, or approved, at each point in the life cycle. An alternative approach is *requirement eleven*, which increase the types of statuses that can be used in some projects (see Table 8.12).

Table 8.12 Requirement eleven

Stated	Confirmed	Communicated	Traced
Approved	Maintained	Prioritized	Analyzed
Verified	Validated	Allocated	

Requirement eleven may also be useful when requirements are in multiple states at the same time, which requires the largest amount of statuses. One technique to monitor several states is *state diagrams* using Unified Modeling Language (UML).

The process of tracking requirements is conducted in the *collect requirements* and *validate scope* processes. The *PMBOK® Guide* approach to the *collect requirements* procedure by Process 5.2 *Collect requirements* was illustrated in Table 8.7.

The *collect requirements* process gives the business analyst the current state, while the *validate scope* process ensures the ongoing monitoring of the requirements. The *PMBOK® Guide* approach to the *validate scope* procedure by Process 5.5 *Validate scope* is illustrated in Table 8.13. The overview of the processes in this domain can be found at the end of this chapter.

Table 8.13 Validate scope

Input	Tools and Techniques	Output
• Project management plan • Requirements document • Requirements traceability matrix • Verify deliveries • Work performance data	• Inspection • Group decision-making techniques	• Accepted deliverables • Change requests • Work performance information • Project document updates

If the project is based upon an agile life cycle—be it the iterative or spiral development model—the approach to the monitoring of requirements varies. In the agile methodologies of Scrum, the monitoring of requirements is conducted in the product backlog, which within each sprint is managed in the sprint backlog, and contains the requirements, called user stories, according to each part of the sprint. The remaining requirements are managed in the user story catalog.

Exercise 8.2—Turn to Your Neighbor: If you are using this book in a study group or have a study buddy, discuss 2-3 main points you took away from this section.

8.4 UPDATE A REQUIREMENTS STATUS

Next, the business analyst needs to update a requirement's status as it moves through its life cycle by communicating with the appropriate stakeholders, and recording changes in the traceability artifacts and tools in order to track requirements toward closure.

The business analyst could use automated software for requirements management, then set up the stakeholders as users and give them the necessary permissions. As requirements are updated throughout the requirements management life cycle and project life cycle, the stakeholders will be informed as traceability artifacts are updated and tracked toward closure.

The requirements status is updated in the requirements documents and as part of the requirements traceability matrix. As illustrated in Table 8.12 depicting requirement eleven, a range of requirement statuses can be applied.

The requirements document is illustrated in Table 8.14, as status is updated with a range of requirements attributes.

Table 8.14 Update a requirements status

Status	ID	Risk	Source	Name	Description	Owner
Confirmed						
Validated						
Allocated						

The requirements document illustrated in Table 8.14 is expanded as it moves through the life cycle. An alternative may be Table 8.15, which can be used for each separate life cycle.

Table 8.15 Update the status of a requirement as it moves through its life cycle

Status	ID	Risk	Source	Name	Description	Owner	Life cycle
Approved							Analysis

Now we have updated the status of a requirement as it moves through its life cycle. Next, we need to communicate that status to the appropriate stakeholders that were identified and analyzed during needs assessment. In addition, stakeholder engagement will be covered further in the following chapter. However, at this stage the stakeholder communication requirements, which is included in the communication management plan, contains the appropriate stakeholder requirements in regard to statuses. Table 8.16 illustrates how the updated requirement's status is communicated with stakeholders. This combines the requirement's status with the communication methods found in the communication management plans as stakeholders need the information in different formats at various times.

Table 8.16 Updating the status of requirements to stakeholders

Status	ID	Name	Description	Life cycle	Stakeholders	How	When
Maintained						E-mail	Daily
Communicated						Website update	Change of status

Furthermore, the recording changes need to be handled by the traceability artifacts and tools, whether automated or manual. The traceability artifacts and tools are:

- Text-based references and hyperlinks
- Trace matrices
- Trace graphs (over different development artifacts)
- Specification trees
- Specialized templates
- Traceability chain (foundation for impact analysis)
- Requirements tools/tracing tools

The process of updating a requirement's status as it moves through its life cycle, by communicating with the appropriate stakeholders, is conducted in the *collect requirements* procedure by Process 5.2 *Collect requirements*, which was illustrated in Table 8.7.

Recording changes in the traceability artifacts and tools in order to track requirements toward closure is handled in the *PMBOK® Guide* approach to *perform integrated change control* by Process 4.5 *Perform integrated change control*, which was illustrated in Table 8.8.

Exercise 8.3—Update: You are in the process of updating Table 8.16. Which of the following items would you most likely see in the table? (The answers are found on page 166.)

1. ID: 232
2. Name: Tyler Barnes
3. Description: Login
4. Life cycle: No
5. Stakeholders: Yes

8.5 COMMUNICATE REQUIREMENTS STATUS

The business analyst needs to communicate a requirement's status to the project manager and stakeholders using communication methods in order to keep them informed of requirements issues, conflicts, changes, risks, and overall status.

An effective communication flow between the project manager and stakeholders is vital for the project's success. One feature of effective communication is that it has the right timing, the right format, and the right medium. Another factor is that efficient communication is only related to required messages. Part of the success for the communication is the communication medium. The communication medium and effective communication distribution are closely related, and several different techniques are efficient and effective—including:

- Sender-receiver models
- Choice of media
- Writing style
- Meeting management techniques
- Presentation techniques
- Facilitation techniques
- Listening techniques

The communication of the requirements status is input to the *manage communications* procedure in the work performance reports. The *PMBOK® Guide* approach to *manage communications* by Process 10.2 *Manage communications* is illustrated in Table 8.17. The overview of the processes in this domain can be found at the end of this chapter.

Table 8.17 Manage communications

Input	Tools and Techniques	Output
• Communication management plan	• Communication technology	• Project communication
• Work performance reports	• Communication models	• Project management plan updates
• Enterprise environmental factor	• Communication methods	• Project document updates
• Organizational process assets	• Information management systems	• Organizational process assets updates
	• Performance reporting	

The major input to the process is the communication management plan, which PMI defines as *a component of the project, program, or portfolio management plan that describes how, when, and by whom information about the project will be administered and disseminated.* In the communication management plan, the considerations for communication channels are included. The formula for calculating the communication channels is $N(N-1)/2$, where N is the number of team members. This leaves 10 communication channels on a team with 5 members: $5(5-1)/2 = 10$.

The communication method is used to convey requirements issues, conflicts, changes, risks and overall status are *a systematic procedure, technique, or process used to transfer information among project stakeholders.* This implies that the business analyst needs to consider interactive communication, push communication, and pull communication, which are the communication methods used as tools and techniques in the manage stakeholders process.

Interactive communication is multidirectional communication and is the most effective. This communication medium would include face-to-face meetings, video conferencing, phone calls, and messenger chats.

Push communication is the broadcasting of distributed communication without any feedback from the recipients. This would include a note to people after a brainstorming workshop, requirements status mail, or similar methods. Push communication is also effective and is often used with stakeholders who in the power/interest grid X, as shown in Table 8.18, are marked as high power/low interest and/or low power/low interest.

Table 8.18 Power/interest grid

Level of Power	High power/low interest	High power/high interest
	Low power/low interest	Low power/high interest
	Level of Interest	

Pull communication is a gathering or collection of data on the intranet or knowledge repository. This communication is passive and can be accessed directly by stakeholders when needed. It would include a website, intranet, and similar mediums.

The application of communication methods—in order to keep stakeholders and the project manager informed of requirements issues, conflicts, changes, risks, and overall status—depends on various factors. Some of those factors would include familiarity with the communication methods, as well as urgency of the communication. If urgency and complexity is high, *interactive* communication will be the best choice since many options may need to be discussed; while a normal requirements status update can be posted on a website where stakeholders can pull the communication when needed.

Some communication methods require a bit of technology and may take time to learn how to use. In the end, it comes down to costs and determining the communication channels stakeholders like best.

Keeping the stakeholders informed is part of the *manage stakeholder engagement* process as emphasis is on communication with stakeholders and ensuring that it is meeting their needs and addressing issues.

The *PMBOK® Guide* approach to the *manage stakeholder engagement* procedure by Process 13.3 *Manage stakeholder engagement* is illustrated in Table 8.19. The overview of the processes in this domain can be found at the end of this chapter.

Table 8.19 Manage stakeholder engagement

Input	Tools and Techniques	Output
• Communication management plan • Work performance reports • Enterprise environmental factors • Organizational process assets	• Communication technology • Communication models • Communication methods • Information management systems • Performance reporting	• Project communication • Project management plan updates • Project document updates • Organizational process assets updates

When working in an agile environment, the communication of the requirements (user stories) status to the product owner is done on a day-to-day basis with interactive communication. However, most communication would also be available on information radiators, work-in-progress boards, and similar communication mediums where the product owner can pull the communication as needed. This also applies for the team members who can pull the communication from within the team.

8.6 MANAGE CHANGES TO REQUIREMENTS

Finally, the business analyst needs to manage changes to requirements by assessing impacts, dependencies, and risks, in accordance with the change control plan, and compare them to the requirements baseline in order to maintain the integrity of the requirements and associated artifacts.

We previously discussed managing changes to requirements and the change control plan. However, let us recap it quickly by examining the *PMBOK® Guide* approach to the *control scope* procedure by Process 5.6 *Control scope*, which is illustrated in Table 8.20, and briefly discuss an important input. The overview of the processes in this domain can be found at the end of this chapter.

Table 8.20 Control scope

Input	Tools and Techniques	Output
• Project management plan • Requirement documents • Requirement traceability matrix • Work performance data • Organizational process assets	• Variance analysis	• Work performance information • Change requests • Project management plan updates • Project documents updates • Organizational process assets updates

The requirements traceability matrix is vital because it can detect the impact of any change or deviation from the requirements baseline. Assessing impacts (impact analysis) is a technique designed to uncover unexpected negative effects of a change, which we will discuss further in Chapter 10. The majority of the changes would most likely affect posterior development artifacts such as test cases and components that need to change. Similarly, the requirements traceability matrix may indicate a good starting point for investigating the dependencies because the requirements are mapped in so changes can be illustrated. The risks of the changes can be assessed by the use of the requirements traceability matrix and requirements document. The requirements will be accepted or denied, and based on that outcome, the project documents are updated (requirements documentation and requirements traceability matrix).

Exercise 8.4—Control Scope: Which of the following is an input to the control scope process? (The answer is found on page 166.)

1. Variance analysis
2. Work performance information
3. Work performance data
4. Change requests

8.7 RELATING PMI-PBA® PRACTICES TO *PMBOK® GUIDE—FIFTH EDITION* PRACTICES

Table 8.21 Project management process groups and knowledge areas

Knowledge areas	Project management process groups				
	Initiating	Planning	Executing	Monitoring and Controlling	Closing
	Domain—Needs Assessment				
Project integration management				4.5 Perform integrated change control	
Project scope management		5.2 Collect requirements		5.5 Validate scope 5.6 Control scope	
Project time management					
Project cost management					
Project quality management					
Project human resource management					
Project communication management		10.2 Communication requirements			
Project risk management					
Project procurement management					
Project stakeholder management			13.3 Manage stakeholder engagement		

8.8 RELATING PMI-PBA® PRACTICES TO AGILE PRACTICES

Traceability and monitoring of user stories is ongoing and transparent in agile methodologies in order to drive value and embrace change. The work is based upon the artifacts of the product backlog and sprint backlog, containing the user stories which are communicated by information radiators, work-in-process boards, and other similar forms of communication, within the team and to the product owner, who communicates with the stakeholders.

The traceability, communication, and monitoring of user stories is conducted on a day-to-day basis within the team and with the product owner and is supported by the Scrum Master. The agile methodologies cover a variation of life cycles. However, Scrum, as illustrated, is highly relevant when dealing with user stories/requirements.

8.9 CHAPTER SUMMARY

Key concepts

- Traceability helps control the force of change and avoid runaway requirements turning into scope creep
- The requirements life cycle can be a complicated process involving a number of phases, and should be aligned with project and program life cycle management

- Requirements statuses are updated and communicated throughout the project life cycle
- The choice of communication methods depends on several factors
- The requirements traceability matrix can detect the impact of any change or deviation from the requirements baseline

Exercise 8.5—Match the Key Words to Their Definitions: Match the business analysis key words to their definitions. You will find the key words in Table 8.22, and their definitions in Table 8.23. You can use Table 8.24 to record your answers and determine your score. You will find the correct answers in Table 8.25 on page 166.

When you have finished reading this chapter, you can refer back to this exercise, and test your knowledge again.

Table 8.22 Key words

No.	Key words
1	Sprint
2	Communication methods
3	Information radiator
4	Product backlog
5	Communication management plan
6	Sprint backlog

Table 8.24 Answer and score sheet

Number of key word	Letter of definition
1	
2	
3	
4	
5	
6	

Table 8.23 Definitions

Letter	Definitions
A	A Scrum artifact. This is the prioritized list of all the features and changes that have yet to be made to the system desired by multiple actors in Scrum.
B	A Scrum artifact. It is the list of features that is currently assigned to a particular sprint.
C	A component of the project, program, or portfolio management plan that describes how, when, and by whom information about the project will be administered and disseminated.
D	The generic term for any of a number of handwritten, drawn, printed, or electronic displays.
E	A Scrum event—30 days in length, it is the procedure of adapting to the changing environmental variables (requirements, time, resources, knowledge, technology, etc.) and must result in a potentially shippable increment of software.
F	A systematic procedure, technique, or process used to transfer information among project stakeholders.

8.10 POSTTEST: TAKE FIVE

The posttest contains five exam-related questions in the PMI-PBA format for you to check your knowledge of the content presented in this chapter, and to check your readiness for the PMI-PBA exam. The answers will be provided in the next section. You should time the posttest and not use more than six or seven minutes.

1. If the project cycle is requirements definition, requirements validation, requirements documentation, and requirements management, which activity below is part of requirements management?

    a) Share data

    b) Test case automation

    c) Authoring

    d) Custom reports

2. Which development model is a variant of the waterfall model?

    a) V-model

    b) B-model

    c) Incremental development model

    d) All of the above

3. If a requirements status is proposed then it:

    a) Is an approved requirement that has been removed

    b) Has been requested by an authorized source

    c) Is a requirement that was proposed, but not planned for implementation

    d) Is work complete

4. The traceability tools are mostly:

    a) Specialized templates

    b) Too expensive to use

    c) Difficult to use

    d) For managing constraints

5. Agile methodologies are based upon which development model?

    a) Spiral

    b) B-model

    c) The waterfall model

    d) V-model

Table 8.25 Correct answers

Key words	Definitions
1	E
2	F
3	D
4	A
5	C
6	B

8.11 POSTTEST: CORRECT ANSWERS

1. Answer: A
2. Answer: D
3. Answer: B
4. Answer: A
5. Answer: A

Answers to *Exercise 8.1*: All of these can be considered experts in terms of *expert judgment*. The definition is purposefully broad.

Answers to *Exercise 8.3*: Items 1, 2, and 3 all make sense while option 4 would need a life cycle term, such as analysis or waterfall. Option 5 would need the name or title of the stakeholders.

Answer to *Exercise 8.4*: Three is the correct answer.

Evaluation Domain 9

TERMS TO KNOW

The list at the beginning of each chapter highlights the key terms you are required to know by the Project Management Institute (PMI). You can start with these terms, and if you already have solid knowledge of them, then you may consider skipping this chapter. However, once you have finished reading this chapter, you can refer back to this list, and test your knowledge. The concepts are:

- Acceptance criteria
- Definition of *done*
- Test-driven development
- Stakeholder signoff

- Statistical quality control
- Quality management and control tools
- Group decision-making techniques

9.1 BRIEF INTRODUCTION: EVALUATION

The Evaluation domain consists of activities to determine how well the developed solution fulfills the defined solution and business needs. This involves validating the solutions and business needs with the use of acceptance criteria. Furthermore, possible solution gaps are identified and managed using quality management and statistical quality control tools and techniques. The evaluation also involves signoff with the stakeholders using group decision-making techniques. However, valuation techniques—being realistic, perceived, or normative—are used to measure the cost and benefits of the developed solution.

Business Analysis for Practitioners (2015) illustrates *solution evaluation* as the following steps:

- Plan for the evaluation of the solution
- Determine what to evaluate
- Establish when and how to validate solution results
- Evaluate acceptance criteria and address defects
- Facilitate the go/no-go decision
- Obtain signoff of the solution
- Evaluate the long-term performance of the solution
- Solution replacement/phase out

9.1.1 Mindset for Evaluation

Business Analysis for Practitioners (2015) introduces a mindset for evaluating which to some degree sums up the activities covered in this chapter. First, *evaluate early and often* is more and more common especially with the agile life cycle. For plan-based projects, the evaluation can be broken into smaller components and evaluated throughout the project, which would reduce the risk, cost of rework, and amount of changes, along with ensuring ongoing stakeholder value. Requirement analysis, traceability, testing, and evaluation have been described as individual components, however, they should be applied as complementary activities. Also, it is important to evaluate with the context of usage and value in mind in order to ensure results can be applied toward day-to-day business, and in order to ensure benefits are obtained from the deliverables. Finally, confirm expected values for software solutions—which implies needed testing by real people with real data, not just automated testing exclusively.

9.2 VALIDATE TEST RESULTS

The business analyst needs to validate the solution's test results, reports, and other test evidence against the requirement acceptance criteria in order to determine whether the solution satisfies the requirements. Simply worded; does the delivered solution meet the business need?

This process is described as part of the *Project Management Body of Knowledge (PMBOK® Guide)* approach to the *control quality* procedure by Process 8.3 *Control quality*. The inputs, tools and techniques, and outputs will follow in a moment, but let's first discuss the thought process behind it.

In order to test and report whether the solution meets business needs, acceptance criteria are used in conjunction with techniques such as problem tracking and root cause analysis. Additional analyses are illustrated in the *control quality* process.

Acceptance criteria are important as they represent a specific and defined list of conditions that must be met before a project has been considered completed, and before the project deliverables can and will be accepted by the business. Furthermore, the acceptance criteria are important because they are used for requirements to produce test plans and test data for valuing the quality of the final solution. The test plans anticipate usage scenarios and include both functional and nonfunctional requirements. If possible, automated tests are used. In many circumstances, scenarios (any level of details), storyboards (steps of a scenario as a sequence of a pictures-paper prototype), and use cases (structure for describing a group of related scenarios) are techniques used to transform acceptance criteria into tests from which test reports can be derived.

Business Analysis for Practitioners (2015) has identified the application of proper metrics for acceptance criteria when evaluating activities as a collaboration point where the business analyst and project manager should work together with stakeholders.

In order to ensure that the requirement acceptance criteria have the right qualities of effective acceptance criteria, and in order to determine whether the solution satisfies the requirements, the following conditions should be met as illustrated in Table 9.1. Requirements that are not supported by well-defined acceptance criteria are likely to cause problems.

Table 9.1   SMART

S	Specific
M	Measurable
A	Achievable
R	Relevant
T	Time-bound

If acceptance criteria are defined for other more complicated areas, such as usability, new conditions need to be defined as illustrated in Table 9.2.

Table 9.2   PLUME

P	Productivity	Time it takes to complete the tasks
L	Learnability	How much training is needed
U	User satisfaction	Subjective responses from users
M	Memorability	Easy to use and remember
E	Error rates	Accuracy in carrying out the tasks

Before examining the result of the process, let us examine the actual *PMBOK® Guide* approach to the *control quality* procedure by Process 8.3 *Control quality*, which is illustrated in Table 9.3. The overview of the processes in this domain can be found at the end of this chapter.

Table 9.3 Control quality

Input	Tools and Techniques	Output
• Project management plan	• Seven basic quality tools	• Quality control measurements
• Quality metrics	• Statistical sampling	• Validated changes
• Quality checklists	• Inspection	• Verified deliverables
• Work performance data	• Approved change requests review	• Work performance information
• Approved change requests		• Change requests
• Deliverables		• Project management plan updates
• Project documents		• Project documents updates
• Organizational process assets		• Organizational process assets update

The acceptance criteria are documented in the requirements document and the project scope statement, in which we have employed the tools and techniques that result in the validation of the solution, stating that it meets the business needs. If this is not the case, the identified defects would result in mitigating, corrective, or preventive actions, which will be taken as change requests to align the requirements with business needs.

When working with agile methodologies, two concepts—test-driven development and the definition of *done*—are highly relevant in this circumstance.

Test-first development is a rapid extreme programming cycle of testing, coding, and refactoring. It is reflected in the equation: test-first design + refactoring = test-driven development. To put it in other words, "Test-driven development is an evolutionary approach to development which combines test-first development where you write a test before you write just enough production code to fulfill that test and refactoring" (Ambler, 2013).

Test-first development is an agile-friendly development practice where the acceptance tests for a module are defined before the module is written. The code is constructed based on passing these tests so that it should only pass when it performs correctly. Test-first development is sometimes called *acceptance test-driven development*. Test-driven development (TDD) is a special case of test-first development. It implies that the acceptance criteria should define the boundaries of a user story and be tested before any coding is done.

The agile concept of the definition of *done* rises above the human tendency to leave things in an almost-finished state. "The team agrees on, and displays prominently somewhere in the team room, a list of criteria that must be met before a product increment (often a user story) is considered *done*. Failure to meet these criteria at the end of a sprint normally implies that the work should not be counted toward that sprint's velocity" (Agile Alliance, 2012). Complying with the definition of *done* means that the work is completed and ready for testing by the product owner.

Exercise 9.1—Question Time: If you are using this book in a study group or have a study buddy, develop 3 questions from the material in this section for your study group or partner to answer.

9.3 ANALYZE SOLUTION GAPS

The business analyst needs to analyze and communicate the solution-identified gaps and deltas using quality assurance tools and methods in order to enable stakeholders to resolve discrepancies between solution scope, requirements, and developed solutions.

During evaluation the business analyst needs to ensure that the statement of the defined result is being achieved, which implies fitness of use for the stakeholders as well as being in accordance with the specifications. This process for analyzing the solution gaps requires ongoing communication with the stakeholders.

The business analyst approach is based upon Total Quality Management authorities Kaoru Ishikawa, Joseph Juran, and W. Edwards Deming, who specify four principles that should guide any organizational interventions intended to improve quality (Hackmann, 1995).

- The first principle is that the quality of products and services depends most of all on the processes by which they are designed and produced.
- The second principle is analysis of variability.
- The third principle is management by fact.
- The fourth principle is learning and continuous improvement.

The business analyst approach may begin in the plan-do-check-act cycle which was developed by W. Edwards Deming and based upon the Shewhart cycle (1939). Figure 9.1 illustrates the plan-do-check-act cycle which is the basis for continuous improvements.

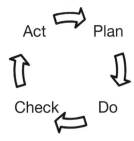

Figure 9.1 Plan-do-check-act cycle

The project and business analyst will *plan* how quality is to be delivered with a comprehensive requirement specification. Next will come the period to *do* the actual work, followed by a time in which to *check* for any solution gaps. If solution gaps are found, the business analyst needs to *act*.

The PMI process of solution assessment by identifying gaps and shortcomings in solutions, and assessing deployed solutions to see how well they meet the original need is part of the *control quality* process. The actual *PMBOK® Guide* approach to the *control quality* procedure by Process 8.3 *Control quality* was illustrated in Table 9.3.

At this stage the business analyst is focused upon evaluating solution performance and correctness of the deliverables, monitoring and recording results, and stating quality requirements to ensure that they have been met with an emphasis on quality management to avoid poor process and product quality. For this purpose, there are several tools to help maintain quality assurance (see Table 9.4).

Table 9.4 Quality management and control tools

Quality management and control tools	
Affinity diagrams	A creativity technique that allows a large number of ideas to be classified into groups for review and analysis.
Process decision program charts (PDPC)	The PDPC is used to understand a goal in relation to the steps for getting to the goal.
Interrelationship diagrams	A quality management tool, interrelationship diagrams provide a process for creative problem solving in moderately complex scenarios that process intertwined logical relationships.
Tree diagrams	A systematic diagram of a decomposition hierarchy used to visualize, as a parent-to-child relationship, a systematic set of rules.
Prioritization matrices	A quality management tool used to identify key issues and evaluate suitable alternatives to define a set of implementation priorities.
Activity network diagrams	A graphical representation of the logical relationship among the project schedule activities.
Matrix diagrams	A quality management and control tool used to perform data analysis within the organizational structure created in the matrix. The matrix diagram seeks to show the strength of relationships between factors, causes, and objectives that exist between the rows and columns that form the matrix.

Quality management and control tools also use a wide range of statistical quality control tools for identifying and analyzing solution gaps (see Table 9.5).

Table 9.5 Statistical quality control

Tool	Description	Identification	Analysis
Cause and effect diagram	Illustrates how various factors can be linked to problems or effects	X	
Control charts	Shows how a process behaves over time		X
Flowcharting	Analyzes how problems occur		X
Histogram	Displays relative frequency of the characteristics		X
Pareto chart	Type of histogram to identify and prioritize problem areas	X	
Run chart	Used to visualize data and contribute to forecasting	X	X
Scatter diagram	Shows pattern of relationships		X
Statistical sampling	Evaluation of a portion of the product	X	

Besides the quality management and control tools and the statistical quality control tools, the following techniques are helpful in analyzing solution gaps:

- Root cause analysis (the 5 Whys)
- Forced field analysis
- Nominal group technique
- Inspections, reviews, peer reviews, audits, and walkthroughs
- GAP analysis (value stream mapping)

Agile project management is very similar in terms of what we want to achieve, but techniques and concepts vary a lot. Quality is an inherent aspect of true agile software development. In agile, we focus on prevention rather than inspections. Prevention is about avoiding errors by means of proper processes, training, checklists, and controls.

The cost of quality varies depending on quality conformance and nonconformance. The cost of conformance is prevention and appraisal, while the cost of nonconformance is internal and external processes when the product is more or less complete.

Since the 1980s, thinking about quality has been inspired by Total Quality Management. W. Edward Deming developed the plan-do-check-act cycle based on the Shewhart cycle (1939), and agile circles employ it. The concept is that we *plan* by setting a standard of practice. The *do* phase observes practice and the *check* phase compares observed practice with standards. The *act* phase then implements changes. This process is often done within a few weeks in agile projects, and variations are found very quickly.

In agile, some people deploy value stream mapping for analyzing solution gaps and for process improvements. This is discussed in Chapter 10.

Exercise 9.2—Gaps: Which of the following techniques are helpful in analyzing solution gaps? (The answer is found on page 180.)

1. Run charts
2. Tree diagrams
3. Statistical sampling
4. Forced field analysis
5. Matrix diagrams

9.4 OBTAIN STAKEHOLDER ACCEPTANCE OF THE SOLUTION

During the evaluation domain, the business analyst must seek to obtain stakeholder signoff on the developed solution by using decision-making techniques in order to proceed with the development.

At this stage the work is more or less complete, which means that we need a process for wrapping up the project to ensure that all of the work is completed, and then compare actual results with project goals; which is the *close project or phase* process. The actual *PMBOK® Guide* approach to the *close project or phase* procedure by Process 4.6 *Close project or phase*, is illustrated in Table 9.6. The overview of the processes in this domain can be found at the end of this chapter.

Business Analysis for Practitioners (2015) has identified determining required signoff practices and auditing with the key stakeholders as collaboration points where the business analyst and the project manager should work together.

Table 9.6 Close project or phase

Input	Tools and Techniques	Output
• Project management plan • Accepted deliverables • Organizational process assets	• Expert judgment • Analytical techniques • Meetings	• Final product, service, or result of transition • Organizational process assets updates

During this stage the business analyst needs a process for obtaining acceptance of completed work, which is done with a formal agreement that is accepted by the stakeholders. This process occurs after quality control. The formal agreement and acceptance by the stakeholders may result in acceptance of the product and may also lead to some changes, which would result in some change requests. This work is conducted in the *validate scope* process. The actual *PMBOK® Guide* approach to the *validate scope* procedure by Process 5.5 *Validate scope* is illustrated in Table 9.7. The overview of the processes in this domain can be found at the end of this chapter.

Table 9.7 Validate scope

Input	Tools and Techniques	Output
• Project management plan • Requirement documentation • Requirement traceability matrix • Verified deliverables • Work performance data	• Inspections • Group decision-making techniques	• Accepted deliverables • Change requests • Work performance information • Project document updates

Part of the formal agreement and acceptance by the stakeholders is the need for group decision-making techniques in order to reach an agreement. Figure 9.2 illustrates group decision-making techniques.

When working in an agile development, stakeholder signoff is conducted at the end of the sprint by the product owner. If the product owner cannot approve the solution, the user stories are returned to the product backlog. The product owner is the final decision maker and can be a dictatorship. Whether or not the development should continue for additional releases or sprints is the decision of the product owner, who should be in close dialogue with the stakeholders.

Exercise 9.3—How to Use This at Work: In groups of two to four people, have participants list ways that they will use the materials presented in this section in their own work environments.

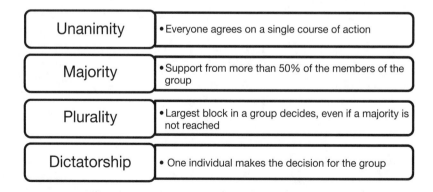

Unanimity	• Everyone agrees on a single course of action
Majority	• Support from more than 50% of the members of the group
Plurality	• Largest block in a group decides, even if a majority is not reached
Dictatorship	• One individual makes the decision for the group

Figure 9.2 Group decision-making techniques

9.5 EVALUATE SOLUTION RESULTS

Finally, in the evaluation domain the business analyst needs to evaluate the deployed solution using valuation techniques in order to determine how well the solution meets the business case and value proposition.

When evaluating the deployed solution using valuation techniques, three types are available:

- Realistic
- Perceived
- Normative

The realistic valuation technique uses fairly objective measurements containing hard data, such as financial methodologies (return on investment, net present value, internal rate of return, break-even, and payback period), which were introduced in the Needs Assessment domain. A majority of this data can be found in the business case and/or the cost benefit analysis, which in many cases is part of the business case. If the solution has been implemented, realistic data should be available for collection.

Realistic valuation techniques are closely related to benefit realization, which is the step where we follow up and measure the value proposition of the business case. This is often just a measurement of the costs of developing the solution compared to the tangible benefits, which are the measurable improvements.

Determining the value derived from the business case and value proposition is used in conjunction with benefit management, which is the process of managing benefits throughout the project. The steps are as follows:

- Identification of benefits
- Definition of benefits
- Tracking of benefits
- Benefit realization
- Optimization of benefits

Perceived valuation techniques are completed using fairly subjective measurements based upon data derived from stakeholders and users involved in the project in a technical, business, or managerial capacity. The perceived valuation technique reflects an individual's view on the benefits to be derived from the system, and is often measured by surveys, focus groups, and interviews. Table 9.8 illustrates how customers and values can be measured.

Table 9.8 Value propositions are the customer's perspective with regard to an organization

		Customers		
		Owner	Partner	End customer
Value categories	Timing			Arrival of products
	Financial		Discount rate	
	Quality	Reputation of organization		

The normative valuation technique uses measurements based upon comparative data from either *best practice* or benchmarking models. The normative valuation technique may involve the development of a prototype or pilot system, or of a model that is used to provide information on what the expected value *should be*.

The evaluation of the deployed solution using a valuation technique—either realistic, perceived, or normative—in order to determine how well the solution meets the business case and value proposition is conducted in the *control quality* process. The actual *PMBOK® Guide* approach to the *control quality* procedure by Process 8.3 *Control quality*, was illustrated in Table 9.3.

In most agile methodologies, the responsibility of evaluating the deployed solution using valuation techniques in order to determine how well the solution meets the business case and value proposition is solely a task for the product owner—who is responsible for the business case and benefit realization of the developed solution.

Exercise 9.4—Decision Maker in Agile? In agile, who is the key decision maker when evaluating the deployed solution? (The answer is found on page 180.)

1. The product owner
2. The Scrum Master
3. The development team
4. The steering committee
5. None of the above

9.6 RELATING PMI-PBA® PRACTICES TO *PMBOK® GUIDE—FIFTH EDITION* PRACTICES

Table 9.9   Project management process groups and knowledge areas

Knowledge areas	Project management process groups				
	Initiating	Planning	Executing	Monitoring and Controlling	Closing
	Domain—Needs Assessment				
Project integration management					4.6 Close project or phase
Project scope management				5.5 Validate scope	
Project time management					
Project cost management					
Project quality management				8.3 Control quality	
Project human resource management					
Project communication management					
Project risk management					
Project procurement management					
Project stakeholder management					

9.7 RELATING PMI-PBA® PRACTICES TO AGILE PRACTICES

In agile methodologies such as Scrum, the evaluation of the solution and benefits are a matter for the product owner, who as the decision maker, is solely responsible for the business case and benefit realization. However, the agile methodologies contain several tools and techniques to deliver high quality, such as TDD and the use of the definition of *done*. Thus, quality is inherent and built into the product and process. For additional measurements of possible solution gaps, the value stream mapping technique is valuable for many teams.

9.8 CHAPTER SUMMARY

Key concepts

- Requirements that are not supported by well-defined acceptance criteria are likely to cause problems
- Acceptance criteria represents a specific and defined list of conditions that must be met before a project has been considered completed and the project deliverables can and will be accepted by the business

- Quality management and statistical quality control tools are the techniques to identify and solve solution gaps
- When evaluating the deployed solution using valuation techniques, three types are available: realistic, perceived, and normative

Exercise 9.5—Match the Key Words to Their Definitions: Match the business analysis key words to their definitions. You will find the key words in Table 9.10, and their definitions in Table 9.11. You can use Table 9.12 to record your answers and determine your score. You will find the correct answers in Table 9.13.

When you have finished reading this chapter, you can refer back to this exercise and test your knowledge again.

Table 9.10 Key words

No.	Key words
1	Process decision program chart
2	Definition of *done*
3	Matrix diagram
4	Tree diagram
5	Acceptance criteria
6	Activity network diagram
7	Interrelationship diagram
8	Affinity diagram
9	Prioritization matrix
10	Test-driven development

Table 9.12 Answer and score sheet

Number of key word	Letter of definition
1	
2	
3	
4	
5	
6	
7	
8	
9	
10	

Table 9.11 Definitions

Letter	Definitions
A	A model used to understand a goal in relation to the steps for getting to the goal.
B	A special case of test-first development.
C	A quality management tool used to identify key issues and evaluate suitable alternatives to define a set of implementation priorities.
D	A quality management tool that provides a process for creative problem solving in moderately complex scenarios that process intertwined logical relationships.
E	Establishes what must be true for the software product in order to be defined as working software.
F	A quality management and control tool used to perform data analysis within the organizational structure.
G	A systematic diagram of a decomposition hierarchy used to visualize, as a parent-to-child relationship, a systematic set of rules.
H	What a system or component must satisfy in order to be accepted by a user, customer, or other authorized entity.
I	A graphical representation of the logical relationship among project schedule activities.
J	A creativity technique that allows a large number of ideas to be classified into groups for review and analysis.

9.9 POSTTEST: TAKE FIVE

The posttest contains five exam-related questions in the PMI-PBA format for you to check your knowledge of the content presented in this chapter, and to check your readiness for the PMI-PBA exam. The answers will be provided in the next section. You should time the posttest and not use more than six or seven minutes.

1. When evaluating the deployed solution using valuation techniques, which one should not be used?
   a) Realistic
   b) Perceived
   c) Normative
   d) Pessimistic

2. Which statistical quality control tools are used for identification?
   a) Control charts
   b) Flowcharting
   c) Cause and effect diagram
   d) Histogram

3. Which of these techniques is *not* used for quality management and control tools during evaluation?
   a) Process decision program charts
   b) Prioritization matrices
   c) Tree diagrams
   d) Impact analysis

4. The plan-do-check-act cycle was developed by:
   a) Kaoru Ishikawa
   b) Joseph Juran
   c) W. Edwards Deming
   d) None of the above

5. When working in agile, which two concepts are relevant in terms of evaluation?
   a) Test-driven development and definition of *done*
   b) Behavior-driven development and software metrics
   c) Agile smells and refactoring
   d) Earned value management and validation

Table 9.13 Correct answers

Key words	Definitions
1	A
2	E
3	F
4	G
5	H
6	I
7	D
8	J
9	C
10	B

9.10 POSTTEST: CORRECT ANSWERS

1. Answer: D
2. Answer: C
3. Answer: D
4. Answer: C
5. Answer: A

Answer to *Exercise 9.2*: Four is the correct option.

Answer to *Exercise 9.4*: One is the correct option as the product owner is solely responsible.

Part 3

Knowledge, Skills, Methodologies, and Standards

PMI-PBA® Knowledge, Skills, Tools, and Techniques

10

TERMS TO KNOW

The list at the beginning of each chapter highlights the key terms you are required to know by the Project Management Institute (PMI). You can start with these terms, and if you already have solid knowledge of them, you may consider skipping this chapter. When you have finished reading the chapter, you can refer back to this list and test your knowledge. The concepts are.

- Analytic tools and techniques
- Backlog management
- Business rule analysis tools and techniques
- Change control tools and techniques
- Collaboration tools and techniques
- Communication skills tools and techniques
- Conflict management and resolution tools and techniques
- Contingency planning
- Data analysis tools and techniques
- Decision-making tools and techniques
- Development methodologies

- Document management tools and techniques
- Elements of a requirements management plan
- Elicitation tools and techniques
- Estimating tools and techniques
- Facilitation tools and techniques
- Interface analysis
- Leadership principles and skills
- Lessons learned and retrospectives
- Measurement tools and techniques
- Negotiations tools and techniques

- Organization assessment
- Planning tools and techniques
- Political and cultural awareness
- Prioritization tools and techniques
- Problem solving and opportunity identification tools and techniques
- Process analysis tools and techniques
- Project methodologies
- Quality management
- Reporting tools and techniques
- Requirements traceability tools and techniques
- Requirement types
- Root cause analysis
- Scheduling tools and techniques
- Stakeholder analysis
- System thinking
- Validation tools and techniques
- Valuation tools and techniques
- Verification tools and techniques
- Version control tools and techniques

10.1 BRIEF INTRODUCTION: KNOWLEDGE CONCEPTS AND SKILLS

The content for the Project Management Institute Professional in Business Analysis (PMI-PBA)® certification exam described in the Examination Content Outline consists of five domains and 40 knowledge concepts and skills. The five domains have been previously discussed, and this chapter will cover the knowledge and skills required to pass the certification exam.

Each knowledge and skill set is aligned with Table 10.1, containing the domains and the dominant development methodologies—waterfall and/or agile—in order to highlight the predominant use of the knowledge and skills. For example, knowledge and skills of backlog management is an agile discipline and would have a marker in that column and in the relevant domain (Traceability and Monitoring).

10.2 TOOLS AND TECHNIQUES OVERVIEW

Business analysis techniques are the style, manner, method, or procedures used to perform tasks or shape output, where one or more tools are employed. The 40 techniques highlighted in this chapter contain a subset of techniques and variations that are used by practitioners of business analysis. However, their application differs from situations and domains or waterfall versus agile.

10.3 ANALYTIC TOOLS AND TECHNIQUES

Technique	Needs Assessment	Planning	Analysis	Traceability and Monitoring	Evaluation	Waterfall	Agile
Analytic tools and techniques			X			X	X

The business analyst needs to take part in developing the schedule, which involves planning a wide range of activities discussed in the domains. A good schedule can reduce the risks of the project, which is the second element of the analytic tools and techniques discussed in this section.

Table 10.1   Knowledge and skills aligned with domains

Techniques	Needs Assessment	Planning	Analysis	Traceability and monitoring	Evaluation	Waterfall	Agile
Analytic tools and techniques			X			X	X
Backlog management				X			X
Business rule analysis tools and techniques			X			X	X
Change control tools and techniques				X		X	X
Collaboration tools and techniques		X				X	X
Communication skills tools and techniques				X		X	X
Conflict management and resolution tools and techniques				X		X	X
Contingency planning		X				X	X
Data analysis tools and techniques			X			X	
Decision-making tools and techniques			X			X	X
Development methodologies		X				X	X
Document management tools and techniques		X				X	
Elements of a requirements management plan		X				X	
Elicitation tools and techniques			X			X	X
Estimating tools and techniques		X				X	X
Facilitation tools and techniques			X			X	X
Interface analysis			X			X	X
Leadership principles and skills	X	X	X	X	X	X	X
Lessons learned and retrospectives					X	X	X
Measurement tools and techniques		X				X	
Negotiations tools and techniques			X			X	X
Organization assessment				X		X	
Planning tools and techniques		X				X	
Political and cultural awareness	X					X	
Prioritization tools and techniques			X			X	X

Table 10.1 Continued

Techniques	Needs Assessment	Planning	Analysis	Traceability and monitoring	Evaluation	Waterfall	Agile
Problem solving and opportunity identification tools and techniques	X					X	X
Process analysis tools and techniques			X			X	
Project methodologies	X	X	X	X	X	X	X
Quality management		X				X	X
Reporting tools and techniques				X		X	X
Requirements traceability tools and techniques				X		X	X
Requirement types	X	X	X	X	X	X	
Root cause analysis			X			X	X
Scheduling tools and techniques		X				X	
Stakeholder analysis	X					X	
System thinking	X	X	X	X	X	X	
Validation tools and techniques					X	X	X
Valuation tools and techniques	X				X	X	X
Verification tools and techniques					X	X	X
Version control tools and techniques		X				X	X

10.3.1 Project Time Management

Project time management involves prerequisite activities to develop a project schedule, which is described in detail in the knowledge area of project time management. The first step is to *plan schedule management,* which is the strategy used to manage the development of the schedule. The plan schedule management process will develop a schedule management plan, which will set the framework for the schedule. When the schedule foundation is settled, the next step is to define the activities. These activities are found in the domain section and are documented on an activity list. The schedule is developed with an approach called rolling wave planning, adaptive planning, or progressive elaboration, which is defined as *the iterative process of increasing the level of detail in the project management plan as a greater amount of information and more accurate estimates become available.*

After defining the activities, the next order of business is to sequence them. This is where the precedence diagramming method is often developed, with the following sequences being used:

- Finish-to-start
- Finish-to-finish

- Start-to-start
- Start-to-finish

The implication of a finish-to-start sequence is that the preceding activities must be finished before the following activity can start. This is the most commonly used sequence. Part of mapping the dependencies is to analyze the dependencies which include:

- Mandatory
- Discretionary
- External
- Internal

Activities in a sequence may have a lead or lag. Lead is the amount of time whereby a successor activity is required to be delayed with respect to a predecessor activity, while lag is the amount of time whereby a successor activity can be advanced with respect to a predecessor activity. A lead of 2 hours is a 2 hour delay before the next activity can start, while a lag of 2 days means that the successor activity can start 2 days before the predecessor activity. When the sequence of the activities is defined, it can be useful for the business analyst, in collaboration with the project manager, to define the milestones, which are a significant point or event in a project, program, or portfolio. A typical milestone is a test, payment, or delivery. The sequenced activities need to be estimated, and this is covered later in Chapter 10. In the next step of the process, the aim is to develop the schedule, which is mostly achieved by creating a Gantt chart. When the Gantt chart is developed, it is relevant to manage the critical path and chain in order to manage the schedule. The critical path is important as it is the sequence of activities that represents the longest path through a project, based on the shortest possible duration. This means that activities that are delayed on the critical path would delay the overall time of the project. Activities outside the critical path cannot affect the final duration of the project unless the critical path is changed. The critical chain is a scheduling method that allows the project team to place buffers on any project schedule path to account for limited resources and project uncertainties. This implies optimizing the critical path with resource considerations, which may or may not change the critical path. If the critical path is facing delays, the techniques of crashing and fast-tracking may help bring the schedule back on track. *Crashing* is *a technique used to shorten the schedule duration for the least incremental cost by adding resources*, while *fast tracking* is *a schedule compression technique in which activities or phases that are normally done in sequence are performed in parallel for at least a portion of their duration*. Table 10.2 illustrates a cost and quality comparison of the two schedule-compression techniques.

Table 10.2 Crashing versus fast tracking

Techniques	Cost and quality characteristics
Crashing schedule	Involves the increased cost of adding resources to critical-path tasks, focusing on least costly first. Risk exposure is minimal.
Fast-tracking schedule	Involves performing critical-path tasks in parallel, or overlapping of phases, activities, or tasks normally performed in sequence. The risks are not achieving a shortened schedule, rework, and added costs.

Table 10.3 illustrates the complete calculations for crashing as normal noncrash costs and crashing costs are measured.

Table 10.3 Calculations for crashing

Activity	Normal time (in weeks)	Time which it can be crashed	Normal costs	Costs per week crashed	Maximum reduction in time (weeks)	Crash costs per week
A	8	5	$25,000	$37,000	3	$4,000
B	7	2	$30,000	$55,000	5	$5,000
C	10	6	$45,000	$85,000	4	$10,000
D	3	2	$30,000	$34,000	1	$4,000

With the project schedule developed, the project manager with help from the business analyst, needs to control the schedule—which is the process of monitoring the status of project activities to update project progress and manage changes to the schedule baseline to achieve the plan. An excellent technique for controlling the schedule is *earned value management*, which is a methodology that combines scope, schedule, and resource measurements to assess project performance and progress.

10.3.2 Project Risk Management

A *risk* is *an uncertain event or condition that, if it occurs, has a positive or negative effect on one or more project objectives*. In order to manage risks in a systematic approach, the first step is to develop a risk management plan, which is a component of the project, program, or portfolio management plan that describes how risk management activities will be structured and performed. The risk management plan describes how and when all risk management activities are handled. The business analyst must take part in identifying risks. Table 10.4 on the next page illustrates the tools and techniques used for identifying risks.

When risks are identified, they need to be assessed, which involves dividing them into qualitative and quantitative risk assessments. The qualitative risk assessment is the first step and is conducted for all identified risks. Each risk is assessed regarding probability and impact. The probability and impact are mapped in the qualitative assessment with the risk appetite, which is the degree of uncertainty that an entity is willing to take on in anticipation of a reward. This is illustrated in the risk matrix in Table 10.5.

Table 10.5 Risk matrix

	5	GREEN	YELLOW	YELLOW	RED	RED
	4	GREEN	GREEN	YELLOW	YELLOW	RED
Probability	3	GREEN	GREEN	YELLOW	YELLOW	YELLOW
	2	GREEN	GREEN	GREEN	GREEN	YELLOW
	1	GREEN	GREEN	GREEN	GREEN	GREEN
		1	2	3	4	5
				Impacts		

While risks are being identified and assessed, the results are documented in the risk register, which is a document in which the results of risk analysis and risk response planning are recorded. The risk register is an active and ongoing document which is updated and used throughout the project. Table 10.6 illustrates the content of a risk register.

Table 10.4   Identify risk techniques

Technique	Description
Brainstorming	Brainstorming is a group or individual creative technique by which efforts are made to find a conclusion for a specific problem by gathering a list of ideas spontaneously contributed by its member(s)
Brainwriting	A written form of brainstorming where each participant writes one risk on a piece of paper before passing it on
Interviews	One-on-one interview on risk identification
Root cause analysis	Technique used to identify the underlying causes of a problem
Delphi	The original version of the Delphi method was first applied in the 1960s and the concept was to ask a range of experts for an estimate. The experts were not located in the same place and were unable to communicate and influence the other expert estimates
Delphi, wideband	Wideband Delphi is a process that a team can use to generate an estimate. The project manager chooses an estimation team and gains consensus among that team on the results. Wideband Delphi is a repeatable estimation process because it consists of a straightforward set of steps that can be performed the same way each time
SWOT analysis	An analysis of strengths, weaknesses, opportunities, and threats to a project or organization
Pre-mortem	The team imagines that a project has succeeded or failed and then works backward to determine what potentially could have lead to that success or failure
Change of perspective—Edward de Bono: Six Thinking Hats	Sequence of methods for the identification of risks and opportunities: 1. Clarification of the problem 2. Putting on the white hat to collect facts and figures relevant to the topic (Flipchart, Post-its on pin wall) 3. Putting on the black hat, e.g., to identify risks
Document-centric techniques	Investigate documentation for risks, i.e., software requirement documentation, contracts, legacy, and other documentation
Survey techniques	Interviews, qualitative and quantitative surveys
Analogy techniques	The basis of this technique is to describe (in terms of a number of variables) the project for which the risk identification is to be made and then to use this description to find other similar projects that have already been completed
Observation techniques	Field observation and apprenticing
Storyboarding/Prototypes	Build a prototype or create a storyboard from which risk can be derived
Focus groups or facilitation	Structured interview of several participants in a facilitated manner
Artifact risk identification	Risk identification based upon solid artifacts, i.e., former car model or item sold

With risks being identified, qualitatively assessed, and documented, some risks, which have extended our risk tolerance by having a high probability and/or high impact, need to be assessed further with a quantitative assessment. Table 10.7 highlights the differences between qualitative and quantitative risk assessment.

Table 10.6 Risk register

Component	Description of the component	Example of the component
ID	Unique identification of the risk	2
Creator	Who identified the risk	Chris Whiffen
Date	Date of risk identification	2014/05/05
Category	Category from RBS	Business
Description	Wording on the risk	Lack of management buy-in
Risk owner	Responsible for handling the risk	CFO
Probability	Probability of occurrence	High (3)
Impact	Impact of risk	Extreme (5)
Expected monetary value (EMV)	Probability i.e., 10% × Impact of $2,500,000	$250,000
Risk detection	Detection rate	Extreme (5)
Risk matrix	The qualitative assessment	Risk matrix
Risk score of P × I × D	The sum of probability, impact, and detection	75
Proximity	Time of occurrence	Within the next 14 days
Triggers	What initiates a response	Extraordinary board meeting
Response category	Risk strategies	Transfer
Action/contingency	Action based upon our strategy	Meet with CEO
Residual rating	Exposure to loss after mitigation	24
Actionee	Who will take action	Scott Nelson
Status	Open or closed	Open
Last reviewed	Date of last review	2015/06/06
Next reviewed	Date for next review	2015/07/07

Table 10.7 Qualitative and quantitative risk analysis

Qualitative risk analysis	Quantitative risk analysis
Addresses individual risks descriptively	Predicts likely business case outcomes based on combined effects of risks
Assesses the discrete probability of occurrence and impact on objectives if it does occur	Uses probability distributions to characterize the risk's probability and impact
Prioritizes individual risks for subsequent treatment	Uses a quantitative method, requires specialized tools
Adds to risk register	Identifies risks with the greatest effect on overall business case risks
Leads to quantitative risk analysis	Estimates likelihood of meeting targets and contingencies needed to achieve desired level of comfort

The quantitative risk assessment includes a wide range of tools and techniques, which to some degree may require slightly more knowledge and additional tool support. The typical quantitative risk assessment techniques are:

- Sensitivity analysis
- Spider plot
- Tornado diagram
- Analytical hierarchy process
- Decision trees
- Monte Carlo analysis
- Probability trees and charts
- Waterfall chart
- Assumptions analysis
- Influence diagram
- Fault tree
- Path convergence
- Force field
- Latin Hypercube
- Multipoint probability analysis

When all risks have been assessed, the project manager, with the involvement of the business analyst, needs to decide upon the risk response. Some risks are negative, thus we aim to avoid or reduce their probability and impact; while others are positive, and we seek to ensure their occurrence or increase their probability and impact. The risk responses are illustrated in Table 10.8.

Table 10.8 Positive and negative risk responses

Risk responses	
Negative	**Positive**
Avoid	Exploitation
Transfer	Sharing
Mitigate	Enhancing
Acceptance	Acceptance

The risk responses are part of the risk register which is updated regularly.

Relating PMI-PBA Practices to *PMBOK® Guide—Fifth Edition* Practices

The analytic tools and techniques can be found in the knowledge area of project time management and project risk management in the *PMBOK® Guide—Fifth Edition*.

Relating PMI-PBA Practices to Agile Practices

When working with agile methodologies, the analytic tools and techniques regarding planning or scheduling and risk management are fairly different from the plan-based approach and are introduced in this section.

Scheduling

We plan to "reduce risks, reduce uncertainties, support better decision making, establish trust and for conveying information" (Cohn, 2011). Even though agile projects concentrate more on execution than planning, projects need to follow the basic process required to execute an agile project. This minimal planning process consists of developing the course of action necessary to attain the product, the release, and the iterative cycle objectives. Agile planning varies from traditional planning as it has more focus on the planning process than the actual plan. The agile plans encourage change; they are easy to modify, and planning is spread throughout the project (Cohn, 2011).

Multiple Levels of Planning

Agile planning begins on a strategic level (Levels 1 and 2: product vision and product roadmap), where focus is on the portfolio and product. The time frame for this part of the planning may consist of many months. The planning for the next 2–3 months includes the team members involved at the tactical level in the release planning. The release planning (Level 3) is planned in greater detail with the operative iteration or sprint (Level 4). Sprint plans cover 2–4 weeks. Finally, plans are broken down into daily sections (Level 5).

Risk Management

Risk management is one of those areas where traditional and agile project management may clash, have some variations in practices, or be even more similar than expected. However, while there is an extensive body of academic literature on traditional risk management, very little research has attempted to rigorously apply this as a lens to study risk management in agile development projects (Coyle et al., 2009).

Risk management involves ongoing activities and it is an important responsibility of the agile project team to identify all potential risks. Risks are events or actions that affect the project positively or negatively. In agile projects, the management of risk happens vigorously and continuously through daily stand-up meetings, retrospectives, Scrum planning meetings, and release planning meetings. Agile projects are business-value-driven and risk-driven. Thus, the product backlog items are not only prioritized based on value and cost, but also on risks.

Before going into details, we need to understand the level of uncertainty we are facing. Most projects face the *fuzzy front end* with a high level of uncertainty early on. The level of uncertainty diminishes, in time, as planning and execution proceeds. We need risk management to deal with the initial high level of uncertainty, or the project could be taking huge risks.

The traditional process starts in the planning phase where decisions are made and documented as to what level and kind of risk the organization is willing to assume or not, and to define how risk management will be performed. The next process is to identify positive and negative risks for the projects. The risks identified in the risk register are then prioritized by probability and impact in a qualitative risk assessment. Some risks will need to be investigated further as they go past our tolerances leading to the quantitative risk assessment process. We then plan risk responses on all quantitatively assessed risks.

The last process includes the monitoring and controlling of risks, which are the ongoing activities of risk management.

The agile risk management process is similar, but terminology and processes are quite different. The agile process has an *identify* process followed by an *assess* phase. *Respond* and *review* are the last two agile processes for risk management. The review phase may be new to traditional project managers, but otherwise we see a fairly similar process of identifying, assessing, and responding to risks.

The traditional plan for risk management has a process that helps to decide how to approach and plan the risk management activities for a project. This is not part of the agile risk management process, yet we still have the primary objective of enabling the team to meet their long-term commitments. In agile, the team is asked to determine the appropriate risk management approach and can result in a less formal process.

Both traditional and agile projects have processes to identify risks in order to determine which "risks are likely to effects the project, and documents the characteristics of each risk. Here the effect includes both the positive effects and negative effects" (Chandramouli et al., 2012). This process is started early on—no later than the planning phase. Identification of risks takes place continuously throughout the project. In agile, the daily stand-up meetings identify continual risks. All project personnel, including customers, should be encouraged to identify risks.

When risks have been identified, they need to be categorized in order to get an overview that high-lights areas where there may be a few or many identified risks. This categorization of risks can be conducted with a risk breakdown structure that is similar in format to the work breakdown structure. Once the risks have been identified, we need to make some assessment on how to proceed with risk management. In traditional project management, this is done by performing a qualitative risk analysis. All risks are assessed in terms of probability and impact.

Some agile practitioners have a similar process where they use qualitative risk analysis. This analysis uses probability impact analysis to prioritize the risks, and the risk register is informally documented using a sprint risk tracker. The result of this process can be documented on the agile risk board, which rates probability and impacts from high to low or from 1 to 5. It offers a good view of the identified risks for all team members. The process in agile can also be conducted on user stories where each story has an impact and probability of high, medium, or low.

Performing quantitative risk assessment is a traditional process, often supported by calculations and simulations such as sensitivity analysis, Monte Carlo simulations, failure mode effect analysis, affinity diagrams, and decision trees. This process of risk assessment is conducted in agile with risk-based spikes.

The agile assess phase is now complete. Next, the agile team needs to consider the respond phase, which corresponds to the planning of risk responses in traditional project management. The respond phase describes how we plan to handle the risk. Common tools and techniques within most frameworks are the same as Michele Sliger and Stacy Broderick mentioned in their book *The Software Project Manager's Bridge to Agility* (2008), which portrays a slightly different view on risk response planning (see Tables 10.9 and 10.10). The terms are fairly similar, but we see major changes in the process.

Table 10.9 Risk mitigation strategies

Traditional	Agile
One or more people are assigned to develop strategies to…	The team brainstorms strategies to…
Avoid	Avoid
Mitigate	Mitigate
Plan contingency	Contain
Accept	Evade

Table 10.10 Additional risk management activities in meetings (*X* means that it should be done every time; *P* means possible, if needed)

Agile processes	Identify	Assess	Respond	Respond	Respond	Review
Risk management in meetings	Identification	Assessment	Create response	Apply response	Risk approval	
Sprint planning	X	X	X			
Daily Scrum	P	P	P			
Sprint review	P	P	P			
Sprint retrospective					X	X

Exercise 10.1—Match the Key Words to Their Definitions: Match the following business analysis key words to their definitions. You will find the key words in Table 10.11 and their definitions in Table 10.12 on the next page. You can use Table 10.13 to record your answers and determine your score. You will find the correct answers in Table 10.14 on page 196.

Table 10.11 Key words

No.	Key words
1	Crashing
2	Risk
3	Progressive elaboration
4	Control schedule
5	Critical path
6	Earned value management
7	Lag
8	Risk register
9	Fast tracking
10	Milestones
11	Risk appetite
12	Critical chain
13	Lead
14	Risk management plan

Table 10.13 Answer and score sheet

Number of key word	Letter of definition
1	
2	
3	
4	
5	
6	
7	
8	
9	
10	
11	
12	
13	
14	

Table 10.12   Definitions

Letter	Definitions
A	A significant point or event in a project, program, or portfolio.
B	A methodology that combines scope, schedule, and resource measurements to assess project performance and progress.
C	The iterative process of increasing the level of detail in the project management plan as greater amounts of information and more accurate estimates become available.
D	A component of the project, program, or portfolio management plan that describes how risk management activities will be structured and performed.
E	The amount of time whereby a successor activity can be advanced with respect to a predecessor activity.
F	A technique used to shorten the schedule duration for the least incremental cost by adding resources.
G	The process of monitoring the status of project activities to update project progress and manage changes to the schedule baseline to achieve the plan.
H	The amount of time whereby a successor activity is required to be delayed with respect to a predecessor activity.
I	The degree of uncertainty an entity is willing to take on in anticipation of a reward.
J	A scheduling method that allows the project team to place buffers on any project schedule path to account for limited resources and project uncertainties.
K	A schedule compression technique in which activities or phases normally done in sequence are performed in parallel for at least a portion of their duration.
L	An uncertain event or condition that, if it occurs, has a positive or negative effect on one or more project objectives.
M	The sequence of activities that represent the longest part through a project, which determines the shortest possible duration.
N	A document in which the results of risk analysis and risk response planning are recorded.

When you have finished reading this chapter, you can refer back to this exercise and test your knowledge again.

Table 10.14 Correct answers

Key words	Definitions
1	F
2	L
3	C
4	G
5	M
6	B
7	E
8	N
9	K
10	A
11	I
12	J
13	H
14	D

10.4 BACKLOG MANAGEMENT

Technique	Needs Assessment	Planning	Analysis	Traceability and Monitoring	Evaluation	Waterfall	Agile
Backlog management				X			X

The origins of Scrum as an agile methodology are found in writings by Takeuchi and Nonaka (Sutherland et. al., 2006). In rugby, a scrum refers to the manner of restarting the game after a minor infraction where players work together to achieve possession of the ball. In 2001, Ken Schwaber and Mike Beedle wrote the book *Agile Software Development with Scrum*, which many consider the official start of Scrum as we know it today.

Roles play a major part in Scrum. The three key roles are the product owner, development team or team member, and the Scrum Master, as illustrated in Table 10.15.

A product owner creates a prioritized wish list called a product backlog. During sprint planning the team pulls a small chunk from the top of that wish list, a sprint backlog, and decides how to implement those pieces. The team has a certain amount of time—a sprint—to complete its work (usually two to four weeks), but meets each day to assess its progress (daily Scrum). Along the way, the Scrum Master keeps the team focused on its goal. At the end of the sprint the work should be potentially shippable as in; ready to hand to a customer, put on a store shelf, or show to a stakeholder. The sprint ends with a sprint review and retrospective. As the next sprint begins, the team chooses another chunk of the product backlog and begins working again.

Table 10.15   Scrum roles

Role	Description
The product owner	Maximizes the value of the product
	Represents the stakeholders
	Voice of the customer
	Communicates the vision
	Prioritizes the product backlog
	Responsible for the outcome
Development team/ team member	Delivers the product
	Self-organizing
	Determines how it will accomplish the work
Scrum Master	Liaison between the product owner and the team
	Advises the product owner
	Supports the development team
	Enforcer of rules and processes

Overall, backlog management is the managing of the requirement specification, which in Scrum is called a *backlog*, defined by PMI as "a listing of product requirement and deliverables to be completed, written as stories, and prioritized by the business to manage and organize the project's work." However, in Scrum, the backlog consists of a product backlog and a sprint backlog. The product backlog is the prioritized list of all the features and changes that have yet to be made to the system as desired by multiple actors, such as customers, marketing and sales, and the project team. The product backlog is the full list of requirements—called user stories in agile methodology. For each sprint a number of user stories are selected for development. These are then placed in the sprint backlog, which is the list of features that is currently assigned to a particular sprint. When all the features are completed, a new iteration of the system is delivered. This means that the sprint backlog is a sub-list of the product backlog.

Relating PMI-PBA Practices to *PMBOK® Guide—Fifth Edition* Practices

Backlog management is not relevant for plan-based projects unless mixed methods are used.

Exercise 10.2—Match the Key Words to Their Definitions: Match the business analysis key words to their definitions. You will find the key words in Table 10.16 and the definitions in Table 10.17. You can use Table 10.18 to record your answers and determine your score. You will find the correct answers in Table 10.19 on page 200.

When you have finished reading this chapter, you can refer back to this exercise and test your knowledge again.

Table 10.16 Key words

No.	Key words
1	Product backlog
2	Risk-adjusted backlog
3	Sprint backlog
4	Product roadmap
5	Backlog
6	Risk-based spikes
7	Product vision statement

Table 10.18 Answer and score sheet

Number of key word	Letter of definition
1	
2	
3	
4	
5	
6	
7	

Table 10.17 Definitions

Letter	Definitions
A	An elevator statement for the product, describing what it is, who would need it, the key reasons someone would pay for it, and what differentiates it in the market.
B	An overview that shows an overall plan with each planned release and the relevant features associated with those releases.
C	The prioritized list of all features and changes that have yet to be made to the system desired by multiple actors, such as customers, marketing and sales, and the project team.
D	Value-generating business features and risk-reduction actions.
E	The list of features currently assigned to a particular sprint. When all the features are completed, a new iteration of the system is delivered.
F	A listing of product requirement and deliverables to be completed, written as stories, and prioritized by the business to manage and organize the project's work.
G	A quick proof of concept used to help the team answer a question and determine a path forward. Can be used to get to failure quickly and then take a different approach.

10.5 BUSINESS RULE ANALYSIS TOOLS AND TECHNIQUES

Technique	Needs Assessment	Planning	Analysis	Traceability and Monitoring	Evaluation	Waterfall	Agile
Business rule analysis tools and techniques			X			X	X

The development of an information technology (IT) system consists of complex logic. The business rule analysis technique is used to define the rules that govern decisions in an organization and that define, constrain, or enable organizational operations. The business rule analysis is expressed as a decision table or decision tree, which are two techniques for representing what the system should do when complex logic and decisions come into play. Furthermore, the decision table or decision tree is an excellent way of documenting requirement and business rules, and helps to avoid overlooking any combinations of conditions.

The decision table is an excellent tool to use in both testing and requirements management. Essentially, it is a structured exercise to formulate requirements when dealing with complex business rules. It detects combinations that are sometimes not found otherwise. However, it is not a complete test case—although test cases can be based upon the decision table. When working with decision tables, automated tools are often employed. Table 10.20 illustrates the look and feel of a decision table.

Table 10.20 Decision table analysis

	Requirement 1	Requirement 2	Requirement 3
Condition			
Withdraw account	True	False	False
Credit granted		True	False
Actions			
Withdraw granted	True	False	False

Decision tree analysis is defined by PMI as "a diagramming and calculation technique for evaluating the implications of the chain of multiple options in the presence of uncertainty." One application for business rule analysis is illustrated in Figure 10.1.

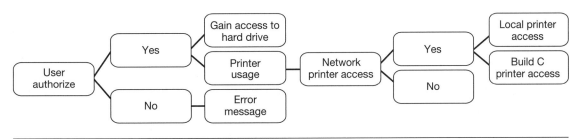

Figure 10.1   Decision tree analysis

Table 10.19 Correct answers

Key words	Definitions
1	C
2	D
3	E
4	B
5	F
6	G
7	A

The decision tree is also used as a decision support tool in quantitative risk analysis and modeling that uses a graph or model of decisions and their possible consequences—including chance event outcomes, resource costs, and utility. Figure 10.2 illustrates the risk analysis application of the decision tree analysis.

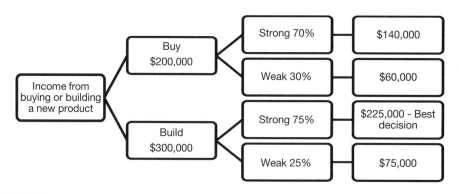

Figure 10.2 Decision tree analysis for risk

Exercise 10.3—Draw a Decision Tree: A Johannesburg farmer needs to make a decision. His orchard is expected to produce 200,000 bushels of peaches that he wishes to sell to a large grocery chain at $50 per bushel as *Grade A* peaches. However, he has great concern about the possibility of early frost damaging his crop. For three of the past five years, the western part of the state where this farmer lives has suffered severe frost. The Department of Agriculture's figures show that the probability of early frost in the orchard area in any given year is 30%. If his crop is damaged, it would not be marketable as fresh fruit, and he would have to sell it to a cannery in Johannesburg for $10 per bushel. He could purchase insurance which would ensure that if his peaches were damaged, he could sell the total crop (both damaged and good fruit) to the insurance company for $25 per bushel. The cost of the insurance would be

$200,000. What are the monetary expectations of the farmer's decision to purchase or to not purchase insurance? (The answer is found on page 271.)

Business rule analysis tools and techniques are mostly used in plan-based projects and in some *PMBOK® Guide—Fifth Edition* practices, but they work well in an agile setting also.

10.6 CHANGE CONTROL TOOLS AND TECHNIQUES

Technique	Needs Assessment	Planning	Analysis	Traceability and Monitoring	Evaluation	Waterfall	Agile
Change control tools and techniques				X		X	X

Change control tools and techniques were already covered in detail in Chapter 6. However, now the emphasis is on the impact analysis and the agile methodologies approach to change control. The impact analysis was highlighted in the analysis knowledge and skills section, but was not covered in detail there. The impact analysis, change impact analysis, solution effect analysis, or software impact analysis has been used for change control since the 1980s. Before going into details, let us recap the change control process in Table 10.21, which is altered based upon Li et al., (2012).

Table 10.21   Change control

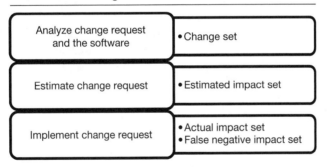

The change control process and in particular, the impact analysis, is a technique designed to unearth the *unexpected* negative effects of a change on an organization, which makes it a key aspect of responsible requirements management. The purpose of the impact analysis is to capture and structure the change in order to control and manage it. This implies understanding the comprehensive consequences of implementing a change and the consequences for the solution. Change control is handling of the change before it is implemented, while change management deals with the consequences after the change has been implemented.

Business Analysis for Practitioners (2015) has identified change control as a collaboration point where the business analyst and project manager should work together to ensure stakeholder needs are met when defining the change control process.

Software change impact analysis involves a collection of techniques for determining the effects of the proposed changes on other parts of the software, and is defined by Arnold and Bohner (1996) as "identifying the potential consequences of a change, or estimating what needs to be modified to accomplish a change." A change made to a software system may result in an undesirable side effect and/or ripple effect. The goal of change impact analysis is to identify the ripple effects and prevent side effects of a proposed change. This requires understanding of traceability, dependency, and the experiential aspects.

The common steps in an impact analysis are as follows:

- Understand the implications (constrains, meaning, and relations)
- Identify all files and documents to be changed
- Identify the activities needed to conduct the change

The impact analysis is often followed by a checklist; for example, when identifying conflicts with existing requirements in order to ensure all implications and activities are covered. These steps are often supplemented with a brainstorming technique. This ensures that all aspects are identified and the results are documented in a cause and effect, Fishbone diagram, or Ishikawa diagram during the *do* phase in the plan-do-check-act (PDCA) cycle. The impact analysis overlaps several other project documents for updates; these being the risk register for the risk assessment, the stakeholder register, and the business case for measuring the constraints and financial measurements. Furthermore, the aspects of impact analysis and change control highlight the importance of traceability, the possible use of a change log, the need for documentation, the use of communication or collaboration tools, and automated software.

With agile methodologies the impact analysis is actually conducted in a similar fashion by the development team. In terms of change control, a formal process with the use of a change control board can also be applied in an agile setting with inclusion of the Scrum roles—product owner, Scrum Master, and development team. However, most changes are controlled on a regular basis in the product backlog and day-to-day in the sprint backlog. Change control in agile methodologies is closely tied to the five levels of planning as changes can be handled at all levels of planning, including change of vision, change of the product roadmap, change in the release planning, change in the sprint backlog, or change in the day-to-day planning. The agile methodologies embrace change and are, in general, much faster and more effective than traditional methods to analyze and adopt these changes.

Exercise 10.4—Turn to Your Neighbor: If you are using this book in a study group or have a study buddy, discuss 2-3 main points you took away from this section.

10.7 COLLABORATION TOOLS AND TECHNIQUES

Technique	Needs Assessment	Planning	Analysis	Traceability and Monitoring	Evaluation	Waterfall	Agile
Collaboration tools and techniques		X				X	X

The choice of collaboration tools and techniques depends mostly upon who is collaborating and whether or not they work at the same location. Collaboration is basically two or more people working together toward a common goal. But in their search for global markets, global talents, and reduced costs, more and more firms are fragmenting geographically, causing difficulties in collaborating within a global environment. This implies a move from collocated teams to more distributed teams which is a challenge for the collaboration. This is what we seek to reduce by the means of tools and techniques.

In the 2008 State of Agile Development survey conducted by Version One, 57% of the respondents stated that their teams were distributed. Furthermore, 41% of the respondents said that they were currently using or planning to combine agile with outsourced development.

Collaboration and communication have close ties because being distributed hinders communication, which is what we seek to reduce with these tools and techniques. In general, face-to-face communication is the most effective form for communication. Furthermore, most teams use an information radiator, which is the generic term for any of a number of handwritten, drawn, printed, or electronic displays that a team places in a highly visible location so that all team members as well as passers-by can see. While writing, reading, typing, or talking, we pick up traces of the ongoing sounds around us, using some background listening mode, even though we are not consciously paying attention—this is osmotic communication. Being collocated, osmotic communication and information radiators are great tools for collaboration. Collaboration benefits from team-based tools and techniques while being collocated. Brainstorming and planning poker are fine tools and techniques for collaboration for estimating and during the daily standup in collocated workplaces while supporting facilitation and consensus seeking. Choosing the right collaboration tools and techniques also depends on whether the communication is synchronous or asynchronous. Figure 10.3 illustrates this.

Sync	Async
In-person	E-mail
Video/screen share	Twitter
Voice call	Facebook
Group chat, virtual worlds, webinars	Wiki technologies, blogs, Linkedin, Google Docs

Figure 10.3 Asynchronous or synchronous communication

Whether the team is collocated or distributed, the amount of collaboration tools and supporting techniques are increasing due to the technological possibilities—as several of the collaboration tools we use at home can also be applied at work. Some of the most common online collaboration tools are:

- Wiki technologies
- Live video conferencing
- Group chat, virtual worlds, webinars, blogs, feeds, LinkedIn
- Twitter, Facebook, Skype, instant messaging, voice call, in-person
- E-mail
- Online document sharing via Google Docs
- Tools to structure, present, visualize, and simulate
- Communication, office, and project management tools

- Modeling tools
- Requirements management tools

Other factors that affect the choice of communication and collaboration technologies are:

- Urgency
- Availability
- Ease of use
- Project environment
- Sensitivity and confidentiality of the information

The use of collaboration tools and techniques may be further complicated if we include the stakeholders. Table 10.22 illustrates the collaboration strategy, which along with the communication management plan also needs to consider the collaboration tools and techniques to apply, depending on the stakeholders and their needs and expectations.

Table 10.22 Collaboration strategy

Planning ability	High	Mitigate concerns	Close collaborations
	Low	Minimal effort	Involve and secure
		Low	High
		Active involvement	

Exercise 10.5—In-Sync Collaboration: Your team has focused on synchronous communication. Which of the following techniques would the team most likely apply? (The answer is found on page 271.)

1. Facebook
2. Google docs
3. Voice calls
4. In-person meetings

10.8 COMMUNICATION SKILLS

Technique	Needs Assessment	Planning	Analysis	Traceability and Monitoring	Evaluation	Waterfall	Agile
Communication skills				X		X	X

Project management and requirements management communication is about knowing how to convey the right message. The impact of the message depends on the right channel which emphasizes the need to tailor the communication. PMI's *2013 Pulse of the Profession®* highlights how effective communications leads to projects that are more successful. Furthermore, the effective communicator is five times more likely to be high in performance as compared to a less effective communicator. This can all be combined with the fact that more than 90% of a traditional project manager's time is spent on communication. The business analyst communicates all the time, whether asking for information, conducting an interview, planning with the team, asking the virtual team for a status update, and so forth.

It is important to tailor the communication to each team member or stakeholder according to the content of the message. The dimensions of project communication may vary as illustrated in Table 10.23.

Table 10.23   The dimensions of project communication

Internal	External
Formal	Informal
Vertical	Horizontal
Official	Unofficial
Written	Oral
Verbal	Nonverbal

The dimensions of project communication can be combined in a number of ways—it may be a formal, written, official, external communication; it could be a letter to a vendor; or it may be an internal, informal, unofficial oral message to a colleague at the coffee machine where you ask them about where to find the printer.

When communicating, the typical communication model contain the following factors:

- Encode
- Transmit message
- Decode
- Acknowledge
- Feedback/response

The sender encodes the message, which is transmitted to the receiver who decodes the message and acknowledges the understanding with feedback in the form of a nod or reply.

The dimensions of project communication include verbal and nonverbal communication. Most people are aware of verbal communication, however, a communication model developed by Professor Albert Mehrabian in 1981 highlights the importance of nonverbal communication. Mehrabian's findings are typically cited or applied as:

- 7% of a message pertaining to feelings and attitudes is in the words that are spoken.
- 38% of a message pertaining to feelings and attitudes is paralinguistic (the way that the words are said).
- 55% of a message pertaining to feelings and attitudes is in the facial expression.

This implies that only 7% of the message is the actual word, while the way the words are said and facial expressions are 93% of the communication.

We will introduce a range of communication methods including interactive, push, and pull, which works in different settings and types of communication. The business analyst and project manager communicate by using all of the types. Effective communication and tailoring of the communication depends upon a range of factors such as:

- Sender-receiver model
- Choice of media
- Writing style (technical writing, business writing)
- Meeting management techniques
- Presentation techniques
- Facilitating techniques
- Questions (open-ended, closed-ended, contextual, and context-free)
- Listening techniques

For instance, perhaps you are doing a presentation for the CEO; the style and content may be more formal which is also dependent upon the corporate culture. While taking part in an online session, you may require more listening techniques.

Exercise 10.6—Try This Presentation Technique: PechaKucha (2014) introduced a simple 20x20 format for slideshow presentations, where you present 20 slides, using 20 seconds per slide. The slides are changing automatically as you speak. Every presentation lasts for 6 minutes and 40 seconds.

Not all kinds of communications have the same effectiveness. A study by Cockburn (2001) clearly illustrates the importance of communication by two people on a whiteboard. This is the most effective communication compared to writing a message on a piece of paper. Figure 10.4 illustrates the effectiveness of communication.

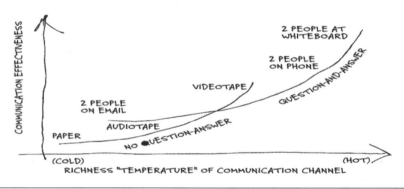

Figure 10.4   Effectiveness of communication—adapted from Cockburn

This stresses the need for the team to be collocated and to find a means to reduce the hindrance of not being in the same room at the same time. Previously, we discussed distributed teams as being one of the challenges in communication, along with the ways in which we can overcome this challenge by the use of collaboration tools and techniques. However, several other barriers to communication also exist that the business analyst needs to take into consideration when tailoring the communication. Some of these are:

- Lack of clear communication channels
- Physical or temporal distance
- Difficulties with technical language
- Distracting environmental factors
- Detrimental attitudes

One-on-one communication has its challenges. Often the business analyst communicates with a range of stakeholders which calls for the use of several types of communication. This is illustrated by the formula for measuring the amount of communication channels needed—$N(N-1)/2$—with N being the *number of stakeholders*. Using 10 as the number of stakeholders would result in 45 communication channels $[10(10-1)/2]$. Reducing the amount of stakeholders to 5 would reduce the amount of communication channels from 45 to 10, which demonstrates the increased complication factor regarding communication with an increase in the number of communication channels.

A central foundation to working with agile is the Agile Software Development Manifesto, which was developed with the purpose of uncovering better ways of developing software. The Agile Software Development Manifesto contains four statements where the left sides of the statements are valued higher than the right sides of the statements. This does not mean that the right sides of the statements are not important; it is just a way of prioritization.

- Individuals and interactions *over* processes and tools
- Working software *over* comprehensive documentation
- Customer collaboration *over* contract negotiation
- Responding to change *over* following a plan

The first statement, *individuals and interactions over processes and tools*, and the third statement, *customer collaboration over contract negotiation*, emphasize the importance of communication in agile methodologies. Whether it is communication within the development team or with the Scrum Master or product owner, the communication is supported by the range of practices which foster communication. These practices may be empowered self-managed teams, daily stand-ups, estimating by playing planning poker, retrospective for lessons learned, and so forth. Overall, the emphasis and need for communication is put in the forefront. This also means that communication skills are especially important when working with agile methodologies.

10.9 CONFLICT MANAGEMENT AND RESOLUTION TOOLS AND TECHNIQUES

Technique	Needs Assessment	Planning	Analysis	Traceability and Monitoring	Evaluation	Waterfall	Agile
Conflict management and resolution tools and techniques				X		X	X

Conflicts are normal and can happen in all requirement and project activities. Conflicts arise from differences that may include values, ideas, motivation, perceptions, desires, or something trivial. We are working closely together with team members from different cultures—and often under pressure. A part of our activities involves negotiations with team members, stakeholders, or vendors over a range of issues. When working in agile, team performances are very visible, and team participation is highly needed. Overall, there are many factors for a conflict and the application of conflict management is needed, which is defined as *handling, controlling, and guiding a conflicting situation to achieve a resolution*.

The steps in conflict management may involve the following activities:

- Conflict identification
- Conflict analysis (who, what, why, when)
- Conflict resolution

The first step is to identify the conflict as it is not always obvious. Often it is difficult to decide whether there is a conflict or not. In most circumstances, conflicts exist but at a fairly low level. When the conflict has been identified, it should be analyzed, which means understanding all the Ws. Who is having a conflict? What is the conflict about? Why and when did it start? What has been done so far? Conflicts may arise for a variety of reasons; some being based on interests, personal issues, values, or just pure happenstance. The last step is conflict resolution—where a mediator or manager tries to solve the conflict with a resolution. Before examining the techniques for solving the conflict, the factors that may influence the conflict resolution methods include:

- Importance
- Time pressure
- Positions taken
- Motivation to resolve conflict

One conflict resolution technique is called *consider-all-facts* (CAF) which examines all the facts, and then a decision matrix is often used to calculate the facts by being irrelevant (0 points) or relevant (10 points). By doing so, agreements can be conducted in terms of possible solutions that best suit the situation. Table 10.24 illustrates this.

Table 10.24   Consider-all-facts decision matrix

	Solution 1	Solution 2
Criterion 1	5	10
Criterion 2	0	5
Sum	5	15

Similar to CAF, the plus-minus-interesting technique (see Table 10.25) measures proposed action pluses (benefits of it), minuses (potential problems), and interesting points that could come from it. Each listed item is assigned a value such as +5 Extremely Favorable, +4 Very Favorable, + 3 Favorable, + 2 Somewhat Favorable, and +1 Slightly Favorable for pluses; -5 Extremely Unfavorable and so forth for minuses; with interesting points being pluses, minuses, or neutral. Sum the three scores to reach a decision.

Table 10.25   Plus-minus-interesting decision matrix

Question: Should we try to reach new and existing customers with direct mail to increase sales in this digital age?					
Pluses	**Rating**	**Minuses**	**Rating**	**Interesting**	**Rating**
Reasonably effective	+3	Very expensive	-5	Digital cheaper, but less effective	-2
Produces inbound volume sales, longer shelf life	+5	Insufficiently trained or inexperienced staff	-3	Status quo is likely to improve if training or coaching is focused on	+5
Rating Total = +3	+8		-8		+3

The Thomas-Kilmann conflict mode and the five general techniques for solving conflicts are fairly similar. The five general conflict resolution techniques are:

- Avoid/withdraw
- Accommodate/smooth
- Compromise/reconcile
- Compete (force/direct)
- Collaborate/problem solve

Exercise 10.7—Five Conflict Management Styles (Adkins, 2006): Read the following statements in Table 10.26 and rate each statement on a scale of 1 to 4—where 1 means rarely, 2 means sometimes, 3 means often, and 4 means always—indicating how likely you are to use the strategy listed in the right hand column. Be sure to answer the questions indicating how you *would* behave rather than how you think you *should* behave.

Table 10.26   Conflict management styles

No.	Question	Answer	Strategy
1	I explore issues with others so as to find solutions that meets everyone's needs		Collaborating
2	I try to negotiate and adopt a give-and-take approach to problem situations		Compromising
3	I try to meet the expectations of others		Accommodating
4	I would argue my case and insist on the merits of my point of view		Competing
5	When there is a disagreement, I gather as much information as I can and keep the lines of communication open		Collaborating
6	When I find myself in an argument, I usually say very little and try to leave as soon as possible		Avoiding
7	I try to see conflicts from both sides. What do I need? What does the other person need? What are the issues involved?		Collaborating
8	I prefer to compromise when solving problems and just move on		Compromising
9	I find conflicts challenging and exhilarating; I enjoy the battle of wits that usually follows		Competing
10	Being at odds with other people makes me feel uncomfortable and anxious		Avoiding
11	I try to accommodate the wishes of my friends and family		Accommodating
12	I can figure out what needs to be done and I am usually right		Competing
13	To break deadlocks, I would meet people halfway		Compromising
14	I may not get what I want but it's a small price to pay for keeping the peace		Accommodating
15	I avoid hard feelings by keeping my disagreements with others to myself		Avoiding

The Thomas-Kilmann conflict mode takes the five general techniques and maps them on two dimensions: (1) assertiveness—the extent to which the person attempts to satisfy his own concerns, and (2) cooperativeness—the extent to which the person attempts to satisfy the other person's concerns. Figure 10.5 illustrates the Thomas-Kilmann conflict mode.

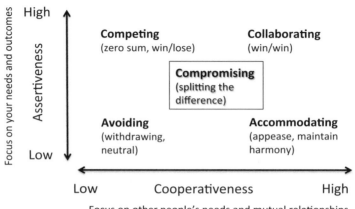

Figure 10.5   The Thomas-Kilmann conflict mode

By *avoiding*, people do not attempt to satisfy their own or others' concerns, while *collaborating* means a win-win situation might be reached as all parties seek to satisfy their own and others' concerns.

The book *Coaching Agile Teams* (2010) by Lyssa Adkins is popular in agile circles for conflict resolution and contains Table 10.27 with its five levels. The idea is that conflicts arise at Level 1 and may escalate if not handled with a conflict resolution process. Some conflicts may skyrocket to Level 5 in no time, while other conflicts may remain on Level 1 for a long time.

Table 10.27   Conflict resolution

Level 1	The lowest level of conflict is Level 1, *Problem to Solve*, which we all know. Information sharing and collaboration takes place as language is open and fact based. The way to deal with these kinds of regular conflicts is through collaboration by seeking consensus and the win-win situation.
Level 2	Conflicts may worsen or start at Level 2, *Disagreement*, where personal protection trumps collaboration, and language is guarded and open to interpretation. The situation may be handled by giving the participants needed support and ensuring the empowerment of the participants to find a good solution without fearing for their safety. We need a cool, calm environment.
Level 3	Things may turn worse with a Level 3, *Contest Conflict*, where winning trumps resolving the issue. Language may include personal attacks. In this situation we need to accommodate and accept the other party's demands and hopefully end the conflict with a negotiation.
Level 4	Level 4, *Crusade*, is really bad. Protecting one's own group becomes the focus, and language is ideological. It is us or them. Winning is the only option. A safe environment must be created to allow time and hopefully some subtle diplomacy to figure out a solution to the conflict.
Level 5	Finally, Level 5, *World War*, is when talks stop and the parties simply seek to destroy each other. We should do whatever is necessary to solve this conflict before someone gets hurt badly. Desperate measures may be needed and often outside help is employed.

In an agile project context, the conflict resolution techniques aim to reach an agreement on a course of action to solve a conflict through voting by team members to reach a solution to a problem based on the conflict analysis. The need for documentation is emphasized even though many people may prefer to forget the conflict. Conflicts may repeat themselves or inappropriate conflict resolution may have taken place in the past, which emphasizes the need for documentation.

The Conflict Resolution Network (2014) has identified 12 conflict resolution skills and techniques that can be easily applied (see Table 10.28).

Table 10.28 12 Conflict resolution skills

The win/win approach	How can we solve this as partners rather than opponents?
Creative response	Transform problems into creative opportunities.
Empathy	Develop communication tools to build rapport. Use listening to clarify understanding.
Appropriate assertiveness	Apply strategies to attack the problem, not the person.
Cooperative power	Eliminate *power over* to build *power with* others.
Managing emotions	Express fear, anger, hurt, and frustration wisely to effect change.
Willingness to resolve	Name personal issues that cloud the picture.
Mapping the conflict	Define the issues needed to chart common needs and concerns.
Development of options	Design creative solutions together.
Introduction to negotiation	Plan and apply effective strategies to reach agreement.
Introduction to mediation	Help conflicting parties to move toward solutions.
Broadening perspectives	Investigate ways to run meetings in conflict resolution mode.

Conflict resolution is highlighted as an important factor of emotional intelligence that more and more teams foster in order to improve teamwork. In this context, communication, active listening, negotiation skills, and soft skills all play an important part.

The need for conflict resolution is highlighted in agile methodologies as teams are self-governed and empowered. This means that the teams should solve their own conflicts, and that, in turn, requires conflict resolution competency within the team.

10.10 CONTINGENCY PLANNING

Technique	Needs Assessment	Planning	Analysis	Traceability and Monitoring	Evaluation	Waterfall	Agile
Contingency planning		X				X	X

The world of projects and requirements are filled with risks and uncertainties, which we aim to reduce by the means of contingency planning. A *contingency* is *an event or occurrence that could affect the execution of the project that may be accounted for with a reserve.* Contingency planning is part of the risk management plan as illustrated in the *PMBOK® Guide—Fifth Edition* Process 11.5 *Plan risk responses*, which is illustrated in Table 10.29.

Table 10.29 Process 11.5 Plan risk responses

Inputs	Tools and Techniques	Output
• Risk management plan • Risk register	• Strategies for negative risks or threats • Strategies for positive risks or opportunities • Contingent response strategies • Expert judgment	• Project management plan updates • Project document updates

The risk management plan is the agreement that specifies how risks will be identified and analyzed—both qualitatively and quantitatively—and how the strategies for negative and positive risks will be applied. The result of the risk assessment is documented in the risk register, which serves as input to the plan risk responses process. Some risks are mitigated in advance in order to reduce or increase the probability and impact of the risk (whether it is a positive or negative risk). In spite of this, some risks may have a high probability and/or high impact that the sponsor cannot tolerate, in which case a contingency plan is developed. Risk responses that have been identified using contingent response strategy are called contingency plans. The contingency plan is developed and maintained until the trigger calls for its execution, which could be in the case of strikes, fire, denial of service attacks, lack of power, and so forth. Contingency responses are the ones that are executed only when certain unwanted events occur. As the contingency plan clearly expresses the people/resources, their responsibilities, and the actions required to implement it, the plan can be executed quickly. In some cases the contingency plans are tested yearly, similar to fire drills. The contingency plan is followed by a contingency buffer, which may include resources or funding to ensure the implementation of the contingency plan. In case the contingency plan is unsuccessful, a fallback plan, which is an additional contingency plan, can be used.

In an agile environment it is the development team's responsibility to ensure the contingency plan is present. However, it is often developed based on a request from the product owner, who must understand the consequence of its implementation.

Exercise 10.8—Find It. Either online or within your work environment, find three different risk management plans for low, medium, and high risk events.

10.11 DATA ANALYSIS TOOLS AND TECHNIQUES

Technique	Needs Assessment	Planning	Analysis	Traceability and Monitoring	Evaluation	Waterfall	Agile
Data analysis tools and techniques			X			X	

Would you build something big without a model or schematic? Data analysis tools and techniques are types of documentation used to model the requirements in a graphical way with a high level of abstraction. Systems are documented from a data, functional, and behavioral perspective, which makes data models important. The data model has the upper hand—meaning that it can model the minor parts of the system that may have a high impact. Language can be misunderstood, whereas data models have the conciseness to describe systems as they really are. Data are gathered over a period of time which allows the data models to prosper from the data quality.

A good data analysis model should be able to live up to the following criteria:

- Completeness
- Nonredundancy
- Enforcement of business rules
- Data reusability
- Stability and flexibility
- Elegance
- Communication
- Integration
- Conflicting objectives

This means that the data models should contain the full model of the system that is enforcing the business rules without reusing the same data. The models must be able to be used over a significant period of time and be able to change with the system. The data models can be used for communication purposes as well as documenting any conflicting objectives or similar concerns.

The most common data analysis tools, data models, and techniques are:

- State diagram
- UML activity diagram
- Class diagram
- Use case diagram
- Data flow
- Entity-relationship diagram
- Interaction diagram
- Decision tables and trees

Several of the data models are illustrated in the domains. The data dictionary is slightly different than the data models as it contains a definition of all the data that resides in the data models. In agile methodologies, a number of data models are used just in case of spikes. However, requirements/user stories are not documented or modeled with data models.

10.12 DECISION-MAKING TOOLS AND TECHNIQUES

Technique	Needs Assessment	Planning	Analysis	Traceability and Monitoring	Evaluation	Waterfall	Agile
Decision-making tools and techniques			X			X	X

"Decision making is the study of identifying and choosing alternatives based on the values and preferences of the decision maker. Making a decision implies that there are alternative choices to be considered, and in such a case we want not only to identify as many of these alternatives as possible, but to choose the one that best fits with our goals, objectives, desires, values, and so on" (Harris, 1980).

The business analyst, the project manager, and stakeholders apply decision-making tools and techniques all the time as they are faced with a range of decisions to make. In order to make a good decision, objectives and goals need to be known and data must be available. With many decisions it is relevant to be familiar with alternative solutions and their pros and cons. Making constant decisions also requires being able to learn from those decisions. Some decision-making tools and techniques focus on the individual, while others are group centered. Some decision-making tools and techniques focus on reaching the right decision, while others have more emphasis on getting a consensus. So far, these decision-making techniques have been introduced:

- Unanimity
- Majority
- Plurality
- Dictatorship

In addition, the decision matrix has been applied in several chapters. Table 10.30 highlights an even wider selection of decision-making tools and techniques.

Table 10.30 Decision-making tools and techniques

T-chart	The T-chart illustrates the plus and minuses on each side of the T.
Pareto	20% of the decisions have 80% of the impact, which the Pareto analysis can help to highlight.
Delphi	Subject matter experts (SMEs) are asked, however, they are not present in the same room so they can't influence the other.
Conjoint analysis	A statistical method for decisions based upon tradeoff.
Multivoting	A wide range of voting to filter the options.
Business strategy analysis (SWOT, PEST, PESTLE)	The use of business strategy analysis for better decision making.
Subject matter experts	Ask the expert for a decision.
Dotmocracy	The use of checklists for decision making.
Range voting	Voting in ranges.

In agile methodologies the development team makes the decision with consensus. However, the product owner also makes many decisions based upon dictatorship, from being the sole responsible business owner.

Exercise 10.9—Not Easy Reaching an Agreement: Your team is working on several options. Ten options are voted on and after multiple voting rounds where the option that gets the least votes is eliminated each round, one option is left standing and agreed upon. What technique has the team applied? (The answer is found on page 271.)

1. Delphi
2. Conjoint analysis

3. Dotmocracy
4. Range voting
5. Multivoting

10.13 DEVELOPMENT METHODOLOGIES

Technique	Needs Assessment	Planning	Analysis	Traceability and Monitoring	Evaluation	Waterfall	Agile
Development methodologies		X				X	X

Software development methodologies based on the waterfall model (Royce, 1970) and the later, spiral model, have a long and proud history. Back in the 1950s most software development projects started out with the waterfall model. The waterfall model had some shortcomings, which resulted in the B-model, the V-model, and the incremental model, as variants or refinements of the waterfall model. However, as many are aware, we witnessed a shift to the spiral model and the agile approach eventually became more dominant. The software development methodologies changed because systems became too expensive, projects took too long to develop, and the software did not serve their intended purposes when they were finally delivered. Overall, the development life cycles and approaches are important as they cover the whole life of a system. The two basic system development life cycle models are the waterfall model and the spiral model.

The waterfall model from 1970 is the "classical" model, sometimes called one-shot or once-through as every stage needs to be checked and signed off before moving on, which imposes a firm structure on the project and activities. The stages are requirements, design, implementation, verification, and maintenance, as illustrated in Figure 10.6. Each stage has two elements, verification and validation.

The traditional plan-based approach as developed in the *PMBOK® Guide—Fifth Edition* is based upon the waterfall model.

A variant of the waterfall model is the *B-model* by Birrell and Ould (1985), which solves some of the shortcomings of waterfall in terms of maintenance and operations. The B-model is illustrated in Figure 10.7.

Another refinement of the waterfall model is the *V-model* illustrated in Figure 10.8 that highlights testing activities early on as the project moves from upper left corner of the V and then down, while constantly checking with the activities on the right side of the V.

Another variant of the waterfall model is the incremental model, which is illustrated in Figure 10.9, and is improved with regard to phased delivery.

The alternative to the waterfall model and its refinements is the spiral model developed by Barry Boehm. Displayed in Figure 10.10, the spiral model is an iterative approach developed by the agile methodologies. This model starts out in the middle and moves outward in short iterations.

The comparative chart (Hoda et al., 2008) in Table 10.31 demonstrates some of the categories where waterfall and spiral vary. This highlights several of the differences between the traditional waterfall-based approach and the agile method based upon the spiral model.

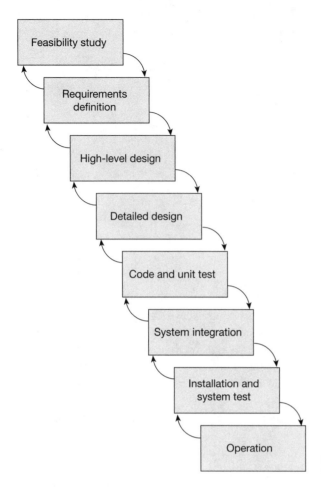

Figure 10.6 Waterfall model

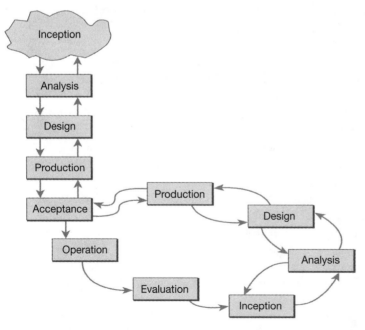

Figure 10.7 The B-model

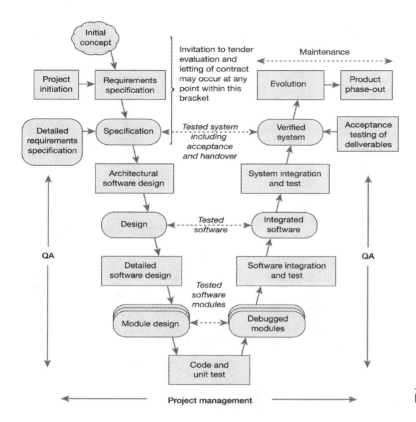

Figure 10.8 The V-model

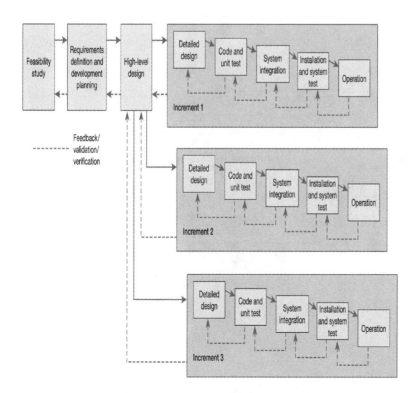

Figure 10.9 The incremental model (phased delivery)

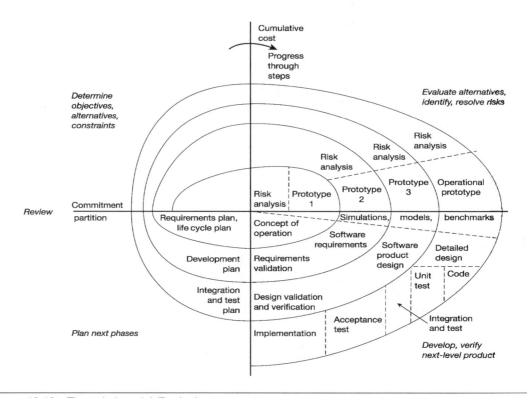

Figure 10.10 The spiral model (Boehm)

Table 10.31 The comparative chart

Categories	Waterfall	Spiral
Development model	Traditional	Iterative
Focus	Process	People
Management	Controlling	Facilitating
Customer involvement	Requirement gathering and delivery phases	On-site and constantly involved
Developers	Work individually within teams	Collaborative or in pairs
Technology	Any	Mostly object oriented
Product features	All included	Most important first
Testing	End of development cycle	Iterative and/or drives code
Documentation	Thorough	Only when needed

10.14 DOCUMENT MANAGEMENT TOOLS AND TECHNIQUES

Technique	Needs Assessment	Planning	Analysis	Traceability and Monitoring	Evaluation	Waterfall	Agile
Document management tools and techniques		X				X	

Document management tools and techniques do not play a direct role in the project management text-books. However, they play a vital role in requirement management and project success. Requirements and project management are document driven, often paper-based, and contain a lot of documents and models. These documents are used in collaboration with stakeholders and team members. This leads to document management as being the foundation for configuration management and versioning, which yet again, plays an important part in regards to traceability.

Document management is defined as the process taken with documents within an organization, with respect to the creation, distribution, and deletion of documents. It is commonly understood that a document can either be represented in electronic form (i.e., Word document, spreadsheet file, movie file, sound clip, etc.), or as a traditional hard copy consisting of any number of pages. Document management in regard to project and requirements management are often related to:

- Hard copy document management;
- Electronic communication management; and
- Electronic project management tools.

Documents are managed in a variety of different document management systems, including:

- Document information systems,
- Integrated document management,
- Electronic document management,
- Enterprise content management,
- Content management and knowledge management, and
- Content management systems.

There are six basic tools and techniques of document management systems. They are:

- Document creating,
- Storage and retrieval,
- Management,
- Version control,
- Workflow, and
- Multiple delivery formats.

Document management is not a single entity or technology, but rather a combination of elements. The day-to-day documentation technique would include the following, which often are used in workshops or similar meetings:

- Notes on flipcharts
- Post-it notes

- Context and use case diagrams
- Rich pictures
- Mind maps

10.15 ELEMENTS OF A REQUIREMENTS MANAGEMENT PLAN

Technique	Needs Assessment	Planning	Analysis	Traceability and Monitoring	Evaluation	Waterfall	Agile
Elements of requirements management plan		X				X	

The elements of a requirements management plan are discussed in Chapter 7.

10.16 ELICITATION TOOLS AND TECHNIQUES

Technique	Needs Assessment	Planning	Analysis	Traceability and Monitoring	Evaluation	Waterfall	Agile
Elicitation tools and techniques			X			X	X

Elicitation tools and techniques are discussed in Chapter 7.

10.17 ESTIMATING TOOLS AND TECHNIQUES

Technique	Needs Assessment	Planning	Analysis	Traceability and Monitoring	Evaluation	Waterfall	Agile
Estimating tools and techniques		X				X	X

Requirements management is filled to the brim with data and numbers. These numbers come from a variation of sources. If estimated data from these sources is not up to the level required, the results of the requirements and project management documents would suffer greatly. In this section, we will introduce estimation methods in order to increase the confidence in the data that are presented in the domains.

Estimation techniques may be considered young disciplines within IT, but they still have a bit of history that leads toward the future. Several sources refer back to Peter V. Norden, Project RAND (Delphi), SEER-SEM, and Frank Freiman (PRICE, 1969), as some of the pioneers of estimation in the 1960s. In the 1970s, recognized techniques such as the Putnam model were developed. Even with a fair range of estimation techniques, Fred Brooks stated in *The Mythical Man-Month* (1975) that "Our estimating techniques are poorly developed. We are uncertain of our estimates." This seems to have haunted us ever since. In the 1970s, the economically based estimation techniques from Wolverton, Walton, and Felix were published, and later the eminent *Function Points* (1979) by Alan Allbrecht. It is also where the first version of *CoCoMo* (1981) by Barry W. Boehm saw the light of day. These estimation techniques are more or less still in use in updated versions.

Estimation is all about estimating the project constraints which includes, but are not limited to, scope, quality, schedule, budget, resources, and risks. The center of attention for academics and everyday project managers has been on estimating time and costs, which are parts of the *PMBOK® Guide*, and includes the project time management and project cost management knowledge areas. The literature of estimation may make it sound like estimation is a walk in the park because most estimation techniques are fairly easy to understand and can be applied to relatively simple projects. However, the testimonials of failures due to poor estimates are long and very expensive according to Fortune 500 companies where only 1 out of 4 projects gets completed on time and within the fixed budget. Chris F. Kemerer claimed that, in 1997, costs were two to three times the estimated amount, and that was the norm. The last 10 to 15 years have confirmed this is still a fact with new and even bigger failures.

In most cases, top management and project managers are fully aware of the fact that precision in estimates varies over time with fairly imprecise estimates—perhaps 50% off in the initiating phase, which decreases to 25% in the planning phase, and hopefully 10% or less in the execution or later phases. This understanding is also contained in the theory of the *cone of uncertainty* or similar models (e.g., Roetzheim, 2000). This underlies the importance of reevaluating estimates as an ongoing process.

Project document estimates are completed very early on in the process, which results in a higher degree of uncertainty, while estimates done during implementation are far less uncertain. This is called the cone of uncertainty as illustrated in Figure 10.11.

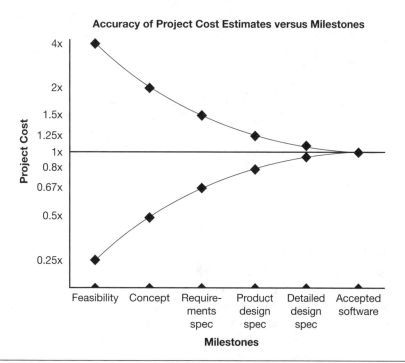

Figure 10.11   Cone of uncertainty

We will introduce several common and quick-to-use estimation methods in order to move from early uncertain estimates to estimates that are far more accurate. These are:

- Analogous estimating
- Parametric estimating
- Delphi
- Expert judgment
- Program evaluation and review technique (PERT)

In addition we will present a range of additional methods, which to some degree, require a bit of training or software support. The estimation methods, sometimes called estimation strategies, can be categorized as illustrated in Figure 10.12.

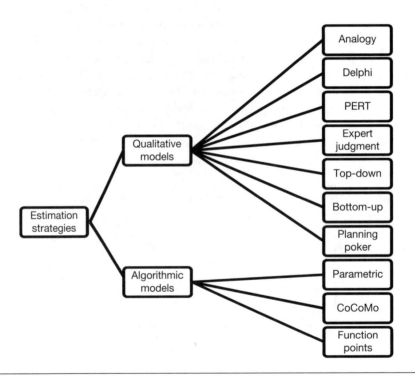

Figure 10.12   Estimation techniques

Analogous Estimating

Analogous estimating is using the actual cost of a previous project as the basis for estimating the cost of the current project, combined with historical information and expert judgment. This method is used to estimate total project costs when there is a limited amount of detailed information about the project. To illustrate this, we would compare an older version with a new version of the same system. We estimate that the new system has twice the functionality as the old system, which was priced at $50,000. This means that the analogy estimate would be $100,000.

Parametric Estimating

Parametric estimating is a cost model that is based on correlation of cost and variables such as weight, size, type of assembly, etc. The benefits are that this method can produce higher levels of accuracy depending upon the sophistication and underlying data. In addition it can be applied to a total project or to segments of a project. In most cases parametric estimating would be more accurate than analogous estimating. The risk is that historical data may not accurately represent the current business case. To illustrate this, assume the price of a house is $12,000 per square meter, and your new house is 300 square meters. This results in a cost estimate of $3,600,000. Combine this with a regression analysis, and the tools may work wonders for your business case.

Delphi

The original version of the Delphi method was first applied in the 1960s. The concept was to ask a range of experts for an estimate. The experts were not located in the same place and were not allowed to communicate or influence each other's estimates. This method is quick to use and combines expert judgment with a range of estimates found in PERT and similar methods. To illustrate this, we would ask three experts to price out a building; the estimates may be $1,000,000, $1,000,000, and $1,300,000. The business case team may then use standard statistical methods on the findings, in terms of average, medium, or similar techniques to find an exact estimate.

Expert Judgment

Expert judgment is simply a method of asking someone who is familiar with and knowledgeable about the application area and the technologies to provide an estimate. Research shows that the judgment of experts tends to be based on analogy.

Program Evaluation and Review Technique

PERT is a three-point estimation method based upon optimistic, most likely, and pessimistic estimates. To get your PERT estimate, add the three estimates together, then divide by three. Or, for a modified PERT estimate, take the most likely estimate times four, and then divide by six. To illustrate this, we use three estimates of 15, 30, and 60. The PERT estimate equals 35; and we calculate an estimate of 32.5 using the modified PERT.

Some of the other slightly more advanced but commonly applied methods are:

- Function points
- CoCoMO II
- Planning poker (agile)
- Top-down
- Bottom-up
- Vendor bids or published data

In order to increase the value of the estimates, the business analyst and teams need to use more than one estimation method as none of them are precise enough. Estimation requires business knowledge, but you can come a long way with good communication skills and with the use of several sources. In order to build up historical data for further activities, the estimates need to be documented and qualified.

Exercise 10.10—Estimating Using Two Techniques: You are estimating activity for the business analysis plan and you are using your experience from earlier projects, which is similar to this one. In addition, you have access to data where you can measure the amount of work that can be done based upon available resources. Which two techniques should you use for this estimating activity? (The answer is found on page 271.)

1. Parametric estimating
2. Function points
3. Planning Poker
4. Delphi
5. Analogue

10.18 FACILITATION TOOLS AND TECHNIQUES

Technique	Needs Assessment	Planning	Analysis	Traceability and Monitoring	Evaluation	Waterfall	Agile
Facilitation tools and techniques			X			X	X

Facilitate means *to make easy*. As a facilitator, your job is to make the meeting easier for the participants. Your main task is to help the team or group increase its effectiveness by improving its processes. A facilitator is an individual who enables groups and organizations to work more effectively, and to collaborate and achieve synergy. Think of the facilitator as the conductor of a symphony, where everyone needs to play the tune. Facilitation tools and techniques are used at the outset of a meeting, often in the form of a workshop. The workshop is a common event in the work of the business analyst, and the business analyst is often taking the role as facilitator even though it is not always the best solution. Workshops and facilitation have broad applications as they are aimed at teams and individuals to assist them in managing the activities and helping them get the desired results. Effective facilitating also involves making the participants comfortable and managing their emotions toward the activity.

A group, team, or amount of participants for a workshop or similar facilitated event may be analyzed using the stages of group development by Tuckman (1965). The model is illustrated in Figure 10.13.

Figure 10.13 Stages of group development

As illustrated, the model contains five stages from forming to adjourning, which in some cases is the team development over a period of time. However, not all groups reach the performing stage. Adjourning is the stage where we close up and finalize the activities. Besides time, the other parameters are energy and productivity, which will increase from the forming stage into the performing stage and is why we seek to move the group to performing as soon as possible. In order to do so, this part will demonstrate a range of facilitation tools and techniques to make this journey happen.

A facilitated event such as a workshop would often include the following stages:

- Plan the workshop
- Conduct the workshop
- Follow up

Plan the workshop

The foundation of an effective workshop or facilitated event is the planning stage, where the facilitator needs to consider the objectives of the workshop, avoidance of an over-ambitious agenda, the number of attendees, the participants' concerns, the structure of the workshop, the duration, the facilitation techniques to be applied, and the practical issues, such as the venue and need for scribes. Planning helps avoid losing control at the event and increases the chances that positive results are achieved.

Conduct the Workshop

Conducting the workshop is a matter of retaining focus and keeping the workshop on track, which often requires that the attendees take an active part in it. The event should be recorded and summarized. Conducting the workshop may depend on the development of the participants. In the forming or storming stage, focus may evolve around group activities and camaraderie, while performing may have a focus on effectiveness—as we all agree on what to do, how to do it, and when to do it. Most facilitated events would include icebreakers, which may be a personal introduction. These may include group agreements, go-rounds, paired listening, role-playing, plus-minus-interest, idea storms, and other similar techniques.

During the event, some of these discovery techniques may be used for information gathering:

- Brainwriting/Post-it exercise
- Brainstorming
- Round robin
- Talking wall
- Greenfile site
- Transporter
- Assumption reversal

In addition, other tools and techniques (explained elsewhere) may also be useful such as:

- Conflict resolution
- Active listening
- Emotional intelligence
- Appreciative inquiry
- Brainstorming techniques
- Consensus affinity and workshops
- Effective meetings
- Problem solving
- Negotiation
- Document techniques
- Decision making

Follow up

The facilitator needs to follow up on the event with documentation, issue notes, and possible feedback from the participants.

When working in an agile environment, it is the Scrum Master's task to facilitate workshops or similar events—sometimes in coordination with the development team and product owner. However, the team is self-governed and responsible for ensuring the results and facilitation of the events. The tools and techniques will focus on communication and collaboration while keeping the amount of formality and documentation that is needed.

Exercise 10.11—How to Use This at Work: In groups of three to four people, have participants list ways that they will use the materials presented in this section back at work.

10.19 INTERFACE ANALYSIS

Technique	Needs Assessment	Planning	Analysis	Traceability and Monitoring	Evaluation	Waterfall	Agile
Interface analysis			X			X	X

Interface analysis demonstrates the interaction between the system and environment. This is a manual analysis that illustrates how the system and environment would work together. Some people call it a test as the purpose is also to verify inputs and outputs. In order to do so, the business analyst needs clear measures, whether they are SMART (specific, measurable, actionable, realistic, and time-bound) or correct, consistent, complete, accurate, and testable.

The requirements interface analysis is performed in three steps—preparation, identification, and definition. The preparation part involves a review of current documentation and visualization of the interfaces. The identification process identifies what interfaces are needed for each stakeholder or system, purpose, type, and any high-level details—and actually visualizes the interface. The definition process involves specifying the interface requirements by describing the inputs and outputs, the associated validation rules, and any events triggering interactions.

Part of the interface analysis is the virtualization in which prototypes may prove useful as evolutionary or throw-away prototypes.

Interoperability serves the same purpose as the interface analysis as it focuses on how the business architecture works together—whether it is on the technical, presentation, or application level. Table 10.32 illustrates this on the system level.

Table 10.32 Intersystem interoperability requirements

Intersystem interoperability requirements		
	System 1	System 2
System 1		3A
System 2	2A	

Agile teams may apply the interface and system interoperability analysis in case of spikes, often in regard to architecture. Prototypes are often applied for demonstrating requirements for the product owner to demonstrate a possible functionality. The use of analysis is the decision of the development team unless it is required by the product owner as it provides value to the business.

10.20 LEADERSHIP PRINCIPLES AND SKILLS

Technique	Needs Assessment	Planning	Analysis	Traceability and Monitoring	Evaluation	Waterfall	Agile
Leadership principles and skills	X	X	X	X	X	X	X

Strong leadership skills are essential for successful projects. Leadership is the interpersonal behavior and work that influences others. Business analysts and project managers can perform well as leaders without being managers. Leadership is the function you perform—and requirements and project management demand strong leadership skills and tools to be successful. Table 10.33 illustrates the difference between a leader and a manager. The competent business analyst or project manager is able to act as a leader while managing the activities.

Table 10.33   Leaders versus managers

Leaders	Managers
Leaders often establish direction for the future, communicate through vision, and forge aligned high-performance teams. The project manager's *leadership function* is specifically used to communicate the project vision.	Managers mainly focus on planning and short-term horizons, devise processes and structures, and solve problems. The project manager plans a project, measures project performance, and solves any roadblock issues.

The style of leadership may depend on the leader's subjective view of other people, whether it is correct or not. Douglas McGregor's (1967) Theory X and Y shown in Table 10.34 explains this using two arch types. People within Theory X generally do not want to work, thus close supervision is needed and the business analyst would need to tell them what to do all the time, while people within Theory Y work for self-fulfillment and personal development.

Table 10.34   McGregor's Theory X and Y

Theory X	Theory Y
People need close supervision	People want independence in their work
People will avoid work when possible	People seek responsibility
People will avoid responsibility	People are motivated by self-fulfillment
People work just for money	People naturally want to work

The style of leadership may also depend on who the leader is.

> *Know the enemy and know yourself; in a hundred battles you will never be in peril. When you are ignorant of the enemy but know yourself, your chances of winning or losing are equal. If ignorant both of your enemy and of yourself, you are certain in every battle to be in peril (Sun Tzu, 250 BC).*

In modern times, identifying the leader's behavior is conducted by a range of possible analyses, including Belbin, Meyers-Briggs, and strength-based leadership (see Table 10.35).

Table 10.35 Behavioral analysis of leaders

Type	Description
Belbin team roles	Belbin team roles are used to identify people's behavioral strengths and weaknesses in the workplace in order to build productive working relationships, select and develop high-performing teams, raise self-awareness and personal effectiveness, build mutual trust and understanding, and aid the team in selection and recruitment processes.
The Meyers-Briggs type indicators	The Meyers-Briggs type indicators (MBTI) are based on Jungian theories (1923) by Isabel Briggs Myers working with her mother, Katharine Briggs. The MBTI is based upon the idea that you have a dominant preference in four areas. Each area has opposite poles. The four preferences are: Extraversion (E) versus Introversion (I); Sensing (S) versus Intuition (N); Thinking (T) versus Feeling (F); and Judging (J) versus Perception (P). Neither preference is wrong. You can do both, but prefer one. All preferences are of equal importance.
Strength-based leadership	In over 30 years of research into leadership and top achievers, Gallup has found that top achievers have one thing in common: they build their academic and personal life on their talents. Based on this research, one of the key promoters, Marcus Buckingham, stresses the idea of strength. Strength comes from teachable knowledge in the form of education, experiences, and awareness, which we combine with teachable skills such as the capacity to perform and practice the steps of an activity. Strength is the ability to provide consistent, near-perfect performance in a given activity. With strength-based leadership, we want everyone on the team to use their strength as much as possible. To do so, we must be aware of our strengths and, equally as important, the strength of our team members.

In 1939, a group of researchers headed by Kurt Lewin identified different styles of leadership—these being autocratic, democratic, and laissez-faire, as illustrated in Table 10.36.

Table 10.36 Kurt Lewin's different styles of leadership

Style of leadership	Description
Autocratic	Being arbitrary, controlling, power-oriented, coercive, punitive, and close-minded
Democratic	Considerate, democratic, consultative and participative, employee-centered, concerned with people, concerned with maintenance of good working relations, supportive and oriented toward facilitating interaction, relationship oriented, and oriented toward group decision making
Laissez-faire	Doing nothing

The identified different styles of leadership shown in Figure 10.14 are used by Tannenbaum and Schmidt to create a leadership model for the leader to lead differently, depending on the participants on the team, group, or at a workshop.

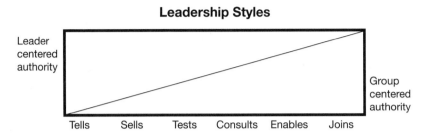

Figure 10.14 Tannenbaum and Schmidt leadership styles

One leadership style is not better than the other. It is simply a toolbox of styles for the business analyst. Some of the factors that influence leadership styles are:

- Task
- Time factor
- Culture
- Employees
- Environment

If the task is well-known or time is limited, the autocratic leadership style may work well. However, if the culture is democratic or we are faced with research, the democratic leadership style may work best.

Leadership of individuals may also be affected by their motivation and competence. The *veteran* SME may be highly competent; yet motivation may be low if the veteran is fed up with the firm—this requires one style of leadership. The *new employee* on the team may have high motivation; but may be low on competency—this would require another style of leadership. This is what Hersey and Blanchard have researched, and Figure 10.15 shows the four styles of leadership depending on motivation and competency.

Leadership and motivation are closely related. Leaders would ask: What motivates people and how can I motivate them? The most common theories of motivation, relevant to requirements and project management are:

- Abraham H. Maslow's hierarchy of needs
- Frederick Herzberg's two-factor theory
- Alderfer's ERG theory
- Douglas McGregor's Theory X and Y
- John Stacey Adams's equity theory
- Victor Vroom's expectancy theory
- Schein approach
- McClelland
- Skinner
- Gibson's overview model
- Porter-Lawler
- Path-goal theory

The leadership style may also depend on the tasks involved, which is what John Adair's three circles aims at solving (see Figure 10.16). The three circles model focuses on different leadership styles depending on who you lead: *individuals* (highlighted by Hersey and Blanchard) versus *team and task* leadership. Some researchers may argue that leaders are born, not made. Also, research shows that people admire leaders who are:

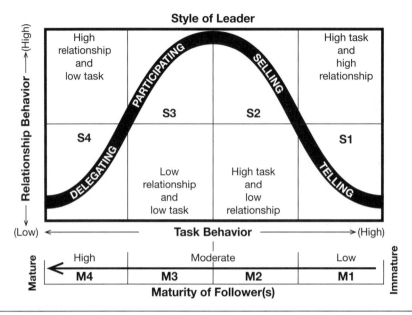

Figure 10.15 Hersey and Blanchard

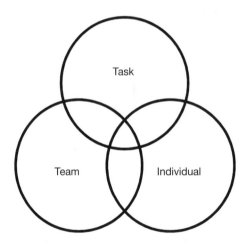

Figure 10.16 John Adair's three circles

- Honest
- Competent
- Forward-looking
- Inspiring

In agile methodologies, teams are self-managed and empowered, which requires yet another type of leadership style. Leadership comes in many forms and shapes with a range of definitions. The concepts of servant and adaptive leadership work well in the agile method. The Scrum Master often acts as servant leader while the product owner may employ adaptive leadership. Furthermore, it is expected that team members also act as leaders within the team.

Adaptive Leadership

In agile, we embrace change. This requires adaptive leadership that deals with changes and problem-solving processes. Adaptive leadership explores why responsiveness is critical to success. Adaptive leadership is dealing daily with change and problem solving. These tasks are at the core of what leaders and managers must do. In agile teams, most challenges are technical where team members are the experts. However, sometimes adaptive challenges arise where someone outside the team must show leadership or the team will suffer.

There are six principles of adaptive leadership:

- Get on the balcony (leaders need to take a step back to gain perspective)
- Identify adaptive challenges
- Regulate distress
- Maintain disciplined attention
- Give the work back to the people
- Protect the voice of leadership from below

Servant Leadership

Servant leadership is a philosophy and set of practices that enrich the lives of individuals, builds better organizations, and ultimately creates a more just and caring world. While servant leadership is a timeless concept, the term *servant leadership* was coined by Robert K. Greenleaf in "The Servant as Leader," an essay that he first published in 1970.

Larry Spears, Executive Director of the Robert K. Greenleaf Center for Servant Leadership, succinctly defines servant leadership as "a new kind of leadership model—a model that puts serving others as the number one priority. Servant leadership emphasizes increased service to others; a holistic approach to work; promoting a sense of community; and the sharing of power in decision making."

The core characteristics of being a servant leader are:

- Listening
- Empathy
- Healing
- Awareness
- Persuasion
- Conceptualization
- Foresight
- Stewardship
- Commitment to the growth of people
- Building community

10.21 LESSONS LEARNED AND RETROSPECTIVES

Technique	Needs Assessment	Planning	Analysis	Traceability and Monitoring	Evaluation	Waterfall	Agile
Lesson learned and retrospectives					X	X	X

Lessons learned and retrospectives are about looking back in time and analyzing the situation in order to learn and improve. However, the time and content of the lessons learned and retrospectives varies as lessons learned are applied in traditional projects, while retrospective is an agile technique. PMI defines lessons learned as "the knowledge gained during a project that shows how project events were addressed or should be addressed in the future with the purpose of improving future performance." In reality, updates to the organizational process assets will happen within most knowledge areas such as Stakeholder and Communication Management. The lessons learned may contain causes of issues, corrective actions, experience and advice, organizational and continuous improvements, learning, capturing actual data, team building, root cause analyses, and historical documents for other project uses, such as an activity list. The lessons learned will be saved in the lessons learned knowledge base, which is a store of historical information about both the outcomes of previous project selection decisions and performances.

The agile approach to lessons learned are retrospectives, which are special meetings where the team gathers after completing an incremental work step to inspect and adapt their methods and teamwork. In traditional projects, lessons learned are mostly documented at the end of the project; while in the agile methodologies retrospectives are ongoing activities that have broader applications as other aspects are included. The purpose of the retrospective is to benefit the team—not for historical reasons.

The most common retrospective, the *iteration retrospective* (Kerth, 2001), occurs at the end of every iteration or sprint. In addition to iteration retrospectives, you can also conduct longer and more intensive retrospectives at crucial milestones such as:

- Release retrospectives
- Project retrospectives
- Surprise retrospectives

The benefits of conducting good iteration retrospectives (Kerth) are:

- Your ability to develop and deliver software steadily improves
- The whole team grows closer and more cohesive
- Each group has more respect for the issues other groups face
- You are honest and open about your successes and failures, and are more comfortable with change

The generic approach to most kinds of retrospectives would be:

- Set the stage
- Gather data
- Generate insights
- Decide what to do
- Close the retrospective

Set the stage is the beginning, where everyone has time to talk. The goals, time box, and approach for the retrospective are discussed. The following activities (Derby et al., 2006) can be used in this process:

- Check-in
- Focus on/focus off
- ESVP (Explorer, Shopper, Vacationer, Prisioner) activity
- Working agreement
- Temperature reading
- Satisfaction histogram

In the *gather data* process, the team examines metrics, charts, stories, meetings, decisions, amount of code refactored, and so forth. The following activities (Derby et al., 2006) can be used in this process:

- Time Line and Variations
- Triple Nickels
- Color-Coded Dots
- Mad, Sad, and Glad
- Satisfaction Histogram
- Team Radar
- Like to Like

In the *generate insight* process, the team asks the *whys*, in order to find patterns, strengths, and issues so as to understand events and circumstances. The following activities (Derby et al., 2006) can be used in this process:

- Brainstorming
- Force Field Analysis
- 5 Whys
- Fishbone
- Pattern and Shifts
- Prioritize with Dots
- Report Out and Synthesis
- Identify Themes
- Learning Matrix

In the *decide what to do* process, the team can create a long list of improvements or experiments from retrospective to retrospective. The result would be a new work agreement for the next iteration. The following activities (Derby et al., 2006) can be used in this process:

- The Retrospective Planning Game
- SMART Goals
- Circle of Questions
- Short Subjects
- Triple Nickels
- Force Field Analysis

Close the retrospective is about documentation, planning, and follow-up so that the team can keep track of the new practices. The following activities (Derby et al., 2006) can be used in this process:

- +/Delta
- Appreciations
- Temperature Readings
- Helped, Hindered, Hypothesis
- ROTI (return on time invested)
- Satisfaction Histogram
- Team Radar
- Learning Matrix
- Short Subjects

An easy-to-use alternative is the starfish retrospective, illustrated in Figure 10.17, which has emphasis on focus points for doing more or less. Learning matrix retrospectives are also similar types of tools.

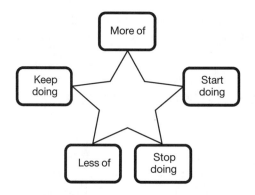

Figure 10.17 Starfish retrospective

Business Analysis for Practitioners (2015) has identified facilitating lessons learned activities as a collaboration point where the business analyst and the project manager should work together. The project manager may gather lessons learned for the whole project, while the business analyst emphasizes lessons learned for the business analyst activities.

10.22 MEASUREMENT TOOLS AND TECHNIQUES

Technique	Needs Assessment	Planning	Analysis	Traceability and Monitoring	Evaluation	Waterfall	Agile
Measurement tools and techniques		X				X	

A range of measurement tools and techniques have been discussed throughout this book. However, now our focus will be on the development of nonfunctional requirements. Nonfunctional requirements, also called *quality requirements*, would often include factors such as:

- Performance
- Availability
- Dependability
- Scalability
- Portability

Nonfunctional requirements are part of the agreements the firm has with internal departments or external customers. The agreements are input in the *Develop project charter* process and would contain one or more of the following types of agreements:

- Service level agreement (SLA)
- Memorandums of understanding (MOU)
- Letter of agreement

- Letter of intent
  - Verbal or written agreements
  - Contract with external customer

In the agreements and as a result of the agreements, the business analyst can derive nonfunctional requirements. Previously we have discussed natural and model language techniques to document requirements where they are functional and nonfunctional. An additional tool to this work is *Planguage*, a key-word-oriented language developed by Tom Gilb, which supports the development of nonfunctional requirements using a language for software development.

In agile methodologies the agreement is the domain of the product owner; who in case of certain requirements of any sort, will bring these to the table and into the product backlog. The team would not be familiar with the agreement as it is the product owner who decides the importance of the agreements. In most cases the development teams would not use or be familiar with Planguage.

10.23 NEGOTIATIONS TOOLS AND TECHNIQUES

Technique	Needs Assessment	Planning	Analysis	Traceability and Monitoring	Evaluation	Waterfall	Agile
Negotiations tools and techniques			X			X	X

Negotiations can be challenging—and it is a challenge that the business analyst faces on a regular basis. Negotiations are defined by PMI as "the process (of communication) and activities (aimed at achieving specific goals) to resolving disputes through consultations (undertake to work together to shape an outcome that meets their interests better than their best alternatives) between involved parties." However, the emphasis here is also on arriving at the settlement of some matter, and less emphasis is placed on disputes. Negotiations and conflicts are related. However, negotiations do not have to end in conflicts—which is one of the goals of this section. Negotiations are also called haggling. Haggling or competitive bargaining is illustrated in Figure 10.18 as simple two-party bargaining.

The business analyst haggles about requirements development, team activities, or during procurement. Negotiations are not about right or wrong, or a matter of winning. Styles and strategies may vary depending on the business analyst's objectives with respect to the negotiations. Negotiations and emotions are

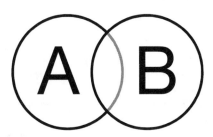

Figure 10.18   Bargaining space

related as negotiations tend to bring the emotions to the forefront. Negotiations can be challenging due to the barriers of lack of trust, culture, spoilers, power, and so forth. Barriers can be created due to the selected tactics, which vary from auction and good/bad cop, to flinch and snow job. Negotiators can be soft, hard, or principled, which may influence their strategy and style. The good negotiators have done their homework, whether it is price checking for identifying zones of possible agreement or brainstorming alternatives.

Weingart has identified four negotiation styles—individualists, cooperators, competitive, and altruists. The individualist seeks to maximize their own gains, cooperators seek a win-win situation, the competitive negotiator aims at increasing the loot and receiving their part, while the rare altruists seek that the other parties get the best possible deal. In Table 10.37, the styles are mixed with strategies: distributive negotiation, integrative negotiation and mixed-motive negotiation (using both distribution and integrative), which to some degree are similar in terms of motives, preferred outcomes, and approach.

Table 10.37 Comparing negotiation styles and strategies

Styles	Distributive negotiation	Integrative negotiation	Mixed-motive negotiation
Individualists	Win/lose; max self interest		Win/lose on top priorities
Cooperators		Win/win for both	Win/win except for top priorities
Competitive	Win/lose; extreme self interest		
Altruists	Lose/win; other's interests		

Figure 10.19 illustrates the modified Kenneth Thomas and Ralph Kilmann classification system to describe negotiating styles using the labels: avoiding, competing, compromising, collaborating, and accommodating.

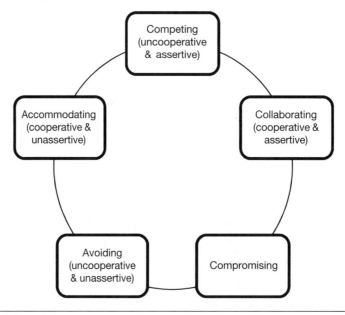

Figure 10.19 Negotiating styles

Fisher and Ury (1991) call their approach *principled negotiation*. Their book *Getting to Yes* contains these four key elements:

- Separate people from the problem
- Focus on interests, not positions
- Invent options for mutual benefit
- Use objective criteria

The principle of *separate people from the problem* deals with the problem of differences in perception. Emotions and communication are other sources of people problems that we have already discussed. Generally, the best way to deal with people problems is to prevent them from arising. People problems are less likely to come up if the parties have a good relationship and think of each other as partners in negotiation rather than as adversaries.

Focusing on interests, not positions means that we need to identify the parties' interests regarding the issue at hand and then discuss them. Too often solutions are picked without considering alternatives. The principle of *inventing options for mutual benefits* aims at satisfying everyone's interests through alternatives. This can be done by brainstorming or other idea generation techniques. In addition we need to separate the invention process from the evaluation stage in order to come up with a good solution for the negotiations. Finally, *using objective criteria* refers to using a process to develop objective criteria for evaluating issues and settling the negotiation.

An additional aspect of the principled negotiation is the *best alternative to a negotiated agreement* (BATNA), which helps stakeholders consider the alternatives.

Exercise 10.12—Negotiations: With whom are business analysts most likely to negotiate with often/daily? (The answer is found on page 271.)

1. The project manager
2. The development team
3. The client
4. The PMO
5. Legal

10.24 ORGANIZATION ASSESSMENT

Technique	Needs Assessment	Planning	Analysis	Traceability and Monitoring	Evaluation	Waterfall	Agile
Organization assessment	X					X	

Organizational assessments follow a systems approach to analyze a proposed change; determine the impacts of the change; assess the organizational structure, including the people and organizational risks associated with the change; and find the readiness of the organizational entities to adopt the change, with a focus on individuals, groups, units, and departments.

There are numerous assessment models and techniques for understanding and analyzing data that focus on organizational culture, structure, capabilities, internal and external environment, and the risks and business benefits of a change. The major elements in these assessment models can be broken down into the following categories: organizational change, people change, and benefit management (discussed in Chapter 5).

Organizational Change

In his book *Beyond Culture*, renowned anthropologist Edward T. Hall (1975) made a typology of cultures in which he distinguishes between *low-context* and *high-context* cultures. Low-context cultures rely on elaborate verbal explanations, putting much emphasis on spoken words, while a high-context culture relies on nonverbal messages and views communication as a means to promote smooth, harmonious relationships. Low-context nationalities are the Swiss, Germans, and Scandinavians—where the verbal explanation often explains the meaning fairly clearly. High-context cultures such as China, Korea, and Japan might speak in riddles. For example, take the Chinese phrase *zou jing kan tian*, which describes sitting in the well and looking at the sky, meaning that you are narrow-minded.

Another renowned anthropologist Geert Hofstede, who is Dutch, conducted one of the early empirical studies of national cultural traits. He collected data on the values and attitudes of 116,000 employees at the IBM Corporation, representing a diverse set of nationalities, ages, and genders. Hofstede conducted two surveys; one in 1968 and another in 1972. Hofstede's theories emphasize four dimensions:

- Individualism versus collectivism
- Power distance
- Uncertainty avoidance
- Masculinity versus femininity

Individualism versus collectivism describes whether a person functions primarily as an individual or within a group. This may be relevant in agile where teamwork is of great importance. It may also pose a challenge if team members feel more connected to other groups of their nationality than to the team. It may cause conflicts, issues of trust, and lack of productivity.

Power distance describes how a society deals with the inequalities in power that exist among people. In some countries there is a great power distance between people working in teams and top management. This may be a problem if the product owner comes from a culture with high power distance, and suddenly finds himself part of the team's work. Power distances in agile teams are rarely an issue with servant leadership, self-empowerment, and team member equality.

Uncertainty avoidance is the extent to which people can tolerate risks and uncertainty in their lives. Working in agile helps reduce risks, but may also create uncertainties as we embrace changes and may not always know more than a few weeks ahead that a sprint or iteration will be completed.

Masculinity versus femininity refers to a society's orientation based on traditional male and female values. Masculine cultures tend to value competitiveness, assertiveness, ambition, and the accumulation of wealth. Feminine cultures emphasize nurturing roles, interdependence among people, and taking care of the less fortunate. Agile is somewhere in between—we like to perform well, but we also need to take care of the team. We keep a high but steady pace so we do not burn out, and measure progress in slightly competitive ways.

Organizational cultural analysis is important for determining the organization's readiness and initiatives for managing change. Kurt Lewin's model of organizational change (see Figure 10.20) contains three stages that a change must complete. First, the situation must be *unfrozen* in order for the *transition* to take place. When change is complete, the environment must be *frozen* again. Kurt Lewin's model of organizational change works well with guidelines from Michael Kotter, who found that transformations may fail during the unfreeze stage if the focus is not on communicating the urgency of the change, building a strong coalition, and having a strong vision. During the transition stage, communication is vital, employees must be empowered, and quick wins should be gained and celebrated whenever possible. The freeze stage consolidates the change.

Figure 10.20   Lewin's model for change

Leavitt developed a less famous change model in 1965 that illustrates how change affects the organization. The elements are technology, structure, people, and tasks, as illustrated in Figure 10.21. What is important is that a new IT system, represented here as technology, affects structures, tasks, and people—which would require training for people, new tasks, and perhaps organizational changes to support the new technology.

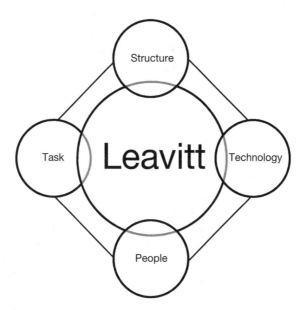

Figure 10.21 Leavitt's change model

People Change

The people change models, illustrated by the SARAH Model, the learning cycle model, and the conscious competence model, demonstrates how people react to change. In Figure 10.22, the Kubler-Ross change curve illustrates the process that employees may experience with a major change in the organization. The first reaction is a shock/honeymoon, then a reaction of denial, frustration, and anger—Why me? The lowest point in morale is the depression or rejection stage—I can't believe it! Then communication and training starts to kick in, and experimentation begins. Eventually, decision and acceptance of the new opportunities happens. The change ends with integration, mastery, and hope; where the change is completed and morale is high.

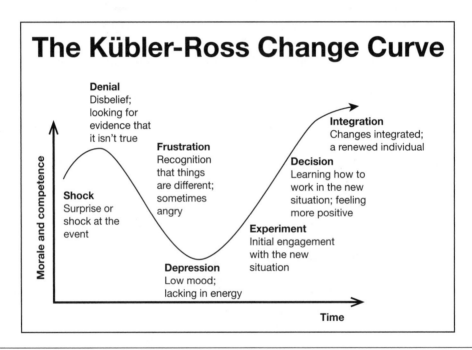

Figure 10.22 The Kubler-Ross change curve

Change requires learning new skills, which Kolb's learning cycle illustrates (see Figure 10.23). The stages in the cycle are concrete experience, observation and reflection, forming abstract concepts, and testing in new situations. In a system context, users must get concrete experience with a new system and have time to think about how they are interacting with it. Typically, users get more and more comfortable and will develop new ways of using it before settling into a consistent work-stream process.

Another approach to learning is the conscious competence model, shown in Figure 10.24, where the first users cannot use the new system and are possibly unaware of the needed competence. Later, the users get to know the system and gain an understanding of what is required. Training kicks in and users become competent and know what they have to do. Finally, users can perform more than they are aware of as the system interaction starts to become natural to them.

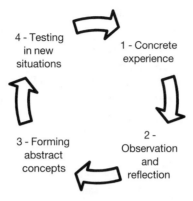

Figure 10.23 Kolb's learning cycle

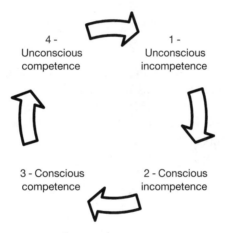

Figure 10.24 Conscious competence model

In agile system development, the organization assessment for organizational readiness for change is the task of the product owner in dialogue with the stakeholders, if needed.

10.25 PLANNING TOOLS AND TECHNIQUES

Technique	Needs Assessment	Planning	Analysis	Traceability and Monitoring	Evaluation	Waterfall	Agile
Planning tools and techniques		X				X	

Early on, the business analyst is involved in organizational changes and is in constant need of knowledge of the firm's strategy and the tactics to reach that strategy. The business strategy and objectives are the overall goals that the firm is aiming to achieve, which are supported at the tactical level where the strategies are made concrete and are executed on a shorter time frame. Tactical decisions are executed on the operational level, which runs the business (see Table 10.38). Strategy decisions have a long time frame, often 3-5 years. The complexity and uncertainty are high as knowledge is limited, being 3-5 years in the future. Tactical planning involves decision making on a 1-2 year time frame, which reduces complexity and uncertainty while increasing the knowledge needed to make the decision. The operational level deals with decisions within days, weeks, and months where the knowledge of the decisions is high and complexity and uncertainty are low.

Table 10.38 Types of decision

Types of Decisions				
	Time	Complexity	Uncertainty	Knowledge
Strategic	Long	High	High	Low
Tactical	Middle	Middle	Middle	Middle
Operational	Short	Low	Low	High

Business Analysis for Practitioners (2015) has identified developing strategies for sequencing elicitation activities as a collaboration point where the business analyst and the project manager should work together to determine how resource availability may impact the project and the overall planning.

The business analyst needs to navigate within the strategic, tactical, and operational planning levels. The input from the planning levels will affect the decision making, and be seen in the agreements being made, as well as the developments of the business cases, which support the firm's strategic and tactical levels. This being said, the project charter will likely contain similar considerations as projects are strategically driven in more and more firms. In order to analyze the strategic and tactical environments, the following should be investigated: external business environment, internal capability, strategy definition, and strategy implementation.

Strategy Analysis: External Business Environment

PEST(EL) analysis examines the external business environment within the following areas:

- Political
- Economic
- Socio-cultural
- Technological
- Environmental (sometimes)
- Legal (sometimes)

Sometimes, it can be useful to include environment and legal external business environment factors. The analysis is often conducted in a workshop where participants brainstorm and describe the considerations within each business factor.

The five forces analysis shown in Figure 10.25 was developed by Michael Porter with the aim of analyzing competition within a given market. The analysis is on the strategic level as it examines threats of new entrants, bargaining power of the buyers, bargaining power of the suppliers, and threats of substitute products and services, which overall describes the rivalry among existing competitors.

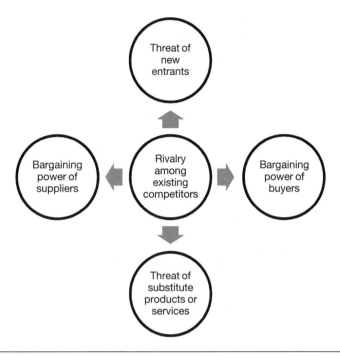

Figure 10.25 Porter's Five Forces Analysis

Table 10.39 contains some of the considerations within each area to be analyzed.

Table 10.39 Four-factor analysis

Threats of new entrants	Bargaining power of the buyers	Bargaining power of the suppliers	Threats of substitute products and services
Barriers to entry	Concentration of the buyers	Strength	Ease of change
Policies	Customer value dependency	Presence	Quality
Distribution		Switching costs	Number of substitute products on the market
Customer loyalty			

Strategy Analysis: Internal Capability

Strategy analysis must likewise examine internal capabilities in order to determine what direction we are going toward and what means are allocated to achieve those goals. The *MOST* analysis examines:

- Mission
- Objectives
- Strategy
- Tactics

The mission describes the rationale and direction, which is transformed into the firm's objectives and goals. The goals are planned for strategically and feature medium- and long-range planning while the tactical level in a MOST analysis has a shorter time frame.

The resource audit analyzes the resources available in the organization and are classified as: tangible resources—often financial and physical resources; intangible resources—reputation and expertise; and human resources—skills, knowledge, and communication. The resources are mapped into five areas as illustrated in Figure 10.26.

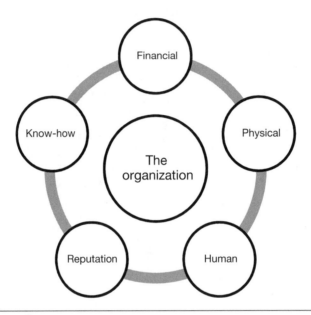

Figure 10.26   Resource audit

A part of strategy analysis and understanding internal capabilities is analyzing products and their positions in a given market. One approach is Boston box analysis (see Table 10.40), which examines the product's market share in a given market and whether overall market growth is high or low. If the market growth is high and the firm's products have a high market share, the situation is a star, which is a very favorable market situation. Low market growth coupled with high market share is called a cash cow, where the firm's products should stay in the market and maximize profit.

Table 10.40   Boston box quadrants

Market growth	High	*Wild cat*	*Star*
	Low	*Dog*	*Cash cow*
		Low	High
		Market share	

As market growth and market share may change rapidly, this analysis should be conducted regularly on the strategic and tactical level. In order to determine which direction is best, the possible risks and rewards should be considered. The risk-return matrix by Edgett and Kleinschmidt (1997) shown in Figure 10.27 illustrates the relationship between risks and rewards, which are often aligned. However, in some cases rewards may be high with less risk, the so-called *oysters*; while *bread and butter* is the reverse situation with low reward and high risk.

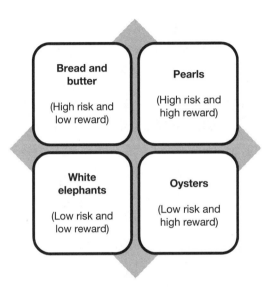

Figure 10.27 Risk-return matrix

Strategy Definition

In order to define the firm's strategy, management needs to fully understand the internal and external environments, which can be conducted by a SWOT (strength, weakness, opportunities, threats) analysis and using the Ansoff's matrix for defining product strategy.

SWOT analysis, as seen in Table 10.41, analyzes internal factors with strengths and weaknesses, and external factors with opportunities and threats. SWOT analysis may be used in conjunction with Porter's five forces, which illustrates several of the external threats, while the resource audit may illustrate internal strengths and weaknesses.

Table 10.41 SWOT analysis

Strength	Weakness
Opportunities	Threats

The Ansoff matrix (see Table 10.42) considers growth strategies for new and existing products within new and existing markets, providing four possible combinations of market strategy: growth via existing products to existing markets with the goal of greater market share (least risk), marketing existing products to new market segments (medium risk), developing new products for existing markets (medium risk), or diversification by going into new markets with new products (most risk).

Table 10.42   Ansoff matrix

Market	New	Market development	Diversification
	Existing	Market penetration	Product development
		Existing	New
		Product	

The Ansoff matrix can be used with Boston Box Analysis. It can also be supplemented with other strategies. However, candidates will not be tested on these other strategies.

Strategy Implementation

The McKinsey 7-S model presents a holistic understanding of the factors involved in organizational change. The factors are:

- Shared value
- Skills
- Staff
- Style

- Strategy
- Systems
- Structure

In addition, the four-view model, which is similar to Leavitt (discussed earlier in this chapter), also highlights factors influencing change:

- Organization
- Processes

- People
- Technology

A change of technology within an organization would influence people, process, and the organization as a whole. When working in agile, planning on a strategic and tactical level is the concern of the product owner, who should keep the development team informed on any directions, considerations, strategies, and goals influencing their tasks. Providing this knowledge to the team is a part of adaptive leadership performed by the product owner.

10.26 POLITICAL AND CULTURAL AWARENESS

Technique	Needs Assessment	Planning	Analysis	Traceability and Monitoring	Evaluation	Waterfall	Agile
Political and cultural awareness	X					X	

With an ever increasing global environment which sets new standards for interpersonal skills, political and cultural awareness are more important than ever for the business analyst. Most teams are scattered across the globe in different time zones, and cultural diversity is ever growing due to the search for competitive advantages. The global environment affects individuals and corporations in which the business analyst needs to navigate in order to be successful. This may affect the speed of working, the decision making, and the communication among team members with management or stakeholders. In some cultures, *now* means now, while in others, it may mean within weeks, which could affect project time management. Some cultures are individual focused, which works well with individual rewards, while other cultures are more group-oriented. In general, communication is difficult in a global environment which puts focus on written documentation in order to avoid misunderstandings. Our diverse environment is more complex which means the opportunities for conflicts increase. The business analyst must have a high degree of professionalism and a global outlook and awareness. Politics are inevitable and the business analyst needs to navigate and make skillful use of politics and power in order to be successful.

Previously, the Blake and Hofstede model was introduced as a model for cultural analysis. Now, Schein's cultural iceberg shown in Figure 10.28, and Johnson and Scholes's cultural web will be introduced to add more techniques and tools for the business analyst.

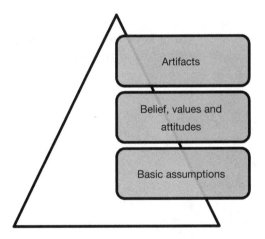

Figure 10.28   Cultural pyramid based upon Schein's cultural iceberg

Culture, globalization, and team diversity are major topics in the literature and play a vital role in our projects and activities. Culture is more or less everything that people have, think, and do as members of a society. It is learned and shared, and forms enduring orientation patterns in a society. People demonstrate their culture through values, ideas, attitudes, behaviors, and symbols.

Our task is to understand how culture affects the project, learn to work within a multicultural environment, study human behavior, follow changes over time, and navigate in the complexity of culture. We do this so that we can apply that understanding to how culture influences habits, values, and communication styles, and how business practices work.

Edgar Henry Schein, a former professor at the MIT Sloan School of Management, conducted research on organizational development and culture. His illustration of the iceberg helps us understand the many layers of culture. Part of a culture is visible and well above the water. These can be items like literature and fine art. Everyone can access it and it becomes common knowledge after a while. The second layer is folk culture. We are aware of it; it is still visible above the water. Humor, cooking, and dressing are examples of the second layer of culture. The last layer is below the surface of the water, the deep culture that we are unaware of. It might include gender roles, nonverbal communication, and similar concepts. These are difficult to master unless we are exposed for many years to people's thoughts, feelings, and experiences.

Johnson and Scholes's cultural web contains a summary of the cultural aspect of an organization that a business analyst needs to consider during most projects. The model includes the following factors:

- Stories
- Symbols
- Power structure
- Organizational structure
- Control systems
- Rituals and routines
- The paradigm

The paradigm is the heart of the culture and the basic assumption in Schein's iceberg. Stories, rituals, routines, and symbols are used throughout the organization as logos, statements, and war stories. The organizational structure is the formal organizational diagram, while the actual power structure might be different. Figure 10.29 illustrates Johnson and Scholes's cultural web.

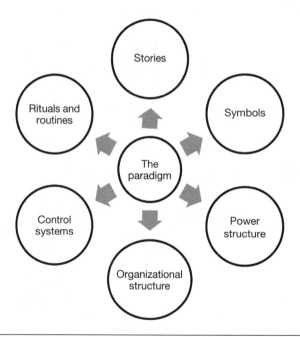

Figure 10.29   Johnson and Scholes's cultural web

When working in agile, political awareness is covered and managed by the product owner. However, cultural awareness has a major impact on the development teams who are also more and more culturally diverse. One technique that development teams use to avoid conflicts and get a common understanding on how to work is through the use of ground rules, which are often unwritten rules about expectations on the project. In agile teams, ground rules are communicated clearly so that everyone knows what is expected of them. Ground rules may include times for working and taking breaks, the *when* and *where* for mobile talks, whether working from home is an option, or the amount of work a team member is expected to deliver on a working day. Ground rules foster communication and sometimes conflicts, but they create a healthy working environment when sorted out and agreed upon because everyone knows exactly what is expected of them—no more and no less.

10.27 PRIORITIZATION TOOLS AND TECHNIQUES

Technique	Needs Assessment	Planning	Analysis	Traceability and Monitoring	Evaluation	Waterfall	Agile
Prioritization tools and techniques			X			X	X

Prioritization tools and techniques are discussed in Chapter 7.

10.28 PROBLEM SOLVING AND OPPORTUNITY IDENTIFICATION TOOLS AND TECHNIQUES

Technique	Needs Assessment	Planning	Analysis	Traceability and Monitoring	Evaluation	Waterfall	Agile
Problem solving and opportunity identification tools and techniques	X					X	X

Mastering business analysis is a lifelong pursuit for those who love problem solving. During the work, problems and opportunities will arise. Information needs to be gathered about these problems and opportunities, which will result in further analysis whether it is for solving a problem or seeking new opportunities. Whether it is requirements which cause scope creeps, test failures, or new possibilities, many of the tools and techniques are similar. To some degree, the problems may be related to quality or scope aspects of the products, where prevention will be sought out if possible as it is cheaper to aim for conformance than nonconformance. On the whole, the need for problem-solving skills arise, whether it is solving problems in teams; developing creative, innovative solutions; showing independence and initiative in identifying problems and solving them; applying a range of strategies to problem solving; or resolving customer concerns in relation to complex project issues.

The tools and techniques for identifying problems and opportunities are focused around information gathering techniques, such as:

- Delphi
- Brainstorming (round robin, brainwriting)
- Interviews or surveys
- Observing
- Analogy
- Expert judgment
- Performance measurement
- Benchmarking
- SWOT analysis
- Creative product development
- Creative readings

The tools and techniques for analyzing problems and opportunities are covered in Table 10.43.

Table 10.43 Resolving problems and opportunities

Techniques	Descriptions
Root cause (Ishikawa, fishbone, cause-effect)	Root cause analysis, cause and effect diagrams, Ishikawa diagrams, or fishbone diagrams are processes or tools for identifying contributing or causal factors that underlie variations in performance associated with adverse events or close calls.
Process maps, system or process flow charts	Process maps, also known as process charting or flow charting, is a process which documents/draws the processes in order to highlight problems and improvements.
Gap analysis—*as-is/to-be*	Gap analysis describes the current state as the *as-is* situation and the future state as the *to-be* situation; in between might include a gap of opportunities or problems to be covered.
Influence diagrams	Influence diagrams identify important variables and relationships in the decision problem. It is a graphical representation that shows all the variables that impact the net present value of a project.
Customer journey map	A graphic representation of the user's experience throughout the system which can illustrate opportunities for improvements.
Failure mode and effect analysis (FMEA)	Systematic approach for failure analysis.
Fault tree analysis	A fault tree is a logical diagram that shows the relation between system failures—i.e., a specific undesirable event in the system—and failures of the components of the system. It is a technique based on deductive logic.
Value engineering	Improve value—cost benefit analysis.
The 5 Whys	We work our way from a problem to a solution by asking *Why?* five times, or until we arrive at the root cause.
Pareto analysis	Pareto analysis, also known as the 80/20 rule, shows how 80% of the problems are due to 20% of the failure, and 20% effort may solve 80% of the problems. However, the remaining 20% requires 80% effort.
Force field analysis	Force field analysis was developed by Kurt Lewin and is a useful decision-making technique used to compensate for failures in system design. It helps you make a decision by analyzing the forces for and against a change, and it helps you communicate the reasoning behind your decision.

An alternative approach is the problem pyramid developed by Robin Goldsmith, which identifies some of the problems with scoping and requirements that the business analyst may face. The steps are:

- Problem, opportunity, or challenge
- Current measure
- Goal measure
- Cause
- Business requirements
- Design

When working in an agile environment, the techniques for identifying problems evolve around cycle times, which is the time that it takes to complete a user story and its possibly escaped defects—which are defects found by the customers that escaped the team's quality control. A broader agile concept is agile smells. When something smells, it is bad. When it is bad, we have a quality issue that we need to fix before the smells evolve. In agile, smells are ways to quickly recognize, describe, and diagnose common problems so that a remedy may be pursued. The agile smells may include: practices take too long, members have fixed roles, or techniques are not used properly. For resolving problems, the agile methodologies rely on verification, validation, refactoring, test-driven development, and the use of spikes, if uncertain of which way to go.

10.29 PROCESS ANALYSIS TOOLS AND TECHNIQUES

Technique	Needs Assessment	Planning	Analysis	Traceability and Monitoring	Evaluation	Waterfall	Agile
Process analysis tools and techniques			X			X	X

Process analysis tools and techniques are discussed in the domains.

10.30 PROJECT METHODOLOGIES

Technique	Needs Assessment	Planning	Analysis	Traceability and Monitoring	Evaluation	Waterfall	Agile
Project methodologies	X	X	X	X	X	X	X

Project methodologies are models that project managers and business analysts employ for the design, planning, implementation, and achievement of project objectives. The project methodologies involved in managing the project management constraints—scope, risk, quality, cost, resources, and schedule—are illustrated in Figure 10.30. Constraints have a relationship, which implies that a change in one will affect the others. For instance, a reduced time schedule may reduce scope, increase risk, reduce quality, require additional resources, and/or increase costs.

Figure 10.30 Project management constraints based upon *I Am Agile* by Klaus Nielsen

No matter which development methodologies the project applies, the project management constraints need to be managed. Management of the constraints may be regarded as fixed or variable. Figure 10.31 illustrates how time and resources are fixed in the waterfall model, while they are flexible with the agile methodologies. This may have a major impact on how we manage our projects.

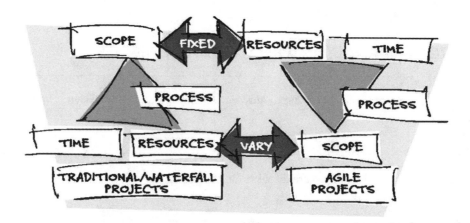

Figure 10.31 Project constraints and development methodologies based upon *I Am Agile* by Klaus Nielsen

This book uses *PMBOK® Guide—Fifth Edition* methodologies, which are based upon waterfall practices while also expanding into agile methodologies. There are different project management methodologies to benefit different projects. At this stage, it is clear how the waterfall approach affects requirements and business analysis (BA) practices. Now, several agile methodologies will be introduced and then discussed to determine how they affect requirements and BA practices.

Scrum

In rugby, a scrum refers to the manner of restarting the game after a minor infraction where players work together, interlocking arms and legs, to take possession of the ball (achieve a common goal). The origins of Scrum (in this context) can be found in an article called "The New New Product Development Game," by Hirotaka Takeuchi and Ikujiro Nonaka published in the *Harvard Business Review* in 1986. Later, Scrum champion Jeff Sutherland worked to smooth these ideas into a formal process for software development. In 2001, Ken Schwaber and Mike Beedle wrote the book *Agile Software Development with Scrum*, which many consider the official start of Scrum as we know it today. Scrum is the most applied agile methodology and is covered in detail in Chapter 13.

Extreme Programming

Extreme Programming (XP) is a self-proclaimed *light methodology* created by Kent Beck in 1999 while he was working on a project for Chrysler. Beck's *Extreme Programming Explained: Embrace Change* (1999) further popularized the concept. The term *extreme* comes from taking these common sense practices and techniques to an extreme level. XP is a set of practices for small- to medium-sized development teams to help ensure quality and high business value in the code they produce, while eliminating excessive overhead.

XP is a discipline of software development based on values. It works by bringing the whole team together in the presence of simple practices with enough feedback to enable the team to see where they are and to tune the practices to their unique situation. The original XP values were simplicity, communication, feedback, and courage. Values are translated into principles, and principles are put into use with activities and practices. The next part of this section will explain XP in terms of the high-level view of the XP project life cycle, the 12 practices, and the five key XP roles. The XP project life cycle is shown in Figure 10.32, and goes from left to right. The beginning is the exploration phase where user stories are created and architectural spikes are made. A spike is a quick experiment to gain knowledge, in this case about the architectural design. The system metaphors are one of the 12 practices. User stories are requirements. Next is the planning phase with a high-level focus on releases. Releases are then broken down into iterations, developed and tested in small chunks, and delivered as small releases.

XP has been described as having 12 practices which implement XP values. The 12 practices are described in Table 10.44.

Kanban Methodology

The *Kanban* method is a change management method, not a framework. Kanban employs a set of management practices for software derived from the Toyota Production System and Goldratt's Theory of Constraints. Kanban is Japanese, and means visual record or card. In Lean, it is used for signal mechanics. Kanban describes a process for driving change in an organization and that process must have sufficient detail as to be repeatable. Kanban was originally applied to software maintenance, then expanded to general software development, and has grown to cover IT operations, IT services, and other areas of knowledge work. There is some belief and hope that Kanban will develop as a general-purpose change-management approach for knowledge worker industries.

David Anderson (2012) defined three foundational Kanban principles:

1. Start with what you do now
2. Agree to pursue incremental, evolutionary change
3. Respect current process, roles, responsibilities, and titles

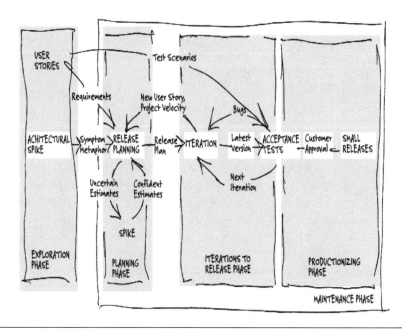

Figure 10.32 XP adapted from *I Am Agile* by Klaus Nielsen

Table 10.44 XP Values

Number	Practice	Descriptions
1	Planning	The programmer estimates the effort needed for implementation of customer stories and the customer decides the scope and timing of releases based on estimates.
2	Small/short releases	An application is developed in a series of small, frequently updated versions. New versions are released anywhere from daily to monthly.
3	Metaphor	The system is defined by a set of metaphors between the customer and the programmers, which describes how the system works.
4	Simple design	The emphasis is on designing the simplest possible solution to implement—unnecessary complexity and extra code are removed immediately.
5	Refactoring	This involves restructuring the system by removing duplication, improving communication, simplifying, and adding flexibility—without changing the functionality of the program.
6	Pair programming	All production code is written by two programmers on one computer.
7	Collective ownership	No single person owns or is responsible for individual code segments; rather, anyone can change any part of the code at any time.
8	Continuous integration	A new piece of code is integrated with the current system as soon as it is ready. When integrating, the system is built again and all tests must pass for the changes to be accepted.
9	40-hour week	No one can work two overtime weeks in a row. A 40-hour work week is the max, otherwise it is treated as a problem.
10	On-site customer	Customer must be available at all times for the development team.
11	Coding standards	Coding rules exist and are followed by the programmers so as to bring consistency and improve communication among the development team.
12	Open workspace	Developers work in a common workspace set up with individual workstations around the periphery and common development machines in the center.

Anderson (2012) also defined five core properties (see Table 10.45) in order to achieve success with this change management method.

Table 10.45 Kanban core properties

Number	Core properties
1	Visualize the workflow
2	Limit WIP
3	Manage/focus on flow
4	Make process policies explicit
5	Improve collaboratively (using models and the scientific method)

The core property *visualize the workflow* uses value stream mapping. *Limiting work-in-progress (WIP)* is where the issue of product quality is discussed. Engaging in too much work at the same time without completing it could cause a bottleneck and have a negative effect on quality. The core property *manage/focus on flow* is found in value stream mapping and WIP. *Making process policies explicit* refers to the use of Kanban boards to demonstrate progress and communication.

Kanban varies from many of the other methodologies (e.g., Scrum) as it does not focus on roles, which is a dominant factor in most methodologies. Kanban contains a wide range of optional aspects, such as team size, burn-down charts, and cross-functional teams. Kanban offers easy-to-use tools, practices, and philosophy, all in one package, and is often used in conjunction with other agile methodologies.

Crystal Methods

Crystal methods were developed by Alistair Cockburn in the early 1990s. He believed that one of the major obstacles facing product development was poor communication, and modeled Crystal methods to address these needs (Cohen, 2003). Cockburn explains his philosophy:

"To the extent that you can replace written documentation with face-to-face interactions, you can reduce the reliance on written work products and improve the likelihood of delivering the system. The more frequently you can deliver running, tested slices of the system, the more you can reduce the reliance on written 'promissory' notes and improve the likelihood of delivering the system." Crystal methodologies are summarized in Table 10.46.

The Crystal family has seven properties. The first four are mandatory for all projects and Crystal family members, while the last three are elective. The seven properties are listed and described in Table 10.47.

Crystal methods consist of five strategies and nine techniques. They are not mandatory but have been found useful in many Crystal family projects. The five strategies and nine techniques are described and explained in Table 10.48.

Table 10.46 Crystal methods

Methodology	Description
Crystal Clear	Small team, no communication structure, no system validation, mandatory policy standards, most tolerant of the crystal methods, low-ceremony, close setting/close communication, regular reflection workshops, frequent delivery, code versioning tools
Crystal Yellow	Same as Crystal Clear, just increased number of people involved, larger budget, and more constraints
Crystal Orange	Big team (40+ people), team structure, medium-sized production projects, time to market is important, not life-critical system, one-two year duration, holistic diversity strategy, mandatory policy standards
Crystal Red	Increased number of people involved (40-80); more at risk so defects have bigger impact
Crystal Maroon	Increased number of people involved, more mission critical defects will have a greater impact than Crystal Red
Crystal Diamond	Increased number of people involved, more mission critical defects will have a greater impact than Crystal Maroon
Crystal Sapphire	Increased number of people involved (1,000+), more mission critical defects will have a greater impact than Crystal Diamond

Table 10.47 Crystal family seven properties

Selected properties	Explanation
Frequent delivery	Delivering running test code to real users, feedback from users, chance to debug, and morale boost through accomplishment
Reflective improvements	Think about what could work better and make the needed changes
Osmotic communication	Information that flows in the background
Personal safety	Being able to talk about what is on one's mind; trust and honesty
Focus	Know what to work on, have the time and space to do the work
Easy access to expert users	Access to experts, reduce reliance on indirect links
Technical environments with automated tests, configuration management, and frequent integration	Have a basic technical environment for frequent delivery

Table 10.48 Strategies and techniques

Strategy/ Technique	Name	Explanation
Strategy	Exploratory 360 degree	Part of charting process to look at envisioned need from many perspectives, sampling the project
Strategy	Early victory	Create small wins in terms of running code, etc., to increase confidence and morale
Strategy	Walking skeleton	Small implementation of the system that performs a small end-to-end functionality
Strategy	Incremental rearchitecture	Revising architecture based upon the walking skeleton
Strategy	Information radiators	Communication displays such as dashboards and whiteboards
Technique	Methodology shaping	Modify practices for unique aspects of each project, including adjusting to scale
Technique	Reflection workshop	Workshop for reflective improvements from lessons learned
Technique	Blitz planning	Jam session, a quick and collaborating project planning technique
Technique	Delphi estimation	Estimates from experts
Technique	Daily stand-up meetings	Meeting to share information; time-boxed as in Scrum
Technique	Essential interaction design	Usage-centered design technique
Technique	Process miniature	A learning technique scaled-down for benchmarking
Technique	Side-by-side programming	A less intense alternative to pair programming
Technique	Burn charts	Plan and report progress of objects planned, started, and completed

Adaptive Systems Development Method

Adaptive software development (ASD), developed by James A. Highsmith, offers an agile and adaptive approach to the internet economy with high-speed and high-change software projects. ASD combines the philosophy and practices of rapid application development with the theory of complex adaptive systems. ASD is a technique for building complex software and systems. The philosophical underpinnings of ASD focus on human collaboration and team self-organization.

The practices of ASD are driven by a belief in continuous adaptation, a different philosophy and a different life cycle, geared toward accepting continuous change as the norm. In ASD, the static plan-design-build life cycle is replaced by a dynamic speculate-collaborate-learn life cycle. It is a life cycle dedicated to continuous learning and oriented toward change. An ASD life cycle has six basic characteristics:

1. Mission-focused
2. Feature-based
3. Iterative
4. Time-boxed
5. Risk-driven
6. Change-tolerant

The ASD framework or adaptive life cycle consists of three phases—speculate, collaborate, and learn. The *speculate* phase is the initiating and planning phase. It also gives room to explore, make clear the realization with which we are unsure, and deviate from plans without fear. Through it all, we plan scope, iterations, and tasks. In the speculate phase, we set the project's mission and objectives, understand constraints, establish the project organization, identify and outline requirements, make initial size and scope estimates, and identify key project risks. The *collaborate* phase is the execution phase where the team tests and codes the solution. The final *learn* phase is a retrospective where the team reflects on what they have discovered. Once the team admits to itself that it is fallible, then learning practices—the learn part of the life cycle—becomes vital for success. The team then has to test its knowledge constantly using practices like project retrospectives and customer focus groups.

Dynamic Systems Development Method

The dynamic systems development method (DSDM) is an agile project management and delivery framework that aims to deliver the right solution at the right time. It focuses on the early delivery of real benefits to a business, user, or customer, while ensuring that the project remains strategically aligned. DSDM is a public domain rapid application development (RAD) method that was developed in the United Kingdom in the mid-1990s through capturing the experience of a large consortium of vendor and user organizations. It is now considered to be the UK's de-facto standard for RAD.

The DSDM is a blend of, and extension to, RAD and iterative development practices. The fundamental idea of DSDM is that instead of replacing functionality in a product, then fixing time and resources to reach that functionality, we manage time and resources and then manage the functionality in relation to the time and resources. DSDM aims at removing the quick and dirty image of RAD by delivering a controlled environment. DSDM is a high-level framework, which gives the developers a wide range of tools and techniques to tailor.

The DSDM development process/life cycle phases include: feasibility, functional model iteration, design and build iteration, and implementation. The first phase, feasibility, aims to investigate the technical and business aspects of completing the project. This phase may use fast prototyping to provide information on the technical feasibility.

Part of the feasibility phase is a business study where business aspects of conducting the project and high-level requirements are identified. A common technique in this phase is a joint application design session for high-level requirements. This phase often takes a few weeks.

The next phase is the iterative functional model iteration, which aims at creating an analysis model, software components, and prototyping activities. Each iteration consists of four activities: identification of tasks, agreement of task allocation, carrying out the tasks, and a review of completed tasks.

The design and build iteration phase adjusts and defines the system for use and implementation. The activities of the functional model iteration continue.

The implementation phase places the system into an operating environment. Users are trained and documentation is created. The output of this process model is a fully functional system that fits the user's requirements, including documentation suitable for maintenance, training schemes, and user manuals.

Lean Software Development

The term *Lean Software Development* was first coined as the title for a conference organized by the ESPRIT initiative in 1992. Independently the following year, Robert Charette suggested the concept of Lean Software Development as part of his work exploring better ways of managing risk in software projects. The term *lean* dates to 1991 and was used by James Womack, Daniel Jones, and Daniel Roos in their book *The Machine That Changed the World: The Story of Lean Production*, as the English language term to describe the management approach used at Toyota. The idea that lean might be applicable in software development was established very early, only 1 to 2 years after the term was first used in association with trends in manufacturing processes and industrial engineering (Microsoft, 2012).

The five-step thought processes for guiding the implementation of lean techniques (Womack, 2012) are:

1. Specify value from the standpoint of the end customer by product family.
2. Identify all the steps in the value stream for each product family, eliminating whenever possible those steps that do not create value.
3. Make the value-creating steps occur in tight sequence so the product will flow smoothly toward the customer.
4. As flow is introduced, let customers pull value from the next upstream activity.
5. Once value is specified, value streams identified, wasted steps removed, and flow and pull introduced, begin the process again and continue it until a state of perfect value is created with no waste.

The principles are applied by using thinking tools, such as *seeing waste* and *value stream mapping* as illustrated in Table 10.49.

Table 10.49 Lean principles

Lean principles	Thinking tools	Comments
Eliminate waste	Tool 1: Seeing waste Tool 2: Value stream mapping	Waste is illustrated later in this chapter
Amplify learning	Tool 3: Feedback Tool 4: Iterations Tool 5: Synchronization Tool 6: Set-based development	The nature of software development
Decide as late as possible	Tool 7: Options thinking Tool 8: The last responsible moment Tool 9: Making decisions	Concurrent development
Deliver as fast as possible	Tool 10: Pull systems Tool 11: Queuing theory Tool 12: Costs of delays	
Empower the team	Tool 13: Self-determination Tool 14: Motivation Tool 15: Leadership Tool 16: Expertise	Beyond scientific management
Build integrity in	Tool 17: Perceived integrity Tool 18: Conceptual integrity Tool 19: Refactoring Tool 20: Testing	Integrity as a foundation
See the whole	Tool 21: Measurements Tool 22: Contracts	System thinking

Feature Driven Development

Feature driven development arose in the late 1990s as a collaboration between Jeff DeLuca, Peter Coad, and Stephen Palmer. Their work is presented in *Java Modeling in Color with UML* (Coad, 1999) and later in *A Practical Guide to Feature-Driven Development* (2002).

"In 1997, Jeff De Luca, an Australian, put together a team for a large lending system project at United Overseas Bank in Singapore. The team included Peter Coad who was well known for his writing on object-oriented analysis and design and the development of a process of software engineering for use with object technology on a large line of business IT projects. He called this process method, 'The Coad Method'. At the heart of The Coad Method was an analysis artifact he dubbed 'a feature.' Features sounded like requirements and were written using domain language which the project sponsors could understand. The concept with features is that each one was written so that the sponsor could agree that the feature had meaning and was required in the system. During the Singapore Project between 1997 and 1999, The Coad Method evolved into feature driven development with the introduction of ideas from the work of Gerald Weinberg, Frederick Brooks, Timothy Lister, and Tom De Marco with some valuable insights on reporting from Jeff De Luca and batching of work from Stephen Palmer" (Anderson, 2004).

Agile Methodologies and Their Affect on Requirements and BA Practices

Agile methods encourage changes in requirements to ensure best value delivery to customers. This means that scope is flexible with agile methodologies and may change at any time. Tables 10.50-10.54 are aligned with the Project Management Institute Agile Certified Practitioner (PMI-ACP)® certification examination content outline, and include the agile tools and techniques along with the domains.

Table 10.50 Needs Assessment

Needs Assessment	
Define business requirement	Agile
5.1 Define business requirements	Interpersonal skills
5.2 Define value proposition	Value-based prioritization
5.3 Develop project goals	Risk management
5.4 Identify stakeholders	Value-driven delivery
5.5 Analyze stakeholders	Agile principles and mindset
	Stakeholder engagement
	Process improvements
	Problem detection and resolution

Table 10.51 Planning

Planning	
Planning	Agile
6.1 Determine project context	Planning, monitoring, and adapting
6.2 Plan requirement traceability	Agile estimation
6.3 Develop requirement management plan	Risk management
6.4 Plan requirement change control	Value-based prioritization
6.5 Plan document control	Value-driven delivery
6.6 Define project expected outcome	Adaptive planning

Table 10.52 Analysis

Analysis	
Analysis	Agile
7.1 Elicit requirements	Planning, monitoring, and adapting
7.2 Elaborate requirements	Agile analysis and design
7.3 Validate requirements	Product quality
7.4 Allocate requirements	Process improvements
7.5 Get requirement signoff	
7.6 Document requirements	
7.7 Verify requirements	
7.8 Specify requirements expected results	

Table 10.53 Traceability and Monitoring

Traceability and Monitoring	
Traceability and Monitoring	Agile
8.1 Track requirements	Communications
8.2 Monitor requirements	Planning, monitoring, and adapting
8.3 Update a requirement status	Process improvements
8.4 Communicate requirement status	Product quality
8.5 Manage changes to requirements	Metrics

Table 10.54 Evaluation

Evaluation	
Evaluation	Agile
9.1 Validate test results	Continuous improvements
9.2 Analyze solution gaps	Process improvements
9.3 Obtain stakeholder acceptance of solution	
9.4 Evaluate solution results	

The agile methodologies do not necessarily cover all aspects of a project as illustrated in Figure 10.33, which shows a comparison of agile methodologies. Only DSDM includes the activities described in the *Needs Assessment* domain. Most agile methodologies cover all aspects and activities from *Planning*, *Analysis*, to *Traceability and Monitoring*, while only DSDM covers the *Evaluation* domain.

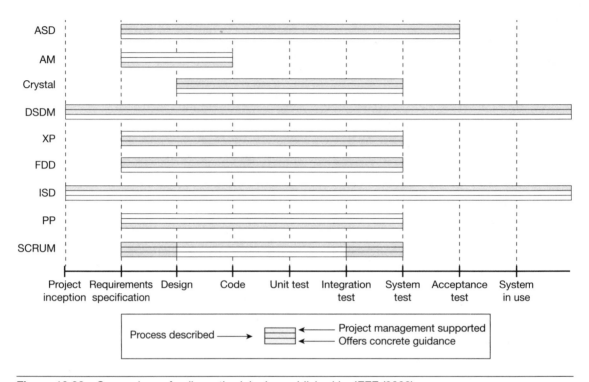

Figure 10.33 Comparison of agile methodologies published by IEEE (2003)

10.31 QUALITY MANAGEMENT

Technique	Needs Assessment	Planning	Analysis	Traceability and Monitoring	Evaluation	Waterfall	Agile
Quality management		X				X	X

Quality management is weaved into many parts of this book and in the domains.

10.32 REPORTING TOOLS AND TECHNIQUES

Technique	Needs Assessment	Planning	Analysis	Traceability and Monitoring	Evaluation	Waterfall	Agile
Reporting tools and techniques				X		X	X

Reporting is the key, official method for communicating to the stakeholders about how project resources are being used, what the progress is, and how project objectives are being met. Reporting methods—such as e-mail, formal reports, and face-to-face meetings and their frequencies—are outlined in the communications management plan and communications requirement analysis.

Reporting communicates all kinds of project information as output from the knowledge areas, which is covered in greater detail in the processes highlighted in the knowledge area of communication. The project manager and business analyst report project information regarding time, cost, risk, scope, and other similar factors on a regular basis—which are included in issues, lessons learned, reports, status, progress, records, presentations, earned value management reports, and similar kinds of reports and information.

Reporting is performed differently for different reports, different outcomes, or different stakeholders, because communication is tailored to its purpose. Reporting is performed against the project baseline, which is the original set of schedule dates, budget amounts, expected work, scope, and quality targets developed in the project planning phase. Project baselines are evaluated against actual performance of the project as the project is executed.

Communications on project activities are collected as work performance data, which is gathered and analyzed for work performance information and work performance reports and is then distributed and managed as illustrated in Tables 10.55 and 10.56.

Table 10.55   Process 10.2 Manage communications

Inputs	Tools and Techniques	Outputs
• Communication management plan • Work performance data • Enterprise environmental factors • Organizational process assets	• Communication technology • Communication models • Communication methods • Information management systems • Performance reporting	• Project communications • Project management plan updates • Project document updates • Organizational process assets updates

Table 10.56   Process 10.3 Control communications

Inputs	Tools and Techniques	Outputs
• Project management plan • Project communications • Issue log • Work information data • Organizational process assets	• Information management systems • Expert judgment • Meetings	• Work performance information • Change requests • Project management plan updates • Project document updates • Organizational process assets updates

The process highlighted also illustrates the need and use of an information management system, which facilitates processes and procedures used to generate or consolidate reports from one or more information management systems and facilitates reports distribution to project stakeholders.

The output for reporting tools and techniques is written, formal communication. However, since communication may take many forms and formats, including informal and verbal, it must be managed in the reporting by the applied tools and techniques.

10.33 REQUIREMENTS TRACEABILITY TOOLS AND TECHNIQUES

Technique	Needs Assessment	Planning	Analysis	Traceability and Monitoring	Evaluation	Waterfall	Agile
Requirements traceability tools and technique				X		X	X

Requirements traceability tools and techniques are discussed in Chapter 7. True requirements traceability is achieved if the origin of each requirement is clear, and if it facilitates the referencing of each requirement in future development or enhancement documentation (IEEE, 1984). Traceability is a technique that provides a relationship between different levels of requirements in the system and plays several important roles, including:

- **Verifying that an implementation fulfills all requirements**: Everything that the customer requested was implemented.
- **Verifying that the application does only what was requested**: Doesn't implement something that the customer never asked for.
- **Impact analysis**: What elements will be affected when we consider adding a new requirement or changing an existing one?
- **Helping with change management**: When some requirements change, we want to know which test cases should be redone to test this change.

The basic techniques (Orlene et al., 1993) for requirements traceability are:

- Cross referencing schemes
- Key phrase dependencies
- Templates
- Requirement traceability matrices
- Matrix sequences
- Hypertext
- Integration documents
- Assumption-based truth maintenance networks
- Constraint networks

10.34 REQUIREMENT TYPES

Technique	Needs Assessment	Planning	Analysis	Traceability and Monitoring	Evaluation	Waterfall	Agile
Requirement types	X	X	X	X	X	X	X

Requirement types are discussed in Chapter 7.

10.35 ROOT CAUSE ANALYSIS

Technique	Needs Assessment	Planning	Analysis	Traceability and Monitoring	Evaluation	Waterfall	Agile
Root cause analysis		X				X	X

Many times, projects have had problems solved with quick fixes, which are repeated over and over. In this case, a Pareto analysis may prove useful to find the root cause as the Pareto 80/20 rules explains that 80% of all problem occurrences are typically linked to only 20 percent of distinctly identified problems. In order to improve upon the situation (save time and money), the team needs to look deeper and identify the root cause in order to fix it for good. A *root cause* is the underlying cause of the problem which, if adequately addressed, will prevent a recurrence of that problem. Root cause analysis is a problem-solving process for conducting an investigation into an identified incident, problem, concern, or nonconformity. Root cause analysis helps identify what, how, and why something happened, thus preventing recurrence. It is also described through a cause and effect diagram, Ishikawa diagram, or fishbone diagram—processes for identifying or contributing causal factors that underlie variations in performance associated with adverse events or close calls. It utilizes interdisciplinary involvement of those closest to and most knowledgeable about the situation. Basically, the root cause analysis can point to several reasons as to why we have a problem, and it may be a valid input as requirements or for the design process. Figure 10.34 illustrates root cause analysis containing a range of causes along the sides, which all point toward an effect.

The five steps in root cause analysis are:

1. Define the nonconformity/identify the problem
2. Investigate the root cause/define/understand the problem
3. Create proposed action plan and define timescales/corrective actions
4. Implement proposed actions/corrective actions
5. Verification and monitoring of effectiveness/monitor the actions

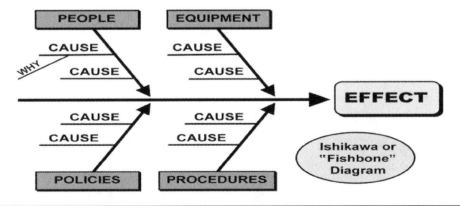

Figure 10.34 Root cause

Table 10.57 highlights the alignment of the steps of a root cause analysis and the techniques applied.

Table 10.57 Steps of a root cause analysis and the tools and techniques

	Identify the problem	Define the problem	Understand the problem	Identify the root cause	Corrective actions	Monitor the actions
Brainstorming	YES	YES				
Cause/effect diagrams		YES			YES	
Pareto diagrams	YES		YES			
Root cause analysis	YES	YES	YES	YES	YES	YES
Scatter diagrams			YES			
Flow charts			YES			
Interviews	YES	YES	YES	YES		
5 Whys	YES	YES	YES	YES	YES	YES
Documents, checklists, and records	YES	YES	YES	YES		

The *5 Whys* is the simplest method for structured root cause analysis (see Figure 10.35).

The method works from a problem to a solution by asking *Why?* five times, or until we arrive at the root cause. Consider this example:

- Problem: The server won't start.
- Why won't the server start? Because the power is not on.
- Why is the power not on? Because the turn-on button is missing.
- Why is the turn-on button missing? Because the cabinet was destroyed.
- Why was the cabinet destroyed? Because I dropped it on the floor.
- Why did you drop it on the floor? Because the floor was wet.
- Solution: I will mop the floor and buy a new cabinet.

A 5 Why root cause analysis can also work amazingly well for a targeted retrospective. An alternative to the proposed methods is the fault tree, which is a systematic graphical representation of possible occurrences of unfavorable outcomes.

Figure 10.35 The 5 Whys

10.36 SCHEDULING TOOLS AND TECHNIQUES

Technique	Needs Assessment	Planning	Analysis	Traceability and Monitoring	Evaluation	Waterfall	Agile
Scheduling tools and techniques		X				X	

Scheduling tools and techniques were discussed earlier in this chapter.

10.37 STAKEHOLDER ANALYSIS

Technique	Needs Assessment	Planning	Analysis	Traceability and Monitoring	Evaluation	Waterfall	Agile
Stakeholder analysis	X					X	

In the Needs Assessment domain, the stakeholder analysis focus has been on stakeholder identification and management. Stakeholders are vital for project success. However, the project manager and business analyst needs to ensure that the right stakeholders are involved, that they are used at the right time, and that stakeholder resources are used in the right way. The stakeholders can be of many different types as illustrated by the stakeholder wheel in Figure 10.36.

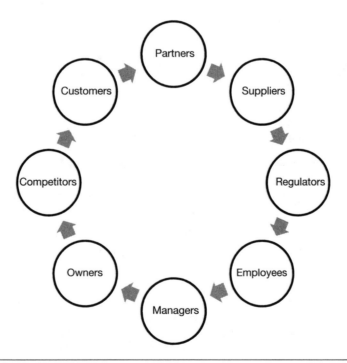

Figure 10.36   The stakeholder wheel

The project manager and business analyst need to ensure that the process of stakeholder identification, analysis, and management is done professionally, i.e., in human resource management. What is sometimes neglected is the use of stakeholder nomination, which should be based upon background research. The project manager and business analyst need to know the kind of stakeholders involved in the project.

Stakeholders are essential for project success. The project manager and the business analyst may benefit from obtaining a job analysis (duties, skills, and requirements) and applying it as input for identifying stakeholders. In addition, the job analysis may indicate which stakeholders can provide signoff. Stakeholders who are *applying* should go through a skills assessment, ensuring that they are qualified, and any training needs should be highlighted. However, this rarely is the case as stakeholder involvement is different in each project so most project owners are honored and pleased if any stakeholder wants to take part in it. However, it is hardly a best practice to forgo the assessment.

During system development and design, the business analyst may use personas and extreme characters for getting a better understanding of requirements. Personas are made up users who are designed for by the team. "When the project calls for it—for instance when user experience is a major factor in project outcomes—the team crafts detailed, synthetic biographies of fictitious users of the future product: these are called *personas*" (Agile Alliance, 2012).

Personas might include:

- Name
- Description
- Picture of a fictional persona (user)—actors

When designing personas:

- Add details
- Be grounded in reality
- Generate focus
- Be tangible and actionable
- Be goal oriented, specific, and relevant

"Personas are not replacements for requirements, but instead augment them" (Griffith, 2012). Sometimes, it is easier to develop a user story with a specific person in mind, like the super geeky, frequently smoking, bearded guy in HR, who after two hours knows all the features of a system—or friendly looking Martha with blond hair, who rarely uses the system. Table 10.58 demonstrates the content of a persona as described above.

Table 10.58 Persona

Random clip art picture	Works as product manager for a mid-sized company	Has managed mature products successfully
	Is 35 years old, holds a marketing degree	Now faces challenge of creating a brand new product
	Has got experience as a product owner of a software product with agile teams	Wants to leverage his agile knowledge but needs advice on creating innovative products using agile techniques
	Has had some Scrum training	

Personas are another application of having knowledge of the stakeholders and should be discussed with them, and in agile methodologies, with the product owner.

10.38 SYSTEM THINKING

Technique	Needs Assessment	Planning	Analysis	Traceability and Monitoring	Evaluation	Waterfall	Agile
System thinking	X	X	X	X	X	X	

System thinking has its foundation in system dynamics. Founded in 1956 by the MIT professor Jay Forrester as a way of thinking that is used to address and make sense of complicated and complex uncertain real-world problems, it is a term that is gaining wider use and acceptance, but it is not widely understood. System thinking is a holistic approach that focuses on the *what* and *why* of current reality over time, across organizational functions and levels, and through various levels of structure in order to effectively and efficiently achieve the results we desire. System thinking is not the same as chaos theory, dissipative structures, operations research, and decision analysis. In system design and development, much depends on correctly determining the requirements. Some requirements are tangible which makes them easier to document in a model or with natural language. However, some requirements or requirement attributes are intangible. In order to document requirements, the business analyst needs to make sense of the complicated problems and purposes along with the requirements. System *thinking* combines analytical thinking and synthetic thinking, where system *analysis* is the application of system thinking. The basic idea in system thinking is to list as many different elements as you can think of and then look for similarities between them.

The benefits of system thinking are:

- Relating people, purpose, process, performance, and systems to their environment
- Understanding complex problem situations
- Maximizing the outcomes achieved
- Helping solve complex and recurring problems
- Avoiding or minimizing the impact of unintended consequences
- Aligning teams, disciplines, specialism, and interest groups
- Managing uncertainty, risk, and opportunity
- Helping balance the needs of the organization's stakeholders
- Impacting how information is shared across the organization

System thinking tools and techniques are value stream mapping, soft systems methodology (SSM), causal mapping, a design structure matrix, and other techniques—all of which can be used together to clarify our thinking in the early stages of requirements engineering. Most tools and techniques include a first step that is analytical and lists as many elements as you can think of and a second step that is synthetic and aims at identifying the common theme or repeating pattern across those elements.

In the late 1960s, Peter Checkland, based in Lancaster, UK, introduced the concept of SSM—a problem-solving methodology which applies systems principles to business and other "soft" problems. It enables intervention in ill-structured problem situations, where relationship-maintaining is at least as important as goal-seeking and answering questions about *what* we should do is as significant as determining *how* to do it. The SSM includes seven stages which are:

- Stages One and Two: Define situation
- Stage Three: Root definition

- Stage Four: Develop a model
- Stages Five, Six, and Seven: Back into the real world (compare model and real world for insights)

10.39 VALIDATION TOOLS AND TECHNIQUES

Technique	Needs Assessment	Planning	Analysis	Traceability and Monitoring	Evaluation	Waterfall	Agile
Validation tools and techniques					X	X	X

Validation tools and techniques are discussed in Chapter 6.

10.40 VALUATION TOOLS AND TECHNIQUES

Technique	Needs Assessment	Planning	Analysis	Traceability and Monitoring	Evaluation	Waterfall	Agile
Valuation tools and techniques	X				X	X	X

Valuation tools and techniques are discussed in Chapter 9.

10.41 VERIFICATION TOOLS AND TECHNIQUES

Technique	Needs Assessment	Planning	Analysis	Traceability and Monitoring	Evaluation	Waterfall	Agile
Verification tools and techniques					X	X	X

Verification tools and techniques are discussed in Chapter 6.

10.42 VERSION CONTROL TOOLS AND TECHNIQUES

Technique	Needs Assessment	Planning	Analysis	Traceability and Monitoring	Evaluation	Waterfall	Agile
Version control tools and techniques		X				X	X

Version control tools and techniques are discussed in Chapter 6.

Answer to *Exercise 10.3*: see below:

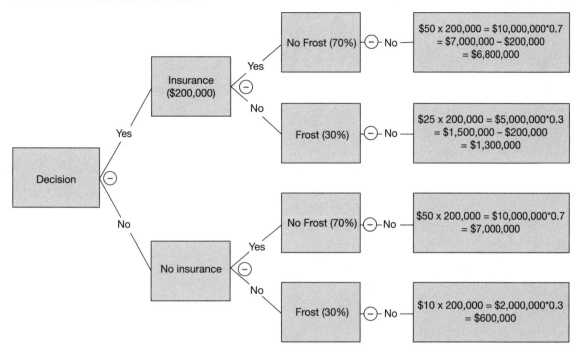

Answer to *Exercise 10.5*: Voice calls and in-person meetings are correct as they foster synchronous communication, while options 1 and 2 are types of asynchronous communication.

Answer to *Exercise 10.9*: Multivoting is correct as the options are reduced by voting multiple times.

Answers to *Exercise 10.10*: Parametric estimating and analogue are correct.

Answers to *Exercise 10.12*: One, two, and three are correct. You may also negotiate with the PMO and legal, however, these negotiations should be limited.

Professional Ethics and Conduct Standards

11

11.1 BRIEF INTRODUCTION: ETHICS AND CONDUCT

The concept of a professional code of ethics and professional conduct has been common throughout history as evidenced by the early use of the Hippocratic Oath within healthcare. *Ethics* has been defined as "involving the systematic application of moral rules, standards, or principles to concrete problems" (Lewis, 1985). People operate under different ethical value systems depending on experiences, religious background, education, and cultural background and values. Ethics involves learning what is right or wrong and then doing the right thing. Aside from the obvious, there are many reasons for ethical behaviors. One of these reasons is the retention of high quality employees. According to a report published on the web, in the business community, companies that actively managed ethical issues outperformed their peers financially by 3.3-7.7 percent over a five-year period. According to Harvard University Business School Professor Max H. Bazerman, ethical lapses in projects contribute to huge losses and brand dilution. An understanding of ethics can also help you to recognize potential ethical difficulties inherent in proposed ideas or suggestions. Ethics, business analyst activities, and project management are closely related and are part of day-to-day project management activities especially when dealing with the objectives of the project, stakeholders, risks, or the project team. We live with the assumption that "the modern day, well-educated, and responsible project managers and business analysts must possess the knowledge and skills to be able to discern and debate ethical issues" (Helgadóttir, 2007).

11.2 PMI AND IIBA STANDARDS

This is where the Project Management Institute (PMI®) Code of Ethics and Professional Conduct and the International Institute of Business Analysis (IIBA®) Code of Ethical Conduct & Professional Standards springs into action. "Codes of ethics are valuable as they both raise awareness of ethical issues and dilemmas that professionals may potentially face and also serve to enhance the public profile of the profession. Furthermore, codes of ethics may provide clarifications about the conduct deemed acceptable in client-professional relationships" (Davison, 2000). In general, ethics can be outcome or process oriented. The PMI Code of Ethics and Professional Conduct seems to be inspired by the outcome-oriented virtues in terms of ethics, the mark of the profession, and utilitarianism, where we conduct our tasks as project managers and business analysts for the benefit of as many people as possible. The process-oriented ethics of deontology and egoism are held at bay, while preserving the natural rights of others and being respectful of their duties takes precedence. Table 11.1 illustrates the nature of ethics (Wood-Harper et al., 2010).

Table 11.1   Nature of ethics

Label	Beneficiary	Objective	Good
Deontological	Not considered	Follow the rules	Follow the rules
Individual consequentiality (egoist ethic)	Individual	Maximize good for individual	Happiness, well-being, fame, riches
Group consequentiality	Group (social group, organization nation)	Maximize good for group	Survival, autonomy, ascendancy
Utilitarian	Society as a whole	Maximize good for human race or all sentient beings	Life, liberty, standard of living

PMI developed the PMI Code of Ethics and Professional Conduct in order to provide some guidance to all PMI members and credential holders so that they can adhere to a high standard of ethical behavior. Ethical behavior is important in satisfying basic human needs because many professionals have a need to work in an ethically sound way. Some academics argue that ethical behavior creates credibility, which can help during the project to make things work. Unethical behavior is a strong force for conflicts in projects, while ethical behavior can unite people and help create a strong basis for good project execution. Ethical behavior is also a robust basis for decision making. IBM's global CEO study *Leading through Connections 2012*, based upon interviews with 1709 CEOs in 64 countries and 18 industries, reveals that when it comes to the organizational attributes that engage employees to draw out the best in their workforces, CEOs are most focused on ethics and values. Ethical behavior has a wide range of long-term gains while the lack of ethical behavior can cause its own wide range of distress for most projects and participants. Table 11.2 illustrates how the ethical approaches of different stakeholders affect their decision making and behavior.

Table 11.2   Ethical approaches of different stakeholders

Stakeholder	Ethics	Example
Government	Group consequentiality	Standards for project management
IT management	Deontological; egoist	Legal compliance and continued funding
Project managers	Egoist; group consequentiality	Salary increase and group harmony
BA consultants	Deontological	Follow management directives
External consultants	Egoist	Make more money

An article by Aiken (Aiken et al., 2004) entitled *Using Codes of Conduct to Resolve Legal Disputes*, highlighted another key aspect of the application of codes of conduct—as court evidence. In most types of contracts, the customer would expect their vendor to follow best practices and codes of conduct within the industry. If things go really bad in the project and in the negotiations that follow, the project may end up in court where the codes of conduct may be applied.

Vision

PMI created a vision for ethical behavior that states, "As practitioners of project management, we are committed to doing what is right and honorable. We set high standards for ourselves, and we aspire to meet these standards in all aspects of our lives—at work, at home, and in service to our profession." This Code of Ethics and Professional Conduct describes the expectations that we have of ourselves and our fellow practitioners in the global project management and business analysis community. It articulates the ideals to which we aspire as well as the behaviors that are mandatory in our professional and volunteer roles (PMI, 2014).

Purpose

The PMI code enhances the profession and helps us become better professionals. "The purpose of this Code is to instill confidence in the project management profession and to help an individual become a better practitioner. We do this by establishing a profession-wide understanding of appropriate behavior. We believe that the credibility and reputation of the profession is shaped by the collective conduct of individual practitioners. We believe that we can advance our profession, both individually and collectively, by embracing this Code of Ethics and Professional Conduct. We also believe that this Code will assist us in making wise decisions, particularly when faced with difficult situations where we may be asked to compromise our integrity or our values. Our hope is that this Code of Ethics and Professional Conduct will serve as a catalyst for others to study, deliberate, and write about ethics and values. Further, we hope that this Code will ultimately be used to build upon and evolve our profession" (PMI, 2014).

It would be the ideal scenario if the Code of Ethics and Professional Conduct could apply to all professionals, including business analysts. However, that is hardly the case as most professionals outside the PMI world are unfamiliar with the PMI code. This implies that the Code of Ethics and Professional Conduct only applies to PMI members and individuals who are not members of PMI, but meet one or more of the following criteria:

- Nonmembers who hold a PMI certification;
- Nonmembers who apply to commence a PMI certification process; and
- Nonmembers who serve PMI in a volunteer capacity (PMI, 2014).

Those who do not follow the Code miss the opportunity to give something back to the profession and improve themselves as professionals. At a formal level, failure to follow the Code may also mean that PMI members can be expelled, but that is a different story altogether.

Structure

The Code of Ethics and Professional Conduct is divided into sections that contain standards of conduct, which are aligned with four values. These values were identified as being the most important with regard to the community and profession:

- Responsibility,
- Respect,
- Fairness, and
- Honesty.

Each section of the PMI Code of Ethics and Professional Conduct includes both aspirational standards and mandatory standards. The aspirational standards describe the conduct that we strive to uphold as practitioners. Although adherence to the aspirational standards is not easily measured, conducting ourselves in accordance with these is an expectation that we have of ourselves as professionals—it is not optional.

The mandatory standards establish firm requirements, and in some cases, limit or prohibit practitioner behavior. Practitioners who do not conduct themselves in accordance with these standards will be subject to disciplinary procedures before PMI's Ethics Review Committee (PMI, 2014).

The first of the four general values is *responsibility*. It is a basic standard for ethical behavior and is spelled out by a number of mandatory and aspirational standards. It is hoped that most business analysts are able to recognize and commit to the mandatory values without having to make too many changes in their lives. The aspirational standards may be slightly more abstract, but they, too, contain many good concepts to bear in mind. A number of mandatory standards of practice are included in the standard of responsibility.

Responsibility

Mandatory standards of responsibility:

- We inform ourselves and uphold the policies, rules, regulations, and laws that govern our work, professional, and volunteer activities.
- We report unethical or illegal conduct to appropriate management and, if necessary, to those affected by the conduct.
- We bring violations of this Code to the attention of the appropriate body for resolution.
- We only file ethics complaints when they are substantiated by facts.
- We pursue disciplinary action against an individual who retaliates against a person raising ethics concerns.

Aspirational standards of responsibility:

- We make decisions and take actions based on the best interests of society, public safety, and the environment.
- We accept only those assignments that are consistent with our background, experience, skills, and qualifications.
- We fulfill the commitments that we undertake—we do what we say we will do.
- When we make errors or omissions, we take ownership and make corrections promptly. When we discover errors or omissions caused by others, we communicate them to the appropriate body as soon they are discovered. We accept accountability for any issues resulting from our errors or omissions, and any resulting consequences.
- We protect proprietary or confidential information that has been entrusted to us.
- We uphold this Code and hold each other accountable to it.

Exercise 11.1—Word Choice: Insert *always*, *do not*, *only*, *sometimes*, *unqualified*, or *qualified* in order to complete the sentences. (The answers are found on page 279.)

- In the case of a contracting arrangement, we _____ bid on work that our organization is _____ to perform, and we assign _____ _____ individuals to perform the work. *What are the four missing words?*
- As practitioners and representatives of our profession, we _____ condone or assist others in engaging in illegal behavior. We _____ report any illegal or unethical conduct. *What are the two missing words?*

Respect

Mandatory standards:

- We negotiate in good faith.
- We do not exercise the power of our expertise or position to influence the decisions or actions of others in order to benefit personally at their expense.
- We do not act in an abusive manner toward others.
- We respect the property rights of others.

Aspirational standards:

- We inform ourselves about the norms and customs of others and avoid engaging in behaviors they might consider disrespectful.
- We listen to others' points of view, seeking to understand them.
- We approach directly those persons with whom we have a conflict or disagreement.
- We conduct ourselves in a professional manner, even when it is not reciprocated.

Fairness

Mandatory standards:

- We proactively and fully disclose any real or potential conflicts of interest to the appropriate stakeholders.
- When we realize that we have a real or potential conflict of interest, we refrain from engaging in the decision-making process or otherwise attempting to influence outcomes, unless or until: we have made full disclosure to the affected stakeholders; we have an approved mitigation plan; and we have obtained the consent of the stakeholders to proceed.
- We do not hire or fire, reward or punish, or award or deny contracts based on personal considerations, including but not limited to, favoritism, nepotism, or bribery.
- We do not discriminate against others based on, but not limited to, gender, race, age, religion, disability, nationality, or sexual orientation.
- We apply the rules of the organization (employer, PMI, or other group) without favoritism or prejudice.

Aspirational standards:

- We demonstrate transparency in our decision-making process.
- We constantly reexamine our impartiality and objectivity, taking corrective action as appropriate.
- We provide equal access to information to those who are authorized to have that information.
- We make opportunities equally available to qualified candidates.

Exercise 11.2—Fairness: Which of the following statements would most involve fairness? (The answer is found on page 279.)

1. We proactively and fully disclose any real or potential conflicts of interest to the appropriate stakeholders
2. We do not act in an abusive manner toward others
3. We only file ethics complaints when they are substantiated by facts
4. We are truthful in our communications and in our conduct

Honesty

Mandatory standards:

- We do not engage in or condone behavior that is designed to deceive others, including but not limited to, making misleading or false statements, stating half-truths, providing information out of context, or withholding information that, if known, would render our statements as misleading or incomplete.
- We do not engage in dishonest behavior with the intention of personal gain or at the expense of another.

Aspirational standards:

- We earnestly seek to understand the truth.
- We are truthful in our communications and in our conduct.
- We provide accurate information in a timely manner.
- We make commitments and promises, implied or explicit, in good faith.
- We strive to create an environment in which others feel safe to tell the truth.

Ethical problems are common in a workplace. As a business analyst, you are required to interact with stakeholders on a regular basis. In the process, you form working relationships with each of the stakeholders. This implies that the business analyst needs to ensure that they treat all stakeholders with fairness. Fairness also involves dealing with suppliers fairly, whether it's related to contracts, pricing, or constructive feedback. As a business analyst, we have a responsibility to clearly demonstrate the inherent value of a business analyst (integrity of the profession). A commitment to each of the values and standards of conduct can have a positive impact on the outcome of the BA practitioner's efforts and the project. The majority of business analysis activities involve records and data, which must be gathered and documented with fairness and honesty no matter what they demonstrate.

The PMI Code of Ethics and Professional Conduct is an important part of working as a business analyst. It highlights some of the considerations and ethics we may take for granted. In a globalized world of business analysts and project managers with dispersed teams consisting of many nationalities, backgrounds, and skill sets, this code of ethics and conduct is the beacon we should all know and follow. The values of responsibility, respect, fairness, and honesty are common behavior and should be a part of ethics around the globe. PMI's vision and purpose for developing its code is to protect and enhance the profession.

Answers to *Exercise 11.1*: *only, qualified, only, qualified* while the answers for the second sentence are *do not* and *always*.

Answers to *Exercise 11.2*: Statement one is correct.

The PMI-PBA® and the PMBOK® Guide

12

12.1 BRIEF INTRODUCTION: *PMBOK® GUIDE*

The Project Management Institute's designation of Professional in Business Analysis (PBA)® is based on the standards outlined in their reference book entitled: *A Guide to the Project Management Body of Knowledge (PMBOK® Guide)—Fifth Edition*, which provides guidelines for managing individual projects and defines project management related concepts. Table 12.1 contains project management process group and knowledge area mapping that is central to the *PMBOK® Guide—Fifth Edition*.

12.2 PROCESS GROUPS AND KNOWLEDGE AREAS

The *PMBOK® Guide* includes five process groups: initiating, planning, executing, monitoring and controlling, and closing. The five process groups incorporate 47 logically grouped project management processes located within the 10 knowledge areas. The knowledge areas are:

1. Project integration management
2. Project scope management
3. Project time management
4. Project cost management
5. Project quality management
6. Project human resource management
7. Project communications management
8. Project risk management
9. Project procurement management
10. Project stakeholder management

Table 12.1 Process group and knowledge area mapping

Knowledge areas	Project management process groups				
	Initiating	Planning	Executing	Monitoring and controlling	Closing
Project integration management	4.1 Develop project charter	4.2 Develop project management plan	4.3 Direct and manage project work	4.4 Monitor and control project work 4.5 Perform integrated change control	4.6 Close project or phase
Project scope management		5.1 Plan scope management 5.2 Collect requirements 5.3 Define scope 5.4 Create WBS		5.5 Validate scope 5.6 Control scope	
Project time management		6.1 Plan schedule management 6.2 Define activities 6.3 Sequence activities 6.4 Estimate activity resources 6.5 Estimate activity durations 6.6 Develop schedule		6.7 Control schedule	
Project cost management		7.1 Plan cost management 7.2 Estimate costs 7.3 Determine budget		7.4 Control costs	
Project quality management		8.1 Plan quality management	8.2 Perform quality assurance	8.3 Control quality	
Project human resource management		9.1 Plan human resource management	9.2 Acquire project team 9.3 Develop project team 9.4 Manage project team		
Project communication management		10.1 Plan communication management	10.2 Manage communications	10.3 Control communications	

Project risk management		11.1 Plan risk management 11.2 Identify risks 11.3 Perform qualitative risk analysis 11.4 Perform quantitative risk analysis 11.5 Plan risk responses		11.6 Control risks	
Project procurement management		12.1 Plan procurement man-agement	12.2 Conduct procurement	12.3 Control procurement	12.4 Close procurement
Project stakeholder management	13.1 Identify stakeholders	13.2 Plan stakeholder man-agement	13.3 Manage stakeholder engagement	13.4 Control stakeholder engagement	

The knowledge area of project integration management is the glue of the framework. The first process is Process 4.1 *Develop project charter* and Table 12.2 illustrates it. Each process contains input which is what is needed to conduct the process; tools and techniques to be used with the input; and output which is the result of the process. In this case, the project charter is the result of the process. The purpose of a project charter is to formally authorize the start of the project. Developing a project charter requires input as well as tools and techniques to develop the output.

Table 12.2 4.1 Develop project charter

Inputs	Tools & Techniques	Outputs
• Project statement of work • Business case • Agreements • Enterprise environmental factors • Organizational process assets	• Expert judgment • Facilitation techniques	• Project charter

12.3 PMI-PBA® OVERVIEW

The PMI-PBA also uses domains which are described in the examination content outline. The content of the examination content outline aligns, to some degree, with the content present in the *PMBOK® Guide*. Table 12.3 highlights this by mapping the five PMI-PBA domains with the processes in the *PMBOK® Guide—Fifth Edition*. This illustrates the knowledge areas of project integration management, project cost management, project stakeholders management, project communication management, and project quality management as being significant for alignment with PMI-PBA domains.

Table 12.3 Domains and knowledge area mapping

Domains				
Needs assessment	**Planning**	**Analysis**	**Traceability and Monitoring**	**Evaluation**
4.1 Develop project charter	4.1 Develop project charter	5.2 Collect requirements	5.2 Collect requirements 4.5 Perform integrated change control	8.3 Control quality
7.1 Plan cost management	5.1 Plan scope management 5.2 Collect requirements	5.2 Collect requirements	5.2 Collect requirements 5.5 Validate scope	8.3 Control quality
	5.1 Plan scope management	5.5 Validate scope	5.2 Collect requirements 4.5 Perform integrated change control	4.6 Close project or phase 5.5 Validate scope
13.1 Identify stakeholders	5.1 Plan scope management 5.6 Control scope	5.3 Define scope 5.4 Create WBS	10.2 Manage communications 13.3 Manage stakeholder engagement	8.3 Control quality
13.1 Identify stakeholders	5.1 Plan scope management 4.5 Perform integrated change control	5.5 Validate scope	5.6 Control scope	
	4.1 Develop project charter	5.2 Collect requirements		
		8.3 Control quality 8.1 Plan quality management		

The PMI-PBA examination content outline contains five domains and 40 knowledge and skills techniques. The knowledge and skills techniques are, to some degree, matched with the 10 knowledge areas illustrated in Table 12.4. This strengthens the emphasis on project integration management and project scope management, while the knowledge area of project procurement management is not part of the PMI-PBA examination content outline in any identified way; neither is it part of the five domains or the 40 knowledge and skills.

Table 12.4   Knowledge and skills, and knowledge area mapping

Knowledge areas	Knowledge and skills
Project integration management	Change control tools and techniques Lessons learned and retrospectives Measurement tools and techniques Requirement traceability tools and techniques Validation tools and techniques Verification tools and techniques Version control tools and techniques
Project scope management	Data analysis tools and techniques Elements of a requirement management plan Elicitation tools and techniques Interface analysis Prioritization tools and techniques Process analysis tools and techniques Requirement types
Project time management	Analytic tools and techniques Decision-making tools and techniques Estimating tools and techniques Scheduling tools and techniques
Project cost management	Estimating tools and techniques Quality management Valuation tools and techniques
Project quality management	Problem solving and opportunity identification tools and techniques Quality management Root cause analysis
Project human resource management	Conflict management and resolution tools and techniques Facilitation tools and techniques Leadership principles and skills Negotiations tools and techniques
Project communication management	Collaboration tools and techniques Communication skills Document management tools and techniques Reporting tools and techniques
Project risk management	Analytic tools and techniques Business rule analysis tools and techniques Contingency planning
Project procurement management	
Project stakeholder management	Stakeholder analysis

This chapter emphasizes the close alignment between the *PMBOK® Guide—Fifth Edition* and the PMI-PBA designation. However, what's most important are the tools and techniques being applied, rather than the actual input and output—as the certification covers plan-based projects that are equally based upon the *PMBOK® Guide* and agile methodologies.

Agile Methodologies and Manifesto 13

13.1 BRIEF INTRODUCTION: AGILE

In Chapter 10, many agile methodologies were introduced with *Scrum* being the most prominently applied. In general the agile methodologies are an umbrella of methodologies, but they all share a common mindset and similar values which are introduced below. Scrum is also covered here in greater detail.

13.2 AGILE PRINCIPLES AND PRACTICES

The use of agile principles and practices in software development is becoming a powerful force in today's workplace. In our quest to develop better products it is imperative that we strive to learn and understand the application of agile development methods. Agile is a philosophy; a mindset that uses organizational models based on people, collaboration, and shared values. The Agile Software Development Manifesto outlines the tenets of agile philosophy.

Agile principles and practices in software development enable practitioners to create and respond to change and to balance flexibility and structure. When compared to traditional waterfall practices, agile software development is distinguished by embracing and reacting to change, learning from mistakes, delivering customer-valued features early and often, and minimizing planning, documentation, and analysis before code.

Agile Software Development Manifesto

"On February 11-13, 2001, at The Lodge at Snowbird ski resort in the Wasatch mountains of Utah, seventeen advocates of lightweight development processes met to talk, ski, relax, and try to find common ground and of course, to eat. What emerged was the Agile Software Development Manifesto. Representatives from Extreme Programming (XP), Scrum, Dynamic Software Development Method (DSDM), Adaptive Software Development, Crystal, Feature-Driven Development, Pragmatic Programming, and others sympathetic to the need for an alternative to documentation driven, heavyweight software development processes convened" (Agile Alliance, 2012).

The Agile Software Development Manifesto was developed with the purpose of uncovering better ways of developing software by doing it ourselves and helping others to do it as well. The Agile Software Development Manifesto contains four statements with the following syntax: We value: <left> over <right>. That is, while there is value in the items on the right, we value the items on the left more.

We are uncovering better ways of developing software by doing it and helping others do it too. Through this process we have come to value:

- Individuals and interactions *over* processes and tools
- Working software *over* comprehensive documentation
- Customer collaboration *over* contract negotiation
- Responding to change *over* following a plan

Individuals and Interactions *over* Processes and Tools

The value and principle of *individuals and interactions over processes and tools* has a strong emphasis on communication, management, and commitment. Project management, requirements management, and communication has been closely aligned for many years. In agile project management, communication is a vital and integral part in various cycles. These cycles can range from every few minutes with pair programming, to every few hours with continuous integration, to every day with a daily stand-up meeting, to iterations with a review and retrospective.

"To create high-performing teams, agile methodologies value individuals and interactions over processes and tools. Practically speaking, all of the agile methodologies seek to increase communication and collaboration through frequent inspect-and-adapt cycles" (Sutherland, 2012).

For the business analyst, this is a new way of working. Requirements will constantly be identified, planned, and analyzed in various releases and sprints since scope is never fixed. The business analyst's work is conducted with the day-to-day cooperation of the development team and the key decision maker, who is also the product owner in Scrum. The business analyst must communicate, negotiate, and manage any conflicts with all the individuals involved in order to ensure the best possible solution.

Working Software *over* Comprehensive Documentation

The principle of *working software over comprehensive documentation* is perhaps the most important value that agile project management offers in the process of delivering small chunks of working software at set intervals. The phrase *working software* may have different meanings from project to project as does the *definition of done* in reference to working software. However, the use of working software is a great way for the project and project team to demonstrate high value and high performance to clients. It can foster increased communication and interactions, thereby supporting other values.

For the business analyst, working software over comprehensive documentation is not the end to documentation as we know it. However, it is a game changer. Requirements management is, to some degree, document- and model-driven—but with agile methodologies, the business analyst *just* needs to develop the needed documentation for the product owner to make the decision, and for the development team to develop the solution. The final result of the partnership is working software rather than extensive software requirement specifications.

Customer Collaboration over Contract Negotiation

"Over the past two decades, project success rates have more than doubled worldwide. These improvements occurred as a result of smaller projects and more frequent deliveries, which allowed customers to provide feedback on working software at regular intervals" (Sutherland, 2012).

For the business analyst this implies the use of verbal skills rather than formal writing skills. However, a limited amount of documentation and contracts may be needed. The work to be included will be discussed with the key decision maker and the development team on a day-to-day basis.

Responding to Change over Following a Plan

"For teams to create products that will please customers and provide business value, teams must respond to change. Industry data shows that over 60 percent of product or project requirements change during the development of software" (Sutherland, 2012). One may argue that customers rarely know what they want until they see working software. If customers do not see working software until the end of a project, it is too late to incorporate their feedback.

For the business analyst the work is an ongoing process where we embrace change and new user stories in order to provide value to the business. User stories are identified day-to-day, while they are prioritized every 2-4 weeks before the next sprint. Not all user stories may be developed because priorities may change.

Agile methods highly emphasize the incorporation of feedback and new information during product development, which allows a high degree of response to change. Agile methodologies are based on the knowledge that, in order to succeed, you must plan to change. That is why there are established processes, such as reviews and retrospectives, that are specifically designed to shift priorities regularly based on customer feedback and business value. The business analyst can take part in a sprint retrospective with the development team and discuss how they can improve cooperation on a more timely basis, rather than at the end when the project is completed.

The Twelve Principles of Agile Software

According to Kent Beck (1999), the Agile Software Development Manifesto is based upon twelve principles of agile software. These values are not just something the creators of the Agile Software Development Manifesto intended to give lip service to, and then forget—they are working values. Each individual agile methodology approaches these values in a slightly different way, but all of these methodologies have specific processes and practices that foster one or more of these principles. In order to understand the underlying values and practical applications of the twelve principles of agile software, review the summary in Table 13.1. This is based upon Bless (2012), but has been adapted to highlight the consequences for the business analyst.

Table 13.1 The 12 principles of agile software

Principle	Practices	Requirements management
Our highest priority is to satisfy the customer through early and continuous delivery of valuable software.	Product backlog Whole team Incremental deployment Small releases Frequent delivery	Backlog management and the ongoing deliveries of identified, planned, and analyzed user stories.
Deliver working software frequently, from a couple of weeks to a couple of months, with a preference for the shorter time-scale.	Incremental deployment Small releases Sprint review Definition of done Acceptance tests	Small releases with incremental development of working software create a constant changing point of reference, which is the working software.
Working software is the primary measure of progress.	Incremental deployment Small releases Definition of *done* Acceptance tests	The measurement is working software as a result of collaboration with product owner and development team rather than individual input.
Welcome changing requirements, even late in development. Agile processes harness change for the customer's competitive advantage.	Sprint planning Planning game Product backlog Customer involvement	Backlog management with a constant increase of new user stories.
Business people and developers must work together daily throughout the project.	Real customer involvement Whole team Osmotic communication Daily Scrum	Day-to-day cooperation with the development team and product owner.
Build projects around motivated individuals. Give them the environment and support they need, and trust them to get the job done.	Servant leadership Motivation	The business analyst must also act as servant leader to motivate the development team to get the work done. This is a team effort.
The most efficient and effective method of conveying information to and within a development team is face-to-face conversation.	Osmotic communication Servant leadership	The business analyst must be with the team and communicate face-to-face as much as possible as it is far more effective.
The best architectures, requirements, and designs emerge from self-organizing teams.	Test-driven development Refactoring Osmotic communication Servant leadership	Requirements are developed in close collaboration with the development team that is going to develop the solution.
Continuous attention to technical excellence and good design enhances agility.	Testing Sprint retrospective Pair programming Test-driven development Refactoring	The business analyst should use pair techniques to foster collaboration and take part in retrospective.

Agile processes promote sustainable development. The sponsors, developers, and users should be able to maintain a constant pace indefinitely.	Real customer involvement Motivation	The business analyst should not pressure the development team more than they can keep a constant speed.
Simplicity—the art of maximizing the amount of work not done—is essential.	Product backlog, refactoring Seeing waste	Backlog management, however, keeps it simple.
At regular intervals, the team reflects on how to become more effective, then tunes and adjusts its behavior accordingly.	Sprint retrospective Root cause analysis Seeing waste Value stream mapping	The business analyst must engage in activities to improve the process and collaboration.

Declaration of Interdependence for Modern Management

In 2005, a group headed by Alistair Cockburn and Jim Highsmith wrote an addendum of project management principles—the declaration of interdependence for modern management—to guide software project management according to agile development methods. The group, not wanting to coin a new buzzword, instead worked out six rules of operation. "The sentences were formed as two clauses, we accomplish X—by doing Y. That is, Y is what you can see us do, and the reason we all care about that is because we're trying to set up X" (Cockburn, 2012), as illustrated in Table 13.2.

Table 13.2 The declaration of interdependence for modern management

The declaration of interdependence for modern management		
Increase return on investment by—making continuous flow of value our focus.	Deliver reliable results by—engaging customers in frequent interactions and shared ownership.	Expect uncertainty and manage for it through—iterations, anticipation, and adaptation.
Unleash creativity and innovation by—recognizing that individuals are the ultimate source of value, and creating an environment where they can make a difference.	Boost performance through—group accountability for results and shared responsibility for team effectiveness.	Improve effectiveness and reliability through—situationally specific strategies, processes, and practices.

The declaration of interdependence (DOI) for modern management is summarized in Table 13.3 based upon an adaption from Cockburn (2012) to demonstrate: what is accomplished, how it is accomplished, and the consequences for requirements management.

"One problem with the DOI is that the six points sound like platitudes" (Cockburn, 2006), as unlike the Agile Manifesto it only identifies causes and effects, but no adverse effects. Only when trying to apply the points do the surprises show up. The application of the DOI is to improve project management as a default mode of management, and is appropriate for self-managed teams.

Figure 13.1 is adapted from Sidkey (2013) and illustrates the process of working agile as a transformation to the agile mindset based upon the manifesto, declaration, and practices with agile tools and techniques—which is *being agile*. Working with the agile techniques without the mindset is just *working agile*.

Table 13.3 Declaration of interdependence for modern management adaptation

Accomplish this	by/through this	and	requirements management
Increased ROI	focusing on *flow of value* (e.g., not *tracking effort*)	continuous (one-piece) flow, preferably	Value-driven requirements
Reliable results	engaging customers in frequent interactions	shared ownership	Collaboration and communication with the development team and product owner daily
Unleash creativity and innovation	recognizing individual human beings as the ultimate source of value	creation of an environment where individual people can make a difference	The business analyst should consider the use of creative techniques and involvement
Manage uncertainty	iterations, anticipation, and adaptation	anticipation and adaptation (i.e., think ahead, plan, iterate, deliver, reflect, adapt)	PDCA
Improve effectiveness and reliability	situationally specific strategies, processes, and practices (i.e., no one answer, folks, get used to it)		The business analyst should embrace the agile practice and use retrospectives for improvements
Boost performance	group accountability for results (i.e., the whole group is singly accountable, no in-team blame)	shared responsibility for team effectiveness	Business analyst shares group accountability with the development team

13.3 SCRUM

We can trace the history and influences of agile project management methodologies back to the early 1900s with Walter Shewhart's plan-do-check-act (PDCA) cycle. By the mid 1900s, his work was modified by people like W. Edwards Deming (SPC, TQM, Toyota Production System) and Peter Drucker (knowledge worker). The late 1900s saw the rise of Womack and Jones (lean thinking), Eli Goldratt (Theory of Constraints), Tom Gilb (Evo), and the Toyota Way.

The evolution of the agile methodologies started in the early 1990s with Crystal methods, Lean Software Development, and DSDM. In the mid 1990s, agile methodologies of Feature Driven Development, XP, and Adaptive Software Development saw the light of day. In early 2001, the Manifesto for Agile Software Development was developed, Scrum in 2002, and the declaration of interdependence in 2005. Frameworks and processes that are based on the Agile Manifesto are called agile methodologies or agile methods. Agile methodology is an umbrella concept encompassing many different, new, and lightweight software development methodologies.

As opposed to heavyweight, plan-driven processes, these new methodologies are lightweight, short-cycled, less wasteful, and focused more on the human aspect of software development. Agile methods are characterized by iterative and incremental development and promote frequent delivery of product features that are prioritized in consultation with customers, aiming to deliver business value in iterations. Agile methods address small, colocated, dedicated, and highly collaborative teams. Scrum and XP are the most widely adopted agile methods. XP focuses on developmental practices, while Scrum mainly covers project management.

The origins of Scrum are found in writings by Takeuchi and Nonaka (Sutherland et al., 2006). (In Rugby, a scrum is a formation of eight multifunctional teammates who *link together* in a common

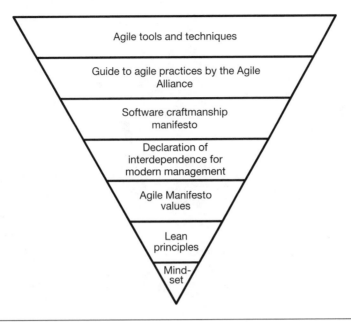

Figure 13.1   Building the right product

mission to gain possession of the ball and advance it to the goal.) A later Scrum champion, Jeff Suther-land, worked at the same time on a similar concept. In 2001, Ken Schwaber and Mike Beedle wrote the book *Agile Software Development with Scrum*, which may be considered the official start of Scrum as we know it today. The theory of Scrum is based upon the three pillars of visibility, inspection, and adaptation, as illustrated in Table 13.4.

Table 13.4   Pillars of scrum

Theory of Scrum	Explanations	Requirement management
Visibility	Visible outcome	Backlog management
Inspection	Timely checks Deviations or differences	Grooming of the backlog
Adaptation	Adjusting a process	Retrospective

The following sections will explain the essential components of Scrum: process, key practices, and roles. Scrum hangs all its practices on an iterative, incremental process skeleton, as illustrated in Figure 13.2.

The Agile Alliance (2012) illustrates the Scrum framework and process succinctly: "A product owner creates a prioritized wish list called a product backlog. During sprint planning, the team pulls a small chunk from the top of that wish list, a sprint backlog, and decides how to implement those pieces. The team has a certain amount of time, a sprint, to complete its work—usually two to four weeks—but meets each day to assess its progress (daily Scrum). Along the way, the Scrum Master keeps the team focused on its goal. At the end of the sprint, the work should be potentially shippable, as in ready to hand to a customer, put on a store shelf, or show to a stakeholder. The sprint ends with a sprint review and

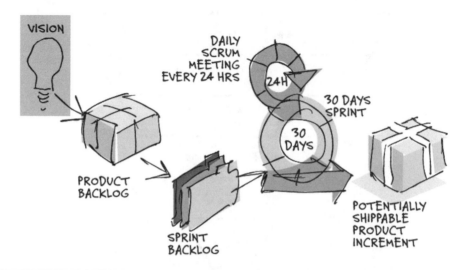

Figure 13.2 Components of Scrum adapted from the Agile Alliance in *I Am Agile* by Klaus Nielsen

retrospective. As the next sprint begins, the team chooses another chunk of the product backlog and begins working again."

For the business analyst, it is important to be familiar with the overall direction of the product vision. Then, the handling of user stories are to be identified, planned, and analyzed in the product backlog, while the user stories for the next sprint are managed in the sprint backlog. The result of the sprint is delivered daily or within 2-4 weeks, which is the typical sprint duration. The key practices of Scrum are captured in Table 13.5 and are adapted from Cohen et al. (2003).

Roles play a major part in Scrum. Three key roles exist—the product owner, development team or team member, and the Scrum Master (see Table 13.6).

The Scrum roles are of vital importance for the business analyst, as the product owner is the key decision maker, while all products from specification to development are conducted in collaboration and communication with the development team. The Scrum Master can help facilitate this collaboration and communication, and help in solving impediments.

Scrum's roles, artifacts, events, and rules are immutable. Implementing only parts of Scrum is possible, but the result is not Scrum. Scrum exists only in its entirety and functions well as a container for other techniques, methodologies, and practices.

Table 13.5 Key practices of Scrum

Scrum methodology	Description
Product backlog (Artifact)	The prioritized list of all features and changes that have yet to be made to the system that were desired by multiple actors, such as customers, marketing and sales, and the project team. The product owner is responsible for maintaining the product backlog.
Sprint retrospective (Event)	Reflection on the process and room for improvements. Read Chapter 3 for more information on retrospectives.
Sprints (Event)	Sprints are 30 days in length; it is the procedure of adapting to the changing environmental variables (requirements, time, resources, knowledge, technology, etc.) and must result in a potentially shippable increment of software. The working tools of the team are sprint planning meetings, sprint backlog, and daily Scrum meetings.
Sprint planning meeting (Event)	A sprint planning meeting is first attended by the customers, users, management, product owner, and Scrum team where a set of goals and functionality are decided on. Next the Scrum Master and the Scrum team focus on how the product is implemented during the sprint.
Sprint backlog (Artifact)	The list of features that is currently assigned to a particular sprint. When all the features are completed, a new iteration of the system is delivered.
Daily Scrum (Event)	A daily meeting lasting approximately 15 minutes, which are organized to keep track of the progress of the Scrum team and address any obstacles faced by the team.
Team size	Development personnel are split into teams of up to seven people. A complete team should at least include a developer, quality assurance engineer, and a documenter.
Iteration length	While Schwaber originally suggested sprint lengths from 1 to 6 weeks, durations are commonly held at 4 weeks.
Support for distributed teams	While Scrum's prescription does not explicitly mention distributed teams or provide built-in support, a project may consist of multiple teams that could easily be distributed.
Definition of *done* (Artifact)	Everyone must agree on the meaning of *done*. Read Chapter 9 for more information on the definition of *done*.
System criticality	Scrum does not explicitly address the issue of criticality.

Table 13.6 Scrum roles

Role	Description
Product owner	Maximizes the value of the product, represents the stakeholders, is the *voice of the customer*, communicates the vision, prioritizes the product backlog, and is responsible for the outcome.
Development team/ team member	Delivers the product and is self-organizing and determines how it will accomplish the work.
Scrum Master	Liaison between the product owner and the team, advises the product owner, supports the development team, and enforces rules and processes.

Web Added Value™

This book has free material available for download from the
Web Added Value™ resource center at *www.jrosspub.com*

Part 4

IIBA CBAP® and IREB CPRE Knowledge Areas and Alignment

The IIBA CBAP® and the *BABOK® Guide* 14

14.1 BRIEF INTRODUCTION: *BABOK® GUIDE*

As mentioned previously, the International Institute of Business Analysis (IIBA®) was founded in Toronto, in 2003, and is globally recognized today for the IIBA standard for the practice of business analysis. The standard for practices are found and verified in the Certified Business Analysis Professional (CBAP®) designation, which is a professional certification for individuals with extensive business analysis experience.

The key concepts of the CBAP® certification exam are mentioned in *A Guide to the Business Analysis Body of Knowledge (BABOK® Guide)*. The first version of the *BABOK® Guide* was released in 2005. *A Guide to the Business Analysis Body of Knowledge v2*, was released in 2009 and an Agile Extension to it was released in 2013. *A Guide to the Business Analysis Body of Knowledge v3* was released during the writing of this study guide in April of 2015. Thus, we follow the *BABOK® Guide v3*. Figure 14.1 illustrates the six knowledge areas. This study guide is designed to be used in conjunction with the *BABOK® Guide v3* and the Agile Extension published by the IIBA. No additional resources are needed to study for and pass the IIBA CBAP® certification exam.

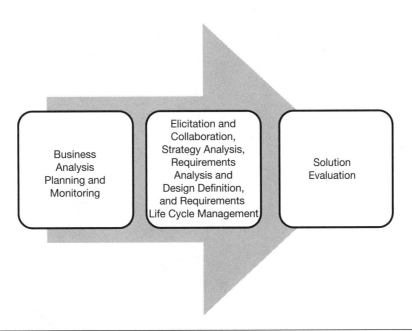

Figure 14.1 IIBA knowledge areas

The knowledge areas are: Business Analysis Planning and Monitoring, Elicitation and Collaboration, Requirements Life Cycle Management, Strategy Analysis, Requirements Analysis and Design Definition, and Solution Evaluation. The six knowledge areas consist of 30 logically related, though not necessarily sequenced tasks. Each knowledge area contains four to six tasks. The specific task describes the activities to accomplish the purpose of the associated knowledge area. Each task contains a purpose, description, inputs, elements, guidelines/tools, techniques, stakeholders, and outputs. Every knowledge area and the tasks to be performed are supported by six underlying competencies, which are needed for effective business analyst performance. The six underlying competencies are a variation of knowledge, skills, and personal competencies. The underlying competencies include a purpose (relevance), definition (skills and expertise involved) and effectiveness measures. The knowledge areas, the 30 tasks, and the six underlying competencies are supported by 50 techniques including purpose (used for), description (how it's used), elements (key concepts), and usage considerations (conditions) which are means to perform business analysis activities. Introduced in the *BABOK® Guide v3* is the use of specialized ways, called perspectives, which are used within business analysis work to provide focus to tasks and techniques relevant for a given context. The contexts are Agile (included in the PMI-PBA), Business Intelligence, Information Technology, Business Architecture, and Business Process Management. Each perspective has the following structure:

- Change scope
- Business analysis scope
- Methodologies, approaches, and techniques
- Underlying competencies
- Impact on knowledge areas

With the *BABOK® Guide v3*, the IIBA introduced the new Business Analyst Core Concept Model, which is a conceptual framework for the business analyst profession highlighting the relationship of the key concepts with the need of evaluating and communicating the concepts (see Figure 14.2). The core concepts of needs, solutions, and value are grouped while stakeholders, changes, and contexts are grouped.

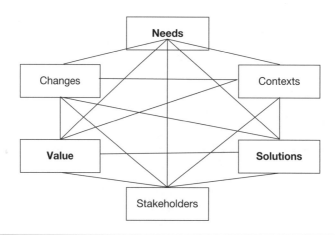

Figure 14.2 IIBA Business Analyst Core Concept Model

When one of the core concepts change, the other core concepts should be reevaluated—as a change in stakeholders may affect the needs, which may affect the solutions and so forth. The core concepts are applied in the knowledge areas and tasks.

The following sections will cover the CBAP® certification examination content aligned with the Project Management Institute Professional in Business Analysis (PMI-PBA)® certification exam—which illustrates a high degree of cohesiveness that also makes this book an effective study guide for the CBAP® certification exam. Please keep in mind that input and output of the tasks are not aligned. Table 14.1 demonstrates the eligibility requirements for the exam.

Table 14.1 Eligibility requirements

Eligibility requirements	IIBA CBAP®
Total work experience	Minimum 7500 hours of BA work experience aligned with the *BABOK® Guide* in the last 10 years
BA work experience	Minimum 900 hours in four of the six knowledge areas
Professional development	Minimum 21 hours of professional development in the past four years
References	Two references from a career manager, client, or CBAP® recipient
Total exam fee	Application fee of $125 plus $325 for IIBA members or $450 for nonmembers
Recertification	Minimum 60 CDUs every 3 years and $120 for renewal

The CBAP® exam is 3.5 hours long and consists of 150 multiple-choice questions with four possible answers to select from.

14.2 IIBA CBAP®: OVERVIEW

The IIBA CBAP® certification exam consists of six knowledge areas, 30 tasks, and 50 techniques, which can, to some degree, be aligned with the five domains, 28 tasks, and 40 knowledge and skills in the PMI-PBA certification exam. This is illustrated in Table 14.2.

Table 14.2 PMI-PBA and IIBA CBAP® high-level alignment

PMI-PBA	IIBA CBAP®
5 domains	6 areas of knowledge
28 tasks	30 tasks
40 knowledge and skills	50 techniques

After examining IIBA knowledge areas and PMI domains, it is evident that the overall body of knowledge is covered in both frameworks and is fairly well aligned (see Table 14.3).

Table 14.3 PMI-PBA and IIBA CBAP® domain and knowledge area alignment

PMI Domains	IIBA
Needs Assessment	Strategy Analysis
Planning	Business Analysis Planning and Monitoring
Analysis	Elicitation and Collaboration
Analysis	Requirements Analysis and Design Definition
Traceability and Monitoring	Requirements Life Cycle Management
Evaluation	Solution Evaluation

The following sections will align the frameworks to an even higher degree in order to create a common point of reference and enable the readers who are preparing for the CBAP® certification exam to judge which sections cover what IIBA related content, and which content is out of scope for the IIBA certification exam. Although the alignment is not completely identifiable or 100% aligned, the core content and techniques are covered in both frameworks to a very significant degree.

14.3 IIBA—BUSINESS ANALYSIS PLANNING AND MONITORING

The IIBA Business Analysis Planning and Monitoring knowledge area emphasizes the initial organization, coordination, planning, and monitoring activities throughout the project (see Table 14.4). These are aligned with the PMI-PBA Planning domain.

Table 14.4 Business Analysis Planning and Monitoring knowledge area aligned with the PMI-PBA (Note: The chapter numbers listed in the table are chapters from this book.)

IIBA	PMI-PBA
3.1 Plan business analysis approach	Chapter 5
3.2 Plan stakeholder engagement	Chapter 5
3.3 Plan business analysis governance	Chapter 6
3.4 Plan business analysis information management	Chapter 6
3.5 Identify business analysis performance improvements	Chapter 6

14.4 IIBA—ELICITATION AND COLLABORATION

The IIBA Elicitation and Collaboration knowledge area contains the core requirements management activities, which are aligned with the Analysis domain in the PMI-PBA certification exam (see Table 14.5).

Table 14.5 Elicitation and Collaboration knowledge area aligned with the PMI-PBA (Note: The chapter numbers listed in the table are chapters from this book.)

IIBA	PMI-PBA
4.1 Prepare for elicitation	Chapter 6
4.2 Conduct elicitation	Chapter 7
4.3 Confirm elicitation results	Chapter 7
4.4 Communicate business analysis information	Chapter 7
4.5 Manage stakeholders collaboration	Chapter 10

14.5 IIBA—REQUIREMENTS LIFE CYCLE MANAGEMENT

The IIBA Requirements Life Cycle Management knowledge area focuses on managing requirements and the reuse and traceability of the requirements, which are aligned with the PMI-PBA Traceability domain (see Table 14.6).

Table 14.6 Requirements Life Cycle Management knowledge area aligned with the PMI-PBA (Note: The chapter numbers listed in the table are chapters from this book.)

IIBA	PMI-PBA
5.1 Trace requirements	Chapter 8
5.2 Maintain requirements	Chapter 8
5.3 Prioritize requirements	Chapter 7
5.4 Assess requirements changes	Chapter 8
5.5 Approve requirements	Chapter 8

14.6 IIBA—STRATEGY ANALYSIS

The IIBA Strategy Analysis knowledge area is the initial focus on needs assessment. It is therefore aligned with the PMI-PBA Needs Assessment domain (see Table 14.7).

Table 14.7 Strategy Analysis knowledge area aligned with the PMI-PBA (Note: The chapter numbers listed in the table are chapters from this book.)

IIBA	PMI-PBA
6.1 Analyze current state	Chapter 5
6.2 Define future state	Chapter 5
6.3 Assess risks	Chapter 10
6.4 Define change strategy	Chapter 5

14.7 IIBA—REQUIREMENTS ANALYSIS AND DESIGN DEFINITION

The IIBA Requirements Analysis and Design Definition knowledge area emphasizes additional aspects of the elicitation and requirement activities, which are part of the Analysis domain in the PMI-PBA certification content (see Table 14.8).

Table 14.8 Requirements Analysis and Design Definition knowledge area aligned with the PMI-PBA (Note: The chapter numbers listed in the table are chapters from this book.)

IIBA	PMI-PBA
7.1 Specify and model requirements	Chapter 7
7.2 Verify requirements	Chapter 8
7.3 Validate requirements	Chapter 8
7.4 Define requirements architecture	Chapter 6
7.5 Define design options	Chapter 6
7.6 Analyze potential value and recommend solution	Chapter 9

14.8 IIBA—SOLUTION EVALUATION

The IIBA Solution Evaluation knowledge area emphasizes measuring the solution and ensuring the transition, which are aligned with the Evaluation domain in the PMI-PBA certification content (see Table 14.9).

Table 14.9 Solution Evaluation knowledge area aligned with the PMI-PBA (Note: The chapter numbers listed in the table are chapters from this book.)

IIBA	PMI-PBA
8.1 Measure solution performance	Chapter 9
8.2 Analyze performance measures	Chapter 7
8.3 Analyze solution limitations	Chapter 9
8.4 Assess enterprise limitations	Chapter 9
8.5 Recommend actions to increase solution value	Chapter 9

14.9 IIBA—UNDERLYING COMPETENCIES

The IIBA underlying competencies are used to support the business analysis in delivering business analysis activities. The concepts are not explicitly referenced in the PMI-PBA certification exam content. However, the content is, to some degree, covered in the PMI-PBA knowledge and skills found in Table 14.10.

Table 14.10 Underlying competencies aligned with PMI-PBA content

IIBA core competencies	IIBA categories	PMI-PBA
Analytical thinking and problem solving	Creative thinking Decision making Learning Problem solving Systems thinking Conceptual thinking Visual thinking	Knowledge and skills
Behavioral characteristics	Ethics Personal accountability Trustworthiness Organization and time management Adaptability	PMI Code of Ethics and Professional Conduct
Business knowledge	Business acumen Industry knowledge Organization knowledge Solution knowledge Methodology knowledge	Certification exam eligibility Knowledge and skills
Communication skills	Verbal communication Non-verbal communication Written communication Listening	Knowledge and skills
Interaction skills	Facilitation Leadership and influence Teamwork Negotiation and conflict resolution Teaching	Knowledge and skills
Tools and technology	Office productivity tools and technology Business analysis tools and technology Communication tools and technology	Knowledge and skills

14.10 IIBA—TECHNIQUES

IIBA techniques are the tools and techniques applied to perform the tasks in the knowledge area. The IIBA techniques are, to a high degree, aligned or similar to the PMI-PBA knowledge and skills, which is illustrated in Table 14.11. The PMI-PBA domains also include techniques, which makes it difficult to align all techniques completely.

There is a high degree of alignment between the major frameworks in the market.

Table 14.11   IIBA techniques aligned with PMI-PBA knowledge and skills

IIBA	PMI-PBA
Acceptance and evaluation criteria definition	Knowledge and skills
Backlog management	Knowledge and skills
Balanced scorecard	Not covered in details
Benchmarking and market analysis	Domain 1—Needs Assessment
Brainstorming	Knowledge and skills
Business capability analysis	Domain 1—Needs Assessment
Business cases	Domain 1—Needs Assessment
Business model canvas	Knowledge and skills
Business rules analysis	Knowledge and skills
Collaborative games	Knowledge and skills
Concept modeling	Knowledge and skills
Data dictionary	Knowledge and skills
Data flow diagrams	Knowledge and skills
Data mining	Not covered in details
Data modeling	Knowledge and skills
Decision analysis	Knowledge and skills
Decision modeling	Knowledge and skills
Document analysis	Knowledge and skills
Estimation	Knowledge and skills
Financial analysis	Domain 5—Evaluation
Focus groups	Knowledge and skills
Functional decomposition	Knowledge and skills
Glossary	Domain 3—Analysis
Interface analysis	Knowledge and skills
Interviews	Knowledge and skills
Items tracking	Knowledge and skills
Lessons learned process	Knowledge and skills
Metrics and key performance indicators	Domain 4—Traceability and Monitoring
Mind mapping	Chapter 3
Nonfunctional requirements analysis	Domain 3—Analysis
Observation	Knowledge and skills
Organization modeling	Knowledge and skills
Prioritization	Domain 3—Analysis
Process analysis	Knowledge and skills
Process modeling	Knowledge and skills
Prototyping	Knowledge and skills

Reviews	Knowledge and skills
Risk analysis and management	Knowledge and skills
Roles and permission matrix	Domain 1—Needs Assessment
Root cause analysis	Knowledge and skills
Scope modeling	Domain 3—Analysis
Sequence diagrams	Domain 3—Analysis
Stakeholder list, maps and personas	Domain 1—Needs Assessment
State modeling	Knowledge and skills
Survey or questionnaire	Domain 3—Analysis
SWOT analysis	Domain 1—Needs Assessment
Use cases and scenarios	Domain 3—Analysis
User stories	Knowledge and skills
Vendor assessment	Domain 1—Needs Assessment
Workshops	Knowledge and skills

The IREB CPRE and Foundation Level Syllabus

15

15.1 BRIEF INTRODUCTION: FOUNDATION LEVEL SYLLABUS

More than 23,000 requirements engineering and business analysis professionals in 59 countries have passed the Certified Professional for Requirements Engineering (CPRE) certification exam since first offered by the International Requirements Engineering Board (IREB) in 2007. Today, many organizations in Europe, particularly in German-speaking countries, consider it a must. The CPRE designation has three certification levels which are the Foundation Level, Advanced Level, and Expert Level. The eligibility requirements for the CPRE Foundation Level exam are illustrated in Table 15.1.

Table 15.1 Eligibility requirements

Eligibility requirements	IREB-CPRE
Total work experience	None
BA work experience	None
Professional development	None
References	None
Total exam fee	$150 for online. The pricing for the certification is fixed by each certification body individually and may differ for different countries.
Recertification	None

The CPRE Foundation Level exam is a 75-minute exam and consists of 45 multiple-choice questions.

15.2 IREB CPRE: OVERVIEW

The CPRE certification is based upon a syllabus version 2.1 with nine main areas, which requires different levels of knowledge, from familiarity to mastery. These main areas are then divided into sublevels. Table 15.2 illustrates the alignment of CPRE certification content with the Project Management Institute Professional in Business Analysis (PMI-PBA)® exam content. Studying Chapters 6 and 7 of this guide will prepare you for the CPRE Foundation Level designation.

All content of the Foundation Level of the CPRE certification is included in this book, except the glossary which is a minor topic; and tool support, which contains types of tools, an introduction to tools, and how to evaluate tools. The glossary and tool support are covered extensively by Klaus Pohl and Chris Rupp in *Requirement Engineering Fundamentals*, which can be found in the reference list.

Table 15.2 IREB CPRE FL and PMI-PBA alignment (Note: The chapter numbers listed in the table are chapters from this book.)

IREB	PMI-PBA
EU 1 Introduction and Foundations	**Chapters 5 & 7**
EU 2 System and System Context	**Chapter 6**
EU 2.1 System, system context and boundaries	Chapter 6.2
EU 2.2 Determining system and context boundaries	Chapter 6.2
EU 3 Requirement Elicitation	**Chapter 7**
EU 3.1 Requirement sources	Chapter 7.2
EU 3.2 Requirement categorization according to Kano	Chapter 7.2
EU 3.3 Elicitation techniques	Chapter 7.2
EU 4 Requirements Documentation	**Chapter 7**
EU 4.1 Document design	Chapter 7.7
EU 4.2 Documentation types	Chapter 7.7
EU 4.3 Document structures	Chapter 7.7
EU 4.4 Use of requirements documents	Chapter 7.7
EU 4.5 Quality criteria for requirements document	Chapter 7
EU 4.6 Quality criteria for requirements	Chapter 7
EU 4.7 Glossary	Not included
EU 5 Documentation of Requirements Using Natural Language	**Chapter 7.7**
EU 5.1 Language effects	Chapter 7.7
EU 5.2 Requirements construction using templates	Chapter 7.7
EU 6 Model-based Documentation of Requirements	**Chapter 7.7**
EU 6.1 The term "Model"	Chapter 7.7
EU 6.2 Goals models	Chapter 7.7
EU 6.3 Use cases	Chapter 7.7
EU 6.4 Three perspectives on requirements	Chapter 7.7
EU 6.5 Requirements modeling in the data perspective	Chapter 7.7
EU 6.6 Requirements modeling in the functional perspective	Chapter 7.7
EU 6.7 Requirements modeling in the behavior perspective	Chapter 7.7
EU 7 Requirements Validation and Negotiations	**Chapter 7.8 & Chapter 10**
EU 7.1 Fundamentals of requirements validation	Chapter 7.8
EU 7.2 Fundamentals of requirements negotiation	Chapter 10
EU 7.3 Quality aspects of requirements	Chapter 7.7
EU 7.4 Principles of requirements validation	Chapter 7.8
EU 7.5 Techniques for requirements validation	Chapter 7.8
EU 7.6 Requirement negotiation	Chapter 10
EU 8 Requirements Management	**Chapters 6 & 7**
EU 8.1 Assigning attributes to requirements	Chapter 7

EU 8.2 Views on requirements	Chapter 7
EU 8.3 Prioritizing requirements	Chapter 7.5
EU 8.4 Requirements traceability	Chapter 6.3
EU 8.5 Versioning of requirements	Chapter 6.6
EU 8.6 Management of requirement changes	Chapter 6.5
EU 9 Tool Support	**Not included**

Part 5

Practice Exam

PMI-PBA® Full Practice Exam

16

16.1 BRIEF INTRODUCTION: SIMULATED PMI-PBA® EXAM

The Project Management Institute Professional in Business Analysis (PMI-PBA) full practice exam consists of 175 questions, which should be completed in no more than 4 hours. Table 16.1 contains the questions and an area for recording your answers. Unless otherwise stated, there is only one correct (or best) answer to each question. Table 16.2 includes the correct answers, explanations, and the chapters in this book where you can find that information in case you need to go back and refresh your memory. You should be able to answer at least 120 questions correctly before moving on to the actual certification exam. Please keep in mind that there is also an online test bank with more PMI-PBA practice exam questions. Directions to the text bank can be found in the Web Added Value (WAV™) Download Resource Center located at www.jrosspub .com/wav.

Table 16.1 PMI-PBA full practice exam

No.	Question	Answer
1	The business analyst validates the solution and business needs with the use of: a) Acceptance criteria b) Software requirements specification c) A traceability matrix d) Test cases	
2	During planning, the business analyst needs to take part in reviewing the business case and the project charter in order to ensure: a) Resources are allocated b) A budget can be developed c) Objectives and goals are clear d) There is funding for the business case	
3	The business analyst manages the life cycle of the requirements, which includes ongoing communication and collaboration with the stakeholders in order to: a) Manage, trace, and monitor the requirements throughout the life cycle b) Manage, trace, and monitor all constraints throughout the life cycle c) Identify, analyze, and monitor the requirements throughout the life cycle d) Monitor and validate the requirements throughout the life cycle	
4	What is *planguage*? a) A key word oriented language for nonfunctional requirements b) A software testing method c) A key word oriented language for developing user stories d) A feature-driven development language	

No.	Question	Answer
5	Which calculations would the business analyst most likely find in the cost-benefit section of the business case? a) Analog estimates b) Return on investment c) Risk analysis d) A budget	
6	How does the business analyst ensure the delivered solution meets the business need? a) Validate the solution b) Ensure signoff c) Verify the solution d) Close project or phase	
7	Which role would you *not* expect to take part in a change control board meeting? a) Quality assurance representative b) Technical helpdesk c) Requirement engineer d) Configuration manager assistant	
8	What is one of the key challenges with requirements elicitation? a) Recording the voice of the customer b) Too many techniques to choose from c) Too little time d) Managing scope	
9	How does the business analyst ensure requirements are delivered as stated? a) Sign off on the contract b) Identify and analyze the requirements c) Track requirements d) Manage and monitor the requirements	
10	Which role is responsible for communicating the needs assessment in Scrum to the development team? a) The development team b) The product owner c) The Scrum Master d) The business analyst	
11	You are waiting on a supplier to install a server. What kind of dependency is this? a) Mandatory b) Discretionary c) External d) Internal	
12	Why is it important for the business analyst to define the system context? a) To know which systems are to be developed b) To know which systems are not included c) Because the system context includes the constraints d) Because the system context includes the systems attributes	
13	Requirements elicitation may derive from stakeholders (individuals or groups) and other sources. Which other sources? a) Legacy systems b) System documentation c) Lessons learned d) All of the above	

No.	Question	Answer
14	Why is it important to document the life of the requirements? a) For lessons learned b) For configuration management issues c) It may assist in managing the budget and schedule d) It may help control scope	
15	You are about to identify opportunities and challenges, and examine cost to the business of an upcoming project. Where would you likely find the answers? a) The budget b) The business case c) The cost-benefit analysis d) The value proposition	
16	Acceptance criteria are important because: a) They represent a specific and defined list of conditions that must be met before a project has been considered completed, and the project deliverables can and will be accepted by the business b) They represent the stakeholder requirements to the defined solution c) They represent the scope of the project d) Test cases are built upon them	
17	Using the Brown Cow Model, the current situation will be found in which section? a) Upper left corner b) Lower left corner c) Lower right corner d) Upper right corner	
18	What is the main task for the *modifier* at a change control board meeting? a) Receives the change request b) Makes the final decision c) Checks changes are made correctly d) Implements the change	
19	Which of the following helps explain why a requirement has been changed? a) Traceability b) Testing c) Contract management d) Scope management	
20	Which risk response/strategy is *best* for handling negative risks? a) Acceptance b) Share c) Avoid d) Enhance	
21	Possible influences of system contexts are processes; however, what kind of processes? a) Technical processes b) Physical processes c) Business processes d) All of the above	
22	If categorizing the requirement using the Kano model, what are the requirements users take for granted? a) Satisfiers b) Delighters c) Dissatisfiers d) None of the above	

No.	Question	Answer
23	Incoming change requests received by the change control board can be classified as: a) Preventive requirement change b) Corrective requirement change c) Internal change d) External change	
24	Traceability is important because it has the ability to: a) Improve quality b) Reduce risk c) Reduce development cost d) All of the above	
25	Needs assessment translates business needs into: a) Goals b) Scope c) Stakeholder needs d) A traceability matrix	
26	You need to elicit the *Satisfiers* from the Kano model. Which techniques would be most suitable? a) Survey techniques b) Observation c) Creativity techniques d) Document-centric techniques	
27	Some of the business analyst tasks with regard to traceability are: a) Collect requirement traceability information b) Update requirement management plan c) Communicate the updated traceability matrix to the stakeholders d) All of the above	
28	You are analyzing stakeholder values. Which of the following would you *not* include? a) Strategy b) Trust c) Collaboration d) Honesty	
29	SMART criteria are short for: a) Specific, Measurable, Achievable, Relevant, and Testable b) Specific, Measurable, Achievable, Resource, and Time-bound c) Specific, Measurable, Achievable, Relevant, and Time-bound d) Specific, Manageable, Achievable, Relevant, and Time-bound	
30	What are the possible consequences of an incorrect or incomplete context analysis? a) Processes will not be documented b) Some systems will not be in the scope statement c) Some systems will be missing while other systems will be wrongly included d) Networks will not be documented	
31	Which factor most influences the choice of elicitation techniques? a) The quality expectations b) The business analyst's lack of experience with a particular elicitation technique c) Distinction between conscious, unconscious, and subconscious requirements d) Opportunity of risks	
32	Which Scrum role determines how developing the solution will be accomplished? a) The Scrum Master b) The project owner c) The stakeholders d) The development team	

No.	Question	Answer
33	As a business analyst, what do you need to examine for prerequirement specification traceability (or backward traceability)? a) Legacy documentation b) Interviews c) Shadowing d) Workshops with stakeholders	
34	Stakeholder analysis is performed to identify which of the following? a) Each stakeholder's interest in the project b) Potential conflicts in stakeholder viewpoint/interests that must be balanced c) Communication needs of each stakeholder throughout the phases of the project d) All of the above	
35	What are business rules used for? a) Define the rules that govern decisions b) Define the rules that govern the team c) Define the rules that govern the business case d) Define the rules that govern the project	
36	'U' for User Satisfaction in PLUME criteria means: a) Ease of use and remembering b) Time it takes to complete the tasks c) Subjective responses from users d) Accuracy in carrying out the tasks	
37	Which of the following activities is *not* typically part of configuration management? a) Configuration identification b) Configuration status accounting c) Configuration verification and audit d) Configuration management analysis	
38	Which of the following analyses are *not* used for change control? a) Impact change analysis b) Solution effect analysis c) Software impact analysis d) Impact configuration analysis	
39	Why would the business analyst use a combination of different techniques for elicitation? a) To reduce costs b) To reduce time c) To reduce resources d) To minimize risk	
40	The future value is $8,000 in 4 years and the interest rate is 5%. What is the present value? a) $7,634. b) $6,775. c) $6,582. d) $8,575.	
41	Postrequirement specification traceability, which examines current or posterior artifacts, is also called: a) Backward traceability b) Forward traceability c) Prerequirement specification traceability d) Late requirement specification traceability	

No.	Question	Answer
42	The system boundary should be identified in order to do what? a) It is the system boundary that separates the system to be developed from its environment b) It is the system boundary that separates the system to be developed and what is already developed c) It is the system boundary that separates the system to be developed in-house from being out-sourced d) It is the system boundary that separates the requirements to be developed from its attributes	
43	Which one of these factors is *not* a disadvantage of survey techniques? a) Lack of access to committed stakeholders b) Observation of nonverbal behavior c) Documentation is subject to interpretation d) Conflicts are unresolved because people only understand their own point of view	
44	Test-first development is a rapid XP cycle of testing, coding, and refactoring. It is reflected in the equation: test-first design + refactoring = ? a) Test behavior development b) Test driven development c) Software metrics d) Code reviews	
45	During the analyzing stakeholder process, stakeholder personalities are outlined. Which of the following techniques should *not* be used? a) MBTI b) Belbin c) Strength-based leadership d) Porter's five forces	
46	Which of the following is a property of a configuration of requirements? a) Testable b) Consistency c) Transparent d) Objective	
47	Which of the following are *not* among the most commonly used traceability tools? a) Trace matrices b) Traceability chain c) Decision trees d) Specification trees	
48	What is osmotic communication? a) Communication around us which we pick up b) Nonverbal communication c) Formal language d) Personalized communication	
49	During stakeholder assessment, stakeholder salience is applied. Legitimacy and urgency has been measured, but what is missing? a) Probability b) Power c) Relationships d) Concerns	
50	A change in requirements most likely arises from: a) A planned change b) Requirement errors c) Changes in company strategy d) External stakeholder requirements	

No.	Question	Answer
51	Which one of these factors is *not* an advantage of brainstorming? a) Generates multiple ideas quickly b) Involves multiple perspectives c) Promotes equal participants d) The true meaning may be misunderstood or ambiguous	
52	What is meant when the status of a requirement is deleted? a) A special request was made by an authorized source b) An approved requirement has been canceled and removed c) A requirement was proposed, but it was not planned for implementation d) Work has been completed	
53	You are using the expert judgment technique to develop the project charter. Who would you consider as an expert? a) Only university professors b) Subject matter experts c) The PMO d) Everyone	
54	Which one of the following factors most affects the choice of communication and collaboration technology? a) Costs b) Availability of technology c) Project environment d) Documentation	
55	The business analyst needs to analyze and communicate the solution's identified gaps and deltas using quality assurance tools and methods in order to enable stakeholders to resolve discrepancies between: a) The project charter and the defined solution b) The business case and the developed solution c) Solution scope and requirements d) Solution scope, requirements, and the developed solution	
56	Is the system boundary likely to be altered during system development? a) No b) Maybe c) Yes	
57	What is the overall purpose of supporting techniques? a) Help balance out the weaknesses and pitfalls of the selected elicitation technique b) Supporting techniques align stakeholders c) Supporting techniques help spice up the techniques with video and layout d) Additional documentation	
58	Customers are primary stakeholders according to the *Onion* model, but which one of the following stakeholders would most likely be considered secondary? a) Employees b) Suppliers c) Media d) Communities	
59	According to Cockburn, of the choices below, what is the most effective form of communication? a) Paper b) Videotape c) Two people using a whiteboard d) Two people on the phone	

No.	Question	Answer
60	The process of tracking requirements is conducted in which PMI process(es)? a) The collect requirements and perform integrated change control process b) Perform integrated change control process c) Collect requirements process d) Verify scope process	
61	Which techniques are used in the control scope process? a) Variance analysis b) Expert judgment c) Meetings d) Change control tools	
62	Which of these prototypes is considered low fidelity? a) Old version or a competitive product b) Clickable version c) Cardboard mockup d) A video of an acted screen	
63	Total Quality Management (TQM) is described by four principles. Which of the following statements is a principle? a) Analysis of variability b) Management by fact c) Learning and continuous improvement d) All of the above	
64	You are taking part in the process of developing the project charter. What is needed as input? a) Project statement of work b) Agreements c) Enterprise environmental factors d) All of the above	
65	The collect requirements process is important for tracking requirements. However, which of these is not an input? a) Scope management plan b) Requirements management plan c) Stakeholder management plan d) Enterprise environmental factors	
66	Sources and sinks help to identify the interfaces the system has with its environment. What is their relationship? a) Sources are outputs to the systems, while sinks are inputs b) Sources are inputs to the systems, while sinks are outputs c) Sources and sinks are both inputs to the system boundary d) Sources and sinks have no relationship	
67	Which of the following information would you *not* expect to find on a change request? a) Description b) Priority c) Title d) Title identifier	
68	Which of these is *not* a typical type of requirement? a) Functional requirement b) Constraints c) Quality requirement d) Risk-based requirement	

No.	Question	Answer
69	Which two dimensions are used in the Thomas-Kilmann conflict mode model? a) Strengths and weaknesses b) Assertiveness and cooperativeness c) Power and conflict d) Collaboration and conflict	
70	The vision document defines: a) High-level scope b) The risk management plan c) All needed inputs to the project charter d) All of the above	
71	How would the business analyst monitor requirements throughout their life cycle? a) Traceability artifacts or tools b) Use models, documentation, and test cases c) All of the above d) None of the above	
72	Which of these common techniques are *not* used for conceptual modeling and requirement analysis? a) Impact analysis b) Business rules analysis c) Scope modeling d) Functional decomposition	
73	Early on, why should the business analyst identify the context boundary? a) The context boundary separates the tasks divided between the project manager and business analyst b) The context boundary separates the relevant and irrelevant parts of a system to be developed c) The context boundary is what separates the relevant part of the environment of a system to be developed from the outsourced development d) The context boundary is what separates the relevant part of the environment of a system to be developed first and last	
74	Which statistical quality control techniques are used for analysis? a) Cause and effect diagram b) Pareto chart c) Statistical sampling d) Scatter diagram	
75	What is an example of a contingency plan? a) A plan in case of time delays b) An emergency plan in case of a fire in the server room c) A plan to raise funds for the business case d) None of the above	
76	Configuration management is: a) A subsystem of the overall project management system b) A configuration management system c) Both of the above d) A subsystem of change management	
77	Which dedicated role would you expect to find at an inspection? a) Project manager b) The business analyst c) Minute-taker d) The PMO	

No.	Question	Answer
78	What is a common data analysis tool, data model, or technique? a) Cause effect analysis b) UML activity diagram c) User stories d) Feature map	
79	To monitor requirements throughout their life cycle depends very much on the project life cycle and related requirements management life cycle. Which of the following models are *not* related to the waterfall approach for monitoring requirements? a) B Model b) V Model c) Spiral model d) Incremental model	
80	Business needs may arise from: a) Market demands b) Social need c) Legal requirements d) All of the above	
81	In addition to quality management and statistical quality control tools, which technique is helpful in analyzing solution gaps? a) Value stream mapping b) Histograms c) Impact analysis d) Business case updates	
82	You have just documented the system context with use case diagrams. What would you confirm it with? a) The software requirement specification b) The business case c) The cost benefit analyst d) Some of the stakeholders	
83	What tool are we working with if we are using *Dotmocracy* for decision making? a) Checklists b) Pareto c) Delphi d) Plurality	
84	Which of these qualitative techniques would be suitable for needs assessment? a) Observation b) Special-purpose records c) Mind maps d) Context diagrams	
85	You have version 0.1 of the software on the shelf and have just developed some major changes. What version number would be suitable for the changed software? a) 0.1 b) 0.2 c) 1.0 d) 1.1	
86	Which decision-making techniques do you use when everyone has to agree upon the decision? a) Unanimity b) Majority c) Plurality d) Dictatorship	

No.	Question	Answer
87	The requirements life cycle would include how many phases? a) Always one b) One or two phases c) Can include a number of phases	
88	The CATWOE analysis involves which of the following factors? a) Client, actor, transformation, world view, owner, and environment b) Client, actor, transformation, world view, owner, and enterprise c) Customer, actor, transformation, world actor, organization, and environment d) Customer, actor, transformation, world view, owner, and environment	
89	Quality is an inherent aspect of true agile software development. In agile, quality focus is on: a) Internal quality b) External quality c) Prevention d) Inspections	
90	Which development model is the oldest? a) The spiral model b) The waterfall model c) The B model d) The ABC model	
91	What are the ideas involved with *tracing*? a) Trace components to the business case b) Trace costs with the business case c) Trace components to their objectives d) Trace goals with the stakeholder requirements	
92	Version control involves: a) Version identification schemes b) Updates of the requirement traceability matrix c) Requirement document updates d) CCB meetings	
93	What are the three broad types of solution development methodologies that business analysts use? a) Structured analysis, object-oriented analysis, and agile b) Business process analysis, object-oriented analysis, and structured analysis c) Data flow diagramming, business process analysis, and object-oriented analysis d) Business process modeling, RUP, and waterfall	
94	Which activities are you *not* likely to find during requirements definition? a) Specification checker b) Authoring c) Traceability d) Visual modeling	
95	If you are estimating with an agile team, which technique would you most likely use? a) Parametric estimating b) Delphi c) Program evaluation and review technique (PERT) d) Planning poker	
96	Which of the following statements *best* describes the purpose of workflow models? a) Used to document the interaction of a user with a solution b) Used to document a graphical presentation of the problem domain c) Used to facilitate the discovery of processes of a system or business d) Used to document how work processes are carried out and to find opportunities for process improvement	

No.	Question	Answer
97	When using agile, when is stakeholder signoff conducted? a) At the end of the sprint b) After a release c) Daily d) As often as possible	
98	What are the typical consequences of requirement traceability on costs? a) No change in cost b) Costs would decrease c) Costs would increase d) Costs would increase by a factor of four	
99	When facilitating, which tools and techniques would be effective? a) Presentation skills b) Idea gathering skills c) Document techniques d) Communication management	
100	Which status is *not* included in requirement eleven? a) Stated b) Tracked c) Confirmed d) Communicated	
101	You have developed a RASCI chart. Who is most likely responsible for identifying stakeholders? a) The business analyst b) The development team c) The sponsor d) The Scrum Master	
102	Requirement baselines are: a) Requirements committed to be tested b) Requirements committed to be implemented c) Requirements within scope d) Requirements out of scope	
103	Which group decision-making style would the product owner most likely apply? a) Unanimity b) Majority c) Plurality d) Dictatorship	
104	Interface analysis demonstrates the interaction between the: a) Requirement and solution b) System and environment c) Scope and business case d) Software and stakeholders	
105	How do you avoid the developers missing a requirement? a) With Scrum, no requirements can be missed b) You can't, however, with requirements traceability you can document whether or not it is the case c) With requirement traceability, it will never happen d) Better train the developers	

No.	Question	Answer
106	According to Hersey and Blanchard, which style is useful for team members who are motivated but not highly skilled? a) S1 b) S2 c) S3 d) S4	
107	Which of the following is a step in benefits management? a) Analyzing benefits b) Measuring benefits c) Validating benefits d) Identification of benefits	
108	What is the net present value (NPV) if the present value is $100,000 and the costs are $100,000? a) −$100,000 b) 0 c) $100,000 d) $200,000	
109	Requirements in Scrum are called: a) Use cases b) Requirements c) Features d) User stories	
110	How are requirements monitored in Scrum? a) Through managing features b) Traceability matrix c) In the product backlog and sprint backlog d) Through managing epics	
111	The normative valuation techniques would include? a) Development of a prototype b) Surveys c) Focus groups d) Interviews	
112	What are the advantages of traceable requirements? a) Certification b) Maintenance c) Both of the above d) Transparency	
113	Examining requirements may uncover errors. The most common are: a) Contradictions b) Ambiguity c) Incompleteness d) All of the above	
114	What should the business analyst do when a requirement status is updated? a) Communicate with the appropriate stakeholders b) Record changes in the backlog c) Both of the above d) None of the above	

No.	Question	Answer
115	You have conducted breakeven and value chain analysis, however, you need to assess the value of an IT investment further. What other tools and techniques should be used? a) Risk analysis b) Sensitivity analysis c) Present value d) Return on investment	
116	Continuous integration, continuous deployment, and continuous improvements can: a) Deliver high quality at low costs b) Deliver high quality at high costs c) Deliver fixed scope at low cost d) Deliver user stories at low risk	
117	You are identifying stakeholder relationships. Which of the following is *not* a typical stakeholder relationship? a) Allied b) Alliance c) Competitive d) Threatening	
118	Which leadership style should Scrum Masters use? a) None, as they are not leaders b) Adaptive leadership c) Servant leadership d) Autocratic	
119	When the business analyst updates a requirement status, what information would he/she likely update? a) Benefits b) Risks c) Auctioneer d) Documentation	
120	What is the name of the traceability process that occurs just before realization of requirements? a) Prerequirement specification b) Postrequirement specification c) Forward traceability d) Backward traceability	
121	What is one of the key challenges with requirements elicitation? a) Geographical location of the stakeholders b) Possible access to key resources c) Both of the above d) The sheer amount of elicitation techniques	
122	You have examined the quality aspects of the content of the requirements and are looking at correctness/adequacy. What question would be good to ask? a) Have all relevant traceability relations been defined? b) Does each requirement contain all necessary information? c) Do the requirements accurately reflect the wishes and needs of the stakeholders? d) Does every requirement contribute to the fulfillment of the defined goals?	
123	As a business analyst, where would you document the appropriate stakeholder requirements in regard to status? a) Communication management plan b) The project plan c) The stakeholders' management strategy d) It is not documented, but only discussed	

No.	Question	Answer
124	In most agile methodologies, who has the responsibility of evaluating the deployed solution using valuation techniques in order to determine how well the solution meets the business case and value proposition? a) The stakeholders b) The Scrum Master c) The product owner d) The development team	
125	Stakeholders are "an individual, group, or organization who may affect, be affected by, or perceive itself to be affected by a decision, activity, or outcome of a project." a) True b) False—not a group c) False—not an organization d) False—not individuals	
126	At what time during the project is it most common for the retrospective to occur? a) At any given time b) At the beginning of every iteration or sprint c) At the end of every iteration or sprint d) At the end of a release	
127	The main goal of elicitation techniques is in supporting the business analyst to: a) Reduce cost b) Reduce time c) Support the business case d) Gain knowledge of stakeholder requirements	
128	You have identified the stakeholders and applied stakeholder salience in order to analyze them. Some stakeholders are identified as dominant, meaning they hold: a) Power and legitimacy b) Legitimacy and urgency c) Power and urgency d) Power, urgency, and legitimacy	
129	During which activities would the business analyst use negotiation techniques? a) Requirements development b) Team activities c) During procurement d) All of the above	
130	Effectively communicating the status of requirements involves: a) Right timing b) Right format c) Right medium d) All of the above	
131	What process outputs are needed to establish the level of traceability necessary to validate and monitor the requirements? a) The project management plan b) Requirements documentation c) Requirements traceability matrix d) Requirements documentation and the requirements traceability matrix	

No.	Question	Answer
132	Sometimes the business analyst may encounter a violation of the quality aspects of the documentation of the requirements, which may cause problems for the acceptance criteria or not reflect the business metrics. What is an example of a violation? a) Contradictions b) Ambiguity c) Lack of communication d) Misunderstandings	
133	Risk is one factor when considering elicitation techniques, what are others? a) The desired level of detail of the requirements b) Training with the elicitation techniques c) Attitude towards the elicitation techniques d) Loyalty	
134	The business case is most important because it: a) Justifies IT investments b) Contains a cost-benefit analysis c) Justifies costs d) Includes financial measurements	
135	Hofstedes dimension of power distance deals with: a) The use of power b) The need for power c) Inequalities in power d) Types of power available	
136	Effective and efficient communication of the status of requirements would *not* require the use of which of the following techniques? a) Presentation techniques b) Facilitation techniques c) Management techniques d) Listening techniques	
137	Requirements documentation includes: a) The business and project objective for traceability b) Requirements identified c) Roles and assignments d) Input for the business case	
138	Which of the following identifies the greatest benefit that requirements traceability offers? a) Supports the ability to trace a requirement through the development life cycle b) Allows the business analyst to understand the interest of all parties that are affected by a change to project requirements c) Aids in scope management, change impact analysis, and risk-based testing d) Allows the business analyst to understand that all impacts of changes to the solution scope are properly considered	
139	Decisions made at the strategic level would have the following complexity: a) High b) Middle c) Low d) All of the above depending on the situation	
140	You have conducted the brainstorming session. However, in need of a supplement in writing, which technique would you use? a) *Onion* model b) Extended brainstorming c) Brainwriting d) Cost-benefit analysis	

No.	Question	Answer
141	When using agile, political awareness is handled by which role? a) The Scrum Master b) The product owner c) The development team d) The stakeholders	
142	What are some of the advantages to using interview techniques? a) Requires access to committed stakeholders b) Requires training and skills to work well c) Documentation is subject to interpretation d) None of the above	
143	Communication channels are increased from 5 external stakeholders and 4 team members to 7 external stakeholders and 5 team members. What is the new amount of communication channels in total? a) 44 b) 55 c) 66 d) 77	
144	What is an alternative to the requirement traceability matrix? a) User stories b) Textual reference c) Impact analysis d) RAM	
145	What is the first of the six principles of validation? a) Validating from different views b) Involving the right stakeholders c) Separating the identification and the correction of errors d) Construction of development artifacts	
146	What is the use of a customer journey map? a) Root cause analysis b) Problem solving and opportunity identification c) Risk analysis d) Map of the product vision	
147	Interactive communication involves: a) Face-to-face meetings b) Website information c) E-mails d) Formal letter	
148	Requirement traceability needs to be conducted: a) Early on and cover it all b) As an ongoing effort c) When time and resources are available d) Once every month	
149	Which constraints are fixed when working with agile? a) Time b) Resources c) Both of the above d) Scope	
150	You are assessing the stakeholders and want to measure their value. How would you do that? a) Ask them b) Conduct a survey c) Observe them d) Use benchmarking techniques	

No.	Question	Answer
151	What factor(s) would you consider when applying communication methods to your project? a) Familiarity b) Urgency c) Both of the above d) Availability of technology	
152	A business analyst work plan, requirements work plan, or business analyst work division strategy are other names for: a) The requirements management plan b) The requirements traceability matrix c) Requirements documentation d) None of the above	
153	When working with the spiral model, which constraints would most likely vary? a) Time b) Resource c) Scope d) Risk	
154	What is the return on investment if benefits are $120,000 and costs are $150,000 a) 10% b) 20% c) −10% d) −20%	
155	Additional elements of validating requirements do *not* involve: a) Checking assumptions b) Checking the business case with sunk costs c) Determining dependencies of solution benefits d) Defining measurable evaluation criteria	
156	In your project documentation, where would the reporting methods and frequency most likely be outlined? a) Communications management plan b) Communications requirement strategy c) Stakeholder management plan d) Stakeholder requirement strategy	
157	Why would you use personas? a) To better understand requirements b) For building test cases c) To derive new requirements d) For user stories development	
158	How many PMBOK knowledge areas are involved in the Needs Assessment domain? a) 1 b) 2 c) 3 d) 4	
159	Which of the following is *not* a benefit of system thinking? a) Maximizing the outcomes achieved b) Analyzing risk and opportunity c) Contingency management d) Aligning specialism and interest groups	

No.	Question	Answer
160	What is the most common reason requirement management plans fail? a) Lack of management support b) Lack of time c) Risks are not identified d) Lack of maturity	
161	You are planning the work and work schedule. The preceding activity must be finished before the next activity can start. Which of the following relationships best describes this? a) Finish-to-Start b) Finish-to-Finish c) Start-to-Start d) Start-to-Finish	
162	You have identified stakeholders with a technique where the team imagines that a project or organization has failed or succeeded. Which technique did you use? a) SWOT analysis b) Delphi c) Pre-mortem d) De Bono	
163	You are working through your project's risk and are analyzing probability and impact. What kind of analysis are you most likely conducting? a) Qualitative risk assessment b) Quantitative risk assessment c) Risk register update d) Risk assessment	
164	You are part of an agile Scrum team and are identifying risk. Which process are you working on? a) Sprint review b) Sprint planning c) Daily Scrum d) Sprint retrospective	
165	If the power is medium in the extended power/interest grid, what is the likely level of interest? a) Very low b) Anywhere from low to high c) Medium d) Very high	
166	In a Scrum team, who enforces the rules and processes? a) The Scrum Master b) The development team c) The stakeholders d) The product owner	
167	Decision trees are used when working on business rules, however, where else would you use them? a) Quality management b) Quantitative risk assessment c) Scope management d) Project time management	
168	You have created a decision table analysis for business rules. What content is in it? a) Requirements and user stories b) Requirements and conditions c) Requirements and test cases d) Requirements and dependencies	

No.	Question	Answer
169	You have assessed stakeholders using the power/interest grid analysis. Which stakeholders can you more or less ignore? a) High power/low interest b) High power/high interest c) Low power/low interest d) Low power/high interest	
170	You are working on the impact analysis and its implications. What are you working with? a) Time and cost constraint issues b) Quality and risk issues c) Constraints and relations issues d) Dependencies and relations issues	
171	Change impact analysis implies identifying the potential consequences of a change, or estimating what needs to be modified to accomplish a change, however, this implies: a) Understanding traceability b) Understanding dependency c) Understanding the experiential aspects of change d) All of the above	
172	What would be considered synchronous communication? a) Skype call b) E-mail c) Letter d) Twitter	
173	What kind of tools would you recommend for increased online collaboration? a) Facebook b) Scrum board c) Task board d) Daily stand-ups	
174	What kind of communication would be most effective within a distributed team? a) Verbal communication b) Nonverbal communication c) Online communication d) Formal written communication	
175	You are identifying stakeholders; which one would you consider as internal? a) Your boss b) Outside counsel c) Your business analyst consultant d) A reporter	

Table 16.2   PMI-PBA full practice exam—answers and explanations

No.	Answer	Explanation	Chapter
1	A	The evaluation consists of activities to determine how well the developed solution fulfills the defined solution and business needs. This involves validating the solutions and business needs with the use of acceptance criteria.	Chapter 9
2	C	We need to review the business case and the project charter to ensure objectives and goals are clear because we need this to set the boundaries for our requirements management work to be conducted.	Chapter 6
3	A	The domain, Traceability and Monitoring, manages the life cycle of the requirements, which includes ongoing communication and collaboration with the stakeholders in order to manage, trace, and monitor the requirements throughout their life cycle.	Chapter 8
4	A	*Planguage*, a key word oriented language developed by Tom Gilb, supports the development of nonfunctional requirements using a language for software development.	Chapter 10
5	B	The business case contains a section on financial measurement, including a cost-benefit analysis where the following measurements are calculated or described: • Present value • Net present value • Future value • Return on investment • Internal rate of return • Payback period	Chapter 5
6	A	The business analyst needs to validate the solution's test results, reports, and other test evidence against the requirements acceptance criteria in order to determine whether the solution satisfies the requirements. In simple terms, does the delivered solution meet the business need?	Chapter 9
7	D	Change manager (chair), contractor, architect, configuration manager, customer representative, product manager, project manager, quality assurance representative, technical support or help desk, and requirements engineer all take part in change control board meetings.	Chapter 6
8	A	One key challenge is for the business analyst to successfully record the voice of the customer.	Chapter 7
9	C	The business analyst needs to track requirements using traceability artifacts and tools; capturing the requirements' status, sources, and relationship (including dependencies) in order to provide evidence that the requirements are delivered as stated.	Chapter 8
10	B	The product owner is responsible and is the decision maker.	Chapter 5
11	C	External	Chapter 10
12	A	The *system context* is defined as "the part of the system environment that is relevant for the definition as well as the understanding of the requirements of a system to be developed." Clearly, this is a major task of a business analyst.	Chapter 6
13	D	Requirements elicitation may derive from any of these sources.	Chapter 7
14	D	As discussed earlier, traceability is important to document the life of the requirements. The documentation or traceability may help control the force of change and avoid runaway requirements which can turn into scope creep.	Chapter 8
15	D	The budget, business case, and cost-benefit analysis are all part of the value proposition.	Chapter 5

No.	Answer	Explanation	Chapter
16	A	Acceptance criteria are important because they represent a specific and defined list of conditions that must be met before a project has been considered completed, and the project deliverables can and will be accepted by the business.	Chapter 9
17	B	The lower left corner is the current (now) situation.	Chapter 7
18	D	The *modifier* implements the change.	Chapter 6
19	A	With traceability, the business analyst can explain why a requirement has been changed and use the documentation as a basis for testing and as ongoing system documentation.	Chapter 8
20	C	Avoiding risk is the best response/strategy when possible. Transfer, mitigate, and acceptance are the other commonly used negative risk response strategies.	Chapter 10
21	D	Technical, physical, and business processes can all influence system contexts.	Chapter 6
22	C	Dissatisfiers—they are properties of the system that are self-evident and taken for granted.	Chapter 7
23	B	They can be classified as corrective requirements change, adaptive requirements change, or exceptional change.	Chapter 6
24	D	Traceability can improve quality, reduce risk, and reduce development costs which may increase our ability to embrace change.	Chapter 8
25	A	Business needs are translated into goals. Goals turn into project and product scope with an agreement on what people want before attempting to create solutions.	Chapter 5
26	A	Survey techniques.	Chapter 7
27	D	Keep track of changes (evolving requirements); collect requirement traceability information; track and report requirement status; update requirement documentation; communicate requirement status and changes; and maintain and update the traceability matrix are all business analysis activities.	Chapter 8
28	A	The values should be high-level such as: vision, servant leadership, trust, collaboration, honesty, learning, courage, openness, adaptability, and leading change.	Chapter 5
29	C	Specific, Measurable, Achievable, Relevant, and Time-bound..	Chapter 9
30	C	The consequences of an ill-defined system context would be that the wrong system or requirements would be considered; requirements would be missing as systems are not within context, while in other cases requirements would be included, but for systems that are not relevant, which would increase costs and workload, reduce the use of the system, and so forth.	Chapter 6
31	C	While lack of experience with a technique, opportunity of risks, time and budget constraints, and stakeholder availability could be influencing factors, the analyst's objective to make distinctions between conscious, unconscious, and subconscious requirements influences the choice of elicitation techniques most.	Chapter 7
32	D	The development team determines how it will accomplish the work.	Chapter 10
33	A	Prerequirement specification traceability, also defined as backward traceability, examines previous artifacts.	Chapter 8
34	D	All the above is the correct answer. Stakeholders have viewpoints, interests, and goals that may be aligned or in conflict. Communication needs of each stakeholder are likely to vary. These need to be identified and then managed.	Chapter 5
35	A	The business rules analysis technique is used to define the rules that govern decisions in an organization, and that define, constrain, or enable organizational operations.	Chapter 10

No.	Answer	Explanation	Chapter
36	C	Subjective responses from users.	Chapter 9
37	D	Configuration identification, configuration status accounting, and configuration verification and audit.	Chapter 6
38	D	The impact analysis, change impact analysis, impact change analysis, solution effect analysis, and software impact analysis are all used for change control.	Chapter 10
39	D	Combining different techniques helps minimize many risks inherent to the project.	Chapter 7
40	C	The formula is = FV / (1 + r)^n. So if the interest rate is 5%, the equation is $8,000 / (1 + 0.05)^4, which equals $6,582.	Chapter 5
41	B	Postrequirement specification traceability, also defined as forward traceability, examines current or posterior artifacts. These may include components and test cases.	Chapter 8
42	A	It is the system boundary that separates the system to be developed from its environment.	Chapter 6
43	B	Possible disadvantages to survey techniques include: lack of access to committed stakeholders and training and skills to work well; documentation is subject to interpretation; conflicts are unresolved because people only understand their own point of view; and stakeholders may not be able to describe the future so they are limited to describing the current situation.	Chapter 7
44	B	Test-first development is a rapid XP cycle of testing, coding, and refactoring. It is reflected in the equation: test-first design + refactoring = test-driven development.	Chapter 9
45	D	The techniques for analyzing stakeholders' personalities are MBTI, Belbin, DISC, strength-based leadership, and similar procedures.	Chapter 5
46	B	Logical connection, consistency, unique identification, immutable, and basis for rollbacks are properties of a configuration of requirements.	Chapter 6
47	C	Text-based references and hyperlinks, trace matrices, trace graphs (over different development artifacts), specification trees, specialized templates, traceability chain (foundation for impact analysis), and requirements tools/tracing tools are all commonly used.	Chapter 8
48	A	While writing, reading, typing, or talking, we pick up traces of the ongoing sounds around us, using some background listening mode, even though we are not consciously paying attention. This is osmotic communication.	Chapter 10
49	B	Stakeholder salience analyzes power, legitimacy, and urgency.	Chapter 5
50	B	Requirement errors, conflicts, inconsistencies, evolving stakeholder knowledge, changing priorities, organizational changes, technological changes, or enterprise environmental factors, such as new laws, are all causes.	Chapter 6
51	D	Generates multiple ideas quickly, involves multiple perspectives, and promotes equal participants are all advantages of brainstorming.	Chapter 7
52	B	An approved requirement has been canceled and removed. Proposed, accepted, verified, postponed, canceled, and implemented requirement status is documented in (a) requirement management tools/repository.	Chapter 8
53	B	Expert judgment can be conducted by everyone with extensive knowledge of the field. These may include (but are not limited to) university professors. The PMO may or may not have subject matter experts while not everyone is necessarily an expert.	Chapter 5
54	C	Project environment is the factor that most affects the choice of communication and collaboration technology. Other factors include urgency, available technology, ease of use, and sensitivity and confidentiality of the information.	Chapter 10

No.	Answer	Explanation	Chapter
55	D	The business analyst needs to analyze and communicate the solution's identified gaps and deltas using quality assurance tools and methods in order to enable stakeholders to resolve discrepancies between solution scope, requirements, and the developed solution.	Chapter 9
56	C	The system boundaries, which separate the system to be developed from its environment, can and most likely would be altered during system development.	Chapter 6
57	A	Support techniques serve as an addition to the elicitation techniques and help balance out the weaknesses and pitfalls of the selected elicitation technique.	Chapter 7
58	C	Communities, employees, suppliers, and customers are primary stakeholders, while the media are secondary.	Chapter 5
59	C	A study by Cockburn (2001) clearly illustrates the importance of communication by two people at a whiteboard. This is more effective compared to writing a message on a piece of paper.	Chapter 10
60	A	The process of tracking requirements is conducted in the collect requirements *and* perform integrated change control processes.	Chapter 8
61	A	Variance analysis.	Chapter 6
62	C	A prototype is not just a prototype—some are low-fidelity prototypes that are fast to create, simple, and low-tech; while high-fidelity prototypes require the use of tools or software that often enables the user to interact with the prototype.	Chapter 7
63	D	The first principle states that the quality of products and services depends most of all on the processes by which they are designed and produced. The second principle is analysis of variability. The third principle is management by fact and the fourth principle is learning and continuous improvement.	Chapter 9
64	D	Project statement of work, business cases, agreements, enterprise environment factors, and organizational process assets are all inputs to the develop project charter process.	Chapter 5
65	D	The scope management plan, requirements management plan, stakeholder management plan, project charter, and stakeholder register are all inputs.	Chapter 8
66	B	Sources are inputs to the systems, while sinks are outputs.	Chapter 6
67	D	Identifier, title, description, justification, date field, priority, and applicant are correct.	Chapter 6
68	D	Risk-based requirements are fictitious.	Chapter 7
69	B	The Thomas-Kilmann conflict mode takes the five general techniques for solving conflicts and maps them on two dimensions: (1) assertiveness, the extent to which the person attempts to satisfy his own concerns, and (2) cooperativeness.	Chapter 10
70	A	The vision document defines the high-level scope and purpose of a program, product, or project. A clear statement of the problem, proposed solution, and the high-level features of a product help establish expectations and reduce risks. The vision document is, in PMI terms, translated into the project scope and product scope.	Chapter 5
71	C	A BA monitors requirements throughout their life cycle using traceability artifacts or tools in order to ensure the appropriate supporting requirements artifacts (such as models, documentation, and test cases) are produced, reviewed, and approved at each point in the life cycle.	Chapter 8
72	A	Business rules analysis, data flow diagrams, data modeling, functional decomposition, organization modeling, process modeling, scenarios and use cases, and scope modeling are all used.	Chapter 7
73	B	The context boundary is what separates the relevant part of the environment of a system to be developed from the irrelevant part.	Chapter 6

No.	Answer	Explanation	Chapter
74	D	Scatter diagrams, run charts, histograms, flowcharting, and control charts are all used for analysis.	Chapter 9
75	B	A contingency plan is a risk response to an event or occurrence (contingency) that could affect the execution of the project.	Chapter 10
76	C	Configuration management, or the configuration management system, is defined as "a subsystem of the overall project management system."	Chapter 6
77	C	Organizer, Moderator, Author, Reader, Inspectors, Recorder, and Minute-taker are all roles taking part.	Chapter 7
78	B	State diagram, UML activity diagram, class diagram, use case diagram, data flow, entity-relationship diagram, interaction diagram, and decision tables and trees are all data analysis tools and techniques.	Chapter 10
79	C	The spiral model is used for agile software development.	Chapter 8
80	D	Business needs may arise from market demands, strategic opportunities/business needs, social needs, environmental considerations, customer requests, technological advancements, legal requirements, or in the context of a strategic plan.	Chapter 5
81	A	Techniques for analyzing solution gaps include: root cause analysis (5 Whys), force field analysis, nominal group technique, inspections, reviews, peer reviews, audits and walkthroughs, and gap analysis (value stream mapping).	Chapter 9
82	B	When the documentation is completed, it's important to confirm or check the diagrams against the business case, organization requirements goals, and project charter that conclude this project and system context loop.	Chapter 6
83	A	We are using checklists for decision making.	Chapter 10
84	A	Qualitative techniques would include interviewing, workshops, and observation.	Chapter 5
85	C	Small changes in a requirement may change the version from 0.1 to 0.2, while larger changes may result in a change from version 0.1 to 1.0.	Chapter 6
86	A	Unanimity.	Chapter 7
87	C	Overall, the requirements life cycle can be a complicated process involving a number of phases.	Chapter 8
88	D	CATWOE analysis involves a customer, actor, transformation, world view, owner, and environment.	Chapter 5
89	C	In agile, we focus on prevention rather than inspections. Prevention is about avoiding errors by means of proper processes, training, checklists, and controls.	Chapter 9
90	B	The waterfall model dates back to the 1970s.	Chapter 10
91	C	The components are traced to their objectives.	Chapter 6
92	A	Version control would include defining a version identification scheme, identifying requirements documents versions, and identifying individual requirement versions.	Chapter 6
93	B	Business process analysis, object-oriented analysis, and structured analysis are the three broad methods. Each has a corresponding set of analysis techniques.	Chapter 10
94	A	Authoring, traceability, and visual modeling are activities in requirements definition.	Chapter 8
95	D	Planning poker is the most common agile estimation technique.	Chapter 10
96	D	Work flow models are used to depict the sequential flow of a work process primarily to find opportunities for improvement.	Chapter 10

No.	Answer	Explanation	Chapter
97	A	When working in an agile development, stakeholder signoff is conducted at the end of the sprint by the product owner.	Chapter 9
98	C	Requirement traceability is a manually intensive task which typically increases development cost.	Chapter 6
99	C	Conflict resolution, problem solving, negotiation, document techniques, and decision making are all used during facilitation.	Chapter 10
100	B	Requirement eleven statuses are: Stated, Confirmed, Communicated, Traced, Approved, Maintained, Prioritized, Analyzed, Verified, Validated, and Allocated.	Chapter 8
101	A	The most likely person responsible for identifying stakeholders is the business analyst. Also emphasized is that it is very unlikely that the development team and the Scrum Master will take part, but the sponsor may have a role; however, he/she may not be responsible.	Chapter 5
102	B	Requirement baselines are requirements committed to be implemented.	Chapter 6
103	D	In agile development, the product owner is the final decision maker and can act as a dictator.	Chapter 9
104	B	Interface analysis demonstrates the interaction between the system and environment.	Chapter 10
105	B	Requirement traceability documents whether or not this is the case.	Chapter 6
106	D	S4.	Chapter 10
107	D	Determining the value derived from the business case and value proposition is used in conjunction with benefits management, which is the process of managing benefits throughout the project. The steps are: identification of benefits, definition of benefits, tracking of benefits, benefit realization, and optimization of benefits.	Chapter 9
108	B	One way to write the formula for NPV is: NPV = present value of future cash flows – costs. In this case, $100,000 – $100,000 = 0.	Chapter 5
109	D	User stories.	Chapter 7
110	C	In the agile methodology Scrum, the monitoring of requirements is conducted in the product backlog and sprint backlog. The agile product backlog is a prioritized features list, containing short descriptions of all functionality desired in the product. The sprint backlog is the list of work derived from the product backlog to be addressed during the next sprint. A sprint (or iteration) is a time-boxed effort; or basic unit of development restricted to a brief and specific duration.	Chapter 8
111	A	The normative valuation techniques use measurement based upon comparative data from either best practice or benchmarking models. The normative valuation techniques may involve the development of a prototype or pilot system, or of a model that is used to provide information on what the expected value should be.	Chapter 9
112	C	The advantages of traceable requirements include verifiability—identification of a gold-plated solution in the system, identification of a gold-plated solution in the requirements, change impact analysis, reuse/reengineering, project tracking, risk reduction, accountability, maintenance, and certification.	Chapter 6
113	D	Examining requirements may uncover errors. The most common are ambiguity, incompleteness, and contradictions.	Chapter 6
114	A	The business analyst needs to update a requirement status as it moves through its life cycle. This is done by communicating with the appropriate stakeholders and recording changes in the traceability artifacts and tools in order to track requirements towards closure.	Chapter 8

No.	Answer	Explanation	Chapter
115	B	Risk analysis is out of place, while calculating the present value and ROI are part of the cost-benefit analysis. Sensitivity analysis is an advanced technique to conduct.	Chapter 5
116	A	Continuous integration, continuous deployment, and continuous improvements can deliver high quality at low costs.	Chapter 7
117	B	The five relationship types are: allied, cooperative, neutral, competitive, and threatening.	Chapter 5
118	C	Servant leadership is used by many Scrum Masters.	Chapter 10
119	B	ID, risk, source, name, description, and owner all are updated.	Chapter 8
120	B	Postrequirement specification.	Chapter 6
121	C	Key challenges are the geographical location of the stakeholders and possible access to these key resources.	Chapter 7
122	C	To gauge correctness/adequacy, ask "Do the requirements accurately reflect the wishes and needs of the stakeholders?"	Chapter 6
123	A	Stakeholder communication requirements are included in the communication management plan, which contains the appropriate stakeholder requirements in regard to status.	Chapter 8
124	C	How well the solution meets the business case and value proposition is solely a task for the product owner, who is responsible for the business case and benefit realization of the developed solution.	Chapter 9
125	A	The definition of stakeholders is "an individual, group, or organization who may affect, be affected by, or perceive itself to be affected by a decision, activity, or outcome of a project." 100% correct.	Chapter 5
126	C	The retrospective is most commonly done at the end of every iteration or sprint.	Chapter 10
127	D	The main goal of all elicitation techniques is that of supporting the business analyst in ascertaining the knowledge and requirements of the stakeholders.	Chapter 7
128	A	Dominant stakeholders hold power and legitimacy.	Chapter 5
129	D	Negotiation would be used during requirements development, team activities, or during procurement.	Chapter 10
130	D	Effective communication requires the right timing, the right format, and the right medium.	Chapter 8
131	D	The output in the collect requirements process is the requirements documentation and the requirements traceability matrix, which is needed to establish the level of traceability necessary to validate and monitor the requirements.	Chapter 6
132	D	Misunderstandings, incompleteness, impairment, and overlooking requirements are all examples.	Chapter 6
133	A	Another influencing factor on the choice of elicitation techniques is the desired level of detail of the requirements.	Chapter 7
134	A	The business case is most important because it justifies IT investments, and includes the cost-benefit analysis and other financial measurements, including all relevant benefits and costs.	Chapter 5
135	C	Power distance describes how a society deals with the inequalities in power that exist among people.	Chapter 10
136	C	Sender-receiver models, choice of media, writing style, meeting management techniques, presentation techniques, facilitation techniques, and listening techniques would all be useful.	Chapter 8

No.	Answer	Explanation	Chapter
137	A	The requirements documentation is "a description of how individual requirements meet the business needs for the project," which includes the business and project objective for traceability.	Chapter 6
138	C	Requirements traceability has many benefits. Structuring requirements for traceability allows the business analyst to take advantage of understanding scope, change, and risk impacts on requirements.	Chapter 10
139	A	High.	Chapter 10
140	C	The *Onion* model and the organization chart are techniques for identifying stakeholders. Extended brainstorming is made-up, while brainwriting is a written version of brainstorming using stickers.	Chapter 5
141	B	When using agile, political awareness is handled and managed by the product owner.	Chapter 10
142	D	Interview techniques allow you to have scripted discussions, promote dialogue, encourage participants, observe nonverbal behavior, and gain immediate feedback.	Chapter 7
143	C	The equation for number of communication channels is: N(N – 1)/2. In this case, 12(12 – 1)/2= 66.	Chapter 8
144	B	The requirement traceability matrix is an effective tool, however, some alternatives are textual reference, hyperlinks, trace graphs (over different development artifacts) or traceability chains (linking relations). Most of these are integrated in automated requirement management tools.	Chapter 6
145	B	The first principle is involving the right stakeholders.	Chapter 6
146	B	Problem solving and opportunity identification.	Chapter 10
147	A	Interactive communication is multidirectional and the most effective. The communication medium would include face-to-face meetings, video conferencing, phone calls, and messenger chats.	Chapter 8
148	B	Requirements traceability is an ongoing effort.	Chapter 6
149	C	In agile development, time and resources are fixed while scope is variable.	Chapter 10
150	A	Stakeholder value can be measured in a number of ways, however, the focus here has been on *asking* them (interviews).	Chapter 5
151	C	The factors would include familiarity with the communication methods and urgency of the communication.	Chapter 8
152	A	The requirements management plan.	Chapter 6
153	C	Scope is variable, while time and resources are fixed.	Chapter 10
154	D	If benefits are $120,000 and costs are $150,000, then $120,000 minus $150,000 = –$30,000/$150,000 = –20% ROI.	Chapter 5
155	B	Checking assumptions, defining measurable evaluation criteria, defining business value, determining dependencies of solution benefits, and evaluating the alignment of the business case with opportunity costs are additional elements of validating requirements.	Chapter 6
156	A	Reporting methods, such as e-mail, formal reports, and face-to-face meetings, and their frequency, are outlined in the communications management plan and communications requirement analysis.	Chapter 10
157	A	During system development and design, the business analysts may use personas and extreme characters for getting a better understanding of requirements. Personas are made up pretend users who are then designed for by the team.	Chapter 10

No.	Answer	Explanation	Chapter
158	C	Project integration management, project cost management, and project stakeholder management.	Chapter 5
159	C	Benefits of system thinking include: managing people, purpose, process and performance; relating systems to their environment; understanding complex problem situations; maximizing the outcomes achieved; avoiding or minimizing the impact of unintended consequences; aligning teams, disciplines, specialism and interest groups; managing uncertainty; and analyzing risk and opportunity to help balance the needs of stakeholders and impact how information is shared across the organization.	Chapter 10
160	D	Although some practitioners lack the resources, knowledge, or skills to develop the plans, the most common reason they fail is lack of maturity.	Chapter 6
161	A	Finish-to-Start.	Chapter 10
162	C	Pre-mortem is the technique where the team imagines that a project or organization has failed or succeeded, and then works backward to determine which stakeholders could lead to the success or failure of the project or organization.	Chapter 5
163	A	Qualitative risk assessment.	Chapter 10
164	B	During sprint planning, risk identification is conducted every time.	Chapter 10
165	B	The level of interest can range anywhere from low to high.	Chapter 5
166	A	The Scrum Master enforces rules and processes within the team.	Chapter 10
167	B	Decision trees are used in quantitative risk assessment.	Chapter 10
168	B	Requirements and conditions.	Chapter 10
169	C	The power/interest grid for analyzing stakeholders has four quadrants illustrated with two dimensions, power and interest. The values are high and low. The stakeholders of low power and low interest may almost be ignored.	Chapter 5
170	C	Constraints and relations issues.	Chapter 10
171	D	The change impact analysis is defined by Bohner and Arnold as "identifying the potential consequences of a change, or estimating what needs to be modified to accomplish a change." This requires understanding traceability, dependency, and the experiential aspects of change.	Chapter 10
172	A	Skype call.	Chapter 10
173	A	Facebook, Wiki technologies, live video conferencing, group chat, Virtual Worlds, webinars, blogs, feeds, LinkedIn, Twitter, Skype, and instant messaging are tools that can be used to increase online collaboration.	Chapter 10
174	A	Communication within a distributed team is often online, nonverbal, and formal; however, effective communication requires verbal communication by skype or similar tools.	Chapter 10
175	A	Internal stakeholders are found within the organization—your boss is the only one among these choices.	Chapter 5

Part 6

Appendices

Glossary and Acronyms

A-1

Acceptance criteria: The criteria that a system or component must satisfy in order to be accepted by a user, customer, or other authorized entity.

Acceptance test-driven development (ATDD): A collaborative practice where users, testers, and developers define automated acceptance criteria early in the development process.

ACP: An acronym for Agile Certified Practitioner.

Active listening: A technique to help you listen well.

Activity network diagrams: A graphical representation of the logical relationship among the project schedule activities.

Adaptive leadership: Leadership that deals with changes and problem solving.

Adaptive planning: *See* progressive elaboration.

Adaptive software development: Popular agile methodologies.

Affinity estimating: An estimation method to generate high-level estimates.

Agile methodologies: Frameworks and processes based on the Agile manifesto (i.e., Scrum).

Agile smells: Ways to describe and quickly recognize and diagnose common problems so that a remedy may be pursued.

Agile Software Development Manifesto: A document created in 2001 that lays out the guiding principles of agile project management.

Agile themes: A collection of stories, an iteration, or a release.

Analogy: A technique for estimation.

Assumption: A factor that is considered to be true, real, or certain without proof or demonstration.

Backlog: In agile, a listing of product requirements and deliverables to be completed, written as stories, and prioritized by the business to manage and organize the project's work.

Baseline: The approved version of a work product that can be changed only through formal change control procedures.

Belbin Team roles: A technique to identify people's behavioral strengths and weaknesses.

Benefit-cost ratio: The ratio of the present value (PV) of benefits to the PV of costs.

Benchmarking: The comparison of actual and planned practices or compared organization practices.

Burn-down chart: A graphical representation of work left to do versus time.

Burn rate: The rate at which resources are consumed.

Burn-up chart: A graphical representation of work accomplished versus time.

Business analysis: The set of activities performed to identify business needs; recommend a relevant solution; and elicit, document, and manage requirements.

Business analysis plan: A sub-plan of the project management plan, defining business analysis activities.

Business case: A documented economic feasibility study used to establish validity of the benefits of a selected component lacking sufficient definition that is used as a basis for the authorization of further project management activities.

Business needs: The impetus for change in an organization.

Business requirements: Requirements that describe the higher level needs of the organization.

Business rules: Constraints about how the organization wants to operate.

Business value: A concept that is unique to each organization and includes tangible and intangible elements. Through the effective use of project, program, and portfolio management disciplines, organizations will possess the ability to employ reliable, established processes to meet enterprise objectives and obtain greater business value from their investment.

Brainstorming: A rapid technique to gather ideas.

Cause and effect diagram: *See* root cause analysis.

Capability: The ability to add value or achieve objectives in an organization.

Change: The act of transformation in response to a need.

Change control board: A formally chartered group responsible for reviewing, evaluating, approving, delaying, or rejecting changes to the project; and for recording and communicating such decisions.

Change control process: Whereby modifications to documents, deliverables, or baselines associated with the project are identified, documented, approved, or rejected.

Change control tools: Manual or automated tools to assist with change and/or configuration management. At a minimum, the tools should support the activities of the change control board.

Change log: A comprehensive list of changes made during the project.

Change request: A formal proposal to modify any document, deliverable, or baseline.

Colocated team: When teams colocate, it means that they are meeting in the same location. This is preferable because it maximizes their ability to communicate.

Communication management plan: A component of the project, program, or portfolio management plan that describes how, when, and by whom information about the project will be administered and disseminated.

Communication methods: A systematic procedure, technique, or process used to transfer information among project stakeholders.

Complex adaptive systems (CAS): A theoretical lens for understanding agile and being capable of adapting to the external environment.

Compliance: Adherence to standards or regulations.

Cone of uncertainty: A term describing the difficulty of estimating early due to unknowns and how that should improve over time.

Configuration management: A subsystem of the overall project management system.

Configuration management system: *See* configuration management.

Conflict resolutions: Methods to solve conflicts.

Constraint: A limited factor that affects the execution of a project, program, portfolio, or process.

Constructive Agile Estimation Algorithm (CAEA): An algorithmic approach for the estimation of cost, size, and duration of a project.

Context: The circumstances that influence, are influenced by, and provide understanding of the change.

Context analysis: Used to separate the system from its environment and highlight those parts that are relevant and affect the requirements.

Context boundary: What separates the relevant part of the environment of a system to be developed from the irrelevant part.

Continuous deployment: Is continuous integration in its purest form—meaning that all code changes are checked in and the entire system is built and tested by the end of each designated time period.

Continuous improvement: Is about maintaining agile project teams to ensure efficiency, effectiveness, individual integrity, and professionalism.

Continuous integration: A concept used to check out code and ensure it runs—and that nothing is broken.

Control limits: A process behavior chart used to determine whether a process is in a state of statistical control.

Control schedule: The process of monitoring the status of project activities to update project progress and manage changes to the schedule baseline to achieve the plan.

Close: The final phase of the agile project management (APM) delivery framework.

Crashing: A technique used to shorten the schedule duration for the least incremental cost by adding resources.

Critical path: The sequence of activities that represents the longest path through a project, which determines the shortest possible duration.

Critical chain: A schedule method that allows the project team to place buffers on any project schedule path to account for limited resources and project uncertainties.

Crystal methods: Popular agile methodologies.

Culture: Learned, shared, and enduring orientation patterns in a society.

Cumulative flow diagram: Displays a visualization of the work status.

Cycle time: The time between two successive deliveries.

Daily plan: More or less similar to daily Scrum.

Daily Scrum: A Scrum event. It is a daily meeting for approximately 15 minutes, often held while standing, which is organized to keep track of the progress of the Scrum team and address any obstacles faced by the team.

Daily standup: *See* Daily Scrum.

Decomposition: A technique that subdivides a problem into its component parts in order to facilitate analysis and understanding of those components.

DEEP: An acronym describing desirable attributes of a product backlog—(D)etailed appropriately, (E)stimable, (E)mergent, and (P)rioritized.

Definition of done: Establishes what must be true for the software product in order to be defined as working software (or *done*).

Deliverable: Any unique and verifiable product, result, or capability.

Disaggregation: Splitting a story or feature into smaller, easier-to-estimate pieces.

Discounted cash flow (DCF) analysis: A method to convert future cash flow into present value cash flow.

Distributed team: A team whose members are distributed in various locations, often around the globe.

Document analysis: An examination of the documentation of an existing system in order to elicit requirements.

Dynamic Systems Development Method (DSDM): An agile project management and delivery framework that aims to deliver the right solution at the right time.

Earned value management (EVM): A methodology that combines scope, schedule, and resource measurements to assess project performance and progress.

Elapsed time: The amount of time it takes to complete a story.

Elicitation: The activity of drawing out information from stakeholders and other sources for the purpose of understanding the needs of the organization in order to address a problem or opportunity.

Emotional intelligence: The ability to recognize one's own and other people's emotions, to discriminate between different feelings and label them appropriately, and to use emotional information to guide thinking and behavior to forge strong and supportive relationships.

Empowerment: The process that enables individuals to take action, control work, and make decisions autonomously.

Enterprise environmental factors: Conditions, not under the immediate control of the team, that influence, constrain, or direct the project, program, or portfolio.

Entity relationship diagram: A business analysis model that is a graphical representation of the relationship between people, objects, places, concepts, or events within that system.

Epic stories: A very large story that may span iterations.

Escaped defects: Defects that escaped quality control inspection but were found by the customer.

Estimation: A rough calculation of the value, number, quantity, or extent of something—time or resource required.

Evaluation: The systematic and objective assessment of a solution.

Evolutionary prototype: A prototype that is continuously modified and updated in response to feedback from stakeholders.

Exploratory testing: An unscripted, free-form validation or evaluation.

Extreme characters: *See* personas.

Extreme programming: A popular agile methodology that is intended to improve software quality and responsiveness.

Facilitation: The art of leading and encouraging people through systematic efforts toward agreed-upon objectives.

Fast tracking: A schedule compression technique in which activities or phases that are normally done in sequence are performed in parallel, for a least a portion of their duration.

Feature: Synonymous with story.

Feature-driven development: A popular agile methodology that blends a number of industry-recognized best practices into a cohesive whole.

Feedback techniques: Techniques that demonstrate part of the solution to the business at an early stage, but still in a quick and easy format.

Fishbone diagram: *See* root cause diagram.

Five levels of planning: High-level description of the planning phases.

Five Whys technique: A form for root cause analysis; used to determine the root cause of a defect or problem by repeating the question "Why?" five times.

Focus groups: An elicitation technique that brings prequalified stakeholders and subject matter experts together.

Force field analysis: A decision-making technique of listing, discussing, and evaluating the various forces for and against a proposed change.

Functional requirement: A requirement concerning the results of a behavior that will be provided by a function of the system.

Future value: The value of an asset at a specific date.

Gap analysis: A technique for understanding the gap between current capabilities and needed capabilities.

Ground rules: Rules about expectations on the project.

Hersey-Blanchard Situational Leadership Theory: The belief that leadership depends upon each individual situation; there is no single *best* style of leadership; and that effective leadership is task-relevant.

High-performing agile teams (HPT): Teams that constantly satisfy the needs of customers, employees, investors, and others in their area of influence.

Ideal time: The time it takes to complete an assignment, story point, or task without impediments of any sort.

Ideal agile team space: *See* team space.

Impact analysis: A technique for evaluating a change in regard to how it will affect other requirements.

Information radiator: The generic term for any of a number of handwritten, drawn, printed, or electronic displays.

Inspection: Scrum pillar with emphasis on timely checks and differences.

Innovation games: Games used for gathering ideas and eliciting requirements.

Internal rate of return (IRR): A way of expressing profit as an interest rate earned.

Interoperability: Ability of systems to communicate by exchanging data or services.

INVEST: Acronym for creating effective user stories (independent, negotiable, valuable, estimable, small, testable).

Ishikawa diagram: *See* root cause diagram.

Iteration planning: Planning iterations by defining the tasks and effort necessary to fulfill the commitment.

Job analysis: A technique used to identify job requirements and competencies needed to perform a certain job effectively.

Kanban: A change management method.

Kanban board: Highly visible agile metrics.

Kano classification: Technique using dissatisfiers, satisfiers, and delighters to prioritize requirements.

Key performance indicators: Metrics to evaluate progress toward objectives.

Lags: The amount of time whereby a successor activity can be advanced with respect to a predecessor activity.

Lead: The amount of time whereby a successor activity is required to be delayed with respect to a predecessor activity.

Lead time: The time between the initiation and delivery of a work item.

Lean Software Development: An agile methodology based upon the concept that efficiencies can be applied and waste can be managed.

Lessons learned: The knowledge gained during the project.

Life cycle: A series of changes an item or object undergoes from inception to retirement.

Metrics: A set of quantifiable measures used to evaluate a solution or business.

Metadata: A description of data to help understand how to use that data.

Meyers-Briggs type indicators (MBTI): Team selection theories based on Jung.

Milestone: A significant point or event in a project, program, or portfolio.

Minimal marketable features (MMF): Features are decomposed into the smallest marketable units of useful deliverable business value.

Modeling language: A set of models and their syntax.

MoSCoW prioritization: Technique used to prioritize requirements. Stands for Must have, Should have, Could have, Would like.

Needs Assessment: A business analysis domain for understanding business goals and objectives along with any issues and opportunities, and then recommending proposals to address them.

Negotiation: Process of discussing and compromising in order to reach the best results.

Net present value (NPV): A way of factoring in the time value of money to calculate a project's worth.

Nonfunctional requirements: Requirements that reveal properties that the product is required to have, including quality properties.

Objective: A strategic position to be attained.

Observation: An elicitation technique that provides a way of obtaining information on how a process is conducted or how a product is used.

Organizational process assets: Plans, processes, policies, procedures, and knowledge bases that are specific to, and used by, the performing organization.

Open team space: *See* team space.

Optimal team size: Application of probable project team size.

Osmotic communication: Ongoing sounds around the team, allowing team members to pick up relevant information through osmosis.

Pair programming: Writing code as a pair together at one workstation.

Parking lot chart: Graphical report highlighting the features (or user stories) in a project.

Payback period (PP): The number of designated time periods it takes to recoup an initial investment.

Peer review: A formal or informal review of a work product to identify errors or opportunities for improvement.

Persona: An archetype user representation.

Perspective-based readings: A kind of validation technique that adopts different perspectives to check requirements, and are typically applied in conjunction with other review techniques.

Process: A systematic series of activities.

Product backlog: This is the prioritized list of all features and changes that have yet to be made to the system desired by multiple actors, such as customers, marketing and sales, and the project team.

Program evaluation and review technique (PERT): Estimation technique that gives three estimates with uncertainties in considerations.

Progressive elaboration: The iterative process of increasing the level of detail in the project management plan as greater amounts of information and more accurate estimates become available.

Proof-of-concept: A model created to validate the design of a solution.

Prototype: A method of obtaining early feedback by providing a working model.

Planning poker: An agile estimation method using numbered cards.

Post-RS traceability: Refers to those aspects of a requirement's life that result from inclusion in the requirement specification (RS).

Pre-RS traceability: Refers to those aspects of a requirement's life prior to inclusion in the RS.

Present value (PV): A way of factoring in the time value of money to calculate a project's worth.

Problem and opportunity analysis: A way of identifying problems and opportunities.

Process decision program charts: A model used to understand a goal in relation to the steps needed to attain that goal.

Product: An artifact that is produced, is quantifiable, and can be either an end item in itself or a component item.

Product backlog: A Scrum artifact. This is the prioritized list of all features and changes that have yet to be made to the system, desired by multiple actors in Scrum.

Product owner: A Scrum role who acts as the voice of the customer and key decision maker.

Product roadmap: An overview that shows an overall plan with each planned release and the relevant features associated with those releases.

Product vision statement: An elevator statement for the product, describing what it is, who would need it, the key reasons someone would pay for it, and what differentiates it in the market.

Profitability index (PI): Also known as profit investment ratio (PIR) or value investment ratio (VIR), it is the ratio of payoff to investment of a proposed project.

Progressive elaboration: The iterative process of increasing the level of detail in the project management plan as greater amounts of information and more accurate estimates become available.

Project: A temporary endeavor undertaken to create a unique product, service, or result.

Project charter: A document issued by the project initiator or sponsor that formally authorizes the existence of a project and provides the project manager with the authority to apply organizational resources to project activities.

Project goals: The desired outcome (performance goal) at a specific end date (time goal), while employing a specific amount of resources (resource goal).

Project management: The application of knowledge, skills, and techniques to execute projects effectively and efficiently.

Project management constraints model: A model of the constraints involved with project management, which include scope, time, cost, risk, quality, and resources.

Project scope: The features and functions that characterize a product, service, or result.

Project scope description: The documented narrative description of the project scope.

Proxies: Customer representatives.

Quality: The degree to which a set of inherent characteristics fulfills needs.

Quality assurance: A set of activities performed to ensure that a process will deliver products that meet an appropriate level of quality.

Quality checklists: A structured tool used to verify that a set of required steps have been performed.

Quality metrics: A description of a project or product attribute, and how to measure it.

Quality requirement: A requirement that pertains to a quality concern that is not covered by functional requirements—also called a nonfunctional requirement.

RACI matrix: A common type of responsibility assignment matrix that uses *responsible, accountable, consulted,* and *informed* statuses to define the involvement of stakeholders in project activities.

Refactoring: A disciplined technique for restructuring an existing body of code—altering its internal structure without changing its external behavior.

Relative sizing: Agile methods for estimation of scales.

Release planning: Planning of releases with deliverables of features, benefits, and value to the customer.

Requirement: A condition or capability to which a system must conform.

Requirements documentation: A description of how individual requirements meet the business need for the project.

Requirements management plan: A component of the project or program management plan that describes how requirements will be analyzed, documented, and managed.

Requirements traceability: Refers to the ability to describe and follow the life of a requirement in both a forward and backward direction.

Requirements traceability matrix: A grid that links product requirements from their origin to the deliverables that satisfy them.

Responsibility assignment matrix: A grid that shows the project resources assigned to each work package.

Retrospective: A look back in time to analyze the situation in order to make improvements.

Return on investment (ROI): Calculation of the percentage of return an organization makes by investing.

Risk: An uncertain event or condition that, if it occurs, has a positive or negative effect on one or more project objectives.

Risk-adjusted backlog: Value-generating business features and risk-reduction actions.

Risk appetite: The degree of uncertainty an entity is willing to take on in anticipation of a reward.

Risk-based spikes: A quick proof of concept that is used to help the team answer a question and determine a path forward. Can be used to get to failure quickly and then take a different approach.

Risk burn-down graph: A chart where the risk to project success that is associated with each feature is displayed.

Risk management plan: A component of the project, program, or portfolio management plan that describes how risk management activities will be structured and performed.

Risk register: A document in which the result of risk analysis and risk response planning are recorded.

Root cause: The underlying cause of the problem which, if adequately addressed, will prevent a recurrence of that problem.

Root cause analysis: Processes for identifying contributing or causal factors that underlie variations in performance that are associated with adverse events or close calls (e.g., cause and effect diagrams, Ishikawa diagrams, and fishbone diagrams).

Rolling wave planning: *See* progressive elaboration.

Running tested features: Metric that forces agility.

Scope: The sum of the products, services, and results to be provided as a project. *See also* project scope and product scope.

Scope model: A model that defines the boundaries of a business domain or solution.

Scrum: A popular agile methodology used as a framework for managing a process.

Scrum Master: A Scrum role. Liaison between the product owner and the team.

Scrum values: Focus, openness, respect, commitment, and courage.

Self-assessment: Stimulate learning and change as well as enthusiasm for development.

Servant leadership: A philosophy and set of practices that enriches the lives of individuals, builds better organizations, and ultimately creates a more just and caring world.

Shu-Ha-Ri: Taken from a Japanese martial art, it describes a progression of learning.

Situation statement: An objective statement of a problem or opportunity.

SMART: Acronym for creating effective goals (specific, measurable, achievable, relevant, and time-sensitive).

Solution: A specific way of satisfying one or more needs in a context.

Solution requirement: A capability or quality of a solution that meets stakeholder requirements. Solution requirements can be divided into two subcategories: functional requirements and nonfunctional requirements (or quality of service requirements).

Software metrics: Measurement of the software product and the process by which it is developed.

Speculate: Second phase of the agile project management (APM) delivery framework.

Splitting user stories: General guidance to make each story provide a vertical slice—some piece of user value—through the system.

Sponsor: A person or group providing resources and support for the project, program, or activity; and is responsible for enabling success.

Sprint: A Scrum event that is 30 days in length. It is the procedure of adapting to the changing environmental variables (requirements, time, resources, knowledge, technology, etc.) and must result in a potentially shippable increment of software.

Sprint backlog: The list of features that is currently assigned to a particular Sprint. When all the features are completed, a new iteration of the system is delivered.

Sprint planning meeting: A Scrum event that is first attended by the customers, users, management, product owner, and Scrum team—where a set of goals and functionality are decided on.

Sprint retrospective: A Scrum event that is used for reflection on the process and to find room for improvement.

Stakeholder: A person, a group, or an organization that is actively involved in the project or whose interests may be positively or negatively affected by the results achieved or by the completion of the project.

Stakeholder analysis: A technique of systematically gathering and analyzing quantitative and qualitative information to determine whose interests should be taken into account throughout the project.

Stakeholder register: A project document including the identification, assessment, and classification of project stakeholders.

Stakeholder requirement: A requirement that describes the need of a stakeholder or group of stakeholders.

Stakeholder salience: Stakeholder identification by power, legitimacy, and urgency.

Statement of work (SOW): A narrative description of products, services, or results to be delivered by the project.

State diagram: A business model that visually illustrates possible different project states.

Story maps: A technique to organize and prioritize user stories.

Story points: A measure of the complexity of the story.

System boundary: Separates the system to be developed from its environment.

System context: The part of the system environment that is relevant for the definition, as well as the understanding of the requirements of a system to be developed.

System thinking: A mental effort to uncover the endogenous sources of system behavior.

SWOT analysis: A planning method used to assess the strengths, weaknesses, opportunities, and threats in a project.

Technique: A defined systematic procedure.

Team space: Space assigned to the team.

Technical debt: Invisible technical negative value to the project.

Test-driven development (TDD): A special case of test-first development.

Test-first development: A rapid XP cycle of testing, coding, and refactoring.

Time box: A previously agreed upon period of time during which a person or a team works steadily toward completion of some goal.

Traceability: The ability to interrelate any uniquely identifiable software engineering artifact to any other, maintain required links over time, and use the resulting network to answer questions of both the software product and its development process.

Transition requirements: Requirements that are temporary capabilities.

Twelve principles of agile software: Working values of agile methodologies.

Unified Modeling Language (UML): A conventional modeling language that is utilized to provide a standard way to visualize the design of a system.

Use case: An analysis model that describes a flow.

Use case diagram: A business analysis model that shows all of the in-scope use cases.

User acceptance test: A method to assess whether or not the delivered solution meets the needs of the stakeholder group that will be using the solution.

User story: A brief statement specifying the software requirements.

User requirements: *See* stakeholder requirement.

User story backlog: *See* product backlog.

User story mapping: *See* story maps.

Validation: Ensures that the software that is being developed or changed satisfies functional and all other requirements.

Value-based prioritization: Project justification.

Value stream mapping (VSM): Method adopted by agile to analyze an entire chain of processes with the goal of eliminating waste and finding gaps for improvement.

Value proposition: A promise of value to be delivered.

Velocity: A measurement of the rate of change in reference to time. At the end of each iteration, the team adds up effort estimates associated with user stories that were completed during that iteration.

Verification: Ensures that every step in the process of building the software delivers the correct product.

Version: A particular form of software.

Version control: The process of maintaining a history of changes.

Vision document: A document that defines the high-level scope and purpose of a program, product, or project.

Walkthrough: A review in which participants step through an artifact or set of artifacts with the intention of validating the requirements or designs, and to identify requirements or design errors, inconsistencies, omissions, inaccuracies, or conflicts.

Work breakdown structure (WBS): A hierarchical decomposition of the total scope of work to be carried out by the project team to accomplish project objectives and create the required deliverables.

Workshop: A facilitated and focused event attended by key stakeholders for the purpose of achieving a defined goal.

WBS directory: A document that provides detailed deliverables, activities, and scheduling information about each component in the work breakdown structure.

Wideband Delphi: Process that a team can use to generate an estimate.

Wireframes: Lightweight nonfunctional user interface design.

Work-in-progress (WIP) report: Used to limit the amount of work being done and concentrate on getting the work done.

WIP limits: A strategy for preventing bottlenecks in software development.

XP: *See* extreme programming.

XP values: Simplicity, communication, feedback, courage, and respect.

Bibliography

A-2

Aiken, P., R. M. Stanley, J. Billings, and L. Anderson. 2004. *Using Codes of Conduct to Resolve Legal Disputes*. Computer.

Ambler, S. W. 2011. *Agile in an Enterprise Environment*. Innovate.

Arnold, R., and S. Bohner. 1996. *Software Change Impact Analysis*. Wiley-IEEE Computer Society Press.

Beck, K. 2000. *Extreme Programming Explained: Embrace Change*, Addison-Wesley.

Beck, K., A. Cockburn, R. Jeffries, and J. Highsmith. 2001. *Agile manifesto*.

Belbin, R. M. 2002. *Management Teams: Why they succeed or fail*. Butterworth-Heinemann, Woburn, UK.

Binti Abdullah, N. N., and S. Honiden. 2007. *Context in Use for Analyzing Conversation Structures on the Web Tied to the Notion of Situatedness*. Modeling and Using Contexts. In Lecture Notes in Artificial Intelligence.

Boehm, B. 2002. *Get Ready for Agile Methods with Care*. Software Development. January 2002.

Boehm, B. W. 1988. *A Spiral Model for Software Development and Enhancement*. Computer 21 (May 1988): 61-72.

Blais, S. 2011. *Business Analysis: Best Practices for Success*. Wiley.

Brooks, Frederick P. 1995. *The Mythical Man-Month: Essays on Software Engineering*, Addison-Wesley Publishing Company, p 178-203.

Burke, R. 2010. *Project Management Techniques*. South Africa: Burke Publishing.

Cadle, J., P. Turner, and D. Paul. 2010. *Business Analysis Techniques: 72 Essential Tools for Success*. British Informatics Society Ltd.

Carkenord, B. 2009. *Seven Steps to Mastering Business Analysis*. J. Ross Publishing.

Cockburn, A., and J. Highsmith. 2001. *Agile software development: The business of innovation*, IEEE Computer. (Sept. 2001) 120-122.

Cohn, M. 2004. *User Stories Applied: For Agile Software Development*.

———. 2005. *Agile Estimating and Planning*. Prentice Hall.

Coulin, C., and D. Zowghi. 2004. *Requirements Elicitation for Complex Systems: Theory and Practice, in Requirements Engineering for Socio-Technical Systems*, edited by Jose Luis Mate and Andres Silva, Idea Group: USA.

Crowe, A. 2012. *The PMI-ACP Exam: How to Pass on Your First Try*. Velociteach.

Davison, R. M. 2000. *Professional Ethics in Information Systems: A Personal Perspective.* Communications of AIS Volume 3, April. Article 8 34. Department of Information Systems. City University of Hong Kong.

Demarco, T., and T. Lister. 2003. *Waltzing With Bears: Managing Risk on Software Projects.* Dorset House.

Department of the Air Force Software Technology Support Center. 2003. *Guidelines for successful acquisition and management of software-intensive systems: Weapon systems, command and control systems, management information systems.*

Derby, E., D. Larsen, and K. Schwaber. 2006. *Agile Retrospectives: Making Good Teams Great.* Pragmatic Bookshelf.

Fernandez, D. M., and S. Wagner. 2013. *Naming the Pain in Requirements Engineering: Design of a Global Family of Surveys and First Results from Germany.* In Evaluation and Assessment in Software Engineering (EASE). 2013.

Fisher, R., W. Ury, and B. Patton. 1991. *Getting to Yes: Negotiating Agreement Without Giving In.* Second Edition. New York: Penguin Books.

Forrester. 2010. *Agile Development: Mainstream Adoption Has Changed Agility* by Dave West and Tom Grant for Application Development & Program Management Professional.

Fowler, M. 1999. *Refactoring: Improving the Design of Existing Code.* Addison-Wesley Professional.

Gotel, O., J. Cleland-Huang, J. Huffman Hayes, A. Zisman, A. Egyed, P. Grunbacher, and G. Antoniol. 2012. *The Quest for Ubiquity: A Roadmap for Software and Systems Traceability Research.* In 21st IEEE International Requirements Engineering.

Gottesdiener, E. 2002. *Requirements by Collaboration.* Addison Wesley: Boston, MA.

———. 2009. *The Software Requirements Memory Jogger: A Pocket Guide to Help Software and Business Teams Develop and Manage Requirements.* Goal Q P C Inc.

Greenleaf, R. K. 1996. *On Becoming a Servant Leader.* San Francisco: Josey-Bass Publishers.

Griffiths, M. 2012. *PMI-ACP Exam Prep, Premier Edition: A Course in a Book for Passing the PMI Agile Certified Practitioner (PMI-ACP) Exam.* Rita Mulcahy Companies.

Haas, K., and R. Hosenlopp. 2012. *Unearthing Business Requirements: Elicitation Tools and Techniques.* Management Concepts, Inc.

Hans, R. T. 2013. *Work Breakdown Structure: A Tool for Software Project Scope Verification.* International Journal of Software Engineering & Applications (IJSEA), Vol. 4, No. 4, July.

Harris, R. 1998. *Introduction to Decision Making.* Virtual Salt.

Hartley, A. 2012. *Requirements Lifecycle Management.* Methodology Planning Guide v1.4.

Hauser, J. R., and D. Clausing. 1988. *The house of quality.* Harvard Business Review, May-June.

Heindl, M., and S. Biffl. 2006. *Risk Management with Enhanced Tracing of Requirements Rationale in Highly Distributed Projects.* GSD. 2006.

Heifetz, R. A., and D. L. Laurie. 1997. *The Work of Leadership.* Harvard Business Review.

Helgadóttir, H. 2007. *The Ethical Dimension of Project Management.* Nordnet. Projects under risk.

Heller, R. 2012. *Challenges in Requirements Management Roundtable.* Three Rivers Chapter. International Council on Systems Engineering.

Highsmith J. 2002. *Agile Software Development Ecosystems*. Boston, MA: Addison-Wesley.

———. 2009. *Agile Project Management: Creative Innovative Products*. Upper Saddle River, NJ: Addison-Wesley.

Highsmith J., K. Orr, and A. Cockburn. 2000. *Extreme Programming, in E-Business Application Delivery*, Feb. 2000.

Hillman, A. 2013. "The Rise in Business-Analytics Degrees." Huffingtonpost.

Hooks, I. F., and K. A. Farry. 2011. *Customer-Centered Products: Creating Successful Products Through Smart Requirements Management*. AMACOM.

IBM Global Business Services. 2012. *Leading through Connections 2012*. Global CEO Study.

IEEE. 1984. *IEEE Guide to Software Requirements Specifications.* ANSI/IEEE Standard 830-1984.

International Institute of Business Analysis. 2009. *A Guide to the Business Analysis Body of Knowledge BABOK® v 2*.

———. 2012. *A Guide to the Business Analysis Body of Knowledge BABOK® Guide v 2*.

———. 2015. *A Guide to the Business Analysis Body of Knowledge BABOK® v 3*.

Jacobson, I., I. Spence, and K. Bittner. 2011. *Use-case 2.0—The Definitive Guide*. Ivar Jacobsen International.

Kerth, N. L. 2001. *Project Retrospectives: A Handbook for Team Reviews*. Dorset House Publishing.

Kruchten, P. 2009. *What Colour Is Your Backlog?* Agile Vancouver Conference.

Kuppuswami, S., K. Vivekanandan, P. Ramaswamy, and P. Rodrigues. 2003. *The Effects of Individual XP Practices on Software Development Effort*, SIGSOFT Softw. Eng. Notes, 28 (2003), p. 6.

Lewis, P. V. 1985. *Defining Business Ethics: Like Nailing Jello to the Wall*, Journal of Business Ethics, (4)5, pp. 377-383.

Magnier, P. (2003) *Value Stream Mapping*. The Lean Enterprise.

Meredith, R. (2010) *Belbin, Team Roles at Work*. Butterworth Heinemann, 2nd ed.

Myers, I., and M. McCaulley. 1985. *Manual: A Guide to the Development and Use of the Myers-Briggs Type Indicator*, Consulting Psychologists Press, California, 1985.

Nielsen, K. 2009. *I am Agile*. Polyteknisk forlag.

———. 2013. *Software Estimation with a Mix of Techniques*. Retrieved from http:/www.pmi.org. Knowledge shelf.

———. 2015. *Mastering the Business Case*. Varius forlag.

Orlena, O. C. Z., and A. C. W. Finkelstein. 1993. *An Analysis of the Requirements Traceability Problem*. Imperial College of Science, Technology & Medicine. Department of Computing.

Pflegeer, S. L. 1998. *Software Engineering Theory and Practice*, Upper Saddle River, NJ: Prentice Hall.

Podeswa, H. 2009. *The Business Analyst's Handbook*. Cengage Learning PTR.

Pohl, K., and C. Rupp. 2011. *Requirements Engineering Fundamentals: A Study Guide for the Certified Professional for Requirements Engineering Exam—Foundation Level*. Rocky Nook.

Poppendieck, M., and T. Poppendieck. 2003. *Lean Software Development: An Agile Toolkit*, Addison-Wesley Professional.

Project Management Institute. 2013. *A Guide to the Project Management Body of Knowledge: PMBOK® Guide.* Project Management Institute; 5 Edition. Newtown Square, PA: Author.

———. 2015. *Business Analysis for Practitioners: A Practice Guide.* Project Management Institute. First Edition. Newtown Square, PA: Author.

Reifer, D. J. 2000. *Requirements Management: The Search for Nirvana*, in IEEE Software, May/June 2000.

Ritter, J. 2012. *Business Case for Agile.* Retrieved from http://www.solutionmatrix.de. Published in Projektmagazin.

Robertson, S., and J. Robertson. 2012. *Mastering the Requirements Process: Getting Requirements Right.* Addison-Wesley Professional.

Rohil, H., and M. Syan. 2012. *Analysis of Agile and Traditional Approach for Software Development.* International Journal of Latest Trends in Engineering and Technology (IJLTET). Vol. 1 Issue 4 November 2012.

Sajid, A., A. Nayyar, and A. Mohsin. 2010. *Modern Trends towards Requirement Elictiation.* NSEC 2010. Proceedings of the 2010 National Software Engineering Conference Article No. 9.

Schein, E. H. 1992. *Organizational Culture and Leadership.* Jossey-Bass Publishers.

Schneider, W. 1998. *Why Good Management Ideas Fail—Understanding Your Corporate Culture.*

Schwaber, K. 2004. *Agile Project Management with Scrum.* Microsoft Press.

Schwaber, K., and M. Beedle. 2002. *Agile Software Development with Scrum.* Upper Saddle River, NJ: Pearson Prentice-Hall.

Schwaber, K., and J. Sutherland. 2011. *The Scrum Guide.* Retrieved from http://www.scrum.org.

Shalloway, G., G. Beaver, and J. R. Trott. 2009. *Lean-Agile Software Development: Achieving Enterprise Agility.* Addison Wesley.

Sharma, V. S., R. R. Ramnani, and S. Sengupta. 2014. *A Framework for Identifying and Analyzing Nonfunctional Requirements from Text.* ACM. Twinpeaks 2014.

Shore, J. 2007. *The Art of Agile Development.* O'Reilly Media.

Simsion, G., and G. Witt. 2004. *Data Modeling Essentials.* Morgan Kaufmann.

Sliger, M., and S. Broderick. 2008. *The Software Project Manager's Bridge to Agility.* Addison Wesley.

Sommerville, I. P., and Sawyer. 2000. *Requirements Engineering a Good Practice Guide.* Wiley, June 2000.

The Standish Group. 2006. *The CHAOS Report.*

Trevino, L. K., and K. A. Nelson. 2007. *Managing Business Ethics: Straight Talk About How To Do It Right.* New York: Wiley & Sons.

Wake, B. 2003. *INVEST in Good Stories, and SMART Tasks.* Retrieved from xp123.com.

Wiegers, K. 2003. *Software Requirements 2.* Microsoft Press.

Wood-Harper, A. T., S. Corder, J. R. G. Wood, and H. Watson. 1996. *How We Profess: Ethical System Analyst.* March 1996/Vol. 39, No. 3 COMMUNICATIONS OF THE ACM.

Index

acceptance test, 136

acceptance test-driven development, 170. *see also* test-first development

Adair, John, 229–230

adaptive leadership, 231

adaptive software development (ASD), 257–258

Adkins, Lyssa, 210

Agile Alliance, 293

agile methodologies, 260–262

    agile principles and practices, 287–291

    introduction, 287

agile principles and practices, 287–292

    Agile Software Development Manifesto, 287–288

    customer collaboration over contract negotiation, 289

    declaration of interdependence for modern management, 291–292

    individuals and interactions over processes and tools, 288

    responding to change over following a plan, 289

    twelve principles of agile software, 289–291

    working software over comprehensive documentation, 288

Agile Software Development Manifesto, 207, 287–288

Agile Software Development with Scrum (Schwaber and Beedle), 196, 253, 293

Allbrecht, Alan, 221

analogous estimating, 222

analysis

    allocating requirements, 122–129

        analytical hierarchy process (AHP), 127–128

        Kano classification, 126–127

        MoSCoW prioritization, 126

        requirement baseline, 128–129

        value proposition using prioritization, 123–126

    categorizing the requirements according to Kano model, 107–108

    creativity techniques, 111

    describing the various elicitation techniques, 108–110

    document-centric techniques, 111–112

    document requirements, 129–138

        document design, 130

        document structure, 134–135

        epic stories, 138

        requirements documentation using conceptual models, 132–134

        requirements documentation using natural language, 131–132

        splitting user stories, 137

        write requirement in agile methodologies, 135–137

    elaborate requirements, 115–119

        conceptual modeling, 118–119

        requirement classification, 116–118

    elicit requirements, 105–115

        categorizing requirements according to Kano model, 107–108

        creativity technique, 111

        describing elicitation techniques, 108–110

        document-centric technique, 111–112

explaining types of requirements sources, 106–107

observation technique, 112

support technique, 113–115

survey technique, 110–111

expected results, 141–142

explaining the types of requirements sources, 106–107

get requirement signoff, 129

observation techniques, 112

overview, 104–105

relating PMI-PBA practices to agile practices, 143–144

relating PMI-PBA practices to *PMBOK® Guide—Fifth Edition* practices, 143

specifying requirements, 141–142

support techniques, 113–115

survey techniques, 110–111

validating requirements, 119–122

verify requirements, 138–140

analytical hierarchy process (AHP), 127–128

Anderson, David, 253

Ansoff's matrix, 245–246

appraisal costs, 141

assets

intangible, 48–49

tangible, 48–49

Association for Computing Machinery (ACM), 10

asynchronous communication, 203

autocratic leadership, 228

backlog, defined, 197

backlog management, 196–198

backward traceability, 151. *see also* prerequirement specification traceability

Bazerman, Max H., 273

Beck, Kent, 289

Beedle, Mike, 196, 253, 293

Belbin team roles, 228

benefit-cost ratio (BCR), 54

benefits, 48–49

best alternative to a negotiated agreement (BATNA), 237

Beyond Culture (Hall), 238

B-model, 215, 216

Boehm, Barry W., 215, 221

Boston box analysis, 244

brainstorming, 111, 142

advantages and disadvantages of using, 111

British Computer Society (BCS), 20

Broderick, Stacy, 193

Brooks, Frederick, 220, 260

Brown Cow Model, 106

business analysis certification organizations, 3–4

Business Analysis for Practitioners: A Practice Guide, 3, 20, 22, 42, 46, 47, 49, 58, 74, 79, 81, 87, 95, 104, 111, 150, 152, 168–169, 173, 201, 234, 242

business analyst certification (PMI-PBA)®, 3

and body of knowledge, 4–5

target groups for, 7

value for individuals, 6

value for organizations, 6

value of, 5–6

business analysts

blueprint, 21

British Computer Society (BCS) definition of, 20

organizational need for, 19–22

project manager and, 21–22

role of, 20–21

business case, defined, 46

business requirements, 116

assessing organizational capacities and gaps, 45

defining the problems and opportunities, 44–45

developing a business case for proposed solutions, 46–47

forming the first phase of the solution scope, 45–46

business rule analysis tools and techniques, 199–201

business value, defined, 47
By, Oddbjørn, 15

Certification of Competency in Business Analysis
    (CCBA®), 5
Certified Business Analysis Professional (CBAP®)
    exam, 3
Certified Professional for Requirements
    Engineering (CPRE)
    Foundation Level (FL) syllabus, 3
change control, 90, 201, 202
    integrated, 88, 154
    planning, 87–91
    tools and techniques, 90, 201–202
change control board (CCB), 89
    participants in, 89
Charette, Robert, 258
Checkland, Peter, 269
Coaching Agile Teams (Adkins), 210
Coad, Peter, 259–260
The Coad Method, 260
Cockburn, Alistair, 255, 291
CoCoMo (Boehm), 221
collaboration points, 22
collaboration tools and techniques, 202–204
collectivism
    vs. individualism, 238
communication barriers, 206
communication management plan, 160
communication skills, 204–207
conceptual modeling, 118–119
conduct standards, 273–279
    purpose, 275
    vision, 275
cone of uncertainty, theory of, 221
configuration identification, 92
configuration management, 91–92. *see also*
    configuration management system
configuration management system, 91–92. *see
    also* configuration management
configuration status accounting, 92
configuration verification and audit, 92

conflict management
    defined, 207
    steps in, 208
    styles, 209
    tools and techniques, 207–211
conflict resolution, 210
    skills, 211
    tools and techniques, 207–211
Conflict Resolution Network, 211
Conscious competence model, 241
conscious knowledge, 107
consider-all-facts (CAF) technique, 208
context analysis, 75
context boundary, 77, 78
contingency, defined, 211
contingency planning, 211–212
Continuing Certification Requirements (CCR)
    program, 9
contract negotiation, 289
control tools
    quality management and, 172
    statistical, 172
costs, 48–49
    of conformance, 141
    of non-conformance, 141
crashing, 187
    calculations for, 188
creativity techniques, 111
crystal methods, 255–257
cultural awareness, 246–249
cultural web model, 247–248
cultures
    high-context, 238
    low-context, 238
customer collaboration, 289
customer journey map, 250

data analysis tools and techniques, 212–213
decision-making tools and techniques, 174, 213–215
decision tree analysis, 199
declaration of interdependence for modern
    management, 291–292

delighters, 107
Delphi method, 223
DeLuca, Jeff, 259–260
De Marco, Tom, 260
Deming, W. Edwards, 171, 173, 292
democratic leadership, 228
development methodologies, 215–218
develop project charter, 74, 234
discounted cash flow (DCF), 54
dissatisfiers, 107
documentation
    quality aspects of, 94
    using conceptual models, 132–134
    using natural language, 131–132
document-centric techniques, 111–112
document control, planning, 91–93
document design, 130
document management
    basic techniques and tools of, 219
    defined, 219
    tools and techniques, 219–220
document requirements, 129–138
    documentation using conceptual models,
        132–134
    documentation using natural language, 131–
        132
    document design, 130
    document structure, 134–135
    epic stories, 138
    splitting user stories, 137
    writing requirement in agile methodologies,
        135–137
documents
    created in each domain, 43
    as requirements sources, 107
document structures, 134–135
    standardized, 134
Drucker, Peter, 292
dynamic systems development method (DSDM),
    258

earned value management, 188

elicitation techniques, 108–110, 220
    advantages and disadvantages of using, 111
    factors influencing choice of, 108–110
    goal of, 108
    risk factors, 108–109
    selection of a suitable, 108
epic stories, 138
ESPRIT initiative, 258
estimating
    analogous, 222
    parametric, 223
    tools and techniques, 220–224
ethics, defined, 273
evaluation
    analyzing solution gaps, 170–173
    mindset for, 168
    obtaining stakeholder acceptance of solution,
        173–174
    overview, 167–168
    relating PMI-PBA practices to agile practices,
        177
    relating PMI-PBA practices to *PMBOK®*
        Guide—Fifth Edition practices, 176
    of solution results, 175–176
    validating test results, 168–170
evolutionary prototype, 121
expert judgment method, 223
Extreme Programming (XP), 253
*Extreme Programming Explained: Embrace
    Change* (Beck), 253

face-to-face communication, 203
facilitation tools and techniques, 224–226
failure mode and effect analysis (FMEA), 250
fault tree analysis, 250
feature driven development, 259–260
femininity *vs.* masculinity, 238
Fishbone diagram, 202
The 5 Whys, 250
focusing on interests, not positions principle, 237
folk culture, 247
Force Field analysis, 250

forward traceability, 151. *see also* postrequirement specification traceability
Foundation Level Syllabus, 309
four-factor analysis, 244
Freiman, Frank, 220
Function Points (Allbrecht), 221
functional requirements, 116
future value (FV), 51
fuzziness, 150

Gantt chart, 187
Gap analysis, 250
Getting to Yes (Fisher and Ury), 237
Gilb, Tom, 235, 292
goal models, 133
Goldratt, Eli, 292
Goldratt's Theory of Constraints, 253
Goldsmith, Robin, 251
Greenleaf, Robert K., 231
group development, stages of, 224
A Guide to the Business Analysis Body of Knowledge (BABOK® Guide) v3, 3
A Guide to the Project Management Body of Knowledge (PMBOK® Guide), Fifth Edition, 7, 299–301
    process groups and knowledge areas, 281–283

Hall, Edward T., 238
Harvard Business Review, 253
high-context cultures, 238
high-fidelity prototypes, 114
Highsmith, Jim, 291
Hirotaka Takeuchi, 253
Hofstede, Geert, 238
horizontal traceability, 151. *see also* mapping dependencies

IAG consulting, 5
I am Agile (Nielsen), 107, 125
IBM Corporation, 238
IIBA-CBAP®
    domains and area of knowledge alignment, 302

eligibility requirements, 301
overview, 301–302
IIBA CBAP® designation
    pretest answers for, 31–33
    pretest questions for, 28–31
Ikujiro Nonaka, 253
individualism
    vs. collectivism, 238
individuals and interactions over processes and tools, 288
influence diagrams, 250
Institute of Electrical and Electronics Engineers (IEEE), 10
intangible assets, 48–49
integrated change control, 88
interactive communication, 160–161
interface analysis, 226–227
internal rate of return (IRR), 51–52
    decision rules, 51
    illustrating with three different discount rates, 52
International Institute of Business Analysis (IIBA), 28, 299
    Business Analysis Planning and Monitoring knowledge, 302
    Certification of Competency in Business Analysis (CCBA®), 5
    Certified Business Analysis Professional (CBAP®) exam, 3
    Elicitation and Collaboration knowledge area, 302–303
    founded in, 4
    membership, 5
    Requirements Analysis and Design Definition knowledge area, 304
    Requirements Life Cycle Management knowledge area, 303
    Solution Evaluation knowledge area, 304
    Strategy Analysis knowledge area, 303
    techniques, 305–307
    underlying competencies, 304–305

International Institute of Business Analysis
        (IIBA) Code of Ethical Conduct &
        Professional Standards, 273–274
    fairness, 277–278
    honesty, 278–279
    respect, 277
    responsibility, 276–277
    structure, 275–276
International Requirements Engineering Board
        (IREB), 3, 6
inventing options for mutual benefits principle,
        237
INVEST in Good Stories (Wake), 136
IREB CPRE
    eligibility requirements, 309
    overview, 309–311
IREB CPRE-FL designation
    pretest answers for, 36–38
    pretest questions for, 33–36
Ishikawa, Kaoru, 171
Ishikawa diagram, 202
ISO Standard 9126 (ISO/IEC 9126), 117
iteration retrospective, 232

Java Modeling in Color with UML, 259
Johnson and Scholes's cultural web, 247–248
Jones, Daniel, 258
journey map, 15
the journey method, 14, 15–16
Juran, Joseph, 171

Kanban Method, 253–255
Kano classification, 126–127
Kano model
    adapted from *I am Agile,* 107
    categories of, 108
    categorizing the requirements according to,
        107–108
    with dysfunctional questions, 127
Kemerer, Chris F., 221
Kilmann, Ralph, 236
knowledge

business analyst certification (PMI-PBA) and,
        4–5
    conscious, 107
    subconscious, 107
    unconscious, 107
Kotter, Michael, 239
Kubler-Ross change curve, 240

laissez-faire, 228
leaders
    behavioral analysis of, 228
    vs. managers, 227
leadership
    adaptive, 231
    described, 227
    Kurt Lewin's different styles of, 228
    and motivation, 229
    principles of, 227–231
    servant, 231
    Tannenbaum and Schmidt styles of, 229
leadership skills, 227–231
Leading through Connections 2012, 274
Lean Software Development, 258–259
LEAN strategy, 55
lessons learned, 232–234
Lewin, Kurt, 228, 239
    model for change, 239
light methodology, 253
limiting work-in-progress (WIP), 255
Lister, Timothy, 260
low-context cultures, 238
low-fidelity prototypes, 114

*The Machine That Changed the World: The Story
        of Lean Production* (Womack, Jones, and
        Roos), 258
making process policies explicit, 255
managers *vs.* leaders, 227
mapping dependencies, 151. *see also* horizontal
        traceability
The March of Folly: From Troy to Vietnam
        (Tuchman), 57

masculinity
  vs. femininity, 238
McConnell, Eric, 5
McGregor, Douglas, 227
McGregor theories of *X* and *Y,* 227
McKinsey 7-S model, 246
McKinsey and Company, 20
measurement tools, 234–235
Mehrabian, Albert, 205
Memo (By), 15
Meyers-Briggs type indicators (MBTI), 228
mind maps, 14, 16
mnemonics, 14
  with BIRDS, 15
model for change, 239
MoSCoW prioritization, 126
MOST analysis, 243–244
motivation and leadership, 229
multidirectional communication, 160
Myers, Isabel Briggs, 228
Myers, Katharine, 228
The Mythical Man-Month (Brooks), 220

natural language, 131–132
needs assessment, 42–43
  analyzing stakeholders, 62–67
  assessing organizational capacities and gaps,
    45
  defining business requirements, 43–47
  defining value proposition, 47–55
  develop project goals, 55–57
  developing a business case for proposed
    solutions, 46–47
  forming the first phase of the solution scope,
    45–46
  identify stakeholders, 57–62
  problems and opportunities, 44–45
  relating PMI-PBA practices to agile practices,
    68–69
  relating PMI-PBA practices to *PMBOK®
    Guide—Fifth Edition* practices, 68
needs assessment domain, defined, 42

negotiations
  defined, 235
  strategies and styles, 236
  tools, 235–237
net present value (NPV), 49–50
  decision rules, 50
network models, for analyzing stakeholders, 66
"The New Product Development Game," 253
Nielsen, Klaus, 107, 125
nonfunctional requirements, 116, 234–235
nonsystematic ad hoc tracing, 79
nonverbal communication, 205
Norden, Peter V., 220

observation techniques, 112
one-on-one communication, 206
Onion diagram, 66
Onion model, 62
  for analyzing stakeholders, 66
operation management, 55
opportunity identification, 249–251
organization assessment, 237–238
organizational capacities and gaps, 45
organizational change, 238–239
organizational need, 19
  business analyst role, 20–21
organizational process assets, 60
organizational strategy, 55
osmotic communication, 203

Palmer, Stephen, 259
parametric estimating, 223
Pareto analysis, 250
PARIS (Participants, Accountable, Review
    needed, Input needed, and Sign-off
    required) model, 67
payback period (PP), 53
  and sensitivity analysis, 53
people change models, 240–241
perform integrated change control process, 87
personas, 268
perspective-based readings, 120

PEST(EL) analysis, 243
plan cost management, 48
plan-do-study-act (PDCA), 292
Planguage, 235
planning
    contingency, 211–212
    defining project expected outcome, 93–96
    determining project context, 74–78
    developing requirement management plan,
        83–86
    multiple levels of, 192
    overview, 73–74
    plan document control, 91–93
    plan requirement change control, 87–91
    relating PMI-PBA practices to agile practices,
        97–98
    relating PMI-PBA practices to *PMBOK®*
        Guide—Fifth Edition practices, 97
    requirement traceability, 78–83
planning tools and techniques, 241–246
    strategy analysis external business
        environment, 243–244
    strategy analysis internal capability, 243–245
    strategy definition, 245–246
    strategy implementation, 246
plan scope management, 81, 84
plus-minus-interesting conflict resolution
        technique, 208
PMBOK® Guide—Fifth Edition. see A Guide to
        the Project Management Body of Knowledge
        (PMBOK® Guide)—Fifth Edition
PMI-PBA certification exam, 184, 283–285,
        301–302
    analytic tools and techniques, 184–191
        project risk management, 188–191
        project time management, 186–188
    backlog management, 196–198
    basics, 13–14
    before, 14–16
    blueprint of, 8
    business rule analysis tools and techniques,
        199–201
    change control tools and techniques, 201–202

collaboration tools and techniques, 202–204
communication skills, 204–207
conflict management and resolution tools and
        techniques, 207–211
content, 7–10
contingency planning, 211–212
data analysis tools and techniques, 212–213
decision-making tools and techniques, 213–
        215
development methodologies, 215–218
document management tools and techniques,
        219–220
during, 17–18
education, 10
elements of a requirements management plan,
        220
elicitation tools and techniques, 220
eligibility requirements, 9
estimating tools and techniques, 220–224
    analogous estimating, 222
    Delphi method, 223
    expert judgment, 223
    parametric estimating, 223
    program evaluation and review technique
        (PERT), 223–224
facilitation tools and techniques, 224–226
    conducting the workshop, 225
    follow up, 226
    planning the workshop, 225
general strategies, 17
interface analysis, 226–227
knowledge concepts, 184
leadership principles and skills, 227–231
lessons learned and retrospectives, 232–234
measurement tools and techniques, 234–235
multiple levels of planning, 192
negotiations tools and techniques, 235–237
organization assessment, 237–241
reference materials for, 11
relating PMI-PBA practices to agile practices,
        191
relating PMI-PBA practices to *PMBOK®*
        Guide—Fifth Edition practices, 191

risk management, 192–196
scheduling, 192
skills, 184
strategies for answering the questions, 18
study tips, 13, 16
PMI-PBA designation
pretest answers for, 26–28
pretest questions for, 23–26
PMI-PBA domains, 8
Pohl, Klaus, 309
political awareness, 246–249
Porter, Michael, 243
Porter's Five Forces Analysis, 244
postrequirement specification traceability, 151.
  see also forward traceability
power distance, 238
A Practical Guide to Feature-Driven Development,
  259
prerequirement specification traceability, 151. *see
  also* backward traceability
present value (PV), 49
pretest answers
  for IIBA CBAP® designation, 31–33
  for IREB CPRE-FL designation, 36–38
  for PMI-PBA designation, 26–28
  sheet to, 27–28, 32–33, 37–38
pretest questions
  IIBA CBAP® designation, 28–31
  for IREB CPRE-FL designation, 33–36
  for PMI-PBA designation, 23–26
prevention cost, 141
principled negotiation, 237
principles of agile software, 289–291
prioritization, 124
  MoSCoW, 126
  tools and techniques, 249
  using urgent and important as parameters, 124
  value proposition using, 123–126
problem solving, 249–251
process analysis, 251
process maps, 250
product scope, 45, 57
product vision, 56

professional ethics, 273–279
  vision, 275
profitability index (PI), 54–55. *see also* profit
  investment ratio (PIR); value investment
  ratio (VIR)
  decision rules, 54
  formula, 54
profit investment ratio (PIR), 54. *see also*
  profitability index (PI)
program evaluation and review technique
  (PERT), 223–224
project charter, 47
  developing, 46, 75
project communication, dimensions of, 205
project context, determining, 74–78
project expected outcome, defining, 93–96
project goals, 55
  developing, 55–57
*Project Management Body of Knowledge
  (PMBOK® Guide),* 3, 46, 114, 168
Project Management Institute (PMI), 3–4, 13
  2013 Pulse of the Profession, 204
  Pulse of the Profession® study, 4–5, 19
Project Management Institute Agile Certified
  Practitioner (PMI-ACP)®, 260
Project Management Institute (PMI) Code of
  Ethics and Professional Conduct, 273–
  274
  honesty, 278–279
  purpose, 275
  structure, 275–276
Project Management Institute Professional in
  Business Analysis (PMI-PBA), 3
project management plan
  and requirement management plan, 84
project manager
  business analyst and, 21–22
project methodologies
  adaptive software development (ASD), 257–
  258
  agile methodologies, 260–262
  Crystal methods, 255–257
  described, 251

dynamic systems development method
(DSDM), 258
Extreme Programming (XP), 253
feature driven development, 259–260
Kanban Method, 253–255
Lean Software Development, 258–259
scrum, 252–253
Project RAND, 220
project risk management, 188–191
project scope description, defined, 45
project time management, 186–188
prototypes, 114
advantages and disadvantages of using, 113
evolutionary, 121
high-fidelity, 114
low-fidelity, 114
techniques for building requirements, 114
throwaway, 121
prototyping inquiry cycle, 113
pull communication, 160
push communication, 160

qualitative risk assessment, 188
quality, defined, 142
quality checklist, defined, 142
quality control, 140
quality management, 262
and control tools, 172
quality metrics, defined, 142
quality requirements, 116, 234–235
quantitative risk assessment, 190, 193

RACI, 65, 67
RAM, 67
ranking technique, 125
RASCI (Responsible, Accountable, Supportive,
Consulted and Informed) model, 67
relative weighting prioritization matrix, 126–127
reporting tools and techniques, 262–263
requirement baseline, 128–129
requirement classification, 116–118
Requirement Engineering Fundamentals (Pohl and
Rupp), 309

requirement management plan, 80–81
developing, 83–86
and other subsidiary plans, 85
project management plan and, 84
requirements
acceptance of, 139
alignment of, 109
allocating, 122–129
business, 116
communicating status of, 159–161
constraints, 116
cost of fixing, 19
created in each domain, 43
document, 129–138
elaborating, 115–119
functional, 116
getting signoff, 129
managing changes to, 161–162
monitoring, 155–157
non-functional, 116
PMI definition of, 116
quality aspects of, 93, 116
solution, 116
specifying, 141–142
stakeholder, 116
steps for construction, 132
three perspectives on, 130
tracking, 150–154
transition, 116
types of, 116
updating status of, 157–159
validating, 119–122
verifying, 138–140
requirements analysis, 115–116. *see also*
requirements engineering
requirements engineering, 108, 115. *see also*
requirements analysis
requirements management plan, elements of, 220
requirements' pyramid adapted from Zielczynski,
43
requirements sources
documents, 107
stakeholders, 106

systems in operation, 107
requirement types, 264
retrospectives, 232–234
return on investment (ROI), 51
    formula, 51
risk
    categorization of, 193
    defined, 188, 192
    identification of, 193
risk management, 192–196
risk mitigation strategies, 194
risk register, 190
risk responses
    negative, 191
    positive, 191
risk-return matrix, 245
Roos, Daniel, 258
root cause analysis, 250, 265–266
Rupp, Chris, 309

SARAH Model, 240
satisfaction
    delighters, 107
    dissatisfiers, 107
    satisfiers, 107
satisfiers, 107
scheduling, 192
    tools and techniques, 266
Schein, Edgar Henry, 247
Schein's cultural iceberg, 247
Schwaber, Ken, 196, 253, 293
Scrum, 252–253, 292–295
    methodology, 295
    roles, 295
SEER-SEM, 220
sensitivity analysis, 53
separate people from the problem principle, 237
"The Servant as Leader," 231
servant leadership, 231
Shewhart, Walter, 292
Shewhart cycle, 173
situation statement, defined, 45
Sliger, Michele, 193

software change impact analysis, 202
The Software Project Manager's Bridge to Agility
        (Sliger and Broderick), 193
software traceability, 150
solution gaps, analyzing, 170–173
solution requirements, 116
solution results, evaluating, 175–176
Spears, Larry, 231
spiral model (Boehm), 218
stakeholder analysis, 63, 267–268
stakeholder management, 58
    fundamental problem of, 59
stakeholder register, 60
stakeholder requirements, 116
stakeholders
    analyzing, 62–67
    contributions of, 64
    external, 61
    goals of, 56
    identifying, 57–62, 63
    impact on, 66
    interests of, 64
    needs of, 63
    obtaining acceptance of solution from, 173–174
    PMI definition of, 58
    power/interest grid, 66
    as requirements sources, 106
    requirements status with, 158
    supporters or opponents, 64
    techniques for identifying, 61
    techniques used to analyze, 65
    tools and techniques for identifying, 60
    value, 63
stakeholder salience, 64
stakeholder value, alignment with, 79
stakeholders' wheel, 59
Standish Group, 19
state diagrams, 156
State of Agile Development survey, 203
Statement of Work (SOW), 46–47
strategy
    definition, 245–246
    implementation, 246

strategy analysis external business environment, 243–244
strategy analysis internal capability, 243–245
strength based leadership, 228
subconscious knowledge, 107
support techniques, 113–115
survey techniques, 110–111
Sutherland, Jeff, 196, 293
SWOT analysis, 245
synchronous communication, 203
system boundary, 76
system context
    defined, 75
    types of aspects within, 77
system thinking, 269–270

tangible assets, 48–49
target groups
    for business analyst certifications, 7
team roles, 228
test-driven development (TDD), 170
test-first development, 170. *see also* acceptance
        test-driven development
test results
    validating, 168–170
theory of cone of uncertainty, 221
theory X of McGregor, 227
theory Y of McGregor, 227
Thomas, Kenneth, 236
Thomas-Kilmann conflict mode, 209, 210
three circles model, 229–230
throwaway prototypes, 121
tools and techniques
    business rule analysis, 199–201
    change control, 201–202
    collaboration, 202–204
    conflict management, 207–211
    conflict resolution, 207–211
    data analysis, 212–213
    decision-making, 213–215
    document management, 219–220
    elicitation, 220

    estimating, 220–224
    facilitation, 224–226
Total Quality Management, 173
Toyota Production System, 253
traceability
    activities (from Anne Hartly Consulting), 156
    advantages of, 80
    artifacts and tools, 158
    backward, 151
    business analyst tasks with, 151
    communication requirements status, 159–161
    defined, 149–150
    forward, 151
    goals of, 151
    horizontal, 151
    and life cycle, 155
    manage changes to requirements, 161–162
    matrix, 82, 120, 161
    monitor requirements, 155–157
    overview, 149–150
    planning, 78–83
    postrequirement specification, 151
    prerequirement specification, 151
    relating PMI-PBA practices to agile practices, 163
    tools and techniques, 152, 264
    track requirements, 150–154
    updating requirements status, 157–159
traceability and monitoring. *see* traceability
traceability tables, 152–153
tracing, 79
    basic, 79
    extended, 79
    nonsystematic ad hoc, 79
transition requirements, 116
Tuchman, Barbara, 57

uncertainty avoidance, 238
unconscious knowledge, 107
Unified Modeling Language (UML), 156
user stories, 135–137
    components of, 136

splitting, 137
U.S. Federal Aviation Administration, 150
Using Codes of Conduct to Resolve Legal Disputes,
    274

validation
    defined, 138
    principles of, 95
    scope, 119, 157, 174
    tools and techniques, 95, 270
    verification and, 138
valuation techniques, 270
    normative, 175–176
    perceived, 175–176
    realistic, 175–176
value engineering, 250
value investment ratio (VIR), 54. *see also*
        profitability index (PI)
value propositions
    benefit-cost ratio (BCR), 54
    benefits and features, 48
    costs and benefits, 48–49
    customer's perspective with regard to
        organization, 47, 175
    defining, 47–55
    discounted cash flow (DCF), 54
    future value (FV), 51
    internal rate of return (IRR), 51–52
    net present value (NPV), 49–50
    payback period (PP), 53
    present value (PV), 49

profitability index, 54–55 (PI)
    return on investment (ROI), 51
    using prioritization, 123–126
verbal communication, 205
verification
    defined, 138
    table, 139
    tools and techniques, 270
version control tools and techniques, 270
Version One, 203
vision document, defined, 45
V-model, 215, 217

Wake, Bill, 136
waterdrop models, for analyzing stakeholders, 66,
    216
WBS directory, 129
Weinberg, Gerald, 260
Wiegers, Karl, 126–127
    relative weighting prioritization matrix,
        126–127
Womack, James, 258
work breakdown structure (WBS)
    creating, 128
    defined, 129
working software over comprehensive
        documentation, 288
workshop
    conducting, 225
    planning, 225